**SOCIAL ORDER AND THE
FEAR OF CRIME IN
CONTEMPORARY TIMES**

CLARENDON STUDIES IN CRIMINOLOGY

Published under the auspices of the Institute of Criminology, University of Cambridge; the Mannheim Centre, London School of Economics; and the Centre for Criminological Research, University of Oxford.

GENERAL EDITOR: IAN LOADER
(*University of Oxford*)

EDITORS: MANUEL EISNER ALISON LIEBLING, AND PER-OLOF WIKSTRÖM
(*University of Cambridge*)

JILL PEAY AND TIM NEWBURN
(*London School of Economics*)

LUCIA ZEDNER AND JULIAN ROBERTS
(*University of Oxford*)

Recent titles in this series:

Black Police Associations: An Analysis of Race and Ethnicity with Constabularies
Holdaway

The Prisoner Society: Power, Adaption, and Social Life in an English Prison
Crewe

Making Sense of Penal Change
Daems

Punishing Persistent Offenders: Exploring Community and Offender Perspections
Roberts

When Children Kill Children: Penal Populism and Political Culture
Green

Social Order and the Fear of Crime in Contemporary Times

STEPHEN FARRALL
JONATHAN JACKSON
EMILY GRAY

OXFORD
UNIVERSITY PRESS

OXFORD
UNIVERSITY PRESS

Great Clarendon Street, Oxford OX2 6DP

Oxford University Press is a department of the University of Oxford.
It furthers the University's objective of excellence in research, scholarship,
and education by publishing worldwide in

Oxford New York

Auckland Cape Town Dar es Salaam Hong Kong Karachi
Kuala Lumpur Madrid Melbourne Mexico City Nairobi
New Delhi Shanghai Taipei Toronto

With offices in

Argentina Austria Brazil Chile Czech Republic France Greece
Guatemala Hungary Italy Japan Poland Portugal Singapore
South Korea Switzerland Thailand Turkey Ukraine Vietnam

Oxford is a registered trade mark of Oxford University Press
in the UK and in certain other countries

Published in the United States
by Oxford University Press Inc., New York

© Stephen Farrall, Jonathan Jackson, and Emily Gray 2009

The moral rights of the authors has been asserted
Database right Oxford University Press (maker)

Crown copyright material is reproduced under Class Licence
Number C01P0000148 with the permission of OPSI
and the Queen's Printer for Scotland

First published 2009

All rights reserved. No part of this publication may be reproduced,
stored in a retrieval system, or transmitted, in any form or by any means,
without the prior permission in writing of Oxford University Press,
or as expressly permitted by law, or under terms agreed with the appropriate
reprographics rights organization. Enquiries concerning reproduction
outside the scope of the above should be sent to the Rights Department,
Oxford University Press, at the address above

You must not circulate this book in any other binding or cover
and you must impose the same condition on any acquirer

British Library Cataloguing in Publication Data
Data available

Library of Congress Cataloging-in-Publication Data
Farrall, Stephen.
  Social order and the fear of crime in contemporary times / Stephan Farrall, Jonathan Jackson, Emily Gray.
     p. cm.
  Includes bibliographical references and index.
  ISBN 978-0-19-954081-5 (hardback : alk. paper) 1. Fear of crime. 2. Crime--Sociological aspects. 3. Sociological jurisprudence. 4. Social psychology. I. Jackson, Jonathan. II. Gray, Emily. III. Title.
  HV6250.25.F36 2009
  362.88--dc22
                                                                                 2009027938

Typeset by Macmillan Publishing Solutions
Printed in Great Britain by the MPG Books Group, Bodmin and King's Lynn

ISBN 978-0-19-954081-5

1 3 5 7 9 10 8 6 4 2

General Editor's Introduction

Clarendon Studies in Criminology aims to provide a forum for outstanding empirical and theoretical work in all aspects of criminology and criminal justice, broadly understood. The Editors welcome submissions from established scholars, as well as excellent PhD work. The Series was inaugurated in 1994, with Roger Hood as its first General Editor, following discussions between Oxford University Press and three Criminology Centres. It is edited under the auspices of these three Criminological Centres: the Cambridge Institute of Criminology, the Mannheim Centre for Criminology at the London School of Economics, and the Centre for Criminology at the University of Oxford. Each supplies members of the Editorial Board and, in turn, the Series Editor.

Social Order and the Fear of Crime in Contemporary Times, by Stephen Farrall, Jonathan Jackson, and Emily Gray, is an important contribution to criminological debate on the 'fear of crime'. The book brings together, and synthesizes into a significant statement on this topic, a series of empirical studies on the impact of crime upon people's lives that the authors have carried out over the last decade. Farrall et al. are acutely aware of the problems involved in measuring fear—indeed they have done more than most in recent years to bring these difficulties to our notice. Yet they manage nonetheless to deploy quantitative measures and analysis to produce new and striking findings on the distribution and effects of social fear and anxiety. This is combined with detailed qualitative investigation of the ways in which people use crime as a vehicle for making sense of, and speaking about, the world around them—its norms and values, its conflicts and divisions, its forms of social and moral ordering, and the manner in which it is regulated and governed. Moreover, this rare bringing together of quantitative and qualitative research is situated in a detailed account of the origins of fear as a discrete political and criminological problem, and the more general rise of crime as an organizing feature of social relations and political life. This is informed by empirical research—in this case interviews with academic and government researchers. But it also draws upon a detailed appraisal of a wide range of relevant literature in criminology, psychology, sociology, and social theory. The result is a book that is likely to be a key and continuing reference point in future debate.

The authors' central claim is that our understanding of what is too often unquestioningly called 'fear of crime' can be deepened if we distinguish between its 'experiential' and 'expressive' dimensions. The theoretical model and empirical analysis they deploy to investigate this distinction finds that the former—worry about crime rooted in daily experience—is rarer than is commonly thought and typically found among people who reside in places where crime, disorder, and attendant social problems are concentrated. A majority of respondents they report as being 'unworried'—a finding that seems especially significant in a climate of public rhetoric and governmental activity that often seems premised on the idea that such people do not in fact exist. The authors refer, finally, to those they categorize as more generally 'anxious' and seek to understand how 'fear of crime' operates, in their words, 'as a lay seismograph of social cohesion and moral consensus', whether in people's immediate neighbourhood or the world beyond. Farrall et al.'s account of this expressive element of 'fear' provides both further evidence and an extended analysis of the claim that 'fear of crime' research is at its best and most illuminating when it attends to the ways in which talk about crime in everyday life registers its entanglement with questions of social order, division, and justice.

The editors welcome this important addition to the Series.

Ian Loader
Oxford,
January 2009

Foreword

In this splendid book, Stephen Farrall, Jonathan Jackson, and Emily Gray think through the many and varied uses to which the term 'fear of crime' has been put, in research, in political discourse, and in everyday conversation. One of their great contributions is the distinction the authors make between 'experiential' and 'expressive' fears. The former is rooted in actual, concrete experience. It is voiced most often by people who live in poor, disorganized, and risky neighbourhoods. They are frequently victimized. Their worries are real, and they have to actively 'manage' their risks by paying attention to them on a daily basis. At the same time, a kind of diffuse anxiety is also commonly expressed by people who do not actually have much day-to-day reason for concern about crime. Their neighbourhoods tend to be stable and civil, their children are (relatively) disciplined, and their personal experience with crime and even visible untidiness is quite limited. At root, both groups are concerned about the same *things*. They do not like it that churches, schools, and neighbourhoods no longer bind us together; that significant numbers of people are willing to tolerate behaviours they find intolerable; that the police are not always able to respond to their immediate problems; and that it can be unwise to place much confidence in the kindness of strangers. But these concerns are not really realized in most communities. It is overwhelmingly the residents of the minority of truly troubled communities that experience the episodes of heart-pounding terror that we commonly associate with 'fear'. For the others, crime is sometimes on their minds.

All of this is important because, of course, fear of crime can have real consequences for individuals and for the communities in which they live. For some, it restricts freedom of movement and undermines neighbourhood cohesion. It stunts capital investment and commercial vitality, and drives those who can afford it as far as they can get from discomforting people and places. Worse (I think), although crime may just sometimes be on the minds of a large majority of the public, there are forces at work that magnify its significance in unexpected places. Concern about crime opens a crack into our private lives through which media images readily burrow with an immediacy unrivalled by any other story line. Mass media generate unrealistic views of the frequency and seriousness of crime, and misrepresent where and for whom risks are concentrated. The featured victims turn out to look like those who are watching or reading, and buying proffered products. Media images perpetuate the view that it is a 'mean world' out there, undermining trust and thus further compounding fear. The malleability of fear also has ugly consequences for our politics. No successful politician lets anyone get to their right on crime. Fear is used strategically to drive wedges that splinter society by race, class, origin, and lifestyle, in order to build winning coalitions around policies protecting inequality. In parallel, political rhetoric undermines the legitimacy of policies and institutions 'that have failed to protect us', further convincing people that they are out there on their own. Instead, politicians proclaim the efficacy of 'keeping a firm hand on the tiller', which of course would be theirs.

All of these are reasons to pay careful attention to fear of crime. Sorting out the 'realistic' roots of fear, and understanding how economic and political forces surrounding the social pockets where crime is actually concentrated serve to put them on display and interpret their significance for the rest of society, is the central mission of this forceful and provocative book.

Wesley Skogan
Professor of Political Science,
Institute for Policy Research, Northwestern University,
January 2009

Acknowledgements

Our debts are many and varied. We would like to start by expressing our deep thanks to the UK's Economic & Social Research Council, which has funded our investigations into the fear of crime on a number of occasions. Farrall first encountered the murky world of anxieties about crime and survey research as part of a grant under the Crime & Social Order programme (award L210252007), while Jackson's explorations for his PhD and postdoctoral research fellowship were funded by the same body (awards R00429834481 and T026271167). The initial piloting of the survey instruments which we rely upon was also funded by the ESRC (award RES000220040); the project which directly led to this book was again funded by the ESRC (as award RES000231108). We would like to express our gratitude to the Council for the generosity of their support over the past ten years or so.

The Home Office, and in particular the British Crime Survey Design Team, deserves a special mention for their willingness to employ the new questions, designed and piloted by Farrall, in the 2003–04 British Crime Survey, and for readily making the data available to us. To this end we thank Alison Walker, Jonathan Allen, Jorgen Lovebakke, and Anna Upson. Each dealt with queries from us throughout (and after) the lifetime of the project and devoted time from their busy schedules to meet with us on various occasions to discuss initial findings and various technical matters.

GERN (Groupe Européen de Recherche sur les Normativés) were kind enough to fund an international one-day conference at Keele University in March 2007 in part devoted to the discussion of the initial results from the project. We extend our thanks to Rene Levy for making these funds available to us, and to Richard Sparks and Mike Hough for agreeing to provide responses to our presentations. We benefited not just from the wider discussion, but also from the other presentations made that day, namely by Werner Greve, Andromachi Tseloni and David Green.

Over the past few years, a number of fellow academics and researchers have been a source of encouragement and criticism (often in equal measure), and we thank all of the following for the time they have given up in order to assist us in ways too numerous to mention: Mike Hough, Richard Sparks, Betsy Stanko, Murray Lee, Jason Ditton, Tony Jefferson, David Gadd, Robbie Sutton, Ian Loader, Susanne Karstedt, Jouni Kuna, Tim Hope, and Wes Skogan (to whom we also owe a further debt for his Foreword).

We have benefited from a number of invitations to present our work and ideas at various forums over the past few years. Aspects of our work—from the embryonic to the fully fledged—have been aired in the following arena: ISTAT Conference, Rome (Italy), 2003; ANU, Canberra, 2004; University of Western Sydney (Australia), 2004; HUENI Conference on social statistics, Helsinki (Finland), 2005; ACPO, Effective Local Policing Conference, Stratford upon Avon, 2005; Statistics Commission Review of Criminal Statistics, London, 2005; European Society of Criminology, Tubingen, 2006; Home Office Conference to mark the 25th Anniversary of the British Crime Survey, Cumberland Lodge, Windsor, 2006; American Society of Criminology Conference, Los Angeles, 2006; Partners Against Crime Taskforce 10th Anniversary Conference, Norwich, 2006; British Crime Survey Users Group, Royal Statistical Society, London, 2006; ESRC Social Contexts and Response to Risk Network, Cambridge University, 2007; ESRC Seminar on New Ways of Approaching the Fear of Crime: Measurement and Policy Applications, London School of Economics, 2007; European Society of Criminology, Bologna, 2007; European Survey Research Association Conference, Prague, 2007; Manning-Gottlieb Media Group, London, 2007; British Society of Criminology, London School of Economics, 2007; Centre for Criminology, Oxford University, 2007; Home Office, London, 2007; Methodology Institute, London School of Economics, London, 2007; Criminología: Causas del Delito Y Procesos de Reacción Al Delito, Universidad Nacional de Edicación a Distancia, Madrid, 2007; American Association for Public Opinion Research, New Orleans, 2008; Royal Statistical Society, London, 2008; and as part of the CRIMPREV seminar, Leeds University, 2008. We would like to thank all of our hosts for both their invitations and their hospitality. We benefited greatly from the chances to present our ideas and from the discussions which followed.

Stephen Farrall
Jonathan Jackson
Emily Gray,
March 2009

Contents

Lists of Figures and Tables   xvii

Part I

1. Introduction   3
   - The Broader Context of Our Study   7
   - The Nature of the Fear of Crime   7
   - The Prominent Position of Crime and Security in Contemporary Times   9
   - The Tension between Government Administration of Justice and Competing Public Perceptions and Demands (The 'Punitive Turn' and 'Penal Populism')   14
   - Our Overall Contribution   17
   - A Quick Summary of the Structure of the Book   18

2. The Provenance of Fear   21
   - The Fear of Crime: The Career of a Concept   21
   - The Beginnings: United States of America during the 1960s and 1970s   23
   - Civil 'Unrest' and the Rise of the 'Crime Problem'   25
   - Britain during the 1970s and 1980s   28
   - Political Interest in Public Anxieties about Crime   30
   - Fear of Crime as a Broader Cultural and Political Theme of 1980s Britain   33
   - Britain during the 1990s   35
   - The Fear of Crime since the Late-1990s   37
   - Explaining the Emergence of the Fear of Crime as a Policy Concern   40
   - Political Economies of Fear   41
   - The Cultural Economy of Fear   42
   - Conclusion   43

3	**What is the Fear of Crime? A Rhetorical Question with No *One* Clear Answer**	45
	Introduction	45
	Measuring the Fear of Crime	46
	Asking about 'Crime' and Specifying an Emotion	48
	Asking about 'Worry' and Specifying a Psychological Account of the Emotion	49
	The Everyday Experience of 'Fear' and 'Worry'	51
	Teasing Apart Frequency and Intensity	52
	Lessons from the Psychology of Survey Response	53
	Presuppositions and Leading Questions	54
	Socially Desirable Responding	54
	Attitudinal Items	55
	Non-Attitudes	56
	Frequency Items	57
	Lessons from the Psychology of 'Everyday Emotions'	60
	Emotional Complexity	60
	How often do we Experience Emotions?	62
	What does it mean to be 'Fearful'?	63
	Emotional Digestion and Appraisal Theory	64
	New Directions in Everyday Emotions Research: Methodological Issues	66
	Lessons from Qualitative Data on the Lived Reality of the Fear of Crime	70
	Feelings as Transitory, Fleeting Experiences	70
	'Fear' in the Absence of Direct Experience	74
	Background Concerns	75
	The Chronically Fearful	76
	To Answer Our Question	78
	Concluding Remarks	79
4	**Theorizing the Fear of Crime: The Cultural and Social Significance of Insecurity**	81
	Introduction	81
	The Victimization Thesis	82
	Imagined Victimization and the Psychology of Risk	85
	Disorder, Cohesion, and Collective Efficacy: The Role of Environmental Perception	91

Structural Change and Macro-Level Influences on Fear	101
Connecting Anxieties about Crime to Other Anxieties (and *Vice Versa*)	106
Towards an Integrative Model of the Fear of Crime	110
Social Perception and the Fear of Crime	111
The Psychology of Risk in the Fear of Crime	112
Experience and Expression in the Fear of Crime	114
A 'Unified' Framework of the Fear of Crime	117

Part II

5	**Conversations about Crime, Place, and Community**	123
	Introduction	123
	A Summary of Our Theoretical Framework	123
	Conversations about Crime, Place, and Community: Sampling and Methodology	124
	Analytic Orientation	125
	The Physical Environment: Crime, 'Place', Change, and Perceptions of Order	127
	Community, Cohesion, and Social Control	133
	Crime Consciousness: Residents' Interpretations of Crime and Risk	141
	Experience and Expression in the Fear of Crime	149
	Experiential fears	150
	Expressive fears	153
	Discussion	157
6	**Types and Intensities of Fear**	163
	Outlining Measures of the Fear of Crime	165
	Basic Frequencies	169
	Worry about robbery	169
	Worry about burglary and car crime	170
	A More Direct Comparison of the Old and New Measures	174
	Combining the Old and New Measures	176
	Implications of the New Measure of 'Fear of Crime'	178
	Correlates of 'Fear': Socio-Demographics and Crime	180
	Multi-Variate Analysis	187
	Consequences of 'Fear': Public Confidence in Policing	197
	Chapter Summary	200

Conclusion		202
Appendix		204
7 Experience and Expression in the Fear of Crime		207
The Story So Far...		207
Outline of the Analyses		210
Analysis of the British Crime Survey		211
Data and Measures		213
Results From the British Crime Survey		217
Analysis of the Local Rural Crime Survey		220
The data		222
Results from the Local Crime Survey		224
Discussion		227

Part III

8 The Anxieties of Affluence		235
Overview		235
Summarizing Our Contribution		235
Crime, Politics, and Insecurity		238
The Nature and Significance of the Fear of Crime		240
The Prominent Position of Crime and Security in Contemporary Times		244
The Tension between Government Administration of Justice and Competing Public Perceptions and Demands (The 'Punitive Turn' and 'Penal Populism')		244
Economic and Social Change and Anxiety		246
Political Culture		252
'Winners' and 'Losers' in Socio-Economic Transformations		254
Psychosocial Understanding of the Fear of Crime		261
What, Then, *Can* the State 'Do'?		262
Methodological Appendix		269
Bibliography		279
Index		303

Lists of Figures and Tables

Figures

4.1	Replication of Ferraro's risk interpretation model of the fear of crime	112
4.2	Summary of Jackson's (2004) model of the fear of crime	115
4.3	A Unified Framework: Experience and Expression in the Fear of Crime	118
5.1	A Unified Framework: Experience and Expression in the Fear of Crime	125
6.1	Worry about robbery, burglary, and car crime (standard measures)	171
6.2	Worry about robbery, burglary, and car crime in the past 12 months using new frequency measures	174
6.3	Worry about crime using new event-sampling measures	175
6.4	Crime and disorder index by fear group	184
6.5	IMD by fear group	185
6.6	Predicted probabilities for age, calculated for men and women separately (Model I)	194
6.7	Predicted probabilities for concerns about disorder and concerns about social cohesion (Model II)	196
6.8	Mediational relationships in the fear of crime	196
6.9	Predicted probabilities for perceived risk (Model III)	197
6.10	Frequency of worry about burglary over 12 months	204
7.1	A Unified Framework: Experience and Expression in the Fear of Crime	209

xviii   List of Figures and Tables

7.2	A Unified Framework: Experience and Expression in the Fear of Crime: SEM of BCS data	221
7.3	A Unified Framework: Experience and Expression in the Fear of Crime: SEM of the local crime survey data	226

Tables

6.1	Standard measure of worry about robbery	170
6.2	New measures of fear of robbery—frequency in the past year?	170
6.3	New measures of fear of robbery—how fearful on last occasion?	171
6.4	Cross-tabulation of the old and new measures	172
6.5	The coding of the answers	177
6.6	Frequency of the four groups by offence type	178
6.7	Frequency of the four groups	178
6.8	How much does crime affect your quality of life?	179
6.9	Bivariate correlates and associates of 'fear'	180
6.10	Bivariate correlates of 'fear'	183
6.11	Bivariate correlates of 'fear' (percentages)	186
6.12	What distinguishes the 'frequently worried', the 'worried', and the 'anxious' from the 'unworried'?	188
6.13	Modelling confidence in the police: old and new measures of fear of crime	199

PART I

In Part I we locate the fear of crime within a wider set of debates surrounding crime and social order in Western societies. This touches on several sets of debates not just in criminology, but also in survey research and question design. It explores not just what the fear of crime 'is', but also unpacks the history of the fear of crime as a concept and object of enquiry. Such debates mean that our journey is not a straightforward one: along the way we shall encounter debates about popular punitiveness; the uses to which politicians have put public anxieties about crime over the years; the latest thinking on the psychology of answering survey questions; the incidence of emotions in everyday lives; and the sorts of processes criminologists have alighted upon when trying to theorise the causes of crime fears. But by the end of Part I we will have outlined the wider background to debates surrounding the fear of crime, described 'where', 'why', and 'when' it emerged, and considered a number of positions on what the fear of crime is and how best to make sense of it.

1
Introduction

'We must travel in the direction of our fears.' (John Berryman, 1942, *A Point of Age*, in *Poems*).

The fear of crime remains a pressing social and political issue in any number of countries across the world. Hundreds of journal articles, books, and book chapters from a variety of social scientific perspectives have been devoted to the issue. Much of the attention is predicated on the status of fear of crime as a negative influence on individuals and communities (see *inter alia* Skogan and Maxfield, 1981; Hale, 1996; Lee, 2007, 2009; Heber, 2007). Pervasive insecurity about crime erodes well-being, promotes precaution, restricts movement, encourages 'flight' from deprived areas, and harms social trust, inter-group relations, and the capacity of communities to exercise social control (Hartnagel, 1979; Lavrakas, 1982; Skogan, 1986; Dolan and Peasgood, 2007; Stafford et al., 2007; Jackson and Gray, 2009).

Criminal justice systems look to reduce crime, render justice, and provide citizens with a sense of safety and fairness. Yet the fear of crime has emerged as a problem *in its own right*—quite separate from crime itself—and this raises some thorny questions. Should governments try to reduce crime-related fears which are out of line with the (for many) 'real' problem of crime? If so how ought this to be achieved? If the fear of crime is caused by a media-inflated (and maybe politically-inflamed, see Loo, 2009) sense of the crime problem, should governments be trying to downplay excessive anxiety (which may only serve, in turn, to fuel punitive sentiments)? If the fear of crime is linked to the perception of and intolerance to anti-social behaviour and so-called 'disorder,' should governments jump on the bandwagon too? If fear of crime is a more acceptable way of expressing intolerance and prejudice towards certain groups in society, how should governments respond? In short, ought the fear of crime to be discounted by governments, or ought it to be embraced in order that it might more readily be addressed and tackled?

Our argument in this book is simple: that the fear of crime is, at once, a more diverse experience and a more expressive phenomenon than has so far been empirically demonstrated. The thesis we develop—first through our assessment of the political and academic debates surrounding public insecurities about crime (Chapter 2); second through our reorganizing and reinterpreting of key literatures (Chapters 3 and 4); and third through our analysis of an extensive and diverse set of data (Chapters 5, 6, and 7) —begins with the idea that the fear of crime manifests in two principal (although not mutually exclusive) 'streams' of everyday experience. Previous survey research has tended to treat the fear of crime as one 'thing'. Yet we show that public emotions register as both a diffuse anxiety and a tangible worry over victimization.

Among those who lived in high crime areas, who had extensive direct and indirect experience of victimization, who were especially concerned about local neighbourhood breakdown, fear tended to present itself as concrete episodes of worry. These were short-lived and thankfully rare events in many people's lives. No matter how frightening, and no matter how much they resonate with and inform subsequent events, they were emotional events isolated in time. And contrary to received wisdom, these worries tended to cluster in individuals who lived in high crime areas. For those who lived in more protected areas (akin perhaps to 'middle England' or 'middle America'), with less experience of crime and less concern about local incivilities or neighbourhood stability, 'fear' was best displayed as a diffuse anxiety—something that Hough (2004) captures nicely when he describes unease and concern as mental states rather than mental events. Such a generalized social attitude is, we argue, more akin to an awareness of risk and a convenient metaphor regarding numerous but connecting social insecurities.

That is the core finding on the 'experience' of fear of crime. But we also argue that fear of crime 'expresses' a specific form of value-laden social perception. We propose that public perceptions of crime articulate a whole set of relational concerns about group values, normative consensus, and moral authority. Trust knits us together. Trust allows us to go about our daily lives in a seemingly secure manner. The data presented in this book are consistent with the idea that public concerns about the threat of crime emerge when citizens lose faith in the local structures of social control, in the shared commitment and connections between people that hold communities together. Thus, at the root of fear of crime may be public unease about the health of local neighbourhood order, as well as broader anxieties about the pace and direction of social change exemplified by concerns about social decline, community fragmentation, and moral authority.

We draw most heavily in this book on data from the British Crime Survey (BCS). But we also report findings from a local crime survey and a series of qualitative interviews that strengthen our conclusions. Building upon the analyses of BCS, the results from our local crime survey suggest that individuals who hold more authoritarian views about law and order—and who are more concerned about long-term deterioration of local community—are more likely to perceive disorder in their environment, and more likely to link these physical cues to problems of (a) social cohesion and consensus and (b) declining quality of social bonds and informal social control. Turning to the qualitative data—and consistent with a number of qualitative studies that we shall encounter in the following pages—we also find that when people talk about crime, they talk about the people who inhabit public space, about the health and stability of their neighbourhood, about the norms, values, and levels of trust that underpin group relations, and the pace and direction of social change more broadly understood.

In short, we argue that people do not separate out the issue of crime from general unease about the state of social stability and the pace and direction of a rapidly changing society (a by-no-means original point, see *inter alia*: Taylor and Jamieson, 1998; Girling et al., 2000). People associate 'crime' with the breakdown of society, the flouting of society's rules, with the erosion of local neighbourhood cohesion and order. To be afraid of crime may therefore be to show disapproval for the way society seems to have loosened its moral standards, and the way society has dampened its shared expectations to conform to a set of traditionally understood rules. Emotions about crime may consequently be bound up in public concerns about social change and the health of the norms and values that are seen to underpin our society. These concerns have spread across society; they have become part of cultural practices and public sensibilities; and crucially, they also affect those who do not face crime on a 'daily' basis, who do not find themselves in threatening situations.

We thus propose that fear of crime operates less as an irrational and misplaced public sense of the crime problem and more as a lay seismograph or barometer of social cohesion and moral consensus (Jackson, 2006). This is not to say that 'fear' does not play a part in clouding judgement and exacerbating distrust—'it' may even be part of a feedback loop that heightens the sense of the crime problem (Lee, 2001; Lee and Farrall, 2009; Stafford et al., 2007; Jackson and Stafford, 2009). Rather, concerns about crime emerge out of these broader concerns about the health of society and the stability, cooperation, and moral consensus of one's community (see *inter alia,* Biderman et al., 1967: 164). And lying behind worries and anxieties about crime are concerns about moral decline (although, of course, panics about moral decline are experienced in every generation), the erosion of social values (even if it is difficult to make a case for longer term decline, given increased rights on issues of gender, race, and sexuality), and the sense of decline of social capital and the norms, values, and mutual respect that underpin trust, cooperation, and shared concern.

We should say one last thing by way of introduction before we develop more fully the broader context of our study. A key strength of this book is the wealth of data that we bring to bear upon the topic at hand. Theoretical development and critical commentary in the fear of crime literature has gathered apace over the past fifteen years or so—especially in Britain, the USA, and Australia. Yet studies that bring empirical evidence together with careful conceptual advancement have been all too rare. Exceptions exist of course (e.g. Taylor et al., 1996; Tulloch et al., 1998; and Girling et al., 2000); and much of our theoretical framework can be traced back to both previous critiques and particularly these theoretical and empirical advances. But our contribution in this book is to develop an *integrative position* on the fear of crime that is (a) supported by a wealth of high-quality quantitative and qualitative data, that (b) takes seriously what we consider to be the best from the interpretive and qualitative turn in fear of crime research (the recent focus on the social and cultural significance of crime), and that (c) provides a much-needed empirical focus on the everyday experience and significance of worry and anxiety about crime.

The Broader Context of Our Study

The empirical work we present in this book contributes to three ongoing criminological debates:

1. The nature of the fear of crime;
2. The prominent position of crime and security in contemporary times; and
3. The tension between government administration of justice and competing public perceptions and demands (the 'punitive turn' and 'penal populism').

We take each in turn.

The Nature of the Fear of Crime

'Fear of crime' is a slippery and contested concept, with doubts remaining over what the 'fear of crime' means as an everyday experience and as a social phenomenon. Beginning with DuBow et al.'s (1979) less than glowing assessment of the clarity and consistency of survey measurement tools, readers of the criminological literature will have regularly encountered commentary from respected scholars on the importance, and slowness, of progress in this regard. Some have even suggested that fear might be as much a methodological artefact as an empirical reality (Ferraro and LeGrange, 1987; Lee, 1999, 2001; Farrall et al., 1997; Farrall and Gadd, 2004). Not only is it unclear which factors drive public perceptions of risk; it is also unclear what is actually being measured. While few argue that public anxieties about crime are not real, and are not therefore a problem, we are left with rather blunt methodological and conceptual tools.

In particular we lack data on the psychological significance of the fear of crime. Survey respondents are typically asked whether they are 'very', 'fairly', 'not very', or 'not at all' worried (or afraid) about becoming a crime victim. Survey respondents are not asked *how often* they worry, nor *when* they worry, nor *what effects* these worries have on their everyday lives. As a consequence, instead of data on the patterning and ecology of events of fear, we are left with only vague 'global' summaries of intensity of worry or feelings of unsafety.[1] So when people say they are 'very worried' about falling victim, should we assume that fear of crime is a constant presence?

A few criminologists have been attuned to the issue of what survey questions about the fear of crime are actually measuring. Warr (2000) suggests that standard summaries represent future-orientated anxiety rather than any summary of past episodes or current feelings of physical fear (see also Sacco, 2005). Jackson (2006) proposes that these questions access individuals' mental image of the risk of victimization; and having a personalized, structured, and emotionally tinged image of risk might be independent of whether they ever actually find themselves in threatening situations. It may be, therefore, that fear of crime is not always reducible to concrete experiences of threat. This is not to say that people do not find themselves in threatening situations and do not worry for their personal safety (as we shall see in Chapter 3). Rather, it is to say that standard measures of fear of crime do not accurately assess these situated and concrete moments; they instead often collate some emotionally-tinged attitude towards risk.

In this book we shed further light on what fear of crime means as an everyday experience and what fear of crime expresses as a social attitude. We discuss some key methodological issues in defining and accessing public feelings about crime. We consider the survey questions commonly used to measure the fear of crime and catalogue broader lessons from the literature on the psychology of survey response. And we explore the various contributions that one might be able to draw upon from qualitative work and methods, notions of public and private accounts (cf. Douglas, 1971), and cross-disciplinary work on everyday emotions.

---

[1] In a general discussion of 'emotional self-report', Robinson and Clore (2002a, 2002b) argue that research into emotion rarely accesses *experiential knowledge* (the specific details surrounding an emotional arousal). The idea is straightforward. Respondents are rarely, after all, feeling the particular emotion they are being asked to report on at the time of the research interview. Research typically evokes generalized beliefs about emotion, and importantly for an understanding of the fear of crime, these beliefs may not neatly map onto experience. Different processes may be involved that invoke different forms of knowledge and involve different strategies of knowledge retrieval.

The Prominent Position of Crime and Security in Contemporary Times

In the UK—as in the US, and many other so-called 'high-crime' societies—the past few decades have seen crime move to centre stage as a social and political issue. Loader (2008: 399) describes the 'rise of crime as a central organizing principle of political authority and social relations'.

Inter alia we have experienced a consumer boom that has produced more to steal, a reduction in situational controls, an increase in young males with time, freedom, and sub-cultures growing around them, and a reduction in the informal social controls that help shape behaviour and discourage rule-breaking (Garland, 2001: 90–99). Accompanying these social and economic changes, we have seen increasing levels of public anxieties about crime, heightened punitive political rhetoric and action relating to both crime and fear of crime, a greater prominence given to the victim in criminal justice policy, greater force given to public opinion in the policy-making process[2], more emphasis given to security and the management of risk, and an expansion of crime prevention and commercialization of crime control through private security.

According to Garland (2001: 148) the 'liberal elites, the educated middle classes and public sector professionals' had little firsthand experience of crime in the 1950s and 1960s:

They occupied low-crime parts of the city and the suburbs. Their children attended schools that were well disciplined and largely free of crime, drugs, and violence. Their daily routines did not often expose them to the threat of crime, nor did fear of crime occupy a prominent place in their consciousness...The professional middle classes were, moreover, an economically prosperous social group, enjoying the security and status afforded by educational certification and professional credentials in the increasingly professional society of the post-war decades. From this vantage point the group was able to adopt a civilized attitude towards crime and criminals. They viewed crime as a social problem linked to, and explicable by, poor social conditions, and susceptible to the professional, expert, social engineering solutions in which they, as a group, now specialized. For this

---

[2] As Garland (2001: 13) remarks: 'The policy-making process has become profoundly *politicized* and *populist*. Policy measures are constructed in ways that appear to value political advantage and public opinion over the views of experts and the evidence of research'. Emphasis in original.

group to adopt a correctionalist, non-punitive attitude was, at once, to disdain the vulgarities of the under-educated, to express compassion for the poor masses, and to further their own professional interests. (pp. 149–50).

A shift was seen in the 1970s and 1980s, however, as the middle class experience of crime was transformed. Crime moved from a problem that afflicted the poor to a daily consideration for many, denting liberal sensibilities about the seriousness of crime. Increasing direct and indirect experience, a mass media raising the salience of crime and 'institutionalising' public concern, and the growing visibility of signs of crime—in the form of physical incivilities, such as vandalism, and social incivilities, such as groups of intimidating youths hanging around in the street—all helped to bring crime and the risk of victimization into people's everyday lives. Events such as the urban riots of the early 1980s in Brixton and Toxteth (alongside media reports and commentary) transformed crime into a major issue, linked it to questions of race and class, and fixed it as a target for more diffuse anxieties about social change. Images of the excluded and disaffected young males of the inner city became resonant as the perception grew of them 'as a newly dangerous, alien class' (2001: 154).

The mass media—in the form of newspapers, television, radio, and more recently the internet—have played a key role in heightening the social significance of crime. Newspapers and other mass media outlets seemingly delight in highlighting increasing crime levels and ignoring decreasing crime levels. But perhaps it is the regular dramatization of the most sensational and shocking criminal events that has the strongest effect on public perceptions and anxieties about crime. 'Fear-inducing accounts' of events—such as the incident in 2002 in Virginia when two snipers killed ten people—are highly publicized. The media dwell on those acts that are especially serious in their consequence, that are morally reprehensible in their character, that are difficult to fathom and explain. Sunstein (2005) has suggested that media representations of risk can lead to 'cascade' effects throughout society as the event becomes 'cognitively available' to an increasing number of people. Especially heinous crimes are more likely to be reported and picked up by members of society, and 'group polarization' processes then lead to people discussing with each other certain events and risks, typically ending up with many individuals holding a rather extreme view of the crime problem and the risk of crime.[3] As Garland argues, the growing visibility of symbols of crime and neighbourhood disorder may also be important in explaining the prominent position of crime and security in cultural and political life. Much criminological research has demonstrated that fear of crime is as much a response to day-to-day encounters with 'symbols associated with crime' as it is about media messages and specific beliefs about crime (Hale, 1996). Perceptions of the likelihood of victimization are thus shaped by these individual evaluations of the social and physical environment, including judgements about (a) social cohesion, trust, and informal social control, (b) incivilities or 'broken windows,' and (c) the values, norms, and morals of the people who make up the community. Feelings of control may therefore extend beyond control of concrete risks (i.e. explicit events of victimization) to control over the social and physical environment: a diffuse sense of unease and lack of control within an unpredictable and disorderly environment. Indeed, Furedi (2006: 5) argues that:

The fear of crime is a distinctive feature of a society where the influence of informal relations and taken-for-granted norms has diminished in influence. It is anxieties about the uncertainties of day-to-day existence that people echo in discussions about the subject of crime. Insecurity towards expected forms of behaviour and suspicion about the motives of others provide a fertile terrain where perceptions of threats can flourish. These perceptions are intensified in circumstances where social isolation has become pervasive.

---

[3] Existing predispositions may determine, in large part, to what individuals give their attention. Individuals hold attitudes towards risk which reflect and strengthen their values, commitment to particular ways of life, and preferred visions of society (see, for example, Douglas and Wildavsky, 1982). Crime threatens social cohesion and moral consensus, and quickly gets linked to individuals and behaviours that are seen to be hostile to social order. People may attend to information about crime risk from the mass media and interpersonal communication because crime speaks to and dramatizes their concerns about social cohesion, relations, and change (Jackson, 2008). Crime may get into such a symbolic tangle with issues of cohesion because the act of crime communicates hostility to the social order of a community and damages its moral fabric. The prevalence of exaggerated levels of crime may thus signal that a community could be suffering from deteriorating standards of behaviour, the diminishing influence of informal social controls, increasing diversification of norms and values, and decreasing levels of trust, reciprocity, and respect.

Crime may also act as a handy receptacle for expressing and distilling broader social anxieties about social change (Bauman, 1999; Taylor and Jamieson, 1998; Girling et al., 2000). Scholars such as Zygmunt Bauman and John Pratt have argued that at a time of rapid social change, of decreasing certainty, of increasing diversity and liberalization, and of decreasing deference to authority, crime becomes a handy receptacle for the broader social anxieties that such broader rapid change engenders. In other words, crime becomes entangled with broader issues of stability and breakdown and the sense that governments have lost the ability to 'steer the ship to safe waters'. Equally, we are increasingly seeing the world through the lens of crime and deviance. Think of Lee's feedback loop (2001) in which fear of crime and government responses to fear of crime only heighten the salience of crime, leading to ever more temptation to pursue punitive criminal justice policies (see pages 30–40 in Chapter 2). Loader and Walker (2007) have drawn our attention to how 'security' has leaked into areas of social life not immediately related to crime. For example, reassurance policing and political rhetoric on anti-social behaviour (ASB) encourages people to view certain social conditions through the lens of crime, policing, and security. However, and as colleagues such as Lucia Zedner (2003) have been quick to point out, security demands are never ending; the more provision is made for security (via 'peep-holes' in front doors, burglar and car alarms, and the such like) the more (a) we are reminded of our (pre-supposed) vulnerability and (b) made to feel that somehow we are entering the lion's den naked when such provisions are unavailable to us. (See also Loader, 2008: 401–2.)

Further afield from these criminological foci—and on which we can do little more than speculate for the present (see Chapter 8 also)—a body of work has started to chart the rise of affluence and the attendant rise of various social problems. That the UK, Europe, and many other parts of the world (both industrialized and developing) have undergone a period of sustained economic changes in the past 40–50 years ought not to be news to anyone. However, there has been a recognition that the (until recently) increasing levels of affluence experienced by many in Europe, North America, and elsewhere may not be making people happier—in fact such developments may be making people less happy and more insecure. Amongst the authors who have articulated the view that increasing affluence may be bad for societies are Avner Offer (2006), Robert

H. Frank (2007), and Oliver James (2007). Offer's arguments are representative of this position: affluence is driven by novelty (2006: vii), whilst abundance causes harm in a number of ways (producing obesity, mental ill-health, violence, economic fraud, and insecurity, 2006: 2). How might such approaches assist us in understanding anxieties about crime?

It was Zolotas (1981: 1) who, along similar lines, claimed that: 'When an industrial society reaches an advanced state of affluence, the rate of increase in social welfare drops below the rate of economic growth, and tends ultimately to become negative.' Put another way, as a society's wealth increases, so increases in welfare ultimately suffer. In short, increases in affluence result in decreases in social welfare, so rises in levels of income past a certain point provide no increases in well-being. Why ought this to be the case? One possible answer is that as income increases, individuals adjust to it and raise their standards—remaining on a 'hedonistic treadmill'. Another possible answer—which resonates with our own concerns—is the thesis put forward by Inglehart: that as a result of their experience of post-war economic security, cohorts of Europeans and North Americans have shifted the preferences from economic to non-economic rewards. As such, economic security encourages us into wanting non-economic goals—including non-economic security. If one measures affluence in terms of the average income per head, then, the US has led the UK by one generation (Offer, 2006: 7). Starting from the end of the 1960s, we witnessed a shift in attitudes away from seeing common welfare and public service as the chief form of well-being towards the view that private benefits were the key sources of well-being (Offer, 2006: 7–8).

Thus, at around this same time there was a shift in the forms of security which people sought (since their immediate economic needs had been met). At around this same time, as others have documented (Loo, 2009), rightwing politicians started to refer to the 'problem of crime'. These sentiments resonated with members of the middle class, who as Frank (2007) noted often felt as if they had lost most during the period of rising affluence. This is also the same approximate point at which we see the widespread recognition (or 'invention' and 'production' for some, see Lee, 2007; Loo, 2009) of the fear of crime in the US and then the UK. Thus, first in the US and then the UK, economic growth led to rising prosperity, which, from around the late 1960s, started to produce not only diminishing rewards, but also increases in levels of anxiety (Offer, 2006: 282).

In this way, the introduction of the fear of crime as an object of enquiry in the late 1960s in the US and the late 1970s in the UK may not simply be because of rising crime rates, but also because of background economic factors and the implications which these had for value systems in industrialized nations. Rising levels of affluence, to which people became habituated and which were then challenged by the oil crisis in the early 1970s, produced increased levels of anxiety. Added to this, according to some authors, was a desire to shift political debates from the socially progressive, welfare-minded concensus which had characterized the post-war period, towards an agenda which would more closely favour neo-conservative policy concerns (Loo, 2009). In this analysis, the rise of the fear of crime was the result of a 'perfect storm': rising affluence, shifts in values as a result of this, an economic crisis in the case of the UK, and an attempt to shift the agenda by the political rightwing in the US and the UK. Although the nature of the data which we have to hand does not easily lend itself to a direct empirical analysis of some of these propositions, we return to these matters in the closing sections of this book, in order to reflect on them.

The Tension between Government Administration of Justice and Competing Public Perceptions and Demands (The 'Punitive Turn' and 'Penal Populism')

To guide democratic societies and ensure order and prosperity, governments must manage natural and human-made hazards. To regulate crime, environmental catastrophe, economic collapse, and other future prospects and uncertain events, governments need rational and technical forms of information and reasoning. Because governments have limited resources, they must give priority to certain issues and decide on appropriate courses of action, ideally according to dispassionate and systematic assessments of likelihood and consequence. But of course not all future events can be known or foreseen. Not all risks can be eliminated entirely.

As both Garland (2001) and Loader (2006b) have argued, prior to (roughly) the mid-1980s it was the liberal elites who took on the role of 'looking after' criminal justice policy. Criminal justice system policy during this era was made through a dispassionate and rational assessment of 'what worked', about the role of rehabilitation, about the allocation of police resources through the targeting of volume crime and especially serious victimization types. However—and as we shall see in Chapter 2—this started to unravel during the late 1970s and throughout the 1980s: the public started to make (and importantly voice) assessments of risk that differed to those produced by rational and technical judgements.

Study after study has shown that the public are more concerned about (media fed?) evocative risks that chime with broader themes of social significance and outrage. Crime, of course, is just one of these. And it is no surprise that citizens fear sensational but rare crimes. When processing information about risk, people often rely upon cognitive heuristics and qualitative judgements rather than engage in more careful, actuarial, numeric assessments of probability and consequence. Such reliance on qualitative judgements—on the emotional valence of a danger, the availability and vividness of relevant imagery, and assessments of control, familiarity, and impact—helps explain why people often *do* worry about some risks which perhaps, if they were all actuaries, they would not (because the objective risk is actually very low but images of the hazard are readily available, evocative, and vivid) and *do not* worry about other risks which they should (because the objective risk is high but the hazard is seen as routine and mundane (for example, car journeys within short distances from one's home).

Such worries, as they relate to crime and disorder, lead to the public clamouring for 'more police on the streets', more 'to be done about knife crime amongst teenagers', 'longer sentences' to be given to murderers and criminals who commit other heinous acts, and the outraged claim that 'life ought to mean life'. In these ways, 'fearfulness' often leads to (or at very least, is temporally associated with) demands for increases in 'punitiveness'. More dispassionate assessments—by policy makers and criminologists alike—often suggest a misplaced and heightened set of public expectations about the levels of control possible that can be a frustrating source of pressure on policy making.

We have thus witnessed the movement from dispassionate, civil servant-led policy (aimed at tackling the problem of crime 'quietly') to 'hot' populist policy, often driven by politicians.

Public anxieties about crime, sensationalist media reportage, and political responses have coalesced around an increasingly illiberal dynamic whereby it would appear that the public have lost trust in their governments' abilities to control crime, punish law-breakers, and ensure safety. Such sentiments, often described as 'penal populism', chime with broader social anxieties about 'moral decay' and the direction and pace of other social changes, and, it would also appear, provide the kindling for demands for punitive actions from the State. As we have attempted to document elsewhere (see Farrall and Lee, 2009: 3–6) the media represent these issues back to the population; governments pander and enter into 'Law and Order arms races', market organizations exploit any potentials for extracting profit, the police are mandated to act in all sorts of new and 're-assuring' ways and so on. Politicians and governments want (and indeed need for reasons of political legitimacy) to create the sense that they have control, that they understand public concerns about crime, that they agree that norms, values, and controls need to be defended, and that the State can after all 'steer the ship'. Hence eye-catching populist schemes and sound bites extolling 'get tough' messages such as 'zero tolerance', 'three strikes and you're out', and 'tough on crime; tough on the causes of crime'.

Governments face numerous dilemmas. One of the trickiest to handle comes when the public raise concerns about certain issues that seemingly outweigh the reality of the problem. Measured and dispassionate crime policy and the debates which surround them produce balanced laws, punishments, and policing. Resources are put into areas with high levels of crime; the police engage in strategies that are known to be efficacious; efforts to rehabilitate offenders supported. But when the public intrude, when there is a clamouring for different sorts and styles of punishment, when the media 'talk up' certain issues, then there is pressure to change policy, to bend the criminal justice system further towards the (supposed) 'needs' of the public. This can be as frustrating for policy makers who believe that the public are overly anxious about crime as it is for academic researchers and less-strident politicians. There arises a situation wherein the public start to distrust their government, whilst, at the same time, some engaged in the work of the government view the public as placing undue pressure on policy-making processes, calling for overly punitive policies simply on the basis of their own misunderstanding and lack of knowledge.

Our contribution to this debate is to encourage policy-makers and police officers (and politicians too, perhaps) to 'stand back' from all this seemingly unending 'demand' for 'safety', 'policing', and other forms of activity aimed at addressing 'all this fear', and to consider what these demands are *really* about. In many cases such demands will refer to problems which need to be tackled, but not in all. And it may be that those who shout loudest have least to shout about (Hope et al., 2001). The resulting problem, of course, then becomes the problems associated with leaving out the voice from one constituency, namely, the loss of legitimacy (see Walklate 2002 for an example of this). Our contribution calls for a less hot-headed and more reasonable debate and set of arguments about crime—perhaps one that is rather difficult to have (Loader, 2006b).

Our Overall Contribution

So—one may reasonably ask—what is our broad and over-arching contribution? What are we saying to policy makers? To politicians? To our fellow academics? In the UK the 'perception gap' or 'reassurance gap' has referred to the refusal of the public to believe that crime has been falling for some time. This distance between 'fear' and 'crime' continues to frustrate, since 'fear' is widely believed to be damaging and irrational. But is worry about crime always damaging? Does not worrying about crime indicate another aspect of the post-welfare state settlement: responsibilization? 'Functional fear' as some have termed it (Jackson and Gray, 2009) may merely be getting on with the job of looking after oneself and one's own. And—as others before us (e.g. Sparks, 1992) have asked—irrational compared to what? The actual incidence of crime? Well, people may not think like that.

How ought governments to respond? Ignore uneducated assessments of risk (and the seemingly punitive demands they bring forth)? Treat the fear of crime as a hyped and stereotypical set of beliefs about crime (intolerance towards young people, media-fuelled beliefs in crime out of control) that must be calmed down, treating it as a problem separate to crime and tackling it through reassurance and education? Wrap up fear and crime in one package and elevate crime and punitive responses? Treat fear of crime as part of a broader battle of cultural cognition?

To a large extent, what governments, academics, policy makers, and pollsters should do depends on the nature of the fear of crime—the topic of this book. Debate in political, social, and academic arenas continues to ebb and flow on the issue of the (ir)rationality and (un)realism of public beliefs about crime. Much of this debate has been unproductive (Sparks, 1992). But the pragmatics and constraints of policy-making mean that the issue rarely seems to go away. Our contribution is the argument that to compare 'fear' to the actual extent of crime is to miss the point (this is by no means an original claim, we concede: see Sparks, 1992). This is especially so since the fear of crime is based not on public assessments of some abstracted crime problem but rather on public assessments of neighbourhood conditions, broader societal change, and circulating representations of criminals and groups in society.

Moreover, there is (we submit) a moral, social value and normative component to the fear of crime. By associating certain individuals, groups, and social conditions with crime, people may be articulating their sense that these run counter to their idea of a stable and cohesive society. Fear of crime may thus be an important attitudinal social indicator, reflecting concerns about the erosion of traditional sources of authority, anxieties about the cohesion and stability of communities, a desire for stronger groups that cooperatively pursue common goals, and concerns about the deterioration in the everyday civil interaction between strangers. But the fear of crime is not only this; it is also a sense of immediate threat to one's security—or to the security of things one holds dear. We misunderstand the fear of crime if we approach it as simply about either crime or a way of making sense of social change. Therefore 'what' one 'does' about 'the fear of crime' depends very much on which element of this phenomenon one wishes to 'tackle'. Hence our exploration of the fear of crime along the lines hinted at above (and outlined in greater depth in subsequent chapters); that is as both a set of discrete, episodic experiences, and as being expressive of another set of feelings and sentiments.

A Quick Summary of the Structure of the Book

It might be worth us devoting at this juncture a few words to the organization of the rest of the book. There are three parts to our

A Quick Summary of the Structure of the Book 19

contribution. The rest of Part I is very much an organizing and marshalling of the key tenets of our core arguments. Chapter 2 outlines the emergence of the fear of crime as a piece of political rhetoric and as an object of criminological interest. Chapter 3 presents arguments—supported by empirical data—which underpin a number of our later claims. These revolve around the design and interpretation of survey questions, the frequency with which basic human emotions (such as fear) are encountered, and the nature of the fear of crime when it comes-a-visiting. Chapter 4 reorganizes a number of the theoretical stances which have been adopted to account for the fear of crime into one theoretical model. By the end of Part I we will have outlined the wider background to debates surrounding the fear of crime, described 'where', 'why', and 'when' it emerged, what the fear of crime is and how best to make sense of it.

Part II commences upon the 'real work' and in so doing we draw upon data from a number of sources, both qualitative and quantitative. Chapter 5 explores the theoretical model we outlined in Chapter 4 using qualitative data. Chapter 6 starts our quantitative investigation of our new approach to the fear of crime—modelling as it does types and intensities of fear. Chapter 7 explores portions of this same data, this time more closely relating it to the theoretical model we developed in Chapter 4 and explored initially in Chapter 5.

Part III contains just one chapter. Chapter 8 recaps what we have learnt from our investigations into the fear of crime. The discussion touches on a number of issues, including economic change, rising affluence, and the notion of 'winners' and 'losers' during periods of socio-economic change, and—of course—the role of these factors in the (re)production of anxiety. We also explore a number of pressing issues, including the frequency with which the fear of crime is encountered within the lives of citizens in industrialized nations such as the US, Canada, Australia, and those in the EU, and what governments can 'do' to address popular anxieties about crime.

2
The Provenance of Fear

'Security is mostly a superstition. It does not exist in nature, nor do the children of men as a whole experience it. Avoiding danger is no safer in the long run than outright exposure.' (Helen Keller, *The Open Door*, 1957).

As a topic of academic research, policy study and public debate, the fear of crime has been with us—at the earliest—since the mid-1960s. Of course, this is not to suggest for one moment that anxieties about crime had *never* surfaced prior to this point. Rather, from the 1960s and 1970s we have witnessed a massive growth in the efforts put into understanding and controlling such fears. Where these fears 'came' from, why they emerged at all, the uses to which they were put, and an understanding of the processes associated with their emergence is the topic of this chapter.

In the first part of this chapter we summarize the development of the fear of crime as a concept and as an object of criminological research. We draw upon qualitative interviews with 28 academic and government criminologists, conducted in 1999 and 2000. Inevitably this section draws heavily from our previous writings on this subject (most notably Jackson, 2004b; Ditton and Farrall, 2000). Following this, in the second part of this chapter, we outline some of the explanations which have been posited for the seemingly inexorable rise of the fear of crime as a topic for and of research. This takes us into uncertain terrain and accordingly the pitfalls are numerous; this part of our chapter necessarily remains informed but speculative. However, the speculation serves as the basis for some intriguing debates about 'where' all of this fear came from, and 'who' or 'what' delivered it to us.

The Fear of Crime: The Career of a Concept

There is ample historical evidence that public concerns about dangerous localities and people are not a new phenomenon (see, amongst others: Curtis, 2001; Pearson, 1983; Shaw, 1931). The consideration of crime has historically formed a part of public consciousness and discourse, a detail often overlooked. For instance, Curtis (2001) analyses the newspaper reporting of the famous 'Jack the Ripper' murders in late nineteenth-century London. He describes how the mass media heightened already high levels of public alarm about crime and examines how the murders were linked to debates regarding the inability of the police to protect the public (no-one was ever caught or prosecuted for the murders) and the growth of a semi-criminal social underclass. This dramatic case reflected a public already fascinated by sensational crimes and typified how such events are 'embedded in a matrix of moral and political imperatives about law and order' (2001: 15).

Of course, the idea that a particular behaviour becomes labelled as criminal according to formally codified legal rules and normatively prescribed codes, and that this occurs according to an array of complex social, institutional, and cultural processes is not new. But moreover, at different times, and in different places, some crimes have come to be seen as representing greater threats to individuals, societies, and governments than others, and the reasons for these disparities may be many, varied, and time- and context-specific. In the UK towards the end of the 1970s for example, Hall et al. (1978) identified a 'moral panic' about the young, black, male robber. This figure operated as a vivid metaphor for the breakdown of social order and stability, a touchstone to racial tensions amongst the white population. More recently, concerns about sex offenders and paedophiles have dominated popular imagination.

Public anxieties about crime thus have a long history; in this respect, the 'fear' of 'crime' is nothing new. Nor do public perceptions of risk exist independently from evaluations of the cultural significance of crime, images of 'the criminal' and understandings about what crime 'says' about society. Consider Pearson's (1983) argument that many generations have expressed their own 'respectable fears' about social groups and behaviours, especially regarding delinquent and criminal youths. These groups and the fears associated with them have often represented to society the notion that its secure, stable moral centre is under threat. Bound up in this concern and the stigmatization of particular groups is the expression of more inchoate anxieties about the direction and character of social change (see also Girling et al., 2000).

If public anxiety about crime has long been with us, if public anxieties have long expressed a range of social concerns—what is new? Well, we think there are one or two distinctive aspects to the modern concept of the 'fear of crime'. Let us turn our minds to the US during the 1960s, where our analysis of the career of the concept of the 'fear of crime' begins.

The Beginnings: United States of America during the 1960s and 1970s

The furthest point back that scholars have traced the genesis of the modern idea of 'fear of crime'—the contemporary manifestation of public attitudes and responses to crime, as an object of study, as a category of description, and as a topic of considerable political salience—was the President's Crime Commission on Law Enforcement and the Administration of Justice (1967) in the United States of America.[1] This Commission was initiated by Lyndon Johnson in 1965, and is sometimes referred to as the Katzenbach Commission after its Chair, Nicholas deB Katzenbach. The main report of the Commission (President's Commission, 1967: 49) commented:

A chief reason that this Commission was organized was that there is widespread public anxiety about crime. In one sense, this entire report is an effort to focus that anxiety on the central problems of crime and criminal justice. A necessary part of that effort has been to study as carefully as possible the anxiety itself. The Commission has tried to find out precisely what aspects of crime Americans are anxious about, whether their anxiety is a realistic response to actual danger, how anxiety affects the daily life of Americans, what actions against crime by the criminal justice system and the government as a whole might best allay public anxiety.

---

[1] Readers are directed towards Harris' (1969) account of the Omnibus Crime Control and Safe Streets Act, 1968, and its passage through the US Congressional process. After President John F. Kennedy was assassinated in 1963, riots flared up in 20 inner-city 'ghettos' and the issue of civil rights boiled over in numerous arenas; disorder and unrest became a source of national anxiety. Race was a hot topic. Stanko (2000) describes how the McCone Commission (1966, and quoted in the President's Commission on Law Enforcement and the Administration of Justice, 1967) examined the cause of unrest, concluding that the structural conditions of poverty and disadvantage in many predominantly black areas were leading to anger, hostility, and resentment. The President's Commission report clearly located white anxieties about crime within the context of racial tension and unrest.

In particular, we turn to the reports of three crime surveys commissioned by this body (Biderman et al., 1967; Ennis, 1967; Reiss, 1967), conducted at the same time as other projects that sought to count unrecorded victimization. These—in part—led to the emergence of National Crime Surveys conducted regularly by the Bureau of Justice Statistics.

For the first time, these (at that point, pilot) studies included questions about public attitudes towards crime and perceptions of their own safety. The report of the first survey (Biderman et al., 1967) contained a chapter entitled 'fear of crime' that reported on the combination of five questions to create an 'index of anxiety' (Biderman et al., 1967: 121). These included subjective reports on the chances of being beaten up, whether neighbours created disturbances, if respondents would move if they could for reasons of 'trouble', and whether safety and moral characteristics were important in their neighbourhood. The measures clearly elicited an unstructured range of attitudes, behavioural intentions, beliefs, and evaluations that were directed towards crime, safety, disorder, and 'moral characteristics'.

A number of important findings and arguments were documented in the report of this study, all revolving around the comparison of public perceptions of the crime problem (using the index) to the reported incidence of crime (using police recorded crime statistics, and crime experienced by the survey respondents). Finding that anxiety did not mirror these statistically estimated risk profiles, the authors argued that attitudes towards 'the gravity of the crime problem and its dangers to themselves' were primarily based on factors 'other than their [people's] own circumstances and experiences' (Biderman et al., 1967: 122). Similarly they argued that 'fear of personal attack', where respondents were asked whether violent crime (such as shootings, stabbings, or rapes) had increased in Washington during the past five years,[2] appeared: '... disproportionate to the relatively low objective probabilities of these dangers in comparison with other perils to life and property' (Biderman et al., 1967: 133–4).

---

[2] Treating beliefs about changing crime rates as synonymous with fear of victimization was not considered problematic or commented on in any way in this report. Similarly, there was no theoretical elaboration of the five measures that were combined to form the index of fear.

Yet despite arguments that public anxieties were *not* based on experience (with an implicit suggestion that they were exaggerated and based on a misunderstanding of the reality of the situation), the concluding chapter of this report attempted to contextualize public anxieties by discussing the symbolic nature of crime (Biderman et al., 1967: 164). The authors argued that citizens' concerns were also understandable because of the meanings and resonance that the incidence of crime has for the moral and social consensus and direction of a neighbourhood or society:

> The special significance of crime is at the social level. The intensity of public reaction to it is understandable in that it reveals weaknesses of the moral order on which not only everyone's safety depends but also almost everything else that is important and precious in life. Crimes therefore have significance in proportion to the extent to which they affront the moral sensibilities of persons…Perceptions of changes in the prevalence of crime can be expected to evoke particularly intense public reactions in that these can be taken as signs of threats to the fundamental moral order. This clearly is the case with much of the current public reaction to news of increasing crime.

It is instructive to take one step back and look at the wider social and political context of this research. The concept of the fear of crime was emerging out of a particular social and political climate: of rising levels of recorded crime; a new government focus on law and order; the commissioning of a series of victim surveys (and the broader context of a State increasingly gathering information about its citizens); racialized concerns about 'black rioting' and 'black crime'; high-level debate about the extent of police powers; and rightwing white concern about the extension of rights to the poor and to black people (see: Harris, 1969; Furstenburg, 1971; Ditton and Farrall, 2000; Stanko, 2000; Loo and Grimes, 2004; Loo, 2009; and Lee, 1999, 2001).

Civil 'Unrest' and the Rise of the 'Crime Problem'

The 1960s were indeed turbulent times for the US: President John F. Kennedy was assassinated in 1963; riots flared up in 20 inner-city 'ghettos' in the mid-1960s; the issue of civil rights boiled over in numerous arenas; disorder and unrest had become national anxieties, with civil rights movement leader Martin Luther King Jr. being assassinated in 1968. The government was understandably concerned about these issues and how they were affecting the general mood of the public. Stanko (2000: 14) describes how the McCone Commission (which reported in 1966, but was quoted in the President's Commission on Law Enforcement and the Administration of Justice, 1967) examined the cause of unrest in US cities, concluding that the structural conditions of poverty and disadvantage in many predominantly black areas were leading to anger, hostility, and resentment. The President's Commission report clearly located white anxieties about crime within this context of racial tension and unrest (Stanko, 2000). It was against the background of urban unrest that a number of Republican politicians started to talk about crime during their campaigning for the 1964 and 1968 Presidential elections. Barry Goldwater (the Republican Party's nominee for President in the 1964 election) raised the topic of 'crime in the streets', whilst Nixon also relied on a law and order programme for his 1968 campaign (ironically given the events of 1972–4); see Loo and Grimes, 2004. Lewis and Salem (1986: 3) commenting on the background, noted that:

> By the late 1960s, the soaring crime rate and the ghetto riots turned the attention of policymakers away from the criminal and towards the victim. The so-called backlash, reflected in public anger at the infusion of funds into the Black community and at the concern with the rights of the criminal rather than those of the victim, led to an interest in alternative approaches to the crime prevention problem that would give primary consideration to the behaviour of those who are threatened by criminal activity.

Fair enough. However, in digging deeper, and in particular in Richard Harris's remarkable—but seemingly little read—book (Harris, 1969), we find further evidence that what we now rather blandly refer to as the 'fear of crime' may have begun life as a rather more unpleasant and inherently racist creature. Harris's account could easily be dismissed were it not for the fact that his book contains a highly favourable Introduction by Nicholas deB. Katzenbach, as mentioned above, the Chairman of the Commission on Law Enforcement and the Administration of Justice.

The book is of great interest as it chronicles the extraordinary American Senatorial shennanigans which preceded the passage of the Omnibus Crime Control and Safe Streets Act on 6 June 1968—a bill that Harris (1969: 14) refers to as 'a piece of demagoguery devised out of malevolence and enacted in hysteria'. Without going into too much detail, suffice it to say that, sponsored by Senator McClellan, the Act was designed to reassert the rights of the white and powerful over the new rights of the poor and black—rights which had then recently been imposed by *Mallory v. United States* (1957), *Gideon v. Wainwright* (1963), *Escobedo v. Illinois* (1964), and *Miranda v. Arizona* (1966). (The *Mallory* decision effectively prevented the police from obtaining confessions, valid or not, by the pressure of holding suspects incommunicado and questioning them intensively and at inordinate length. *Gideon* stipulated that if a defendant in a criminal case could not afford a lawyer the State had to provide one. The *Escobedo* case required that a suspect be allowed to consult a lawyer when a police investigation switched from the exploratory to the accusatory. And *Miranda* that a suspect in custody must be warned prior to any questioning that he has the right to remain silent).

So, the 'public alarm' about crime emerged, via the manipulation of the Nixonian 'silent majority', from rightwing white concern about the extension of rights to the poor and the black. Indeed, in one of the very first academic articles on the subject, Frank Furstenburg comments (1971: 601) 'fear of crime is the symptom of the silent majority's lashing back'. In an admirably clear statement, Furstenburg elucidates the findings from the Presidential Commission, and presents some of the paradoxes that have become the staple diet of fear of crime research: that anxiety about crime is not always commensurate with the risk of victimization (with fear, ironically, being the most intense among inner-city low-income blacks); and that those least in danger are the most afraid.

Against *this* backdrop, then, public anxieties are more explicable. Crime gathered its resonance not just from the *meaning* of the event itself, but also from wider social change in society (and, of course, although in a more diffuse way, as an image of that society, which it typifies, expresses, and informs the citizenry about itself). Added to this was a growing awareness by conservative politicians of these feelings and of their emerging salience in the minds of ordinary people. Citizens believed that crime was a problem; that they themselves were more at risk than previously; and that these issues reflected broader changes and threats in society. Self-reported attitudes in surveys expressed a range of judgements, values, and everyday experiences of emotion and perceptions of risk, and articulated responses to and interpretations of a range of connected changes in society that shaped the importance, salience, and cultural meaning of crime. But the initial focus on the wider context of fear of crime gradually became lost in research and debate. As Stanko (2000: 16) proposes, 'the social tensions that gave rise to the creation of the crime survey initially—that of White American anxiety about personal safety within a climate of racialised frustration—have been forgotten in the rush to embrace the democratic possibilities of the crime survey'.

The label 'fear of crime' was born out of these early studies. It emerged as an object of social scientific investigation against a backdrop of increasing governmental interest in 'Law and Order' (cf. Lee, 1999, 2001, 2007) and a State in the throes of becoming ever more a 'knowledge society' (see Melanson, 1973; Lee, 2001, 2007), accruing increasing amounts of information about its citizens. With growing sophistication of statistical collection and analysis, combined with the political will to understand and intervene in the lives of its population, so a context emerged where national surveys were commissioned.

The debate quickly honed in on the relationship between fear, experience of crime, and 'objective' risk. Surveys allowed the populace to articulate their feelings, beliefs, and behaviours in a rather ill-defined and unstructured manner. The resulting data were ordered and interpreted using a set of restrictive and normative precepts and propositions concerning the rationality or otherwise of public perceptions. Were people 'too' anxious? (and, latterly, what was the 'correct' level of fear?) How did anxiety levels compare to official estimates of the actual threat? Biderman et al.'s (1967) interpretation of the data as an expression of wider concerns about moral and social order suggested that the questions were engaging with more than just public experience of 'fear' relating to their perceptions of the immediate threat of crime. But this notion (that fear of crime might not be reducible to actuarial assessments of risk) was quickly lost.

Britain during the 1970s and 1980s

Let us now shift focus to the British experience—and in particular to start to draw upon some of Jackson's interviews with UK-based experts on the fear of crime (the nature of these interviews is outlined in our Methodological Appendix). Jackson (2004) interviewed 28 such experts about the fear of crime as part of his earlier research into this topic. A number of interviewees identified two features of the social scientific literature in the 1970s as being salient to the conceptual development of the fear of crime in the UK during the 1970s and 1980s (also see: Lee, 1999, 2001). Both were radical positions: the so-called 'moral panic theorists' within criminology, and feminist sociologists and criminologists (operating against a backdrop of women's movements more generally). Although the term 'fear of crime' was not used, these analyses increased the salience of the topic of public anxiety within criminology, bringing it forward as an issue to be explained and diagnosed. They created what Lee (2001: 232, 2007) describes as 'a phenomenon that now required criminological explanation', as well as providing a set of concepts and perspectives that would resurface in later debates. One interviewee pointed to the US as the origin of the fear of crime:

> When the Americans started doing the crime surveys in the 1960s, [fear] became more of an issue because all of a sudden once you can quantify something, even if you don't agree with the way it has been quantified, people sort of leap in, and want to analyse it.

The notion of a moral panic was used to analyse how public concerns about crime and deviance can be stirred up by the mass media, and how the hyping of these issues can serve an ideological purpose (Hall et al., 1978). They examined what they identified as a moral panic over young, black, and male robbers that developed in the latter part of the 1970s. A central part of their thesis was that robbery became a metaphor for a breakdown of order and cohesion, of declining stability and standards of living. It was also capable of condensing racial tensions amongst the white population. In this way, as others have noted (e.g. Hay, 1996), Thatcher used and reconstructed the existing *industrial* crisis as being a crisis of *law and order*. Similarly Pearson (1983) described how the history of public debate about delinquency and youth crime in the UK has involved notions of generational decline in terms of family, community, authority, tradition, and morality, so that young offenders symbolize a kind of modern emptiness. Comparable descriptions of this malaise can be identified in public documents from the eighteenth and nineteenth centuries.

The other intellectual current involved feminist scholarship, which collectively (and correctly) brought attention to male violence, abuse, and harassment of women, all against a wider critique of patriarchy. Put simply, feminist arguments about violence, victimization, and their effects stressed the pervasive and insidious nature of experience and of fears. Directly and indirectly, male abuse acted as a form of social control. Female concerns certainly ought not to be seen as misplaced or exaggerated. Rather, as women's refuges and rape crisis centres were opening and the women's movements in general were raising public and political awareness of male abuse, a body of literature was highlighting the inherently gendered nature of such violence and its reality in women's lives (see Connell, 1987; Dobash and Dobash, 1979, 1992; Gordon and Riger, 1988).

Political Interest in Public Anxieties about Crime

The late 1970s saw crime and public concerns about crime in Britain become increasingly salient in social and political issues. As Rock (1990: 254) describes, the Home Office, noting the rising crime rates, became more and more concerned about possible knock-on effects for the criminal justice system and the seemingly intractable nature of the crime problem. It '...had become defensive about its performance. It was said to be "locked into a gloomy cycle", spending more without apparent effect' (1990: 255). Again, Jackson's interviewees provide similar accounts:

Now, there is an argument that one of the functions of the British Crime Survey, as far as the Home Office was concerned, was to try and play down on this, to say 'it's not quite as bad as you thought it was'...

Interestingly, in the UK things were starting to mirror the US politicization of the fear of crime—with rightwing parties again leading the way. In her final election broadcast on the eve of the 1979 election, Margaret Thatcher (then the Conservative party leader who was about to win a landslide victory) referred to the importance for citizens of 'feeling safe in the streets' (Riddell, 1985: 193). As one of Jackson's interviewees stated 'You've only got to look at the way Thatcher used [the concept of the fear of crime] before the '79 Election – "people afraid to walk the streets", "we're not going to give in to this", "we're not going to be cowed"...'. Another interviewee, formerly a senior government official, said Mrs Thatcher was 'a Prime Minister who had, for the first time I think, seriously made crime and putting down crime an election issue in the '79 election'. Other experts felt that is was partly responsible for her election victory: 'there was this major conflation of fear of crime and crime and hooliganism and industrial unrest and protest and so on by Margaret Thatcher in the build up to the 1979 election and it undoubtedly did figure as an important factor in the Conservative victory'. Prior to the 1979 election, she had also claimed that the country wanted 'less tax and more law and order' (Evans, 1997: 75; Savage, 1990: 89). In making such statements, Thatcher served to make legitimate the prejudices of Tory activists (Riddell, 1985: 193), and, we suspect, vocalized a set of concerns which were held by the electorate, although perhaps had not yet been fully articulated into a coherent discourse (see Farrall, 2006 more generally).

The public were becoming more vociferous about crime and their concerns, yet there was also a sense—at least in some sections of government—that these anxieties were somehow misplaced. One of Jackson's interviewees remarked that 'I think throughout the '70s there was an awareness of the sort of get tough on crime pressures and a sense that they were misplaced. That was a core Home Office ideology, I think'. In other words, that these anxieties were contributing to a set of 'get tough' attitudes amongst politicians. The context was government thinking that its citizens had begun to feel unprotected by the State. Rock (1990: 257–8) observes that:

> It was supposed that public confidence was the foundation upon which crimes were reported, co-operation with the police was secured, victims and witnesses came forward, vigilantism and anarchy were discouraged, public fear was suppressed, and governments were respected. Without public confidence, it was argued, the criminal justice system would have to be presented in an even more severe guise.

It was felt that policy and the public needed facts and reassurance to calm down excessive concern and elevated demands that were being stoked up by public debate. The British Crime Survey was commissioned by the government, and would measure the 'dark figure' of unreported and unrecorded incidents, but also show that most crime in the country was trivial, non-violent, and mundane. As one interviewee remarked '...the British Crime Survey was doing ideological work as well as producing factual information about crime'.

The first sweep (and all subsequent sweeps) contained a measure of 'fear for personal safety' (Hough and Mayhew, 1983: 34) replicated from Ennis (1967): 'How safe do you feel walking alone in this area after dark?' Analysis of these data produced findings that mirrored many of those in the US. High levels of anxiety, particularly amongst women and the elderly, gave rise to what became known as the 'risk-fear paradox'.

The Home Office moved quickly to downplay the meaning of these findings. This reflected their own orthodox position that public fears were misplaced, exaggerated, and that they were '…a serious problem which needs to be tackled separately from the incidence of crime itself' (Hough and Mayhew, 1983: 26). The authors continued '…excessive anxiety about crime not only impoverishes people's lives, but also makes it difficult to secure rational discussion of criminal policy' (Hough and Mayhew, 1983: 33–4). If public fear of crime exceeded the *actual* reality then re-education and public involvement in community safety became a serious and important policy objective. To downplay public concern could also be to downplay embarrassing levels of concern by a government proud of its 'Law and Order' image. A number of interviewees argued that it was politically expedient to partly displace the problem of crime onto the fear of crime. But the Home Office's stance was also partly a function of frustration that uninformed public opinion might deleteriously affect more reasoned Home Office policy, coupled with a sense that crime was *not* as serious a problem as public opinion might have it.

However, certain sections of academia did not buy the Home Office line. As one interviewee remarked: 'essentially one of the critiques for me is what crime surveys do in conceptualising victimization—it homogenises it, it turns people into the average and generic victim…and what I was doing was saying, you can't do that for women. You've got to understand that gender isn't about being generic'. Alongside these feminist concerns were those raised by some on the political left of academia: namely that crime *was* a serious problem for many of those living in lower socio-economic neighbourhoods. As one interviewee said:

I think to some extent they [the Home Office BCS team] were [trying to reduce public concern over crime] and they tended to give averages like, you know, you would only get robbed once every, I don't know how many years it was, 35 years or something…Yeah, and that's the sort of average that Jock Young and Co. scorned. But I mean obviously that was the first victim survey, the average was the average for the whole country. And once you break it down, by definition an average includes that which is very high as well as that which is very low. It is perfectly fair to say in some areas that it's an unacceptably high risk and that sharpens an awareness of where those areas are.

Another interviewee, one who was closely involved in the left realist and local crime survey movement, claimed that these movements were '...very much a critique or a correction of the British Crime Survey. So it was very deliberately an attempt to, in a sense, have empirical ammunition or empirical findings which would address some of the problems that the Home Office was using the British Crime Survey for'. This, in the words of a further interviewee, shifted the debate away from the direction the Home Office had hoped for, and towards further evidence that crime was indeed an important issue for some people in some locales:

And the political point was that as Jock Young put it...well, two things, one of which was the [British] Crime Survey produced blancmange, what he called blancmange figures—in other words it levelled out the distinction between different parts of the country and different communities and localities. And that if you actually proceeded in another means, in other words, if you produced rather detailed studies of particular locations, of which the most famous is on Merseyside and Islington, then you discover two things. You discover there is no such thing as the statistically average citizen who has low crime risks, and you discover that the fear of crime might actually be in his words rational rather than irrational [...] I think he saw what the Home Office was up to was an attempt to kind of deny the problem of crime because he thought it suited the Conservative government to issue such a denial. Because it's not politically expedient for the party of law and order to be in charge at times of escalating crime rates.

Fear of Crime as a Broader Cultural and Political Theme of 1980s Britain

Meanwhile, crime rates continued to rise in Britain. As others (e.g. Garland, 2001) have argued, beginning in the 1970s, crime moved from a problem that afflicted the poor to increasingly become a daily consideration for many. Liberal sensibilities about the seriousness of crime as a problem were dented as victimization became a prominent issue for the middle classes. Increasing direct and indirect experience, a mass media raising the salience of crime and 'institutionalizing' public concern, and the growing visibility of signs of crime—in the form of physical incivilities, such as vandalism, and social incivilities, such as groups of intimidating youths hanging around in the street— all helped to bring crime and the risk of victimization into people's everyday lives. As Garland (2001: 153) puts it, 'rising crime rates ceased to be a statistical abstraction and took on a vivid personal meaning in popular consciousness and individual psychology'. Events such as the urban riots of the early 1980s in Brixton and Toxteth (alongside media reports and commentary) transformed crime into a major issue, linked it to questions of race and class, and fixed it as a target for more diffuse anxieties about social change. In particular, images of the excluded and disaffected young males of the inner city became resonant as the perception grew of them 'as a newly dangerous, alien class' (2001: 154). As Garland (2001: 154) notes '…diffuse middle-class anxieties [became shaped] into a more focused set of attitudes and understandings, identifying the culprits, naming the problem, setting up scapegoats'.

In addition to the above, and as pointed out by another interviewee, the fear of crime has been adopted as a further money-making tool by some sections of industry:

The fear of crime now, I think, has got well out of hand. I mean it's sort of been industrialised you know, with insurance companies and so on, have made great use of it, you know, trying to whip up people's concerns about household insurance and so on. It's built into insurance policies so that you know, you've got to be security conscious. Lock number whatever it is, has to be fitted, otherwise you're not covered.

During this decade, the issue of the fear of crime became infused with two other discourses and policy formations. First, there was a real increase in expenditure on the criminal justice system and crime control in general as 'Law and Order' emerged as a politically charged topic. For Garland (2001: 11): 'the emotional temperature of policy-making ha[d] shifted from cool to hot… the new discourse of crime policy consistently invokes an angry public, tired of living in fear, demanding strong measures of punishment and protection'. Along with a greater concentration on the victim, some of Jackson's interviewees argued that the empirical 'discovery' of fear of crime was invoked to support 'tougher' neo-conservative political agendas and policies, exemplified by the vast increase in the funding of the criminal justice system (see also Lee, 1999). However, there were divergent views on this matter. Other interviewees argued that the Home Office actually pursued relatively liberal policies during this decade, despite the popular punitive rhetoric. Second, the fear of crime became linked to crime prevention. Again, another interviewee—formerly a senior government official—provided an insider's account of this process:

The agenda on fear of crime is partly sort of amalgamated with the agenda on crime prevention and encouraging security and the sort of early crime prevention work on situational prevention and strengthening security and closed circuit television and all these things which were thought to make people feel safer as well as the substantive effects that some of them were hoped to have on crime itself.

Thus the government encouraged the public to be more crime literate (Garland, 1996), to be more responsible for both crime and their fears. The idea that people themselves should take responsibility for reducing the risk of victimization meant that crime policies became individualized as the agenda moved into one of 'responsibilization'. People, it was argued, should act cautiously and sensibly, restricting their own lifestyle if it meant it made them safer and decreased the chances of their victimization. 'At its most extreme, the discourse of victim carelessness operates as a way of removing responsibility from a failing police service, and poor political tactics' (Lee, 1999: 240). Paradoxically, the rapid proliferation of CCTV cameras and other aspects of crime prevention may have contributed to public concerns by encouraging: '... mutual suspicion and a profoundly anti-communitarian fortress mentality' (Gilling, 1997: 186).

Academic and policy-orientated research, the mass media, and political rhetoric and response all had the effect of further sensitizing the public to crime and fear once again (cf.: Lee, 1999: 240). Raising the salience of crime and reifying the category of 'fear of crime' (feeding back into the social world largely through the media) may have helped frame the topic in an emotional manner. It may have further encouraged the use of the notion of crime to express concerns about related social issues such as poverty, race and social cohesion. Another potential effect was the recognition and classification of certain behaviours as criminal. Furedi (1998) argues that the public have been encouraged to see a number of interpersonal relations as potentially victimizing, and ourselves as vulnerable and susceptible to harm or injury. Thus, a whole range of experiences can be seen in a new light: as disruptive and threatening.

Britain during the 1990s

Many of Jackson's interviewees argued that 1992 saw a clear break in governmental policy on law and order—a break which was augmented by the murder in February 1993 of James Bulger. Tony Blair became Shadow Home Secretary and, as one interviewee stated, declared an intention 'to take crime and public concerns about crime seriously'.[3] This had been because of the Tories' earlier 'tough stance' on crime, and had had the effect of making Labour look weak on law and order:

> The other effect of the Conservatives' use of law and order in the '70s was to terrify the Labour Party. And I think...whether it would happen anyway, as part of the sort of New Labour, I know, but they clearly were determined that they were not going to be portrayed as weak on law and order, because it had been used so effectively against them.

This in turn precipitated a mirror change in the Conservative Party, who had by that time also changed leader, dropping Thatcher in favour of the less strident John Major. The early 1990s consequently saw a decline in interest amongst policy making in the fear of crime as a topic discrete from crime. One interviewee spoke directly of this movement:

> From the late-70s through probably to Douglas Hurd [Home Secretary September 1985-October 1989], there was a sense of the media and some politicians stoking up needless concern and that really came to a fairly abrupt halt in the early '90s. Partly because of Tony Blair, the Shadow Home Secretary, adopting New Labour's position about tough on crime, tough on the causes of crime. And the last thing he'd want to say is that people are worrying about nothing. And that precipitated a mirror reaction from Ken Baker, Ken Clarke and Michael Howard [subsequent Home Secretaries], who couldn't possibly start saying fear of crime is exaggerated, inflated and so on. So 1992 is where there was a clear break in the continuity of policy and where perspectives on fear changed at a political level.

The emphasis was less on the management of fear through public education and more on public emotions as an indicator of the impact of crime. The BCS would provide information on where priorities lay in tackling crime levels. In this sense, the instrument became more like a consumer survey, eliciting levels of public satisfaction with the criminal justice system and indicating areas of priority—in a similar way to the local surveys of the 1980s.

The fear of crime remained a salient issue in official government statements, of course, but it became bound up with the idea that the public were rightly concerned and demanded action. But

---

[3] A theme in the interviews was the attribution of some success to the Left Realists, one of whose remits was to encourage the Labour Party to take these issues more seriously.

tension concerning the proportionality of public perceptions bubbled underneath. As Reiner et al. (2000: 107) argued 'The media have consistently been seen by policy makers as a major source of the problem, stimulating unrealistic and irrational fears by exaggerating and sensationalising the risks and seriousness of crime'.

From the early 1990s onwards, the Labour Party began to outmanoeuvre the Conservative government with increasingly rightwing policies of their own. This stimulated what one interviewee called an 'arms race' between incumbent and opposition, from Michael Howard to the present day, with parliament regularly being packed with crime bills. During this time, public fear of crime was regularly used in a grandstanding manner to justify popular-punitive solutions to issues of law and order. This at a time of a number of changes in criminal justice system policy, partly in response to public demands. The first was increased pressure for police foot patrols. While it is often argued, in Britain at least, that high-visibility patrols are generally not an effective way of preventing or detecting crime, the public generally seems to like them. They may even be important in sustaining police legitimacy. The second change has been the proliferation of the installation and use of CCTV cameras, partly as a response to perceived levels of public fear of crime.

The Fear of Crime since the Late-1990s

In terms of the period since the late-1990s, two important things need to be referred to during our 'history of the present' as it relates to the UK's experience of the fear of crime. The first is the UK's Economic and Social Research Council's Crime and Social Order research programme of the mid- to late-1990s. The second is the election in 1997 of a Labour government. Let us take each in turn.

Following the debates around what the fear of crime 'was', what it 'meant' and why the relationship between risk and fear levels appeared to be so complex, the UK's ESRC commissioned a programme of research entitled Crime and Social Order. A number of the projects funded under this programme touched on the fear of crime. The Crime and Social Order programme ended towards the end of the 1990s. Various of the projects which had explored the fear of crime ended on notes which suggested that the fear of crime was a confused and congested topic (which indeed it was and still is). Tony Jefferson and Wendy Hollway (2000) pointed to the importance of making sense of individual biographies when exploring the fear of crime. Others, such as Evi Girling, Richard Sparks, and Ian Loader (Loader et al., 2000: 66) suggested that public sensibilities and 'crime talk' constituted 'a means of registering and making intelligible what might otherwise remain some unsettling, yet difficult to grasp, mutations in the social and moral order'. This involved, they suggested, the use of metaphor and narrative about social change and the folding of stories, anecdotes, gossip, career, and personal biography together with perceptions of national change and decline. Yet others, e.g. the team led by Jason Ditton, reported that they had encountered so many problems with the key items used to measure the fear of crime that they had lost faith in such work (Farrall et al., 1997). By this time, however, the fear of crime had already become an object of government interest (Lee, 1999).

Mirroring an increasing emphasis on the role of disorder, and the notion that the public was sick of everyday incivility, policy began to shift towards more strongly linking fear of crime, anti-social behaviour, and the incidence of crime. These issues became fused under the banner of 'community safety' (see Crawford, 1998). The Crime and Disorder Act (1998) formulated the concept for the first time within public policy. Giving local authorities and the police joint statutory responsibility for crime, this legislation dictated that local agencies were now responsible for carrying out 'audits' of community safety in their local area, including the measurement of fear of crime and some evaluation of the effect of strategies.

Central elements of the Crime and Disorder Act (1998) aimed to improve the ability of multi-agencies to address disorder, particularly relating to young people. These included a number of orders: child safety, anti-social behaviour, and parenting. They also included provisions for local child curfews and powers for the police to remove truants. There was consequently an increasing link within public policy between disorder, youth, crime, and public concerns about each. But, as Harcourt (2001) points out, 'criminalizing' disorder—presenting it as a fixed category rather than an interpretative activity with heterogeneous meaning—encourages stereotypes that link certain non-criminal behaviours, performed by people of certain social categories, to crime itself (Roberts, 1999). As one interviewee pondered, perhaps this both reflected and encouraged decreasing margins of tolerance in certain sections of the populace to 'infringements' of privacy, quietness, and the intrusion of signs that the world is not disorderly, out of one's control. Embodying change, of inter-generational difference, young people can represent unwelcome changes in norms, values, and standards. They are both a real cause for concern, and an easy and often misunderstood target. And, as Hall et al. (1978) and Pearson (1983) show, this is not a new phenomenon.

The twin effects of the ESRC's Crime and Social Order programme and the election of a Labour government which had developed a strong commitment to tackling crime were not hard to predict: academic criminologists in the UK dropped the fear of crime as a research topic (Key Performance Indicators are not the most exciting of research topics a criminologist could focus on, after all),[4] leaving it to local governments, police services, and similar agencies to try to make sense of. So as academic research on the fear of crime in the UK pretty much dried up completely, so the fear of crime 'industry' switched homes—leaving academe and taking up residence in central government departments before forming a key plank of the local Crime and Safety Audits inspired by the 1998 Crime and Disorder Act (see also Lee, 2009 for a review of the situation in Australia). At around this time, too, the British Crime Survey became an annual survey and the design was changed so that more reliable estimates could be provided for local police areas—enabling the BCS and the fear of crime to become part of the growing 'audit culture'. Indeed, as Elizabeth Burney (2005) contends, the conspicuous rise in anti-social behaviour (ASB) policy throughout the 1990s and into the twenty first century has been legitimized through a community safety agenda, irrespective of evidence that suggests the weak foundation for the sequential aspect of the 'broken windows' claim (on which it has been promoted)—that social and physical disorder *causes* a subsequent spurt in predatory crime (see also Skogan, 1990). Nevertheless, New Labour have pursued populist politics

---

[4] Evidence for this comes from an analysis of academic papers with the 'fear of crime' as a topic listed in the Web of Knowledge (June 2008). From 1970 until 2001 there is a clear and steady growth in such papers from 3 in 1970 to 79 in 2001. From that point, however, there is a steady decline towards 60 articles per annum. Given the (roughly) two- to three-year lag between fieldwork, writing, and publication, we see this as proof that research in the fear of crime started to go off the boil from the late 1990s.

and given the police and local authorities more power than ever before to manage public disorder. Burney concludes that ASB policy and legislation 'leaves no doubt that the marginalised poor have been the main objects of control and consequences often disproportionate to the actions that triggered the intervention' (p 14) and compares the erosion of civil liberties and the rule of law to developments to curb international terrorism. Topics related to popular concerns about crime have emerged and receded at staggering rates—especially in the media since the 1990s. No less ephemeral have been some of the governmental responses to such concerns. Tony Blair's respect agenda came and went (as did the notion that troublemakers ought to be marched to cash point machines for on-the-spot fines). Concerns about youths wearing sweat tops with hoods ('hoodies') came and went as a cause of crime too, as did terms like 'community-led policing', 'neighbourhood-led policing', 'intelligence-led policing', and 're-assurance policing'. Less transitory, but no less related to the fear of crime, has been the slow but steady rise in penal populism (Pratt, 2007). Pratt argues that rising fear of crime and reduced confidence in the criminal justice system led to the rise in penal populism from the early 1980s (2007: 60–3). In part this rise in anti-rehabilitative practices is part of wider shifts in attitudes towards offenders. But in part it is also a reflection of a general loss of trust in governments and their ability to control and regulate crime. The exact causes of such sentiments are beyond the scope of our current task. But one thing is clear: that the fear of crime both as a label for describing feelings and as a set of feelings themselves underlies much of the increasingly punitive (not to mention) vindictive tone of debates in this arena.

Explaining the Emergence of the Fear of Crime as a Policy Concern

Let us now summarize the main accounts for the rise of the fear of crime as a policy concern. Our focus is drawn to a number of explanations: those which deal with the political economy of fear of crime and long-term structural explanations, and those which deal with the cultural economy, namely the psychological processes that underpin social and risk perception, and the broader social significance of crime.

Political Economies of Fear

As described earlier, some (e.g. Loo and Grimes, 2004; Loo, 2009) have argued that the fear of crime was essentially hyped up by rightwing politicians in order to win them votes during national assembly elections. Whilst rightwing politicians' immediate objective was to steal votes from the Democrats, they also had a longer-term aim of altering the overall political climate. Thus a putative public fear of crime was constructed and hyped by rightwing politicians in an effort to reverse the gains made by the Sixties insurgencies. In other words, the battle was over reshaping the overall political climate and political alignments and not simply an attempt to grab votes. That is, it was an effort to shift the terms of the debate away from social justice and towards 'let's get those criminals' (or as John Ehrlichman, Nixon's Special Counsel, admitted 'We'll go after the racists. That subliminal appeal to the anti-African American voter was always present in Nixon's statements and speeches', Ehrlichman, 1970: 233, cited in Loo, 2009: 25). The fear of crime thus, whilst reflecting some pre-existing set of concerns or anxiety, became something that appropriately-minded politicians could use to stoke up public feelings on certain topics. This process became, over time, self-perpetuating, as Lee (2001: 480–1) suggests when he refers to a fear of crime 'feed-back loop', which

...operate[s] symbiotically to produce and intensify crime fear and the research related to it; that research into victims produces and maintains the criminological concept of 'fear of crime' quantitatively and discursively; that this information operates to identify fear as a legitimate object of governance or governmental regulation; that the techniques of regulation imagine particular types of citizens—*fearing subjects*; that these attempts to govern 'fear of crime' actually inform the citizenry that they are indeed fearful; that this sensitises the citizenry to 'fear of crime'; that the law and order lobby and populist politicians use this supposed fearing population to justify a tougher approach on crime, a point on which they grandstand, and in doing so sensitise citizens to fear once again; and that this spurs more research into 'fear of crime' and so on.

In this approach, the fear of crime approaches something of an elite-constructed and publicly-maintained exaggeration of the reality of public anxieties. Whether one believes or not the suggestion that this was 'engineered' by elites (Loo and Grimes, 2004: 50) or Lee's less forceful stance is another matter.

The Cultural Economy of Fear

Garland (2001) has argued that the last few decades saw crime move from a problem that afflicted the poor to increasingly become a daily consideration for many. Liberal sensibilities about the seriousness of crime as a problem were dented, as victimization became a prominent fact for the middle classes. Increasing direct and indirect experience, mass media raising the salience of crime and 'institutionalizing' public concern, and the growing visibility of signs of crime—in the form of physical incivilities, such as vandalism, and social incivilities, such as groups of intimidating youths hanging around in the street—all helped to bring crime and the perceived risk of victimization into people's everyday lives. As Garland (2001: 153–4) puts it, 'rising crime rates ceased to be a statistical abstraction and took on a vivid personal meaning in popular consciousness and individual psychology...diffuse middle-class anxieties [became shaped] into a more focused set of attitudes and understandings, identifying the culprits, naming the problem, setting up scapegoats'. Images of excluded and disaffected young males of the inner city became resonant as the perception grew of them 'as a newly dangerous, alien class' (2001: 154). Crime reflected and refracted a whole host of social issues and problems.

Such an explanation is plausible, focusing as it does on the social meaning of crime that gathered during this period, analysing how cultural significance connects to public attitudes and concerns about social change and social relations. Yet the remit of the fear of crime work in the 1980s and early 1990s was politically charged, mobilizing around the question: Were public perceptions of risk irrational? This was partly because of the real increase in expenditure on the criminal justice system and crime control in the 1980s. Along with a greater concentration on the victim, the empirical 'discovery' of fear of crime was invoked to support 'tougher' neo-conservative political agendas and policies, exemplified by the vast increase in the funding of the criminal justice system (Lee, 1999). At the same time, those who wished crime policy to be less authoritarian sought to downplay public anxieties, arguing that policy should not be based on inaccurate public perceptions.

With the 1990s came a change of emphasis away from the 'rationality question'—in the UK at least. The fear of crime began to be treated as a legitimate problem, no longer independent of crime. It was increasingly seen as a public response to anti-social behaviour and incivilities. Together, fear of crime and disorder became part and parcel of police dealings. Now the police undertake more high-visibility patrols and tackle what are sometimes called 'quality of life' issues, all the while engaging in what might rather uncharitably be termed 'public relation activities'. Currently the fear of crime is a performance indicator for the police and for the Home Office, its reduction forming a key aspect of high-profile reassurance interventions and the day-to-day operation of the criminal justice system.

Taylor and Jamieson (1998) take a slightly different, but not unrelated tack, arguing that the high rates of fear of crime witnessed in the UK in the mid-1990s were symptomatic of the UK's fall from a world-leading economic power to a net importer of goods and services (1998: 152). This sense of economic decline led to a sense of widespread insecurity, especially as it related to employment. These 'fears of [social] falling' are caused they argue by the sudden changes in the economy at that time, but are condensed into more easily expressed fears about crime and those individuals associated with it in this moral discourse ('yobs', homeless people, 'young people', ethnic minorities, 'foreigners', and so on).

Conclusion

Where, then, did the fear of crime 'come from'? It strikes us that the origins, although far from being entirely clear, can be distilled into a rough chronology. The fear of crime (as we know it today) initially emerged, via the manipulation of the Nixonian 'silent majority' by rightwing US politicians, from middle-American white concern at the extension of political and legal rights to the poor and the black (itself a welcome result of the civil rights movement in the US during the 1960s, of course). These concerns were employed by rightwing politicians in the US, who used them in election campaigns in the mid- to late-1960s. Just as crime policies can travel, so too do objects of enquiry, and the fear of crime was no different in this respect. The fear of crime made the journey from the US to the UK in the late 1970s and early 1980s. Partly this was the result of social upheaval in the UK which was (again) employed by rightwing politicians in election campaigns. However, it was also partly the result of members of the British Crime Survey team taking advice from their US colleagues as to what ought to be included in any survey and, importantly, the desire amongst some in the Home Office to provide a counter to sensationalist media reports and the more excessive of the Conservative law and order policies.

Yet, and probably to the surprise of those in the Home Office, not everyone shared their hope that the BCS could be used to dampen down public concern about crime—left realists and feminists in the UK certainly did not, and set about their own (local) crime surveys and qualitative research strategies in order to highlight the lived reality of crime and the fear of crime (giving further credibility to the academic and policy relevance of the fear of crime). The same left realists were also—at least according to some—responsible for the adoption of crime as a focal point for policy action for New Labour under Tony Blair. Many of these policies called for reductions not just in crime but also the fear of crime as part of the measures by which they were evaluated.

By now, the fear of crime genie was well and truly out of the crime survey bottle. In the context of an ever-growing news media, hungry for stories about crime in particular, so the fear of crime entered public discourse in such a way that would make it hard to dislodge. Even the less populist sections of the press were keen to report stories about trends in crime, especially given the seeming inability of anyone to do very much about this. In so doing, and reporting basic reports of worry about various crimes, so the media, perhaps unwittingly, perhaps not, promulgated the notion that some 25-40 per cent of the surveyed population were anxious about becoming a victim of any number of crime types. Of course, politicians continued to rely upon the fear of crime to stoke up anxieties in order to win votes by grandstanding on 'tough' policies. Commercial firms adopted a similar approach when selling security services or insurance policies. In this light, perhaps, one can locate our recent and current work as continuing the ideological work started by the British Crime Survey. Various of our articles (e.g. Farrall, 2004a and b; Farrall and Gadd, 2004; Farrall, Jackson and Gray, 2006) have attempted to shift the debates away from debates about who feels most fearful or how best these fears can be tackled and instead to paint a picture of the fear of crime which better captures the lived reality of fear: rarely experienced, episodic, and short lived.

3
What is the Fear of Crime? A Rhetorical Question with No *One* Clear Answer

'Present fears are less than horrible imaginings' (Shakespeare, *Macbeth*).

Introduction

But what *is* the fear of crime?

This seemingly simple question has rarely been addressed on a systematic empirical basis. In this chapter we explore some of the approaches to the topic at hand and some of the methodological issues which need to be grappled with in order for us to answer this question. In so doing we will need to explore the unfolding quantitative measurement of the fear of crime and its legacy for the current approaches to its measurement. Such an approach inevitably means that we must engage with the fact that the survey is the dominant *modus operandi* of research in this field. However, along the way to our answer to the above question, we draw lessons from three areas of—we think—great importance. These are the psychology of survey response, the psychology of everyday emotions, and closer to home still, qualitative data on the lived reality of feelings of fear and anxiety.

Technical problems have certainly dogged this field of enquiry, and as we shall see, some criminologists believe that methodological limitations have posed serious implications for the validity of the body of knowledge that public policy relies upon (e.g. Ferraro and LaGrange, 1987; Farrall et al., 1997; Farrall, 2004; Lee, 1999 and 2001). Others argue that theoretical underspecification has restricted the breadth and depth of definition and explanation, leaving us with a contested and congested concept (e.g. Girling et al., 2000). Public concerns and perceptions do seem messier and more multi-faceted than current methods and concepts disclose. In particular, the fear of crime has social and psychological dimensions that require interdisciplinary analysis and innovative methodological inroads. Yet the vast majority of research in this area has lacked such ambition.

By considering research from a multi-disciplinary perspective, we explore how standard research tools have simultaneously misunderstood and misrepresented the nature of this social problem. Failing to appreciate the complexity, antecedents, and effects of fear of crime; failing to contextualize worries with other day-to-day concerns; using the rather blunt construction 'how worried are you'—all this has confused and prejudiced our comprehension of worry about crime in people's everyday lives.

Measuring the Fear of Crime

As we saw in Chapter 2, public concerns about the social and moral order of society and the pace and direction of social change are nothing new (Curtis, 2001; Pearson, 1983; Shaw, 1931). Analysing the period which saw the 'Jack the Ripper' murders in nineteenth century London, Curtis (2001) describes how the mass media heightened pre-existing public alarm about crime and linked debates between public protection and the inability of the police to manage a semi-criminal social underclass. The case typified how such events are 'embedded in a matrix of moral and political imperatives about law and order' (2001: 15). Similarly, the late nineteenth century saw widespread concern with the 'dangerous classes' (Godfrey et al., 2007, Chapter 1).

And, as we also saw in the previous chapter, the contemporary manifestation of the fear of crime as an object of study and a category of description can be traced back to the President's Crime Commission on Law Enforcement and the Administration of Justice (1967) in the US. Three crime surveys commissioned by this body (Biderman et al., 1967; Ennis, 1967; Reiss, 1967) sought to count unrecorded victimization, partly leading to the emergence of National Crime Surveys. Because the belief that the public was anxious about crime also motivated the organization of the Commission itself, the three surveys included questions about public attitudes towards crime and perceptions of their own safety. The report of the first survey (Biderman et al., 1967) refers to 'anxiety about crime' and includes one of the first operational definitions of fear—a combination of the following five rather idiosyncratic questions (which are worth reading closely) to create an 'index of anxiety' (Biderman et al., 1967: 121):

- 'What was it about the neighborhood that was most important? [Response alternatives: 'Safety or moral characteristics'; and 'Convenience or aesthetic characteristics']';
- 'When you think about the chances of getting beaten up would you say this neighborhood is [Response alternatives: 'Very safe'; 'About average'; 'Less safe than most'; 'One of the worst'; and 'Don't know']';
- 'Is there so much trouble that you would move if you could? (For those who did not characterize neighborhood as very safe.) [Response alternatives: 'Yes'; and 'No']';
- 'Are most of your neighbors quiet or are there some who create disturbances? [Response alternatives: 'All quiet'; 'Few disturbances'; and 'Many disturbances']'; and finally,
- 'Do you think that crime has been getting better or worse here in Washington during the past year? [Response alternatives: 'Better'; 'Worse'; and 'Same']'

Another of these pilot studies commissioned by the President's Commission fielded a different set of measures. Among the items were: 'How safe do you feel walking alone in your neighborhood after dark?'; 'Have you wanted to go somewhere recently but stayed home because it was unsafe?'; 'How concerned are you about having your home broken into?'; and, 'How likely is it a person walking around here at night be held up or attacked?' (Ennis, 1967).

While the questions of Biderman et al. (1967) and Ennis (1967) were a somewhat uneven and unstructured collection of indicators—lacking a clear theoretical specification—they did have the advantage of conceptualizing public attitudes in a multidimensional manner. Indeed, the concluding chapter of Biderman et al. (1967: 164) made a fascinating attempt to contextualize public anxieties by discussing the inherently *symbolic* nature of crime—noting that such anxieties uncover popular assessments of the prevailing moral order.

Over time, variants of questions about perceptions of safety on the street became standard, and ironically it is these measures which have attracted the most critical comment. Garofalo and Laub (1978) pointed out that safety questions (a) did not mention crime, (b) failed to provide a specific geographical reference, and (c) provided a hypothetical situation. They argued that the measures therefore tap into broader symbolic issues above and beyond the 'fear' of actually becoming a victim of crime. Concern for community included: '...the fear of actual criminal acts as well as the feeling that one's social situation is unstable, anxiety about strangers, the belief that one's moral beliefs are being offended'. (Biderman et al., 1967: 250). The Figgie Report (Figgie, 1980) continued this theme, differentiating between 'formless' fear (measured by perceptions of safety and abstract threats to one's security) and 'concrete' fear (self-reported concern about becoming a victim of various personal crimes).

Asking about 'Crime' and Specifying an Emotion

Not unsurprisingly then, the 1970s saw criminologists arguing that there was more to the 'fear of crime' than simply the 'fear' of 'crime' (see also: Hunter, 1978; Wilson, 1976). Evidence began to accrue that people assessed the threat of victimization partly through the interpretation of symbols of crime in their immediate surroundings—what Biderman et al. (1967: 160) referred to as 'highly visible signs of what [people] regard as disorderly and disreputable'. From one perspective, then, perceived safety questions were right to focus on broader definitions of urban unease—of which the threat of crime was only related to in part (for defences of these measures see: Maxfield, 1984; Skogan and Maxfield, 1981).

Yet the lack of precision in perceived safety questions continued to concern some scholars. In an influential article Ferraro and LaGrange (1987) argued that the perceived safety question measured judgements of risk (albeit in a vague and diffuse manner) rather than any emotional reaction. This is hardly hairsplitting: these measures conflate measures of 'fear' with measures of judgements of threat. Indicators of emotion and perceptions of risk may be related, of course, but not strongly enough to indicate that the constructs being measured are the same thing (Warr and Stafford, 1983; Warr, 1984). Moreover, different measures of 'fear' yield inconsistent empirical relationships. Perceived safety measures elicit different predictors than indicators of worry, perceived risk, and fear. Take the much-repeated statement that the elderly are more afraid of crime than the young. This is borne out by research that uses the perceived safety question: the elderly tend to feel less safe walking alone after dark than other age groups. However, if you ask people how worried or afraid they are of becoming a victim of a number of different crimes, the age effect generally disappears (see *inter alia* Hough and Mayhew, 1985; Ferraro and LaGrange, 1987; Chadee and Ditton, 2003). For Ferraro and LaGrange (1987: 82) 'Researchers' proclivity to term various types of perceptions about crime as the fear of crime has all too frequently resulted in misspecification of models and/ or a confounded variable problem.'

Ferraro and LaGrange (1987: 715) subsequently recommended that future measures of the fear of crime have the following characteristics: (1) use 'how afraid'—a 'helpful way to examine an emotional state of fear'; (2) make reference to crime—do not use implied meaning as they are probably not valid indicators (i.e. not just refer to 'safety'); (3) refer to specific crimes; (4) do not use a hypothetical format; and (5) state 'in your everyday life' to bring 'a touch of reality to the questions'. In later work, Ferraro (1995) nicely demonstrated the utility of differentiating between perceived risk and fear. Applying insights from symbolic interactionism, he found that ecological information—such as perceptions of incivilities and poverty, and socially shared information about the reputation of an area—predicted the perceived risk of crime.[1] Perceived risk then predicted fear and constrained behaviour.

Asking about 'Worry' and Specifying a Psychological Account of the Emotion

Despite such advances, US surveys still regularly field perceived safety questions (exceptions include Taylor and Hale, 1986; Sacco, 1993; Ross and Jang, 2000; Williams et al., 2000). It is only in the UK that a variant of Ferraro's (1995) measures are standard (Hough, 1995), where the British Crime Survey has long included

---

[1] Intriguingly, the work of Ferraro (1995) comes back to the issue first raised by Biderman et al. (1967: 164). Ferraro (1995) found that fear of crime was predicted by lay interpretations of incivilities, which are '. . .low-level breaches of community standards that signal an erosion of conventionally accepted norms and values'. Jackson (2004) found the same pattern in a UK-based study, but also showed that the social perspective of the perceiver explained why some people judged particular ambiguous stimuli as 'disorderly' and representational of criminal threat, while other people in the same environment judged the same stimuli as malign and unthreatening (cf. Sampson and Raudenbush, 2004; Carvalho and Lewis, 2003; Harcourt, 2001; Girling et al., 2000).

measures of worry about falling victim of various crimes, as well as perceptions of likelihood of these things happening.

The specification of 'worry' rather than 'fear' in the BCS measures is noteworthy, particularly because psychological research suggests that 'worry' is more appropriate than 'fear' in regard to the risk of crime. Fear is a physical response to an immediate threat, and no doubt some individuals, in some instances, experience this strong emotion. But worry may better describe more common emotional responses, because worry describes both rumination about future events and immediate response to current situations. Worry can also be functional and problem-solving, as well as damaging and debilitating, and a review of the psychological literature on worry provides the following, revealing definition:

As a phenomenon, [worry] can range from an innocuous activity possibly associated with positive consequences (i.e. solution finding), through to a distressing and uncontrollable process like the excessive and chronic worry recognized as the cardinal feature of generalized anxiety disorder (GAD). It has been defined broadly as repetitive thought activity, which is usually negative and frequently related to feared future outcomes or events[2] (Gladstone and Parker, 2003: 347).

As measurement tools, psychologists typically use trait questionnaires such as the Penn State Worry Questionnaire (Meyer et al., 1990) and the Worry Domains Questionnaire (Tallis et al., 1992).[3] These tools can be supplemented by 'ecological momentary assessment methods' (Verkuil et al., 2007) that could involve a worry log (respondents register their worries over a six-day period) or something like Kahneman et al.'s (2004) 'day reconstruction method' and 'event reconstruction method'.

---

[2] Intriguingly for fear of crime research, this definition suggests that what might be called *dysfunctional* or *damaging* worry is characterized by frequent events, underlining the utility of asking people about the regularity with which they worry.

[3] The PSWQ measures pathological worry and the worry process, asking individuals to agree or disagree to statements such as: (a) 'I worry all the time', (b) 'My worries overwhelm me', (c) 'Many situations make me worry', and (d) 'I know I shouldn't worry about things, but I just can't help it'. By contrast, the WDQ measures the content of worries and taps into constructive worrying, asking individuals whether they worry that they (for example): (a) 'lack confidence', (b) 'can't afford to pay bills', (c) 'cannot be assertive or express their opinions', and (d) 'haven't achieved much'.

The Everyday Experience of 'Fear' and 'Worry'

Together the above techniques produce data on the everyday experience of emotion and its patterning or ecological distribution (see below). By contrast, crime surveys (such as the BCS) produce data that are more difficult to interpret. Specifically, the use of the broad measures (How safe do you feel...? How afraid are you...? How worried are you...?) has arguably left us knowing little about the frequency or intensity of specific moments of emotion, or about where such events take place and why.[4] We also do not know if emotions are functional (problem-solving, leading to cautious behaviour) or damaging (reducing psychological well-being). Moreover, respondents may interpret the meaning of the emotion (whether it is worry or fear) differently—sometimes consistent to psychological theory, other times not.

One possibility is that surveys tap not into a self-report of current or past 'feelings' but rather into a more future-orientated anxiety or a general representation of risk. Warr (2000: 453) has recently suggested that fear is 'an emotion, a feeling of alarm or dread caused by an awareness or expectation of danger', and given that respondents of crime surveys will rarely be feeling immediate threat during the time of the survey, measures are more likely to capture anxiety (reactions to future or past events) rather than fear. Sacco (2005: 125) concurs: 'Typically, researchers do not have access to people when they are actually afraid (and thus reacting physiologically). Instead, criminologists have focused on anticipated rather than actual fear. They have thus tended to think about fear more as an attitude or a perception than as a physical response'.[5]

---

[4] Perceived safety questions ask what respondents anticipate they might feel in a certain situation (Skogan, 1981).

[5] Robinson and Clore's (2002a, 2002b) discussion of emotional self-report raises the additional possibility that such measures tap into 'identity-related beliefs'—essentially, individuals ask themselves whether they are the sort of person who is 'worried' or 'afraid.' It is also worth noting that Warr (2000: 459) believes that asking people about their behaviours may more accurately assess the impact of crime-risk on people's everyday lives—yet even here 'the behaviours through which fear makes itself known are not easily identifiable or detectable'.

Teasing Apart Frequency and Intensity

In one of the most recent empirical investigations of measures, Farrall et al. (1997) asked 64 respondents a series of survey questions relating to worry, perceived risk of crime, perceived safety, victimization experiences, and worries about other non-crime issues. Approximately one month later, these respondents were asked the same questions again, this time in qualitative interviews. 'Mismatches' or inconsistencies in the responses given by respondents on sweep one and two were common. Specifically, 'mismatches' were defined as instances where an individual gave different answers depending upon the nature of the interview being undertaken. Only 15 out of 64 sets of interviews did not produce mismatches. A significant number (where answers differed to a moderate to strong degree) were related to the nature of the methodology—e.g. 46 out of a total of 114 mismatches were generated between 'open' and 'closed' questions. In the majority of these cases, survey measures exaggerated the day-to-day experience of concern or worry. The authors concluded:

... the results of fear of crime surveys appear to be a function of the way the topic is *researched*, rather than the way it *is*. The traditional methods used are methods which seem consistently to over-emphasize the levels and extent of the fear of crime. It seems that levels of fear of crime, and, to a lesser extent, of victimization itself, have been hugely overestimated (Farrall et al., 1997: 676).

Two follow-up studies concluded that questions about the *frequency* of worrying episodes better captured the everyday experience of worry about crime. In these studies Farrall and colleagues (Farrall and Gadd, 2004; Gray et al., 2008) developed and tested a new set of measures with two novel aspects: (a) the use of a filter question, followed by (b) an assessment of the frequency in the past year and the intensity of the most recent event. Farrall and Gadd (2004) found that frequency questions yielded smaller estimates of the fear of crime than 'old' standard questions (i.e. 'worry about...' or the 'safety walking' items). Jackson et al. (2006) found that the discrepancy in the levels of fear identified by the old and new measures suggested that some people reported being *worried* (using standard measures) without actually *having worried recently* (using new measures).

These findings point to a pressing need to uncover what people mean when they say to a survey interviewer that they are worried about being victimized. The findings speak to concerns often expressed in the literature about the specificity and theoretical clarity of the concept of the fear of crime, and of widespread methodological confusion. With this in mind, we begin with a consideration of some of the key lessons from the literature concerning how respondents interpret and respond to survey questions.

Lessons from the Psychology of Survey Response

In the past few years, although developing out of work started in the late 1970s and early 1980s, a considerable body of research and theorizing about the ways in which respondents answer survey questions has emerged. This body of work examines surveys and the ways in which respondents answer them from a psychological perspective (e.g. Zaller and Feldman, 1992; Tourangeau, Rips and Rasinski, 2000). This approach argues that the processes by which people answer questions as part of a survey can be understood in terms of cognitive models. The ways in which people understand and interpret questions, the ways in which they decide if they can give an answer, or go about selecting an answer (often from a range on offer) are part and parcel of the ways in which people ordinarily process information cognitively. This approach (often referred to as the cognitive aspects of survey methodology movement) develops and builds upon earlier psychological models, adding to them an understanding of how people make judgements about issues and an improved understanding of the cognitive processes involved in decision making.

Thinking on the psychology of survey response is heavily influenced by the work of Tourangeau et al. (2000). Their model emphasizes four major components of survey response. These are: comprehension of the survey question; retrieval of relevant information; the formation of a judgement based on that information, and, finally, the selection and reporting of an answer. Depending upon how thorough the respondent is when selecting their answer(s) they may break down these four aspects into further tasks (see Tourangeau et al., 2000) and they may repeat or return to these tasks when selecting an answer. Now is not the place for a full rehearsal of the model proposed by Tourangeau et al. (2000); however, their work and thinking (especially as it pertains to questions which ask about the frequency with which some event occurred and attitudinal questions) has important messages for us in terms of how we approach the questions designed as part of our earlier forays into this field (see Farrall and Gadd, 2004).

Presuppositions and Leading Questions

All survey questions involve, to some extent, presuppositions. That is, that they assume that the respondent has an opinion about a topic or has experienced a certain social situation and can recall it in sufficient detail to be able to provide reliable answers about it. Questions which are particularly poorly worded and which suggest that the respondent is expected to have an opinion or even ought to lean towards one particular opinion are often referred to as leading questions. Such questions can cause respondents to 'recall' events as if the presupposition were true (Tourangeau et al., 2000: 42), i.e. they can encourage respondents to provide answers which confirm the bias contained in the question. The presupposition is not rejected unless the respondent believes it to be false (so those, for example, with no firm opinion on the topic, may tend to agree with it). In some specific cases, in which, for example, the question refers to an event or a situation about which the respondent has no opinion, the respondent may infer that this is an issue about which they *ought* to have an opinion (since, in the mind of the respondent, surveys would not ask about trivial or unimportant issues). Similarly, the codes presented to respondents may be interpreted by them as indicating the usual set of responses which people give to the question at hand. Respondents then 'locate' themselves on the scale presented to them in terms of where they feel they fit relative to others.

Socially Desirable Responding

Some questions have a tendency to elicit socially desirable responses. These are answers which do not necessarily reflect the respondent's true feelings, but rather, the answer which they feel best fits the image of themselves which they wish to portray to the interviewer. Evidence from a number of surveys suggests that respondents manipulate their answers (either wittingly or unwittingly) in order to present themselves in a favourable light with the interviewer. For example, few respondents would wish to admit to poor levels of personal hygiene, and so may exaggerate the number of times they showered or the amount of soap they consumed in a particular period. Closer to home, Sutton and Farrall (2005, 2009) found that men were more likely than women to underreport their concerns about becoming a victim of crime to such an extent that when this was taken into account, men's fears outstripped women's. This finding was curious since it has commonly been believed that women report greater levels of fear of crime since they are (generally) physically weaker than males of a comparable age and may have had rape foremost in their minds when answering questions about crime (Stanko, 1990). However, if confirmed, the finding that men may have suppressed their fear levels when reporting demonstrates that answers to survey questions ought not to be treated uncritically.

Attitudinal Items

Attitudinal questions are those questions which ask respondents for their opinion about a particular topic or behaviour, or to state the extent to which they agree or disagree with a statement. As such, attitudinal items do not often refer to objective facts and almost always present the respondent with a pre-coded set of responses ('strongly agree' to 'strongly disagree' or 'not at all' to 'almost always', for example).

Traditional approaches to the ways in which respondents answered attitudinal survey questions suggested that, after reading and comprehending the question, people 'consulted' some pre-existing set of values which were easily available and relatively stable (Tourangeau et al., 2000: 165–96). However, such a view has problems. First of all, many studies have suggested that attitudes are not stable, and secondly, the model assumed that the respondent 'had' a set of values or an opinion from which they were able to extract an answer. It appears, from a number of publications, that the answers to some attitude questions were simply 'made up' on the spot. As Zaller (1992: 76) notes, this is hardly surprising since few people are regularly asked to provide either their political opinions (for example) or to account for them, hence in-depth expressions of views on a subject by the majority of the public are rare.

Tourangeau et al. (2000: 178–94) therefore propose an alternative model of the ways in which respondents answer attitudinal survey questions. Their answers, they suggest, are 'a haphazard' collection of beliefs, feelings, impressions, and general values about the issue at hand. Attitudes are a 'database' of these feelings about the issue. Attitudes are therefore a kind of memory structure (Tourangeau et al., 2000: 194) which contains existing evaluations of the topic at hand. Depending upon which memories are retrieved, respondents may simply restate an existing evaluation of the topic at hand, extend it to cover a new or related subject matter(s), or produce a new attitudinal response. These feelings etc. can be influenced by a number of factors (such as personal experiences, societal level debates on the topic, for example). The ease with which the respondent is able to retrieve relevant beliefs and feelings influences their abilities to provide an answer to the question. The accessibility with which beliefs etc. are recalled is in turn influenced by a range of factors such as the respondent's interest in the topic, the wording of the question, the instructions given to them, their perceptions of the question and of the questionnaire in general, and the questions which preceded the one being answered. Issues surrounding the social desirability of questions cannot be ignored either (see above). At an individual level, therefore, answers to attitudinal questions are inherently unstable, since they are based on a sampling of beliefs and this sampling will not always produce the same response. In addition, over time, an attitude will change as new experiences, beliefs, and feelings are encountered.

Non-Attitudes

A further body of work (Bishop et al., 1986; Sterngold et al., 1994; Osborne and Rose, 1999) suggests that surveys can create the illusion of an informed public with opinions on particular topics. These opinions are captured through the desire on the part of respondents to help interviewers, which leads to them giving answers to questions about which they may have no opinion, or only a poor understanding of the topic at hand. Although widely acknowledged to represent a serious problem since Converse identified them (Converse, 1964), there are some who argue that the issue of non-attitudes has been overstated (e.g. Schuman and Presser, 1996) and that even non-attitudes reflected dispositions towards the topic at hand.

Non-attitudes—the expression of opinions on a fictitious topic, or the reporting of values on a topic about which one has no values—appear to arise from a combination of poor question design (Bishop et al., 1986; Jackson et al. forthcoming) and the respondent's desire to cooperate with tasks (such as taking part in a survey). Although respondents may be poorly informed, surveys appear to be for the common good, and, as such, respondents may attempt to give answers which they hope will be both helpful and constructive. When filter questions are used to screen out respondents who may have no opinion about or experience of a particular subject prior to them being asked for an evaluation of that topic, the overall frequency of answers is altered (see Farrall and Gadd, 2004). This suggests that even if a respondent has no opinion about a topic, she or he will 'make one up on the spot' (Zaller and Feldman, 1992; Tourangeau et al., 2000). If the topic is salient enough in the minds of politicians and social commentators and resonates at some level with popular beliefs, then, over time, the topic may become one which is 'produced' via repeated surveys on that topic (Osborne and Rose, 1999). Few commentators have explicitly linked these processes with the fear of crime, although Lee (2001) is one who has done. Lee (2001: 480–1) argued that the fear of crime was chronically reproduced as an object of social and political discourse and debate—a process he referred to as the 'fear of crime' feed-back loop.

This, taken together, suggests an uncomfortable possibility; namely that poor question wording, respondents' desire to co-operate with surveys, and media and political interest in crime and the fear of crime have contributed to a scenario in which the fear is continually 'recreated' both socially as a topic for debate and at the individual level as a set of experience-able phenomena. Surveys in this situation may not merely measure fear, they may actually create and recreate it. As such, surveys may, via poor design, generate the impression of a large proportion of the populous who 'fear' crime and this may become adopted by members of the public to describe and articulate their own experiences during which they have felt uncomfortable in some way as a result of an episode which could be described as 'crime-related'.

Frequency Items

Frequency items are those questions which ask respondents to recall (usually over some set period of time) how many times they experienced an event or undertook some form of activity. For example: 'In the past twelve months, how often have you travelled abroad for the purposes of work?' Here we summarize Tourangeau et al.'s thinking on some of these issues (2000: 136–64). There are a number of ways of approaching responses to survey questions which ask for a frequency to be provided. One way, possibly the least refined, is to simply assume that the answer given is an *accurate count*. For example, the respondent answering the question above may have attempted to recall each trip over the past year and then reported this figure. Alternatively, if the event is rare it may be memorable (for example, n of friends' weddings attended in the past year, or burglaries in the previous six months). On the other hand, if the event is common for the respondent in question (e.g. n of times eating at home in the past month) then the precise count may become harder to produce accurately and the respondent may resort to guessing or some form of estimation. Some questions will not need respondents to put much effort into recalling a figure, while others will. For example, respondents can reasonably be expected to recall the number of children they have had, or their own age (which is merely a count of years lived). The evidence suggests that, excluding those counts which are relatively straightforward (e.g. n of children), the exact count model is an imprecise assessment of the way people recall and report counts: people simply do not carry around in them a tally of the n of times they have been out to eat in the past month (for example).

Another way to approach the meaning of the answers to frequency questions is to assume that the answer is an *estimation* of the number of times an event took place. For example, thinking back over the past year, a respondent may estimate that they have been abroad for work six times during that period. How they reached this estimation is a source of further debate. It could be that respondents think back over the entire reference period and recall as many events as possible, and then report this, or then additionally assess how reliable they think their memory is and moderate the count in the light of their assessment about their memory. A further strategy might be for respondents to think back over the past month, produce a count, and then multiply this by twelve (assuming an even distribution over the year). Or they might think back over the longer period of time and then multiply the count by four or three or two depending on the period recalled (three, four, or six months). A further variant would operate via 'decomposition', whereby the count is produced by dividing the behaviour asked about (say, trips taken by train) into specific categories of travel—with friends, alone, with work colleagues, and so on. These separate counts are then summed to produce one global count of n of train journeys. Of course, had the questions used terms like 'roughly', 'about', or 'approximately', the chances of the answering being an estimation are increased, since these words imply that an exact count is not required and that a 'guestimation' is sufficient.

If the question includes a set of possible responses which are made available to the respondent, say, as cards shown to them or as part of the question (e.g. 0, 1–4, 5–10, 11–15, and so on), then the respondent may 'anchor' themselves at the mid-point (a sort of default position), and then adjust their answer up or downwards depending on their own judgement of the frequency with which they have experienced the referent of the question. Alternatively, assuming that the topic asked about is one which has a socially desirable answer (say, the n of trips taken to the dentist in the past year), respondents may report something approximating to this answer or may anchor on this answer and then moderate up/down. The current thinking (Tourangeau et al., 2000: 50) is to ask for a raw count, since offering codes can lead to respondents anchoring and adjusting.

Finally, respondents' answers to frequency questions may simply be guesses, plucked at random. If answers to frequency questions where a raw count is recorded do involve a significant element of guessing, then these will tend to 'round-up' at typical rounding points, such as five, ten, fifteen, twenty, and so on (Tourangeau et al., 2000: 150). Research suggests that those who give zero answers or report 'not at all' attempt to recall specific episodes and fail to remember any (Tourangeau et al., 2000: 157). Of course, the same respondent may use any number of these strategies during a single survey, varying them according to the question asked and their ease of recall. For example, asked how many children s/he has, a respondent is likely to be able to give an answer without needing to recall each child, but later when asked how many months s/he has needed to claim social security as a result of their being unemployed in the past five years, may need to count specific months or produce an estimation.

Lessons from the Psychology of 'Everyday Emotions'

The second area of contemporary research and debate which we draw upon again derives much of its inspiration from the work of psychologists. Research into emotions has become an increasingly prominent issue in the humanities, social sciences, and psychology (see Davidson et al., 2003; Turner and Stets, 2005), and there is now a large and expanding body of research on emotion emanating from these disciplines. In the criminological arena we have been able to draw upon the legacy of Durkheim and Elias who debated the relationship between human emotions and crime, punishment, and social control. More recently, as Karstedt (2002) insists, there has been a 'return of emotions' in criminal justice via the increasingly prominent voice of the victim, the use of restorative justice, and increasingly emotionalized cultures of late modern societies (see Wouters, 1986; Williams, 2001). However, despite the apparent emotionality of crime and criminology, there are relatively few empirical studies that investigate the part that the broad emotional palette has to play in influencing our responses to crime or even the causation of crime and violence. Meanwhile, there is an increasingly rich and diverse understanding of 'everyday emotions' outside the criminological field; one of the largest studies of real-life emotions involved a series of surveys which focused on describing the probabilities of experiencing certain emotions in everyday life and on the socio-demographic and situational factors that influence these probabilities (Scherer et al., 2002). This body of work has also encompassed a number of ethnographic studies concerned with 'how emotions work' (Katz, 1999), how emotions are 'managed' across the settings of everyday life (Hochschild, 1983), and the development of a diverse 'sociology of emotions' (Kemper, 1990; Wouters, 1992; Williams and Bendelow, 1998). These contributions are noteworthy; not least because they offer a conceptual vocabulary that may well have much to offer criminological research, but also because they address pertinent methodological questions concerning the ecological and external validity.

Emotional Complexity

As noted above, Scherer et al.'s influential work examined the incidence of emotions in ordinary 'everyday' life, the potential risk factors, and the typical appraisal and reaction patterns. The study employed a population survey methodology in which data were canvassed from more than 1,000 German and French speaking adults. There were two waves of the study, conducted four years apart. Participants were asked to report an emotional event that happened the day before as well as to verbally label the experience. The emotional complexity of these responses was expressed by no less than 775 different words and phrases participants used to describe their emotions. In fact, this work demonstrated that there are numerous ways in which people interpret and understand their emotional responses. Scherer et al. (2004) stated that there were as many emotions as there are 'appraisal combinations' or interpretations. Along these lines Ben-Ze've (2000) and Katz (2004) have also highlighted the complexity and enormous diversity of human emotion in normal day-to-day life.

Nevertheless, despite the vivid assortment of emotions reported by participants in Scherer et al.'s study, both sweeps, four years apart, produced very similar distributions of emotional descriptions and frequencies. This work mapped a wide array of emotional activity, but also revealed structural regularity. Moreover, individuals were better able to manage and adapt to significant world events than one might have expected.

Ben-Ze've (2000) has distinguished five main types of everyday affective phenomena: emotions (such as fear, envy, anger, and guilt), sentiments or enduring emotions (enduring grief or love), moods (such as being cheerful, gloomy, down), affective traits, (such as trait anger or shyness etc.), and affective disorders (such as depression and anxiety). Although there is considerable overlap between the various 'types', the distinction between them is important as it represents the possible reasons why an individual might respond to stimuli in a certain way; someone who is fearful of crime when being followed at night is different to someone who is arbitrarily scared of crime due to a psychiatric condition.

According to Turner and Stets (2005), everyday emotions are influenced by a range of factors, all of which should be taken into consideration. Emotions involve certain elements. These include: (1) biological reaction of key body systems such as the nervous system in the brain or hormonal influences (raised heart rate, tears etc.); (2) socially constructed cultural definitions and checks on what emotions 'should' be experienced and expressed in a given situation (social desirability); (3) the application of common linguistic labels provided by culture and an individual's semantic ability to describe an event or feeling; (4) the external expression of emotions through facial, vocal, and/or linguistic actions; and (5) perceptions and appraisals of contextual objects or events. In short, being in a state of fearing crime should be considered a multi-dimensional event. However, the authors also suggest that not all of these elements need to be present for emotions to exist. For example, people have unconscious emotional memories which trigger biological actions, which may later prompt physical cues to themselves and others. At other times, individuals may repress their emotions with the result that they do not experience the emotion or signal it to others at any level.

How often do we Experience Emotions?

Wilhelm's (2001) and Myrtek's (2004) work conclude that most people experience some kind of emotion on a daily basis. Similarly, Scherer et al. (2004) found that one in two individuals are likely to experience at least one strong emotion on any given day. The most frequent emotions were happiness (9.1 per cent) and anger (8.6 per cent), which reflect results in similar studies. The most pertinent results to those of us in the fear of crime arena indicate the low frequency of 'basic' emotions, thought to be central to everyday thinking.[6] Fear was a relatively rare emotion; 1.2 per cent of the respondents reported experiencing fear on the previous day, although anxiety was more common (6.5 per cent). Scherer et al. noted that while it is possible that less intense experiences of fear did occur, they could not have been consciously remembered or perceived. They conclude: 'Serious fear situations are few and far between in the normal course of events' (2004: 520). Indeed, Averill (2004) has also reflected that fear is an infrequent emotion and rarely experienced outright. Similarly, other 'basic emotions' registered low frequencies: love was 0.8 per cent, hate 0.2 per cent, jealously 0.2 per cent, hope 0.1 per cent, envy 0.1 per cent, shame 0.1 per cent, and contempt in at less than one tenth of 1 per cent. While these emotions may be considered normal 'expressive'

---

[6] Although there are cultural differences in how emotions are expressed and interpreted, it has been widely excepted that some emotions are basic and universal. Many writers (see Darwin, 1872; Emde, 1980; Turner, 1996) have agreed that happiness, fear, anger, and sadness are universal (Turner and Stets, 2005).

fodder in popular culture and to have a strong motivational force on our daily behaviour, they may actually be much *less* common than we think they are. Other commentators have mused that we may expect certain emotions to be more prevalent than they actually are because of their symbolism and significance;

Fear, love, hate, jealousy, hope, envy, shame and contempt are perceived to be frequent since they appear to have tremendous impact upon our behaviour. While these emotions seem to shape our behaviour in many circumstances, the findings of the study under discussion (Scherer et al., 2004) indicate that they may have less impact than we think. Similarly aeroplane accidents are perceived to be more frequent than their actual occurrence because their immediate impact—the death of so many people at one time—is so great and attracts large media attention. Accordingly we consider their impact upon our life as more profound than it actually is (Ben-Ze've and Revhon, 2004: 583).

Perhaps the low occurrence of 'basic emotions' (including fear) signifies the growing importance of other social and cultural emotional considerations. While historically basic emotions have been considered the most important, due to their evolutionary function, modern life has posed new emotional stimuli, involving particularly complex social, political, and philosophical factors. As Ben-Ze've comments: 'social comparative concerns have become as crucial as the self-preservative biological concerns and cannot be reduced to them' (2000: 104). However, as Scherer et al. remind us, that despite being a rare event, the significance of fear as an emotion should not be underestimated. Fear is described as a 'phylogenetically continuous emotion' which produces important biological, emotional responses essential for the maintenance of health and the avoidance of imminent danger: 'the fact that it is apparently a relatively rare event, at least in modern Western democracies, does not detract from its important role in the emotional repertoire of humans' (Scherer et al., 2004: 557).

What does it mean to be 'Fearful'?

If fear is rare, what does it actually mean to think about crime and fear of crime in everyday life? Similar to the approaches adopted in the above-mentioned studies, Gabriel and Greve (2003) argue that fear of crime research needs to utilize approaches that are sensitive to the intricacies of fear as experienced by individuals.

They argue that it is essential to distinguish conceptually between fear which is due to a 'personal trait' and a 'momentary affective' state. There are clear and important differences, the authors maintain, between a fear of crime that passes quickly in response to very specific surroundings, and a general disposition or trait of being afraid of becoming a victim of crime. Individuals who have dispositional fear consider more situations as being significant indicators of crime, are more likely to experience fear in a given situation, and probably more intensely. The importance of this contribution is that the distinction demonstrates that fear of crime can be experienced very differently in terms of individual relevance, explanation, and consequences. Along these lines, some people may experience fear on a regular on-going basis on account of their individual characteristics and psyche—perhaps parochially described as 'nervous' or 'vulnerable', while others are more likely to respond to specific stimulus.

Furthermore, not all behaviours indicative of fear will have been prompted by a fearful experience. For example, taking out insurance, locking one's car and home may be an everyday precautionary action taken to minimize one's risk of crime, but is not necessarily provoked by a fear-inciting situation. These sorts of 'safety precautions' are taken daily by the vast majority of people without an accompanying emotional theme-tune—similar to decisions to take exercise, moderate alcohol intake, or eat well to maintain general well-being and avoid the onset of ill-health.

Emotional Digestion and Appraisal Theory

In responding to Scherer et al.'s study, Goldie (2004) makes the point that emotional responses do not always immediately follow an event. For example, if you are robbed on the street, you may not feel a sense of anger until much later—perhaps days or even weeks after the episode—when the full impact of the action has had time to 'settle' and 'digest' in your mind.[7] As Goldie explains:

In much of our life—the life of the mind—the 'event' is not so tightly connected to the emotion that it elicits. We feel emotions in looking backwards at events that took place long ago in our own lives: nostalgia, grief, sadness, regret and shame. . .

---

[7] Post-traumatic stress disorder, which may indeed follow an incident of serious personal violence, is not, by definition, felt until some time after the event.

Goldie (2004) goes on to argue that emotion-eliciting events can consist of different types of incidence, they may be felt 'in the moment' or following an event or crime, for example; they may be registered by the individual's unconscious mind, recalled later from memory, or even fabricated and inflated by imagination and reappraised at will. Accordingly, some experiences of the fear of crime may be difficult for a respondent to 'anchor' in their memory or talk about accurately. Indeed, Goldie (2004) highlights the subjective interpretation of thinking about facts and events that shape our emotional responses. A central point in emotion research and specifically 'appraisal theory' is that the very same event may be considered highly significant by one individual and irrelevant by another, depending on their personal, cultural, and biological characteristics at that point in time. One person may become scared of crime because there are numerous teenagers hanging around the local streets, whereas others may feel a sense of belonging to a local community where young people are visible and playing outside. Even *imagining* a situation of potential danger may elicit fear or worry in one person but not in another (Warr, 1984).

Interestingly, there are numerous studies which have documented profound discrepancies between people's concurrent and retrospective reports of emotional experiences (Gilbert and Ebert, 2002; Robinson and Clore 2002a, 2002b). Researchers have concluded that this is due, in part, to the highly fluctuating nature of emotions over time, as well as from place to place (Brandstatter, 1983; Fredrickson and Kahneman, 1993); the nature of memory (Scherer et al., 2004) and the way respondents integrate subtle nuances of their experiences when they are recounting historical emotional events (Kahneman, 1994). Exploring how respondents recall knowledge, Robinson and Clore (2002a, 2002b) distinguish between episodic and semantic knowledge; when people report their *current* or very recent feelings they are accessing their 'episodic' memory which is grounded in the specifics of time and place. Conversely, reports of feelings experienced in the past (more than two weeks previously) are drawing on 'semantic' knowledge. This information is conceptual in nature and draws upon people's general beliefs related with this particular event. The actual experience may not figure prominently in these semantic reports because the experience is no longer accessible to the memory. Indeed, semantic knowledge allows respondents to characterize themselves, 'in general'. This dynamic is supported by similar studies which have confirmed that people have fashioned beliefs and ideas about themselves which can be divorced from experiences in their everyday life (Klein, Babey and Sherman, 1997; Marsh and Yeung, 1998). Moreover, Robinson and Clore (2002a) maintain that individual beliefs about emotion are more heavily influenced by semantic, rather than episodic, knowledge. As such, when surveys pose the question 'how worried are you about burglary', the wording of this question is more likely to elicit vague 'global' summaries of intensity of worry or fear. Warr (2000) suggests that these summaries represent future orientated anxiety rather than a summary of past episodes or current feelings of physical fear (see also Sacco, 2005).

Critically, the research presented herein has encountered a divergence between self-reported levels of fear (see Chapter 6 below). We have found that more general estimates of fear of crime do not neatly map onto experiential time-focused accounts of crime-fears. Specifically some 88 per cent of respondents confirmed that they were worried (to some degree) about domestic burglary when presented with a standard (semantic) survey question—perhaps because they have a vivid and accessible image of risk. Yet when asked an additional time-limited question, 65 per cent of the same sample reported that in the past 12 months they had *not experienced* any events of worry about burglary. We conclude that the results point towards one of two manifestations of fear—one based on *expressive* or semantic inspired fear, and the other more grounded in the daily *experience* of everyday life, a dynamic we will cover in more detail as we progress.

New Directions in Everyday Emotions Research: Methodological Issues

While work in the field of everyday emotions has opened up new ways of looking at emotional responses and provided a multi-dimensional view of our emotional life, it has also raised a series of methodological questions concerned with the internal as well as the construct validity of such methods. If everyday emotions are revealed to be complex thought processes which individuals experience in very personal and diverse ways, exploring the incidence and experience of the fear of crime is also a multi-faceted and methodologically challenging arena. Being alert to the issues identified here will not only increase the general validity of any study, but also will better inform our understanding of how people understand, process, and 'manage' their fears about crime.

Evidently, we need to exercise greater sensitivity and seek more accuracy in the way we understand and interpret survey reactions on the fear of crime. How often do people actually encounter feelings of 'fear'—are other less severe reactions more appropriate? How intense is this reaction and what are the implications for respondents—how do they cope with fear? If we were to let participants speak in their own language would they use the term fear and if not, how would they describe their feelings? Specifically, attempts to acquire knowledge about the frequencies of emotions in daily life are confronted with conceptual problems, such as how moods and unspecific emotional states can be distinguished from emotions. Even though studies may ask respondents to only report incidences in which they felt 'fear' or 'worry', it is very likely that participants will also report what they perceive to be similar states, such as 'anxiety', 'dissatisfaction', or 'mild concern', for example. Are we at risk of misinterpreting any reaction as a specifically fearful one? Clearly, we need to pay close attention not just to the presence of these emotions but also their intensity and frequency.

In order to produce a more authentic picture of what fear of crime actually means to respondents, data collection efforts need to minimize the potential for measurement errors. Cognitive interviewing techniques were designed by an interdisciplinary team of methodologists and psychologists in the 1980s for the very purpose of estimating the impact of measurement errors. Specifically, the overall aim is to use cognitive theory to understand how respondents perceive and interpret questions and to identify potential problems that may arise in prospective survey questionnaires. For example, an interviewer will probe the comprehension of the question; the ability of the respondent to recall relevant information; the decision process involved in reaching answers to questions and how these processes operate in the context of a research process. Cognitive interviews are a useful means for pre-testing questionnaires, particularly where the subject matter is sensitive or complex. As such, cognitive interviewing techniques might be a particularly valuable method in fear of crime research, usefully employed to allow researchers to go 'back to basics' and investigate what fear of crime tools are actually measuring.

68   What is the Fear of Crime?

We have sought to demonstrate how notions of 'fear' and 'worry' in criminological circles and within popular culture require thoughtful expansion. Fear of crime has commonly been considered in exclusively negative terms, as a social *problem* which impacts on people's quality of life and sense of safety. However, some degree of worrying about crime is both an inevitable and ordinary experience for most people. As Gladstone and Parker (2003) note, worry is not a typically pathological process, it has functional properties, such as prompting the mental reminder to lock the house or check the burglar alarm. When people say they are worried about crime it is very likely that some of these respondents at least are describing a type of worry which is not detrimental to their well-being, but has motivational qualities which leads them to take common precautions, such as locking their car, taking insurance, or purchasing security lights for their property. These actions may indicate they are aware or alert to the possibility of becoming a victim, but do not necessarily mean these respondents are experiencing feelings of fear, anxiety, or vulnerability. Indeed, it is clear that further research is required to explore the multiple personalities of fear and what it represents to people in the course of their daily lives.

However rich and diverse respondents' descriptions are, we should be aware that it is particularly difficult to elicit these through survey methods. Specifically, the recall of an event or experience depends on its proximity and recent events are more accessible. One method for minimizing response error is to employ a narrow time frame in interview or survey questions which limits respondents to a specific reference period which they will be able to recall more accurately. For example, 'in the last 12 months have you worried about...?' Nevertheless, retrievals are influenced by a tendency to reconstruct events or experiences so as to make them consistent with memories and subsequent interpretations. Respondents are unlikely to be succinct or clear when describing their past emotional experiences in which numerous thoughts and feelings may have been intertwined. Consider this example: a person may become *worried* that their car has been stolen when they cannot locate it in an unfamiliar car park they find *disorientating*, he or she becomes *scared* of not being able to get home late at night and then feels *concerned* about the consequent financial implications as they search for their car. Eventually the person is *resigned* to the fact that the car has been stolen and begins to think about making alternative arrangements and later *relieved* when they realize they were confused and it was parked on a different floor. In this situation a respondent has gone through a range of brief emotional encounters and asking them to summarize this into one word or phrase is highly reductive. Indeed, much of the difficulty in defining and studying emotion is due to the extraordinary changeability of the process, which can be hard to pin down into specific researchable 'chunks'. The use of multiple research methods including both qualitative and quantitative techniques which allow respondents more freedom to define their own and various emotional reactions to crime may help us to better understand the properties of fear of crime and the consequent impact of such emotions on individual perceptions.

Work in emotions research also suggests that respondents are more likely to recall negative experiences than they are to recall positive ones. If a researcher asks a respondent about their last experience of fear or worry about crime they may only recall the most memorable and possibly the most serious experience. For example, a respondent is more likely to remember a time when they were concerned about being robbed, rather than a time when they briefly thought something may have been stolen from their car. Scherer et al. (2004) report that respondents have a tendency to associate the term 'event' in a survey with the most dramatic incidence they can recall. As such, delicate internal thoughts, perhaps about less serious crimes or more subtle worries, are easily missed. Accordingly it is essential that (1) different crimes are considered separately and (2) we assume that less intense experiences of fear of crime are not consciously remembered and consequently have a reduced contribution to the overall count.

Research into 'everyday emotions' has demonstrated how much we can learn about the manner in which people respond emotionally and how to best capture these processes through empirical research. Although such endeavours may be methodologically and conceptually challenging, these techniques could be very useful for fear of crime work. If we are to continue with this endeavour, ways forward might include drawing upon the research on the psychology of emotional self-report and risk, the sociology of everyday emotions, and public sensibilities to crime. Meanwhile, we turn to a growing body of equally relevant work in relation to quantitative survey-based research.

Lessons from Qualitative Data on the Lived Reality of the Fear of Crime

A brief departure to some qualitative data from two previous ESRC-funded studies that members of the current author-team have conducted will provide useful examples of the discussion thus far. This way we can begin to explore the lived reality of the topic at hand, before we launch more fully into the empirical material in Part two. Our data speak to what it is like to feel fearful of crime: What are the contours of this experience? Is it an everyday event, or something which ebbs and flows? In order to answer these (and similar) questions we rely on in-depth interviews with respondents interviewed as part of earlier projects (see our Methodological Appendix for an outline of the data sets). All of the extracts from interviews with those living in and around Glasgow (see Farrall et al. 1997 for an outline of the methodology) are from those characterized as expressing both subjectively high fear and high risk of victimization. The Glaswegians were interviewed between the autumn of 1995 and the spring of 1996 by Stephen Farrall and Elizabeth Gilchrist. The interviews with those living in London were conducted in 2000 by Jonathan Jackson.[8]

Feelings as Transitory, Fleeting Experiences

Some experiences were reported as having a very short duration, and certainly represented uncommon events. As the respondent below (a male living in the West End of Glasgow) reported:

A chair came flying over our hedge one night. Now I don't know where it came from 'cause I went shooting out to punch somebody's lights out and there was nobody there [laughs]. I don't know where they went, maybe they were round the corner laughing at me, but this chair came and landed in the garden, now I'm not entirely sure whether it either came out of an upstairs window, but I don't think [so], I don't see how it could've done and bounced off our wall and landed in our front garden, I think somebody must've wheeched it over the hedge. That's quite a risky thing in some ways in that you get a bit of a fright but looking back on it, you think that was somebody a bit bevvied having a bit of a laugh, you know,

---

[8] Our interviewees are referred to by code numbers only. K = Kelvinside, B = Bearsden, G = Gorbals and D = Drumchapel (all in or around Glasgow) and H = Hounslow (London). Interviewers are identified by initials, SF = Stephen Farrall, JJ = Jon Jackson and LG = Elizabeth Gilchrist.

that was the end of it. I felt threatened for about two seconds at the time but now, nah, it was somebody pissed as a fart, 'yeah let's toss this chair, I can't be bothered carrying it anymore', that sort of thing, you know. They probably stole it out a bar or something. That's the end of the story. K102 (male, under 30, white)

The 'flying chair' strikes the respondent as shocking because it took him unawares and a few moments passed before he realized it did not represent a criminal or immediate danger. Once he came to the conclusion it no longer posed a 'threat' the emotion of the event, while memorable, quickly dissolved. It does not appear to have had any long-term impact on the respondent. The passing nature of crime fears was raised by other respondents; the following two quotes describe how worries about burglary came to mind during the moments when respondents were actively taking safety precautions (locking up) or leaving their homes. However, these feelings dissipated once their focus switched to other matters.

D15 (male, over 50, white)

When you go out [of your home] it's the worry, like I say, you might go out and then you'll start to wonder 'did I lock this?, did I lock that?' but after you're out a while, it goes away, you forget. You forget about it till you come back you know or if you're maybe taking longer than you thought you would, you're hurrying back you know. That's what it is to worry about it. [laughs]

JJ

... you're saying you often think about being burgled and there's times when ...

H01 (female, over 50, white)

When I go out, I don't think of it, it's only when I physically go out, you know, I know I've got to lock the doors and it does make me cross because ... and when my son comes home from school and I'm out, he can't get in, so he's sitting on the doorstep waiting for me. I used to let my mum have a key but I took my keys off my mum. I'm the only person now that's actually got a deadlock key. And I always make sure that's on and that makes me angry, the fact that I have to sort of, it's like a bolt hole, you know, and you've got to lock everything up before you. Life shouldn't be like that, you shouldn't have to lock everything up and you know ... once I've gone out, I'm not worried. But when I'm initially locking the door, it does make me angry.

D32 (male, 30s–40s, white)

As I say [I only worry] when I go away for, like say, the weekend or a week or something like that and then I worry but any other time is, no.

Conversely others suggested that it did not occur to them to worry about burglary until they experienced the crime first hand:

SF

Was this something which you'd worried about before it happened?

D05 (female, 30s–40s, white)

Never, never . . . I was here for seven years before that and I could go out and in and not bother until that, but that is still in my mind.

The key message from these interviews was that the lived reality of worry about crime was most often described as a fleeting, routine, and uncommon event. It is also worth noting that some respondents described the emotional impact of victimization as similarly short-lived:

SF

You said you were very cross [about having his car vandalized], understandably. How long did it take you to calm down?

D15 (male, over 50, white)

How long did it take me to calm down, I don't know. . .

SF

Was it a matter of minutes or was it, like, maybe a couple of days?

D15

Naw, it was till I got a hold of them all and found out if any of them done it. After that I just said 'well they said they never done it, I cannae do anything about it'.

Another respondent said:

So I just came in and said to my husband 'the bloody bike's been stolen' and that was it, I reported it to the police, I felt really, really annoyed, just because it was new, and I'd never really sort of used it. I knew it was another £50 excess to pay on it, so that was it, it just annoyed me, but it's gone, it's over, frustration, and then it goes and something else takes its place quite quickly. B131 (female, 30s–40s, white)

Other extracts suggested that the framework of 'fear' overstated the reality of the emotional experience, which for some people was more accurately described as commonplace concerns or momentary worries.

It's not so much worry it's just, I don't know, I just, I suppose I just think about it. I don't sit down actually *worry* about it, it just, if it comes into my head I'll think 'Oh that would be, I wouldn't really like that to happen to me' but it's not so much something that plays on my mind all the time. I don't think worry's quite the right word. K99 (male, under 30, white)

SF

One of the other questions which I asked you about was how much you worried about somebody robbing you or assaulting you or making threats to do either.

B166 (male, over 50, white)

I have a sense of caution about making it easy for somebody to do that and to, erm, I would say, yes you probably do think about it, once or twice during the week.

SF

Would you say you worried about it or just that you thought about it?

B166

Thought about it, I don't worry about it too much. The moment when you think about it you have a moment's anxiety perhaps, but it's not a constant worry at the moment.

It's just a thought in the back'ae yer mind, 'I hope ma car's OK while I'm away'. G76 (female, 30s–40s, white)

It is worth bearing in mind that some of the above quotes were sourced from respondents who initially stated they had 'high' levels of fear—when presented with the first round of traditional quantitative questions. It is only during open-ended qualitative interviewing that we were able to tease apart more precise details about their emotional responses to crime. That many of these quotes suggest their experience of fearful episodes is transitory, infrequent, and often very short lived is thus particularly significant. Of course, this is hardly surprising. We do not live in a society in which crime is a daily feature of everyone's life (although, of course, there may be a heightened *awareness* of the risks posed by crime, this does not often lead to outright fear, merely a calculated set of behavioural responses, as argued by Garland, 2001). Despite

74 What is the Fear of Crime?

this, however, we did find some instances in which respondents' even fleeting or vicarious experiences of crime led on to more sustained feelings. Take the cases below, for example:

[After the burglary] I never felt unsafe in the house, I never ever felt that, just, aye, unsafe at leaving it, that's it an' that takes a long, long time to get over. G76 (female, 30s–40s, white)

I suppose after it's happened, you're more aware, you're made more aware of burglary in general and you perhaps worry about it more and as I say, when you know someone who's been burgled, you tend to think about it more often and then eventually go back to just hardly ever thinking about it but if it actually happened to you, you'd be totally conscious of it for ages afterwards and perhaps it would start to rule your life, you know, you'd always be leaving lights on and perhaps someone staying in when everyone else goes out and fitting lots of locks on the doors and stuff and just going completely over the top. K99 (male, under 30, white)

Even here, though, our respondent K99 (who had experienced an attempted break-in at his parents' house some years before the interview was conducted and who seemed little bothered by it) reports that he imagines that after hearing from friends about their burglary, for a while he would have an increased awareness of the possibility of being burgled himself, but that over time this would subside. Similar experiences were reported by Farrall (2004a) when discussing his own experiences of victimization. None of this is to suggest, however, that there are no individuals in society who experience fear on a daily basis. Stanko (1990) reports that the experiences of female victims of domestic abuse often prompt high levels of anxiety about crime, and presumably similar rates of fear could be expected amongst some ethnic minorities, gay people, and/or religious groups—Muslims living in the US or Europe being the most obvious example in the present climate. However, our basic point stands outwith this: fear of 'run-of-the-mill' crime would appear to be infrequent and short lived.

'Fear' in the Absence of Direct Experience

Some of our 'fearful' respondents, when interviewed in-depth about their fears, provided answers which suggested that, in fact, they were not fearful of crime at all—rather they empathized with those who *had* been victimized:

[My neighbour] came to my door and told me, that her front door was lying open, and she's frightened to go in. So I went in with her. And I felt so sorry for her. Because the things that were taken, I mean, she didn't have much in her house, just a wee woman that stays on her own, she didn't have much. They took a new gas fire that she saved up all her 20 pences for, a new electric fire that she'd saved up for that too, they took them, two fires and went into the bedroom and took wee personal things, as I say, she didn't have much, just wee personal things . . . And I couldn't control her, she was broken hearted she was, and you know it's a horrible feeling, the mere fact that somebody's been in my drawers and opened her cupboards, she says, it'll never be the same. Plus she wasn't insured. That made it worse, and oh she was devastated, and so was I when I saw her. The state she was in, so that was the only experience that I've ever known anybody's house was broken into. Because it wasn't my house and I felt it for her, it was horrible.

This episode—some six years before the interview was conducted-had significant consequences for our respondent, as she detailed later in her interview:

Oh I was getting every time I heard a noise in the corridor that I was opening the door. And it was innocent . . . somebody just maybe walking by or something like that, that only happened . . . it lasted for quite a while then you get lackadaisical, you get bored with it, that's what happened, but that was an awful episode, it was a shame, I felt sorry for her. G89 (female, over 50, white)

Eventually the intensity of these anxieties subsided and the respondent became less 'alert' to the presence of noises in the corridor, but continued to feel empathy for her neighbour when she reflected upon the event.

Background Concerns

For some whom we interviewed, including some of those whose experiences were fleeting, their feelings about crime were more akin to a concern about the way 'society was heading'. These feelings do not seem to represent 'personal fears' as such, but rather to represent opinions about societal-level change, the causes of this, and what can be done to limit the less desirable aspects of these changes.

I would say I was more, *concerned* with the cause than the whole structure of . . . what seems to be, er, *causing* crime to be on the increase . . . and to my mind it's not just parental control, drugs, violence on television, lack of control by, oh, schools being allowed to control, having discipline. I think it's a combination of all these factors, plus the limitations that some of the courts have and, in anybody that does commit anyone who is put on probation, not probation, what is the word when they're waiting for trial again . . . [SF: remand]. Remand, that's right, the real danger of remand and let out on bail, pending a court case, they've picked up new tricks . . . I think what judges are allowed to mete out in terms of punishment, the quality of punishments for certain crimes. Especially in case of firearms where, and for the elderly where they get, beaten up and things like that. B166 (male, over 50, white)

Yes, it's part of society's general deterioration to more violence than perhaps we would be accepting, I'm not personally going around worried, I'm just concerned. B152 (female, 30s–40s, white)

I mean, I've got an Arab next door, I've got a Somalian lady next door to there, Welsh opposite and we all get on great. There's no problem, but when you get, we seem to have got an influx of people and they seem very aggressive. I don't really know how to put it into words, but it's becoming a 'them and us'. You can actually see it you know, and you listen to people and it's becoming, it's becoming like that; 'them and us'. H18 (female, 30s–40s, white)

Well I think, actually to be honest with you, I think you don't really worry so much for yourself, you worry for your kids, you know what I mean, you worry for like your kids, you know, like it's a changing world an' you worry what's out there for them, you know, that I think really that's it, you're no just so worried for yourself, it's more your kids you're worried about. G76 (female, 30s–40s, white)

These concerns, as such, then do not represent heart-stopping, terror-loaded moments when citizens fear for their lives or the integrity of their home and possessions, but rather represent quite reasonable expressions of valid and not disinterested views on the society in which they live. In fact, if citizens expressed the opposite (a sort of 'Crime? Who cares what happens? I don't care if dangerous offenders are released to victimize ex-partners or ethnic minorities', an 'I'm alright, Jack' attitude) we would be the worse for it, and, one suspects, there would be a public debate not about the fear of crime, but about citizen *apathy* to crime.

The Chronically Fearful

This is not to suggest, of course, that there were not those who reported feeling extremely fearful. The following respondent suggested that she had felt fearful about burglary for some period of time:

[I've] always been worried about it, it's just more now but I was always, I've always been worried about it, I don't go out, don't stay out late because I'm, sometimes I'm frightened to come home ye know. I've just always had that fear in the back of my mind that it could happen. D34 (female, under 30, white)

Her feelings of 'dread' and anxiety—which she describes in unambiguous detail—occur not only when she is away from the property, but at night, keeping her awake as she ruminates on external noises or lack of security:

I do dread it, even through the night an' I'm in my bed I actually think about it because I live alone with my daughter an' I've always got this fear, this sounds stupid but this fear that somebody could break in this living room while I'm in my bed even sleeping an' my daughter's in the other room. Sometimes I cannae even sleep because an' that, you know. It's probably in my mind but you hear that many people outside an' you know if the wind's blowing you hear like cans blowing about an' papers, you think it's actually somebody in your house, you think it's somebody that's gonnie come to your, I mean the close isnae secure you know there's no back door.

Understandably, the respondent's anxieties are set in the context of her own experience of being burgled, as well as her knowledge of other local burglaries or neighbours who share her concern about the safety of their homes:

There's quite a few in the close that I've spoke to after my house got broken into, in fact I'm not the only one in the close, the boy at the top's house got broken into as well and the boy next door, they're all kinda worried about it.

Not only did local crime rates and shared stories embed themselves in the mind of this individual, but, she explains, different seasons of the year pose particular threats. Christmas, for example, a time when houses are filled with presents and additional monies or goods might make one more vulnerable to burglary:

I think everybody worries about it this time of year [the autumn]. I mean Christmas Eve I just don't even go tae bed you know [laughs]. You hear that many stories people get up in the morning, their kids' Christmas presents, that's actually happened to a friend of mine, she got up on Christmas morning an' there was not a present under the tree for her kids cause they'd been through the night . . . so more so this time'a year 'cause people know you've got kids, yer spending money, yer buying, whether it's TVs whatever you're buying for them, toys even, even just their clothes. In fact I've just bought my daughter a pair'a boots for Christmas when the house got broken intae an' they were in her room an' when I went intae my room to check if the boy had taken anything the boots were actually lying at my room door just ready to get carted out the door so they were even looking, I mean kids boots you know he was even wanting to take them as well so more so this time'a year.

For this respondent, her fear of crime impacts on many domains of her life—it is not an exclusive concern about burglary. She limits her movements after dark; is suspicious of groups, 'gangs', and 'junkies', and speeds her walking pace if she feels the presence of strangers:

As I said I don't go out late at night because it's more likely to happen then I suppose cause there's gangs like hang about the corners, the shops round the corner an' there's a chip shop which I think attracts people anyway and an off sales which attracts them so I try and avoid these kinda places, you know, I just go as far as two streets away cause I have got a fear of, anybody walks down the street behind me I'm off! [laughs]. I'm home in two seconds. I just don't trust anybody that I don't know their face, I just don't. There's too many junkies, drunks going about that probably maybe even know me could do the same thing cause they don't know what they're doing, they're that spaced out half the time, you know they're bouncing round there you know [laughs] . . . they don't know whit they're daein'.

To Answer Our Question

What, then, *is* the fear of crime? Here we provide—ranked in order of most to least fearful—our answer to the question 'What is the fear of crime as played out in the lives of ordinary citizens?'. We contend that the 'fear of crime', as a lived experience, includes the following, then:

- Those, thankfully rare, moments when one realizes that one is in a situation in which victimization is a very serious possibility (or imagines this occurrence). This may occur immediately prior to any victimization, or immediately after the victimization or threat has been recognized.
- The puncturing of mundane feelings of security by sudden shock events which alert one to the fact that whilst crime happens, it can happen to oneself too and that, as such, one is not immune from victimization. These sudden shocks can take the form of actual victimization, hearing about the victimization

of specified others, or the defused sense that one is in an area which is a 'hot spot' for trouble of some sort.
- Those nagging doubts about locking front doors, closing windows, and (in essence) leaving one's home alone for a period of time which ebb and flow during the trip away (being more heightened at points of departure and return) and successively reducing over time as one becomes habituated to leaving the home unattended but finding it intact on return.
- An awareness that crime is a possibility, and that, therefore, extra precautions ought sensibly to be taken.
- A set of feelings which are orientated towards the problem of crime for society. These are quite separate *emotionally* from one's own experiences, but possibly strongly linked to them on an experiential level. One's own victimization experiences do not dictate whether or not one will perceive crime as a problem for society (although, as these experiences accumulate, so they increase the chances that crime will be perceived as a serious problem) since even those who have experienced relatively little victimization will have an opinion about the problem of crime for society.

As such, and as a lived experience, the fear of crime represents a *continuum* of feelings which are distributed along a spectrum between two distinctly different ideal typical emotional reactions. At one end, the most emotive aspect is the experience(s) of having felt fearful in a specific situation. At the other is a set of attitudes or opinions which are brought forth when people are asked to discuss their feelings about crime. This 'invocation of attitude'—which surveys provoke and measure—we shall refer to as the 'expressive' dimension of the fear of crime (in contrast to the 'experiential' dimension).

Concluding Remarks

The way a construct is measured reflects the way it is conceptualized, and the fear of crime construct and its appropriate indicators have been developed considerably over the years. Yet debate continues about the nature and scope of fear of crime. The concept covers a wide range of different experiences, attitudes, and vulnerabilities, and questionnaires unsurprisingly struggle to capture its entirety. It is even possible that standard approaches inadvertently exaggerated the fear of crime problem (Lee, 1999; Farrall and Gadd, 2004); distorted the nature of fear as it is experienced in everyday life (Gabriel and Greve, 2003; Farrall et al., 1997); and failed to recognize the functional as well as expressive aspects of the language of crime fears (Jackson, 2006). Research into 'everyday emotions' and the 'psychology of survey response' has much to offer criminologists conducting fear of crime research. Exploring these literatures we conclude that fear is an infrequent emotion in response to crime (others have suggested *any* stimuli, Scherer et al., 2004). There is, unsurprisingly, an enormous complexity and diversity of human emotion in general and about crime in particular; emotions (including those about crime) have multi-dimensional antecedents. The heightened significance and impact of fear may be leading people (including academics) to perceive emotions like fear to be a more frequent occurrence in everyday life than is actually the case. As research in memory and recall has found, negative memories are much more salient and easy to recall *in general*; and, that when asked about a nonspecific event (i.e. worry about crime) respondents will employ the most dramatic individual instance that they can recall (which will often turn out to be the most emotional and resonant).

While it may be difficult to produce *precise* evidence about the frequency or intensity of fear of crime, there is considerable room for methodological improvement in order to capture important detail and describe the significant characteristics of these responses. We have shown that more work needs to be done if we are to tease out the reality of this social phenomenon—to examine its variety, its effects, its causes, and its nature. Such empirical study promises to produce more valid and reliable research tools—tools that will facilitate more theoretically sophisticated modes of explanation of this important social and political issue of the day.

4

Theorizing the Fear of Crime: The Cultural and Social Significance of Insecurity

'Fears trace a map of a society's values; we need fear to know who we are and what we do not want to be.' (Marina Warner, *No Go the Bogeyman*, Chatto and Windus, 1998).

Introduction

As well as receiving much attention at an empirical and descriptive level, the fear of crime has of course received considerable theoretical attention: attempts to discover the causes of fear, to highlight the processes that underpin social and risk perception, have continued apace. Theoretical work, as one might well imagine, does not always proceed smoothly, and efforts have met with varying degrees of empirical success. Indeed, few of the theoretical models have been sufficiently ambitious to fully appreciate this complex social phenomenon.

This chapter outlines the theoretical positions adopted to explain the fear of crime. We start by outlining the broad theoretical approaches taken to account for levels of fear of crime since the 1960s. We are not, of course, the first to attempt such a review: Chris Hale in his gargantuan review of the fear of crime literature (Hale, 1996) suggested that there were four broad dimensions to the theoretical attempts to explaining the fear of crime: those which focused on vulnerability, another set which concentrated on victimization experiences, an emerging body of work which drew out the relationship between the environment and feelings of insecurity and, lastly, a small field of research which emphasized the role of psychological factors in the production of anxiety. Our first contribution in this chapter is to both update Hale's review and apply our own way of thinking on the literature. We structure our review into five sections:

- The victimization thesis;
- Imagined victimization and the psychology of risk;
- Disorder, cohesion, and collective efficacy—environmental perception;
- Structural change and macro-level influences on fear; and,
- Connecting anxieties about crime to other types of anxiety.

We then, in preparation for subsequent chapters (especially Chapters 5 and 7) and as the second contribution of this chapter, outline the framework that we pursue in the rest of this project—a framework that draws upon a range of insights generated by both quantitative and qualitative research in this area. Inevitably, given the number of authors working in this field, the range of countries from which such authors originate, and the development of the field over near-on 50 years, these theories are not perhaps quite as distinct as our review here suggests. However, in the manner of previous reviews (most notably Bennett, 1990; Hale, 1996; Vanderveen, 2006), we shall take a broad-brushed approach. We start with those theories which highlighted victimization as a root cause of fear.

The Victimization Thesis

The victimization perspective is based on the principle that fear of crime within a community is caused by the level of criminal activity or by what people hear about activity—either from conversations with others or from the mass media. (Bennett, 1990: 14).

One of the earliest approaches to explaining the fear of crime posited that the statistically estimated risk of crime and actual direct personal experience of victimization were both key to understanding why some people report being anxious about crime while others do not (Lewis and Salem, 1980). Thus the fear of crime was seen as partly the *product* of victimization. The more *actual* victimization experiences (experienced directly), or the more *likely* victimization was, the more fearful an individual will be (see *inter alia* Balkin, 1979; Liska et al., 1988; Skogan, 1987). This model is by far the simplest model of fear: levels of fear of crime within a community are caused by the level of criminal activity within that community.

Yet this theoretical position has only been partially supported by the empirical data at hand (Hale, 1996: 104). There is some evidence (e.g. Garofalo, 1979; Skogan, 1981; Stafford and Galle, 1984; Liska et al., 1988; Covington and Taylor, 1991; Hough, 1995; McCoy et al., 1996; Kury and Ferdinand, 1998; Rountree, 1998) that direct victimization experience is related to worry about certain types of crime. But such experience seems but a small part of any powerful explanation of the fear of crime. Weak correlations between fear and both levels of crime and individual experience of victimization have given rise to the risk-fear paradox: more people worry about crime than are likely to fall victim and the wrong people seem to be worrying (Conklin, 1975; DuBow et al., 1979; Hale, 1996). The 'crime causes fear' explanation therefore seems inadequate—at least in isolation.

The risk-fear paradox is also evidenced by the fact that some of the social groups most at risk of victimization are relatively fearless (e.g. young males) and some of the social groups least likely to be victimized are relatively fearful (e.g. older females, although in the UK worry decreases as age increases). Some criminologists have responded by arguing that it is *relative* harm that influences expressed fear levels. Others have suggested that the nature of the victimization experienced by those groups found to be most fearful (women and the elderly) was inaccessible to quantitative research procedures (Stanko, 1985 and 1988). Others still have argued that victimization will actually *reduce* fear of crime by demystifying the unknown and still others have suggested that it is the *amount* of victimization that is important (Agnew, 1985). Still others, for example, found that the victimization thesis worked for violent offences, but not property offences (Miethe and Lee, 1984). Conversely, Smith and Hill (1991) found that, after weighting for the seriousness of the victimization, property victimization, not personal victimization, was significantly related to fear levels.

It could be—as suggested by Agnew (1985)—that victimization is neutralized by victims in the same way that offenders negate feelings of guilt (see Hale, 1996, for a discussion of this work; see also Winkel, 1998). Surveying crime victims, Tyler and Rasinski (1984; see also Tyler, 1980) found that perceptions of risk and worry about future victimization was associated with both what individuals learnt from their particular experience of crime (i.e. how much the experience told them about the likelihood of victimization occurring again in the future, how much they learnt about the crime, and how much they learnt about how to protect themselves in the future) and the emotional reactions they had to the experience (upset, stunned, outraged, frightened, and shocked). Innes and Jones (2006) found empirical evidence that a high crime community they were studying had become 'normalized' to the threats and dangers posed by the substantial levels of crime in their area.

However, a range of methodological issues has hampered the search for the impact of victimization on fear. First, Sutton and Farrall (2005, 2009) found that men appeared to suppress their fear levels and that when this was allowed for, men (rather than women) were the more fearful. Given that men are more likely to be victimized than women, this suggests that there may well be a victimization-fear link, but that it has been hidden by male suppression of anxiety in interview situations. Second, crime survey respondents are typically only asked about victimization experiences that have occurred during the past 12 months: an experience might have an impact for a larger period than just 12 months. Third, as Bowling (1993) argues, victimization surveys reduce victimization to snapshots of a single event rather than the more fluid process that it might involve. As such the 'true' nature of both the victimization and the extent to which these emotions endure over time, may not be adequately captured by the research methods currently employed to study the fear of crime. Fourth, research over the past few decades has tended to use inconsistent measures of the fear of crime which might account for the inconclusive picture of the relationship between crime and fear (LaGrange et al., 1992). Indeed, as we shall demonstrate, when the frequency of fear is measured (instead of the overall intensity of fear) one finds stronger associations between worry and each of: crime levels, victimization experience, and knowing a victim of crime.

Finally, as mentioned earlier, legal definitions of victimization tend to exclude unpleasant experiences that might be relevant to public unease such as intimidation, obscene phone calls, and sexual harassment; identity-related victimization (i.e. crime committed because of the gender, sexuality, race, or other such attribute of the victim) is dealt with only cursorily. See, for example, Kelly, 1987, 1988 (cited in Vanderveen 2006: 118–20) and Phillips (1999, 2000) who discuss the complexities of unwanted behaviour and daily harassment for women, where male attention can feel aggressive and contradictory. Such a 'continuum of violence' (Kelly, 1987) has relatively minor acts of abuse at one end ('flashing' and minor forms of sexual abuse) and acts like rape at the other (see also Stanko, 1985, 1987, 1990, 1997; Gardner, 1990; Pain, 1993, 1997; Madriz, 1997; Hollander, 2001, 2002). As such, even minor acts are fear-provoking as these remind women of the possibility of more serious forms of violence.

Whatever the explanation for the findings generated by this avenue of research (and in our experience it is likely to be a combination of all of these and other possibilities), the claim that the fear of crime is simply (or solely) the result of victimization seems both simplistic and unwarranted by the available data.

Imagined Victimization and the Psychology of Risk

The second model states that people worry when they can imagine themselves falling victim. Hearing about events, knowing others who have been victimized—these are thought to raise perceptions of the risk of victimization (Skogan and Maxfield, 1981; Tyler, 1980, 1984; Covington and Taylor, 1991; LaGrange et al., 1992; Ferraro, 1995; Hough, 1995; Chiricos et al., 1997). Taylor and Hale (1986: 152–3) describe this as 'crime "multiplier" processes operating in the residential environment that would "spread" the impacts of criminal events'. Skogan (1986: 203) refers to direct and indirect victimization as 'primary and secondary knowledge of neighbourhood crime rates'. The evidence which exists suggests that hearing of friends' or neighbours' victimization increases anxiety is so strong that Hale (1996) concludes that indirect experiences of crime may play a stronger role in anxieties about victimization than direct experience. Box et al. (1988) found evidence to suggest that indirect victimization increased fear, whilst direct victimization did not, as did Arnold (1991). Indirect victimization thus seems to partly explain higher overall levels of fear. However, Skogan (1986: 211) offers a cautionary note: '. . . many residents of a neighbourhood only know of [crime] indirectly via channels that may inflate, deflate, or garble the picture'.

Hearing about unpleasant events may stimulate personal perceptions of risk which are themselves complex and multi-faceted (for a discussion of how the risk perception literature might shed light on the fear of crime, see Jackson, 2006, 2008). Sketching out a schema for vulnerability in the fear of crime, Killias (1990) identifies three dimensions: exposure to risk, the anticipation of serious consequences, and the loss of control ('that is, lack of effective defence, protective measures, and/or possibilities of escape', 1990: 98). All of these are necessary to produce fear, although each individually is not sufficient according to Killias. Moreover, these dimensions of vulnerability may combine to form complex interaction effects. Each dimension of threat is also associated with physical, social, and situational aspects of vulnerability. For example, more serious consequences are expected to occur amongst women, the elderly, and people in bad health (physical factors), amongst victims without networks of social support (social factors), and in deserted areas where no help is available (situational factors).[1]

Support has been found for this model. Jackson (in press) showed that some aspects of Killias's (1990) dimensions of vulnerability explained differential levels of fear of crime between age and gender groups. Perceived risk was defined as: assessments of likelihood ('how likely do you think it is that you will be burgled in the next year?'); control ('how much do you feel able to control whether you are burgled?'); and consequence ('how much impact would being burgled have on your life?'). Also measured were relative-risk judgements, where individuals are asked whether their own social group (here defined according to age and gender) are more or less likely to become a victim of crime than other social groups. Gender effects were explained by both differential levels of vulnerability (control, consequence, and self-rated physical vulnerability) and by differential assessments of the likelihood of crime (individual- and relative-levels). Thus, the reason why women worried more than men was partly to do with the fact that women typically felt less able to control victimization and anticipated more severe consequences, and the fact that women typically felt that the risk was more likely to occur to them and to women in general (but see Sutton and Farrall, 2005, 2009).

Warr's (1987) model of 'sensitivity to risk' predicts that the influence of likelihood on fear was moderated by perceptions of seriousness of the given crime-type. Analysing US data, he found that when people judged crime to be especially serious in its effect, a

---

[1] To explore one aspect of this model Killias and Clerici (2000) drew upon data from a sample survey of Swiss nationals to show that respondent assessments of their physical ability to defend themselves were an important predictor of anticipated feelings of safety in a number of situations.

lower level of perceived likelihood was needed to stimulate some level of personal fear: individuals were thus more 'sensitive' to a given level of perceived risk when they viewed the consequences of victimization to be especially serious. As such: '. . . circumstances or events that appear innocuous or comparatively minor to males or younger persons are apt to be viewed as more dangerous to females and the elderly because of the offences they imply or portend' (Warr, 1994: 19). The heterogeneity of different types of crime—with regard to 'relevance, explanation and consequences' (Gabriel and Greve, 2003: 6)—may mean that the same crime could have a different anticipated resonance or impact from one individual to the next. For example, one person may associate burglary with the risk of physical or sexual assault; another person may associate burglary with the loss of material goods and a great deal of inconvenience. Similarly, Ferraro (1995: 87) argues that sexual harassment: '. . . may shadow other types of victimization among women. Rape may operate like any other master offence among women, especially younger women who have the highest rate of rape, heightening fear reactions for other forms of crime'.

A recent development of the risk sensitivity model found that subjective probabilities strongly predicted the frequency of worry, but also that control and consequence played two key roles: (a) each shaped the judgement of likelihood; and (b) each moderated the impact of likelihood on worry (Jackson, 2009). Judgements of control and consequence thus operated as differential sensitivity to the risk of criminal victimization: when individuals judged crime to be especially serious in its personal impact, and when individuals judged that they have little control over the event, a lower level of perceived likelihood was needed to raise the frequency of worry.[2]

---

[2] Feelings of control may extend beyond control of risk to control over the social and physical environment. An environment seen to be unpredictable, unfamiliar, and beyond the control of oneself or one's community may generate a sense of disquiet and an instinctive need to scan the environment for signs of trouble—a sense that '. . . anything could happen'. Tulloch (2003: 475) used qualitative methods to show that her '. . . participants deploy discursively constructs of locus of control and self-efficacy that are more commonly identified through psychometric measurement'. Mirroring Carvalho and Lewis (2003), Tulloch (2003: 475) found that those who were fearful saw themselves at the 'mercy of powerful others (criminal gangs, predatory males, armed gunmen, paedophiles, etc.) and chance (through the random lottery-like nature of attacks)'. In contrast, the unfearful individual felt protected, claiming high levels of control over their environment, feeling that others were not aggressively dominating public space.

In sum, looking across the findings from these studies, a key dynamic to fear of crime emerges, involving both sensitivity to the impact of victimization (Ferraro, 1995; Warr, 1984, 1985) and control over its occurrence (Tulloch, 2003; Jackson, 2004a, 2009). Those with fewer resources (typically posited to be females, the elderly, and those in lower socio-economic groups) may be less able to protect themselves and deal with the consequences, and therefore more likely to report anxiety about victimization (for notes on the role of poor health, see Jackson and Stafford, 2009). As such, when individuals felt crime to be especially serious in its impact and especially difficult to control, then a lower level of perceived likelihood is needed to stimulate fear or worry (Warr, 1987). Sacco (1993) found that levels of social support provided by friends (but not by family) were associated with worry about crime; however, the effect was weak and positive, suggesting that high levels of attachment to others is more threatening because it affects others as well as oneself.

Thus far we have discussed 'indirect victimization'—the impact of hearing about crime through local interpersonal communication—and in particular a series of studies into the important mediating role of perceived risk. We have described how judgements of control, consequence, and likelihood not only interact in differential vulnerability in the fear of crime, they also mediate the influence of perceptions of the environment and hearing about crime on any subsequent anxieties, worries, or fears. Yet we have not, as yet, considered the influence of the mass media on the fear of crime.

The media is of course a major source of information about the world, but according to Hale (1996): 'Conflicting positions arise in studies of the impact of the media in general on fear'. Hearing about crime through the media may make victimization imaginable—especially if it is 'brought home' when the victim is seen to be similar to oneself or the event occurs in familiar circumstances (see Winkel and Vrij, 1990). Media crime reports dramatize, sensationalize, and report only the most serious crime, setting agendas which frame public opinion and revealing a risky and dangerous world (Smith, 1985, 1986). But direct evidence is mixed on the role of reading certain types of newspapers, or watching the news or dramas. Tyler (1980, 1984; Tyler and Cook, 1984) found that mass media reports and hearing about crime from family friends had different impacts on the perceived societal and personal risk levels. This means that any one person can be influenced by (for example) the media to feel that the risk for society is larger than previously thought, but this heightened risk judgement will not greatly affect personal risk judgement.

The impact of the mass media on fear of crime might stem from circulating images of especially dramatic and frightening criminal events that are seen as somehow personally relevant to the individual (Winkel and Vrij, 1990). If the reader of a newspaper, for example, identifies with the described victim, or feels that their own neighbourhood bears resemblance to the one described, then the image of risk may be taken up and personalized. In a related study, Stapel et al. (1994; see also Stapel and Velthuijsen, 1996) found subjects who received car crash information and who shared social identity with the victims provided elevated estimates of risk compared to those who had no basis for assumed similarity.

In examining the dynamics involved in such circulating representations of risk (such as crime report of a particular criminal event), the loose collection of concepts organized by the Social Amplification of Risk Framework (SARF) might be useful. According to Pidgeon et al. (2003: 2): '[SARF] aims to examine broadly, and in social and historical context, how risk and risk events interact with psychology, social, institutional, and cultural processes in ways that amplify and attenuate risk perceptions and concerns, and thereby shape risk behaviour, influence institutional processes, and affect risk consequences'. The goal is to understand why some hazards and events come to be of social and political relevance, even while experts judge them to be relatively unimportant (risk amplification), and why other events (to experts, more serious events) induce comparatively low levels of concern and activity (risk attenuation).

Perhaps the greatest strength of SARF is its attention to communication processes. The framework states that risk signals are received, interpreted, and passed on at a series of 'amplifier' stations and diffused through different channels. Kasperson et al. (2003: 15) argue that: '... as a key part of [the] communication process, risk, risks events, and the characteristics of both become portrayed through various risk signals (images, signs, and symbols), which in turn interact with a wide range of psychological, social, institutional, or cultural processes in ways that intensify or attenuate perceptions of risk and its manageability'. While the media are primary amplifiers, stations can also include individuals, groups, and organizations such as activist groups or government agencies, driven by their interests and functions. The results are signals that are increased or decreased in intensity, transformed in their cultural content.

Part of the explanation for why crime is such a popular topic of the mass media, and such a salient and vivid public issue, may lie in the way in which crime condenses and dramatizes our sense of the social world. Those researching communication would argue that a plural set of media amplify or attenuate risks if they resonate with public feelings and mood—if the symbols and representations deployed capture existing public concerns and frames of reference (Horlick-Jones et al., 2003). Issues are more likely to receive media attention if they can be easily integrated into a narrative that motivates interlinked processes (Wiedemann et al., 2003):

- Connecting: links are made between new events and already familiar instances and narratives, providing a readily available frame in which to understand novel phenomena.
- Contextualizing: links are made to more abstract but still resonant contemporary issues.
- Anchoring: the imagery and connotations of an event are placed within popular anxieties and fears.

The reception and engagement with such media may make the risk more available and salient when stories chime with existing public concerns and debates about social cohesion and moral consensus (Jackson, 2006). People may attend to information about crime risk from the mass media and interpersonal communication because crime speaks to and dramatizes their concerns about social cohesion. Crime may get into such a symbolic tangle with issues of cohesion because the act of crime communicates hostility to the social order of a community and damages its moral fabric (Jackson et al., 2006). The prevalence of crime may thus signal the community to be suffering from deteriorating standards of behaviour, diminishing power of informal social control, increasing diversification of norms and values, and decreasing levels of trust, reciprocity, and respect (Jackson, 2008).

Finally, we should note that the 'imaginable victimization' explanation—as just outlined—is consistent with an influential account of the trajectory of crime control policy over the past few decades in the US and UK. Garland (2001) argues that crime has moved from a problem that afflicted only the poor to a daily consideration for many. Liberal sensibilities about the seriousness of crime as a problem have been dented as victimization became a fact for the middle classes. Increasing direct and indirect experience, mass media raising the salience of crime and 'institutionalizing' public concern, and the growing visibility of signs of crime—in the form of physical incivilities, such as vandalism, and social incivilities, such as groups of intimidating youths hanging around in the street—all helped to bring crime and the perceived risk of victimization into people's everyday lives. As Garland (2001: 153–4) puts it, 'rising crime rates ceased to be a statistical abstraction and took on a vivid personal meaning in popular consciousness and individual psychology . . . diffuse middle-class anxieties [became shaped] into a more focused set of attitudes and understandings, identifying the culprits, naming the problem, setting up scapegoats'.

Disorder, Cohesion, and Collective Efficacy: The Role of Environmental Perception

Also consistent with Garland (2001) is the idea that signs of neighbourhood breakdown and the deterioration of social controls influence public perceptions of crime risk (see also Lewis and Maxfield, 1980; Lewis and Salem, 1980, 1981; and Ferraro, 1995). 'Disorder' is any aspect of the social and physical environment that indicates to the observer (a) a lack of control and concern and (b) the values and intentions of others that share the space (Skogan and Maxfield, 1981; Wilson and Kelling, 1982; Taylor et al., 1985; Smith, 1986; Lewis and Salem, 1986; Taylor and Hale, 1986; Box et al., 1988; Skogan, 1990; Covington and Taylor, 1991; LaGrange et al., 1992; Ferraro, 1995; Perkins and Taylor, 1996; Rountree and Land 1996a, 1996b; Taylor, 1999; Innes, 2004; Robinson et al., 2003; Jackson, 2004a; Jackson and Sunshine, 2007). According to Ferraro (1995, p 15), incivilities are '. . . low-level breaches of community standards that signal an erosion of conventionally accepted norms and values'. Analysing data from a nationally-representative survey of US citizens, he found that incivilities provided ecological information that shaped citizens' perceptions of the chances of victimization; perception of risk then influenced people's expressed fear of crime.

A plethora of other studies have associated urban environmental cues with the fear of crime (Wilson, 1968; Hunter, 1978; Lewis and Maxfield, 1980; Jones et al., 1986; and Bannister, 1993). These cues include the following: poor lighting (Tien et al.,

1979; Hassinger, 1985; Jones et al., 1986; Pain, 1993); graffiti (Maxfield, 1987); litter (Maxfield, 1987; Burgess, 1994); vandalism (Jones et al., 1986; Pain, 1993; Burgess, 1994); hiding places for criminals (Tucker et al., 1979; Hassinger, 1985); poor state of buildings (Hassinger, 1985; Maxfield, 1987); disorderly or disreputable behaviour (Biderman et al., 1967); areas adjoining vacant areas such as car parks, parks, or factories (van der Wurff and Stringer, 1988; Valentine, 1989); the positioning of shrubberies (Pain, 1993); numbers of people that are present in the area (Valentine, 1989; Burgess, 1994); noise pollution (LaGrange et al., 1992); dogs and 'dog shit' (Burgess, 1994); perceptions of the people in the area (Merry, 1981; Maxfield, 1987; van der Wurff and Stringer, 1988); discarded needles (Burgess, 1994); and the presence of empty or abandoned streets (Lewis and Maxfield, 1980). Clearly the cues mentioned above fall into two broad categories, social cues and physical cues (LaGrange et al., 1992: 312). Social cues include such things as 'disreputable behaviour', noise pollution, and perceptions about the people in the area, whilst physical cues include stray dogs, vandalism, and discarded needles (for example).

Warr (1990) provides insights into readings of environmental cues via the work of Goffman (1971) who shows that humans habitually scan the environment for potential danger signs and attackers. He focuses upon three cues: fear of the unknown; darkness-related 'blind spots' (loss of visual control); and the presence (or otherwise) or 'others'. All of these cues involve (to varying degrees) elements of social control. With the first of these, fear of the unknown, Warr interprets Goffman as pointing to mastery of the environment as equalling feelings of safety. Warr illustrates this point by noting how a group of young males may be understood to be waiting for a bus in a 'familiar' area, whilst in an unknown area this cue may carry a vastly different meaning (1990: 893). Working through Goffman's concept of the *Umwelt* (or 'bubble of awareness'), Warr shows that the 'blind spots' that darkness creates for humans are a source of potential fear for many people. Finally, Warr argues that the individual needs to be able to interpret the actions of others as being 'safe' or 'unthreatening' in order to reassure themselves of their safety. Through the work of Warr, the fear of crime can be interpreted as being related to the individual's ability to derive a sense of security from the immediate environment (via the reading of cues). Hence new areas or new events in familiar areas (1990: 893–4) will (potentially at least) provoke fear until their meaning is fully understood by the individual. Feelings of security may thus be gained from both formal and informal provisions of social control. Hence if control is seen to have been exerted, a sense of security is engendered. If control is *not* seen to have been exerted, then (logically) a sense of *insecurity* is more likely to be engendered. This model helps us to explain the relationship between the micro-environment and the fear of crime in two ways. First, directly, signs of crime can indicate real risk of crime. Second, indirectly, as the fear of crime is not provoked by the features of the urban environment (i.e. the cues) in themselves, rather they are *symbolic* of the capacity of the community to exercise informal social control. The importance of a neighbourhood's capacity to regulate its residents has been frequently cited (Bursik, 1988; Bursik and Grasmick, 1993; Sampson and Raudenbush, 1999). Jacobs (1961: 31–2) clearly articulates this position when she writes: 'The public peace . . . is not kept primarily by the police, necessary as the police are. It is kept primarily by the intricate, almost unconscious, network of voluntary controls and standards among the people themselves and [is] enforced by the people themselves'. As Sampson et al. (1997: 918–9) have it, this is:

. . . the differential ability of neighborhoods to realize the common values of residents and maintain effective social controls . . . Although social control is often a response to deviant behaviour, it should not be equated with formal regulation or forced conformity by institutions such as the police and courts. Rather, social control refers generally to the capacity of a group to regulate its members according to desired principles—to realize collective, as opposed to forced, goals . . . the willingness of local residents to intervene for the common good depends in large part on conditions of mutual trust and solidarity among neighbours. Indeed, one is unlikely to intervene in a neighbourhood context in which the rules are unclear and people mistrust or fear one another.

As such, high levels of community efficacy, social cohesion, and a tight social structure (with low levels of anonymity and distrust) might inhibit fear of crime. Ross and Jang (2000) found that informal social ties 'buffered' the impact of disorder on fear and mistrust. Similarly, Jackson (2004) found that judgements of social cohesion and informal social control predicted perceptions of risk in the same way as judgements of disorder; trusting people and community efficacy led to low perceptions of risk. Such judgements about crime—and subsequent cognitive and emotional representations of the risk of victimization—were strongly shaped by assessments of social control, and since different people sharing the same environment came to different conclusions about disorder, cohesion, and collective efficacy, it would appear that the fear of crime operates as a barometer of mutual trust and solidarity (Jackson, 2004a; cf. Bannister, 1993). Recall here the 'community concern' model (Conklin, 1975) which states that fear of crime reflects an atomization of community and a concern for community disintegration. It should be noted, however, that Villarreal and Silva (2006), in a study of neighbourhoods in Brazil, found that social cohesion was associated with higher levels of fear (although few other variables were included in the models). The authors argued that high social cohesion means a greater spread of information regarding crime (Covington and Taylor, 1991, also found that social bonds increased fear; Kanan and Pruitt, 2002 found that social bonds had no effect on fear or perceived risk).

Smith (1987) notes the impact of lack of control on social interaction between people living in urban areas. She writes (1986: 128) that 'fear is greatest among people who perceive their communities to be in decline when they are powerless to intervene' and adds that these feelings of lack of control are partly due to '... the uncertainties generated by a wide range of other urban events' (1987: 10) and as such represent displaced anxieties (Furstenburg, 1971 and 1972). She goes on to note that these displaced anxieties have as their sources (amongst other things) dissatisfaction with urban life which includes deterioration of community life, poor services, and social isolation. She concludes that '... it has to be recognised that such anxiety is primarily a characteristic of the neighbourhood, not of the social groups within it' (1987: 9). However, it has also been argued that some communities may 'tolerate' or become acclimatized to a certain degree of criminal activity because many of those involved in this behaviour are perceived as not 'all bad' (Pattillo, 1998). Additionally, tolerance may operate as a form of adaptation to social and economic deprivation; there may be greater acceptance of crime in neighbourhoods which suffer the adverse effects of poverty (see Anderson, 1999; Markowitz and Felson, 1998; Sampson and Jeglum-Bartusch, 1998).

In the influential 'broken windows' theory of urban decline, Wilson and Kelling (1982) argued that low-level disorder actually led to more serious crime, as well as eroding the social fabric of the community (see also Skogan, 1990). In their analysis they indicated a causal link between minor incivilities and offences which go unchecked by the community or local agencies, with greater and more serious criminal activity. However, the nature of the relationship between crime and disorder has been the subject of considerable debate and is still unclear. Harcourt (2001) challenged this thesis by pointing out that empirical data have been unable to verify the prediction by Wilson and Kelling that there was a direct relationship between disorder, fear, and crime. Similarly, Taylor's data (2000) found that changes in levels of physical decline, social disorder, and racial composition did not lead to increased crime (although economic decline was shown to have a positive relationship instead).

Although the 'broken windows' theory was heavily debated, the idea that visible signs of disorder were a particular problem for local communities continued. Moreover, disorder rather than crime may have a particularly potent impact on people's sense of ontological security. Burney (2005: 5) stresses that 'there is long-standing evidence that people (or some people in some places) are psychologically more affected by disorderly behaviour and messy environments than they are by more serious crime'. In terms of the specific potency disorder has on public sensibilities, further research carried out by Innes (2004) suggests that some crimes and disorders (such as serious domestic violence) may pass relatively unnoticed by the general public, while other incidents are widely perceived to indicate or 'signal' a latent threat to the safety of the community. Drawing on symbolic interactionist sociology he develops the concept of 'signal crimes and disorders' which are important in terms of how people interpret threats to their security and demonstrate how social space is symbolically constructed. Intriguingly, in empirical surveys carried using the 'signal crimes' concept (see Innes et al., 2004, 2005), respondents listed various local disorders (persistent graffiti, youths always hanging around in a particular place shouting insults to passers-by etc.) as being actually more threatening to local safety than some more serious crimes like domestic burglary.

It should also be recalled that the mechanisms by which people perceive their environment not only include 'primary' or first-person assessments, but also 'secondary' sources of information. Skogan (1986) suggests that discussing 'stories' with neighbours and knowing local victims of crime or anti-social behaviour appears to affect levels of fear and individual estimates of perceived risk of victimization (Bishop and Klecka, 1978; Tyler, 1980; Lavrakas, Herz and Salem, 1981; Skogan and Maxfield, 1981). As such, local networks provide a means of communicating and exchanging stories about regional events and conditions. They can convey messages of personal significance or potential vulnerability which are incorporated in an individual's appraisal of their environment (Tyler, 1984).

In one of the first reports on the fear of crime, Biderman et al. (1967) suggests that public beliefs about crime stem largely from 'the highly visible signs of what *they regard as* disorderly and disreputable behaviour in their community' (emphasis added). Investigating such interpretative activity, Jackson (2004) found that some people judged particular ambiguous stimuli as 'disorderly' and representational of criminal threat, while other people in the same environment judged the same stimuli as benign and unthreatening. Data from a local crime survey showed that respondents who held more authoritarian views about law and order, and who were concerned about a long-term deterioration of community, were more likely to perceive disorder in their environment (see also Dowds and Ahrendt, 1995). They were also more likely to link these physical cues to problems of social cohesion and consensus, of declining quality of social bonds and informal social control. In a similar vein, Warr introduced the concept of 'perceptually contemporaneous offences', which refers to the connection some individuals make about certain offences being associated with other potentially more serious crimes; for example he suggests older people worry about begging, because they assume it is a 'prelude to other more serious offences (e.g. assault or robbery)' (1984: 695). As such, when people interpret and define their sense of safety, they not only incorporate both objective and subjective dimensions, but also include what they reasonably expect will happen in the future. Through the reading of 'cues' and their consequences, perceptions of disorder involve a series of interpretative exercises, influenced by personal experience or observation, as well as secondary knowledge of crime and disorder.

Exactly how researchers explore perceptions of disorder and the methods by which participants evaluate their environment is an important concern here. The vast majority of studies which examine disorder use subjective assessments drawn from individual survey responses. In particular, social cues such as 'youths' or 'drunkards' may be variously assessed by respondents; for example one person's 'thug' may be another's peer, similarly graffiti may be considered both a positive or negative addition to one's environment.[3] Warr (1990) makes the point that 'cues' are not always easy for the individual to interpret, as they are not self-evident nor self-explanatory. Curiously, only rarely do studies make systematic or objective reference to the environment from which the disorder is borne, and only a small number of studies have examined both subjective and objective measures of disorder. Taking a multi-level approach, Sampson and Raudenbush (2004) brought together personal interviews, census data, police records, and video-taped social observations situated within 500-block groups in Chicago to explore the basis on which individuals formed perceptions of disorder.[4] Intriguingly, the data suggested that perceptions of disorder were shaped by racial stigmatization of urban ghettos and the association of geographically segregated minority groups with crime and disorder. Chiricos et al. (1997), in a Florida-based study, also found that perceived racial composition (but, interestingly, not actual racial composition) was a significant predictor of fear of crime among whites but not among African-Americans (see also Covington and Taylor's 1991 Baltimore study, although this did not estimate separate effects for whites and blacks, and Skogan, 1995). Indeed, feeling that one is in the racial minority in one's neighbourhood was also correlated with higher levels of fear for whites but not for blacks (Chiricos et al., 1997).

So far we have discussed perception of disorder and the impact of perception on judgements of risk of crime. However, a number of US-based studies have addressed the impact of 'objective conditions' on fear by training observers to make detailed observations of neighbourhoods (Taylor et al., 1985; Taylor and Hale, 1986; Maxfield, 1987; Covington and Taylor, 1991;

---

[3] Striking evidence of the cultural approval of *some* forms of graffiti comes in various British local governments' decision to protect the urban 'street artwork' of 'Banksy', the 'graffiti artist' hailing from Bristol.

[4] Also using both subjective and objective measures; Maxfield (1987) found observed measures of physical neighbourhood decay related more strongly to fear than perceived vulnerability or victimization. Also, Perkins (1990) corroborated the link between fear and certain observed incivilities (i.e. litter) using block level data (see also Taylor *et al.*, 1985; Taylor and Hale, 1986; Covington and Taylor, 1991; Perkins and Taylor, 1996).

Perkins and Taylor, 1996). Early studies showed mixed results. However, Perkins and Taylor (1996) found that individual and trained observer ratings had roughly equal ability to predict fear. Covington and Taylor (1991) also identified an effect of 'objective conditions' on fear, but showed that perceived incivility was three times more predictive of fear than observed incivility. Disorder and its relationship to fear seems therefore to be 'in the eye of the beholder' (cf. Harcourt, 2001): anxieties about crime might be dependent not just on the local environment, but the respondent's *relationship* to that environment and others who inhabit it. Thus, what people *do*, *see*, and *encounter* in an environment and how they *react* to this is based upon their knowledge about that area (Bannister, 1993) and is therefore perhaps more important than purely counting 'broken windows'.

Taylor et al. (1985) investigated the relationship between residents and their interpretation of physical decay in an attempt to explore individual and structural relationships between fear and environmental cues. They found that the interpretation of environmental cues differed according to the socio-economic status of the area. In neither high- nor low-income areas were cues related to the fear of crime. In middle-income areas these cues were related to urban decay and social decline and hence the fear of crime. They conclude that ' . . . in the neighbourhoods where socio-economic status is neither so high as to guarantee confidence, nor so low as to guarantee pessimism, a good or bad physical environment has a crucial impact on how people view the neighbourhood' (1985: 274). Smith (1986: 128) adds weight to this argument with her comment that the answer to why the fear of crime is ' . . . in some places debilitating, whilst at others it represents simply a healthy awareness of the risks of victimization' is to be found in ' . . . the character of the urban environment (built and social) within which fear is experienced'. The thesis is that these cues are not in themselves fear provoking, but they produce fear amongst the population as many people equate incivilities with criminal activities. Implicit support for this approach comes from interventions which have been aimed at tackling some of these cues and which have resulted in reductions in reported fear levels. Tien et al. (1979) report that improvements in the levels of street lighting decreased the fear of crime.

Finally—and as hinted at above—there is evidence from the US and the UK that people have different levels of tolerance towards the cues in one's environment that signify a weak (or strong) social order, and potentially therefore crime and victimization (Carvalho and Lewis, 2003; Sampson and Raudenbush, 2004; Jackson, 2004a; Jackson et al., 2009; Franzini et al., 2008). Indeed, some UK research suggests that such sensitivity to disorder (the tendency to view, for example, the young people hanging around the streets as a problem) is both rooted in existing social concerns about the pace and direction of social change (cf. Girling et al., 2000) and local neighbourhood cohesion (cf. Bannister, 1993; Jackson, 2004a), and expresses therefore a lay seismograph of neighbourhood stability and breakdown. To view the young people in the streets as a problem and as representing the potential for criminal activity is to designate them and the norms and values they represent as hostile to social order and therefore as a threat to moral consensus.

The idea is not only that people ascribe meaning to disorder they see in front of them (i.e. disorder signals a lack of concern for public order and low levels of informal social control), but that ambiguous cues also need to be defined by the observer as 'disorderly' *in the first place*. Some individuals might judge certain stimuli as 'disorderly' while other individuals in the same environment might not; Sampson and Raudenbush (2004) explored the basis on which individuals formed perceptions of disorder (see also Franzini et al., 2008).[5] The authors reasoned that citizens interpreted objective signs of disorder (measurable signs of litter, vandalism, graffiti etc.) through existing and historical stereotypes of race and deprivation.[6] This work demonstrated that observers not only associated disorderly cues to notions of race and deprivation, but that they had existing cognitive representations or stereotypes that linked blacks and disadvantaged minority groups with 'social images, including but not limited to crime, violence, disorder, welfare, and undesirability as neighbors'. As Loury

---

[5] Maxfield (1987) also used subjective and objective measures. He found observed measures of physical neighbourhood decay related more strongly to fear than perceived vulnerability or victimization. Perkins (1990) corroborated the link between fear and certain observed incivilities (i.e. litter) using block level data (see also Taylor *et al.*, 1985; Taylor and Hale, 1986; Covington and Taylor, 1991; Perkins and Taylor, 1996).

[6] Other work has found perceived racial composition to be a significant predictor of perceptions of the neighbourhood crime level (Quillian and Pager, 2001) and fear of crime (Chiricos *et al.*, 1997; St. John and Heald-Moore, 1996).

(2002) stresses, racial origin is a directly observable feature which can not only serve to stigmatize the individual, but also the areas they inhabit. In effect, an individual's existing attitudes, beliefs, or prejudices provide a filter through which they experience and interpret their environment.

Similarly, Jackson's (2004) UK study found that the social perspective of the perceiver explained why some people judged particular stimuli as 'disorderly' and representational of criminal threat, while others in the same environment judged the same stimuli as malign and unthreatening. But here, respondents who held more authoritarian views about law and order, and were concerned about a long-term deterioration of community, were more likely to perceive disorder in their environment. They were also more likely to associate these physical cues with problems of social cohesion, the decline of a 'social consensus', and declines in both the quality of social bonds and informal social control. The symbolic nature of social order generated meaning in the context of their relationship to long-term social change and people's anxieties about cohesion and moral consensus (cf. Tyler and Boeckmann, 1997; Jackson and Sunshine, 2007). Follow-up work then explored the feedback between, on the one hand, perceptions of disorder, and on the other hand, fear of crime and concerns about social cohesion (Jackson et al., 2009). Analysis of data from the 2003/2004 British Crime Survey showed that not only did individuals come to different conclusions about the same neighbourhood stimuli, but also that both fear of crime and concerns about social cohesion shape sensitivity to the problematic nature of neighbourhood stimuli. For example, the judgement that 'youths hanging around in the street' was an especially big problem in one's neighbourhood (and therefore constituted neighbourhood disorder) was not just to report the presence of these youths, but also to express the judgement that their presence and behaviour was beyond local conventional norms of acceptability and signalled low levels of collective efficacy.

In another study, Carvalho and Lewis's (2003: 791) qualitative work explored how reactions such as fear, safety, and anger were dependent on personal distancing from issues of crime and disorder:

The more distant the relationship, the less salient these problems, as dangers, are in the context of daily routines and the less they intrude in one's life. With close relationships, crime and incivilities occupy a central position in one's daily life. These problems appear isolated, detached from other domains of life, imposing themselves onto the person as dangerous (raising fear) or as bothersome (raising anger). With distant relationships, on the other hand, crime/incivilities are peripheral to the person. The dangers of these problems are part of life, and qualities other than their dangerousness are apparent. Peripheral relationships with crime/incivilities accompany a neutral reaction of safety (neither fear nor revolt).

Carvalho and Lewis's (2003: 791) qualitative data suggested that individuals can neutralize dangers when they view crime/incivilities as 'banal events . . . Dangers are contextualized temporally, referred to the past, with the idea that they have been there, they have existed, and they are ordinary'. Dangers might also be neutralized when they are 'delimited': 'when they lose their random character (thus, the potential to affect just anyone) and become restricted to certain places of the neighbourhood and times of the day (physical delimitation), or to groups of people (social delimitation)' (p 794).

Structural Change and Macro-Level Influences on Fear

Macro-level influences on fear include changes at the neighbourhood level and changes at the societal level. We begin with changes at the neighbourhood level.

Describing the US, Skogan (1986: 203) argues that: 'fear of crime in declining neighbourhoods does not always accurately reflect actual crime levels. It is derived from primary and secondary knowledge of neighbourhood crime rates, observable evidence of physical and social disorder, and prejudices arising from changes in neighbourhood ethnic composition'. Skogan takes one step back to outline a number of factors which trigger neighbourhood decline: disinvestment; demolition and construction; demagoguery (where certain individuals profit from fragile and decaying urban conditions); and deindustrialization. Migration is also key in driving neighbourhood change, as people move out of areas characterized by mounting crime and fear:

> Flight from neighborhoods may carry away somewhat less fearful residents, leaving those who are more fearful—but stuck there—to deal with the area's problems. A few elderly and long-time residents may remain behind after this transition because they are unwilling to move or cannot sell their homes for enough to buy another in a nicer neighbourhood. They find themselves surrounded by unfamiliar people whom they did not choose to live with. Loneliness and lack of community attachment are significant sources of fear among the urban elderly (Jaycox, 1978; Yin, 1980),

especially among women (Silvermann and Kennedy, 1985). Interestingly, it appears that perceived social diversity (measured by questions about whether neighbors are 'the same' or 'different' from the respondent) has a strong effect on fear only among the elderly (Kennedy and Silverman, 1985). (Skogan, 1986: 208)

Neighbourhood decline may thus stimulate fear through increased victimization, second-hand information about crime, greater levels of disorder, deterioration of the built environment, and increased group conflict over 'neighbourhood "turf"' (p 214). Skogan describes how group conflict can result from increased ethnic diversity and comes with greater demand for living space, which may actually translate into neighbourhood crime (see also Merry, 1981). Indeed, concerns about crime may actually serve as code (Skogan calls this an 'outlet') for concerns about race and a fear of racial change (see Bursik and Grasmick, 1993). Chiricos et al. (1997) found that while actual racial composition had no impact on stated fear of crime (controlling for other factors), perceived racial composition was associated with elevated levels of risk perception and thus higher levels of fear, and this was so amongst whites but not amongst African-Americans (see also: Taub et al., 1984; Moeller, 1989; Skogan, 1995; St. John and Heald-Moore, 1996). As Skogan (1986: 215) speculates: 'Outsiders who are in the process of violating a community's space can threaten a broad range of values and conjure up many stereotypes about their behaviour'. In the words of Sacco (2005: 135):

. . . increases in levels of ethnic or racial heterogeneity contribute to a sense of discomfort on the part of neighborhood residents who feel that their neighborhood is undergoing a decline. Dramatic increases in the numbers of 'strangers' make the environment seem less familiar and perhaps more threatening . . . [indeed] while it may be 'politically incorrect' to express racist attitudes openly, expressions of anxiety about crime and criminals are usually regarded as perfectly appropriate forms of public discussion.[7]

---

[7] Sampson and Raudenbush (2004) brought together personal interview data, census data, police records, and video-taped social observations situated within 500 block groups in Chicago to explore the basis on which individuals formed perceptions of disorder. Their analysis suggested that respondents incorporated ingrained and stigmatized beliefs about racial groups within their appraisal of disorder. In other words, underpinning the notion 'disorder' is implicit stereotyping that links race, deprivation, and social breakdown.

Greenberg (1986) sketches out an 'economic-viability' model of the fear of crime which moves to the foreground public confidence in the trajectory of economic well-being in their neighbourhood. Greenberg's hypothesis was that 'concern about the economic future of the neighbourhood may make individuals feel vulnerable to events that are beyond their control, one of which is crime' (p 48). Greenberg found that perceptions of disorder and confidence in neighbourhood economic well-being both predicted levels of fear—indeed, they both mediated the impact of neighbourhood crime levels on fear.

Taylor and Jamieson (1998) take a slightly different, but not unrelated, tack when arguing that the high rates of fear of crime witnessed in the UK in the mid-1990s were symptomatic of the UK's fall from a world-leading economic power to a net importer of goods and services (p 152). In some respects, this thesis is a historically-informed, politically-embedded, macro-level version of the social control/social structural thesis. The sense of economic decline Taylor and Jamieson discuss, they say, led to a sense of widespread insecurity, especially as it related to employment. These 'fears of [social] falling' are caused, they argue, by the sudden changes in the economy at that time, but are condensed into more easily expressed fears about crime and those individuals associated with it in this moral discourse ('yobs', homeless people, 'young people', ethnic minorities, 'foreigners', and so on).

Dowds and Ahrendt (1995) provide evidence that perception that the world was changing in undesirable ways and beliefs that the social changes experienced were unwelcome were indeed related to the fear of crime. Embedding their work in a wider context of authoritarianism, Dowds and Ahrendt argue that the fear of crime can be understood as the fear of social change and the disintegration of society. These beliefs, as well as supporting the argument put forward by Taylor and Jamieson, return us to the issue of the political usage of the fear of crime, since authoritarianism was associated with 'anti-welfarism', punitiveness, and social conformity, and was found to be most prevalent amongst the middle aged and elderly. Jackson (2004) found, first, a set of social and political attitudes influenced the identification of disorder *in the first place* (respondents who held more authoritarian views about law and order, and who were concerned about a long-term deterioration of community, were more likely to perceive disorder in their environment; they were also more likely to link these physical cues to problems of social cohesion and consensus, of declining quality of social bonds and informal social control), and second, that concerns about disorder then strongly influenced the fear of crime.

Other scholars have sought to explain why the fear of crime has become so 'woven into the lived culture and ordinary practice of situated actors' as Hope and Sparks (2000: 9) put it. Although some (e.g. McConville and Shepard, 1992: 58) found that the fear of crime was not 'such a prominent feature in most people's lives', adding that 'if it figures at all, [it] is a background consideration' (p 59), the commonly held position is that fears about crime became an ever more pressing concern. Arguably anxieties about crime have remained at the front of the public's mind since 'responsibilisation strategies' (Garland, 2001: 124–7) began to shift the responsibility for crime control from formal institutions to individuals, organizations, and their use of commercial security products. Garland and Sparks (2000: 199) refer to the emergence of a 'crime complex' whereby citizens become '. . . attuned to the crime problem and many exhibit high levels of fear and anxiety. They are caught up in institutions and daily practices that require them to take on the identity of (actual or potential) crime victims and to think, feel and act accordingly'. These analytic frameworks help us understand how concerns about crime have perforated the public's consciousness, impacting on their daily cognitive and behavioural processes. This in turn has facilitated the 'commodification of security' (Loader, 1999) for the purposes of crime control and led to an expanding role for private security companies. More recently Bauman (2006) has described the 'securitarian obsession'—an obsession that pervades the social relations and political life of Western societies today where substantial numbers of individuals, politicians, and organizations are attracted to demanding ever-increasing levels of security from anti-social behaviour, crime, and terrorism.

As Lee (2001: 480) argues, 'attempts to govern "fear of crime" actually inform the citizenry that they are indeed fearful'. The term 'the fear of crime', it has been recognized, has been used to justify various crime control policies which some on the libertarian left have found hard to accept. When introducing more punitive sentences, restrictions on the rights of the accused, or more intensive forms of supervision and surveillance, politicians have sought to justify the proposed measures in terms of reducing the fear of crime (Fattah, 1993: 61). In part, perhaps, this has always been one of the uses of the fear of crime (Harris, 1969, would suggest that this was the case). As noted in Chapter 3, some accordingly (e.g. Loo and Grimes, 2004) have argued that the fear of crime was essentially hyped up by rightwing politicians in order to win them votes during national assembly elections. There is, it must be said, some evidence to support this line. The first politicians to refer to the fear of crime during electoral campaigns were Barry Goldwater and Richard Nixon when (respectively) contesting the 1964 and 1968 US Presidential elections.[8] In the UK, the first politician who made political capital out of the fear of crime was Margaret Thatcher in the 1979 general election, when she referred to 'feeling safe in the streets' (Riddell, 1985: 193). Prior to that too, she had claimed that the country wanted 'less tax and more law and order' (Evans, 1997: 75; Savage, 1990: 89). In making such statements, Thatcher probably served only to make legitimate the prejudices of Tory activists (Riddell, 1985: 193). However, in so doing, she brought the issue of concern about crime into the political realm. Once politicized, the left in the UK and the Democrats in the US could do little other than to follow suit and to also highlight their own crime policies, culminating in Blair's expressed desire to be 'tough on crime and tough on the causes of crime' during the 1997 general election.[9] The fear of crime thus became something that, whilst reflecting some pre-existing set of concerns or anxiety, could be used by appropriately-minded politicians to stoke up public feelings on certain topics. This process became, over time, self-perpetuating, Lee's fear of crime 'feed-back loop' (2001: 480–1). In this approach, the fear of crime approaches something of an elite-constructed and publicly-maintained exaggeration of the reality of public anxieties. Whether one believes or not the suggestion that this was 'engineered' by elites (Loo and Grimes, 2004: 50) or Lee's less forceful stance is another matter. Evidence, however, does suggest that the population has learnt that crime 'must be' a problem (McConville and Shepard, 1992: 63; Taylor, 1990: 26).

[8] A similar strategy was employed by George Bush (Snr); see Scheingold, 1995.
[9] Blair actually used this sound bite for the first time during the Labour Party's Conference in the autumn of 1993.

Connecting Anxieties about Crime to Other Anxieties (and *Vice Versa*)

The idea that the fear of crime expresses other anxieties is not a new one: '... what has been measured and conceptualized as "fear of crime" has its roots in something more diffuse than the perceived threat of some specific danger in the immediate environment. In some sense the public appears to be concerned about crime. But the concern seems to be about something abstract rather than concrete' (Garofalo and Laub, 1978: 245; see also Merry, 1981; Smith, 1986; Bursik and Grasmick, 1993). In part taking seriously this notion, and in part responding to largely derivative and atheoretical body of survey research, a series of qualitative studies was conducted by a number of British criminologists in the 1990s.

Girling et al. (2000) argue that public sentiment towards crime is embedded in people's local and lived environment. They set out to:

... pursue the idea that people's everyday talk about crime and order (its intensity, the vocabularies used, the imagery mobilised, the associations that are made) both depends upon, and helps to constitute their sense of place; that it takes the form of stories and anecdotes that fold together elements of biography, community career, and perceptions of national change and decline... [stories] are one of the means by which people routinely come to acquire a sense, not only of crime, but also of the place in which they live—its habitability, its inward tensions and divisions and its future prospects. (Girling et al., 2000: 170)

Examining public perceptions and responses to crime in 'Middle England', the same authors found concerns about crime chimed with:

... a fear that the exclusive pastoral corner of the English social and spatial landscape in which they have invested heavily, both materially and emotionally, can no longer exempt itself (as it properly should) from the malign currents that flow through the wider world, and that its established social and moral order is being threatened, perhaps even eroded, by a combination of outsiders (professional criminals) and strangers (drug-using, disorderly local youths). (Loader et al., 2000: 66–7)

Local residents deemed most crime and disorder small-scale. Yet they also identified three threats: burglary, car crime, and teenage disorder. Crucially, it was what these represented that made them salient and gave them meaning as much as likelihood of their occurrence or the consequences of the potential events themselves. The first two threats had their roots in outsiders largely from Manchester and Liverpool, two nearby cities, coming into Prestbury because of its 'rich-pickings'. The final threat seemed, in fact, more troubling. Teenagers loitering around: '... threatened to erode *from within* the idea of Prestbury as a safe home, free of the troubles that bedevil so much of contemporary English society elsewhere' (Loader et al., 2000: 71).

Other qualitative studies have looked at how individuals construct 'mental maps' of localities that are used to both represent and avoid certain areas (e.g. Lupton and Tulloch, 1999; Taylor, 1996; Taylor and Jamieson, 1998), and draw on representations of social relations and individuals inhabiting and passing through public space. Taylor et al. (1996) suggest that precautionary mental maps of the locality and representations of potential criminals are constructed and shared by neighbourhood residents; Smith's work (1986) comes to similar conclusions, suggesting that crime-related information flows most easily between socially and spatially proximate individuals. Moreover, Taylor et al. (1996) found that interviewees identified a particular area in Manchester called Moss Side as a 'symbolic location of crime', as public concern over increasing social inequality took on racialized themes of an urban underclass (Moss Side is an area which has historically been associated with an Afro-Caribbean presence, drugs, and guns). They argued that crime can act in a metaphorical capacity for (other) related concerns about the locality. Such neighbourhood issues could include unemployment, the deterioration of the physical environment, increased social diversity and social disorder cues. In this way, fear of crime can be seen as a metaphor for 'urban (mis)fortunes'; the ways in which one understands and represents one's locality, with its perceived levels of safety, socio-economic conditions, and civil character.

Just as studies have examined the cultural meanings of crime, particularly with respect to how we perceive our own and other neighbourhoods, so qualitative research has investigated how social relations and perceptions of other people are important. Young (1999) observes that we live in an era of great mobility, so we have less direct knowledge about those around us, and in a more socially and culturally diverse society, this can lead to less perceived predictability of behaviour. Lupton and Tulloch (1999) argue for the importance of the figure of the 'unpredictable stranger'. This can act as a kind of 'folk devil' (Cohen, 1972) —they become the target of generalized as well as more specific worries, fears, and anxieties. The figure and its effect are largely based on uncertainty: individuals did not know a particular individual and thus cannot gauge how he (this figure is invariably thought of as a male) might respond or act. They argue that people were more afraid of this figure when moving in public spaces, because they felt that they had far less control over others in such spaces than when in their own homes, and they are far more likely to encounter strangers in the 'outside world' than when they are in their homes.

In an ethnographic study carried out in Boston in the US, Merry argues that crime 'serves as an idiom for expressing and legitimating the fear of the strange and the unknown' (Merry, 1981: 151). She found that an important aspect of the monitoring of threat and danger was perceptions and inferences about others. Indeed, racial and class groupings were most significant. Talk about crime in the media, in gossip, and in rumour, served to both designate certain areas and people dangerous and, more obscurely, to define and continually reproduce social relations in an area (Merry, 1981). Hale (1996: 113), too, notes that research suggests that people feel less safe in urban areas, arguing that:

. . . the impact that the increased population density and heterogeneity of urban life has on social ties [can lead] to both isolation and loneliness and to increased anti-social behaviour. Encounters in urban settings are encounters with strangers, in both a cultural and personal sense. Increased social diversity leads to greater social uncertainty. On this interpretation fear of crime is fear of strangers, the downside of the opportunity offered by the city for cultural adventure.

Evans et al. (1996) approached the fear of crime through an appreciation of the way trust manifests itself in a community. They argue that 'whom one trusts, when and by how much' provides a valuable insight into how they manage their routine daily lives. Being seen as 'local' created a sense of safety from victimization, and being familiar with the neighbourhood indicated who was safe to co-operate with. Yet, conversely, fear of crime can result in changing attitudes towards uncertainty and ambiguity in human behaviour: a movement to see others as threatening and representational of crime (Furedi, 1998). It may increase the propensity to employ certain mechanisms to identify and categorize strangers and groups (and indeed certain locations or environments) by certain traits, connoting threat, danger, and crime.

No review of recent work on the fear of crime would be complete without some discussion of that body of work which takes as its starting point the key ideas emanating from psychoanalysis. In a nutshell, this body of work argues that all individuals suffer from anxiety, and that this anxiety comes from a range of sources. Individuals need to 'defend' themselves against such anxieties and this will often mean that individuals are drawn to those discourses which offer ways of controlling such anxieties. However, the ways in which individuals are attracted to different discourses and the reasons for their being attracted to one discourse rather than another are partly dependent upon their personal experiences and biographies (Hollway and Jefferson, 1997: 261). As such, argue Hollway and Jefferson, the fear of crime is 'an unconscious displacement of other fears which are far more intractable' (1997: 263). In this way, anxieties which perhaps cannot be properly identified or fully understood by the individual in question are projected onto a 'knowable' and 'nameable' fear—in this case the fear of crime.

Crime is a convenient receptacle for anxieties associated with modern living for a number of reasons. First, it represents one of the last remaining 'others' in a complex society. The 'criminal other' represents a traditional 'bogeyman' where anxieties can be safely projected and attacked. What sets the 'criminal other' apart from, for example, the 'racial other' is that in modern societies many people know, often as family members, people from ethnic minorities and, as such, processes of racial othering are harder to undergo. In addition, widespread social condemnation of explicitly racist opinions has made this all the harder anyway. This has not happened, however, with those people identified as 'criminal'. Thus the 'criminal other' represents a convenient location for the storing of anxieties (Scheingold, 1995: 155). Second, the fear of crime discourse brings with it a whole series of actions which can be undertaken (padlocking gates, securing cars with steering locks, and so on) which promote control and as such serve to provide relief against the fear of being victimized, thus providing the fearful subject with a sense of control over uncertainty (Hollway and Jefferson, 1997; Lupton, 1999: 14). As Hollway and Jefferson conclude:

In a late-modern world of uncertainty, ambivalence, chaos even; of risks that are omnipresent but invisible, fear of crime might provide some rather modern reassurances: the knowability of the criminal; the decisionability of response; the mastery of control of anxiety; the externality of the source of misfortune and the consequent opportunity for 'real blaming' (the 'other', not myself [or some other less controllable unity—e.g. economic and social change], is responsible for my predicament) (1997: 264 [additional comments added]).

But why ought modern societies to be so afflicted by all of these unknowable and unactionable fears? The work of Bauman offers some clues in this respect. Bauman (2000) argues that in the modern world security is traded in against the exercise of free choice (driven by market forces) and that this creates, as a by-product, anxiety. These anxieties are then channelled into issues surrounding law and order (2000: 213). Governments, however, are relatively powerless in the face of both the market and the anxieties it engenders; they have conceded power to the market and its 'forces' which, in an increasingly globalized system of capital transfer, are harder and harder for any one government to control and almost impossible to predict with any degree of certainty. Instead, governments focus on efforts to 'do something' (2000: 215), which often translates as increasingly harsh punishments and increases in the statutes of criminal offences (Scheingold, 1995: 156). One might add, following Lee, that this serves only to highlight the apparent 'need' for such policies. Of course, many of these policies will either fail (in the long-term) or will make no discernible impact on the problem at hand. This is partly because, in our opinion, many of the policies aimed at tackling crime since the 1970s are ill-conceived, or, following Hollway, Jefferson, and Bauman, *not* the prime source of many of the fears anyway, since this is the anxiety brought on by social and economic changes.

Towards an Integrative Model of the Fear of Crime

The social sciences have been derided for their inability to produce consensus on anything but the most basic of issues, and have borne witness to wars of strategic positioning in which heavily-entrenched positions are fiercely guarded and basic knowledge is left, in many cases, undeveloped. Each way of viewing the world makes some things visible whilst rendering other aspects invisible, or at least slightly out of focus. Our aim has been to avoid such fruitless activities. Seeking to build upon the insights from a range of positions, the remainder of this chapter outlines our theoretical framework. This is based most heavily on the work of Ferraro (1995) (and others, such as Girling et al., Garland, Jackson, Taylor and Jamieson, Greenberg) and builds upon many of the previous models put forward to account for feelings of fear of crime. The model developed herein will be the focus of our own quantitative and qualitative data analysis. As such its theoretical basis and our rationale for employing these features will be drawn out in a more detailed manner below. Our aim in building this 'integrated' model being to provide a more rounded and thorough understanding of the fear of crime and those processes associated which have been identified as being causally related to it.

Social Perception and the Fear of Crime

Ferraro's (1995) US study uses insights derived from symbolic interactionism to flesh out how interpretations of incivilities and perceptions of structural aspects of a community provide information that subsequently shapes subjective estimates of the chances of victimization. Ferraro (1995: 9) elaborates that the situation: '... includes a person's physical location and activities as well as actual crime prevalence, the physical environment, and victimization experiences and reports'. Central to individuals' evaluations of risk is the way in which they make sense of their world—how they define their situation through the formation of judgements and interpretations. Perceived risk and fear of crime are thus located within the actor's definition of the situation— their subjective experience placed in its social context. These are themselves fluid and under the process of re-interpretation as new information is gained through interaction.

In lay judgements of situations, criminal activity, and threat, therefore, two broad classes of stimuli are important. The first is the physical and social environment, the second is shared information about crime and danger in that environment. Considering how such beliefs and interpretations shape the appraisal of threat of victimization, our thinking, following Ferraro (1995), specifies that incivilities provide ecological information that in turn shapes perceptions of the chances of victimization. Furthermore, areas that have reputations for crime or suffer from problems of poverty are treated as 'signals' of potential danger. Finally, the actor reacts in a number of different ways to perceiving danger. Fear is one response to perceived danger. Other reactions include: '... constrained behaviour, community or political activism, compensatory defensive actions, and avoidance behaviours including relocation' (Ferraro, 1995: 12). The model is summarized in Figure 4.1.

Ferraro's theory was tested via a telephone survey of a nationally representative sample of the US population living in a household with a telephone (and carried out in 1990). Respondents were asked for their 'zip code' (equivalent to the UK's postcode), thus identifying their state and county of residence. Using what are widely known as the *Uniform Crime Reports* (UCR; Federal Bureau of Investigation, 1989) the offences known to the police at the county level were identified for each respondent (Ferraro, 1995: 8). Analysis of the data provided showed support for the model.

The Psychology of Risk in the Fear of Crime

Ferraro's (1995) work remains important not only because it integrates key insights from a rather piecemeal literature, but also because it stresses the wealth of interpretative activity at play in the fear of crime. Moreover, it raises some rather interesting questions. The first of these is: what are the psychological processes underpinning emotion and risk perception? Whilst recognizing that the psychological definition of fear is as a physical emotion that responds to the identification of perceived immediate danger, Ferraro (1995: 4) defined fear of crime as: '. . . an emotional response of dread or anxiety to crime or symbols that a person associates with crime'.

Figure 4.1 Replication of Ferraro's risk interpretation model of the fear of crime

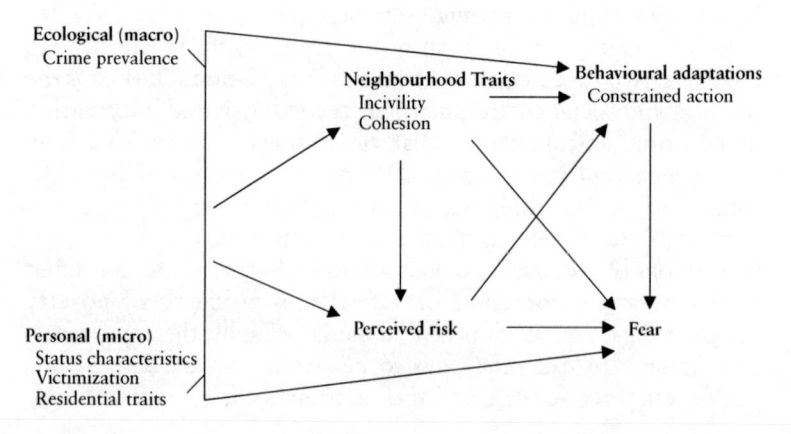

The Psychology of Risk in the Fear of Crime

Fear was measured by asking how 'afraid' respondents were of a number of crimes, implicitly assuming that respondents understood 'fear' as dread or anxiety rather than a physical reaction to immediate threat—something more amorphous. One limitation of this strategy is that it does not easily facilitate an elaboration of the processes underpinning emotion and risk perception.

An alternative approach is to be more specific about the core emotion. This allows one to draw upon psychological theory on the nature of and the processes which underpin 'fear'. Worry comprises both an emotional evaluation of an immediate situation (interpreting cues in the environment that signify a sense of the possibility of threat) and an anticipatory state (a concern about potential danger, of imminent and distal threat, or events yet to transpire). Jackson (2004) found that the frequency of worry about personal crime was shaped by an appraisal of threat comprising perceptions of likelihood, control, and consequences.

Warr's (1987) 'risk sensitivity' model provides further insight. He found that the influence of likelihood on fear was moderated by perceptions of seriousness of the given crime type: when people judged crime to be especially serious in its effect, a lower level of perceived likelihood was needed to stimulate some level of personal fear. Individuals were thus more 'sensitive' to a given level of perceived risk when they viewed the consequences of victimization to be especially serious. A follow-up study subsequently confirmed that perceived likelihood played a key role in explaining the frequency of worry (Jackson, 2009). But crucially, while control and consequence played small roles in predicting worry, these judgements exerted two striking influences. First, both control and consequence predicted judgements of likelihood. Cognitive heuristics may be at play here: people substitute a hard question ('How likely do you think it is that you will be burgled in the next year?') with easier questions ('Can I imagine being burgled?' 'Is burglary a risk that is vivid, dramatic, and especially serious in its consequence?'). Second, both control and consequence moderated the influence of likelihood on worry. Thus, when people judged crime to be especially serious in its effect, and when they judge themselves to have little control over its incidence, a lower level of perceived likelihood is needed to stimulate personal fear.

A psychological account is important in examining potential feedback between emotion, risk perception, and social perception (see Jackson, 2006, 2008); even if a cross-sectional survey is not an ideal vehicle for empirical test. Emotions provide information and guide attention; they direct attention towards belief-relevant information (Clore and Gasper, 2000); they create and shape beliefs, amplifying or altering them, and, in some cases, making them resistant to change (Frijda et al., 2000). In a heightened emotional state, one might more quickly see risk in ambiguity, and more quickly associate people, situations, and environments with crime. Worry might thus stimulate a preoccupation with negative information and future unpleasant outcomes, increasing the scanning of the environment for salient material relating to threat (Matthews, 1990), and making ambiguous events more threatening (Butler and Mathews, 1983, 1987; Russell and Davey, 1993). In short, those people who are emotionally animated about crime may be more likely to see disorder in their environment, and more likely to link disorder to the threat of crime, net of actual levels of crime and disorder (Jackson et al., 2009). Thus the fear of crime maintains itself at the individual level through perceptual and interpretive processes.

Experience and Expression in the Fear of Crime

A second (and related) question raised by Ferraro's model is: what shapes assessments of disorder above and beyond neighbourhood characteristics? One needs to bear in mind that fears about crime are dependent not just on the local environment, but the respondent's *relationship* to that environment and those who also inhabit and people it. What people *do, see,* and *encounter* in an environment and how they *react* to this is based upon their knowledge about that area (Bannister, 1993) and is therefore perhaps more important than purely counting 'broken windows'. Sampson and Raudenbush (2004) showed that perceptions of disorder were shaped by racial stigmatization of urban ghettos and the wider association of geographically segregated minority groups with crime and disorder. Jackson (2004) found that the social perspective of the perceiver explained why some people judged particular ambiguous stimuli as 'disorderly' and representational of criminal threat, while other people in the same environment judged the same stimuli as malign and unthreatening. Data from a local crime survey showed that respondents who held more authoritarian views about law and order, and who were concerned about a long-term deterioration of community, were more likely to perceive disorder in their environment (Jackson, 2004a; see also Dowds and Ahrendt, 1995). They were also more likely to associate these physical cues with problems of social cohesion, the decline of a 'social consensus', and declines in both the quality of social bonds and informal social control. Therefore, the symbolic nature of aspects of social order generated meaning in the context of their relationship to long-term social change and people's anxieties about cohesion and moral consensus. Figure 4.2 summarizes the model.

So, people 'read' the environment to draw information about the state of the local community and the norms and values displayed by people who inhabit that community and who pass through public space. Such information is used to draw inferences about intentions and possibilities, about the extent of crime, and the personal risk of victimization. When crime is seen as possible and likely, this interacts with the *personal sense* of consequence and control—individuals may feel able to control whether they find themselves in difficult situations, or they may feel able to deal with the event and any subsequent consequences. Those who feel especially vulnerable (i.e. judge themselves as a likely target/victim, feel they are unable to control whether it happens, and assess the possible consequences to be severe) will worry frequently about crime, especially if their precautionary activities do not help them manage their feelings of vulnerability.

Figure 4.2 Summary of Jackson's (2004) model of the fear of crime

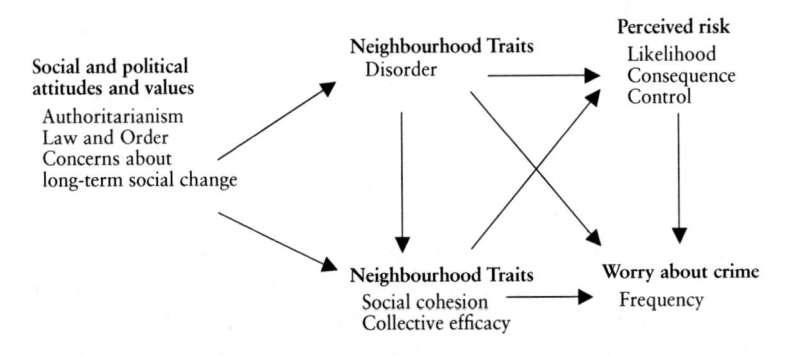

Social and political attitudes and values
Authoritarianism
Law and Order
Concerns about long-term social change

Neighbourhood Traits
Disorder

Neighbourhood Traits
Social cohesion
Collective efficacy

Perceived risk
Likelihood
Consequence
Control

Worry about crime
Frequency

nb: This study took place in one homogeneous area so respondents shared the same environment; social and political attitudes and values thus orientated how people made sense of neighbourhood disorder, cohesion, and collective efficacy.

The mass media and interpersonal communication are obvious sources of second-hand information about crime. Stories are told, narratives outlined—perpetrators, victims, and motives named and discussed. Surveying crime victims, Tyler and Rasinski (1984; see also Tyler, 1980) found that perceptions of risk and worry about future victimization were associated with both what individuals learnt from their particular experience of crime (how much the experience told them about the likelihood of victimization occurring again in the future, how much they learnt from the crime, and how much they learnt about how to protect themselves in the future) and the emotional reactions they had to the experience (whether they were upset, stunned, outraged, frightened, and shocked). In the last of three studies, Tyler and Rasinski (1984) also found the same processes at play when individuals read a report of a particular crime, thus suggesting that informativeness and affect are important mediators of the impact of first-hand *and* second-hand experience on fear of crime. Also important is the notion of 'stimulus similarity', which describes how the reader of a newspaper (for example) might identify with the described victim or feel that their own neighbourhood bears resemblance to the one described (Winkel and Vrij, 1990).

Sunstein (2005) argues that hearing about events has an impact on public perceptions of risk through an interaction between availability and social mechanisms which generate so-called 'availability cascades':

[these are] social cascades, or simply cascades, through which expressed perceptions trigger chains of individual responses that make these perceptions appear increasingly plausible through their rising availability in public discourse. Availability cascades may be accompanied by countermechanisms that keep perceptions consistent with the relevant facts. Under certain circumstances, however, they generate persistent social *availability errors*—widespread mistaken beliefs grounded in interactions between the availability heuristic and the social mechanisms we describe. [emphasis in original] (Kuran and Sunstein, 1999: 685)

Thus, 'fear-inducing accounts' of events—such as the incident in 2002 in Virginia when two snipers killed ten people—are likely to be highly publicized, noticed, and repeated, leading to cascade effects as the event becomes available to an increasing number of people. Furthermore, 'group polarization' describes how, when individuals discuss with each other certain events and risks, they typically end up with a more extreme view (p 98).

Sunstein (2005: 93) also speculates that existing predispositions may determine in large part what individuals pay attention to. One example he gives relates to genetic modification of food. Those who are predisposed to be fearful of this issue are more likely to seek out information about genetic modification. People may attend to information about crime risk from the mass media and interpersonal communication because crime speaks to and dramatizes their concerns about social cohesion, relations, and change. Crime may get into such a symbolic tangle with issues of cohesion because the act of crime communicates hostility to the social order of a community and damages its moral fabric. The prevalence of crime may thus signal the community to be suffering from deteriorating standards of behaviour, diminishing power of informal social control, increasing diversification of norms and values, and decreasing levels of trust, reciprocity, and respect.

This is consistent with the arguments of a number of criminologists who conducted qualitative research in this area during the 1990s. Fear of crime can be embedded in a model which saw feelings of insecurity as a comprehensive pattern of interpretation of the surrounding social world. Crime may serve as a vivid marker of the breakdown of social organization and moral norms; things seen to be hostile to social order become associated with crime (Jackson and Sunshine, 2007); crime acts as a proxy for the status of society's underlying moral order and social organization. Emotions about crime may thus partly arise as a desire to re-establish rules and behaviour that underpin social organization, and censure those who violate the rules (see Elster, 2004: 155). As such, 'crime may be one of those forms of "danger on the borders" which gives form to a community's sense of itself...' (Girling et al., 2000: 16).

A 'Unified' Framework of the Fear of Crime

The suggestions and findings explored above have been built into our own framework—which we present here as a 'unified' framework of the fear of crime. This framework we summarize in Figure 4.3.

Our framework starts by assuming—in line with the social control, vulnerability theses, and in particular Ferraro (1995)—that even at the most basic of levels the fear of crime is in some way related to actual levels of crime in society and local communities.

118 Theorizing the Fear of Crime

Figure 4.3 A Unified Framework: Experience and Expression in the Fear of Crime

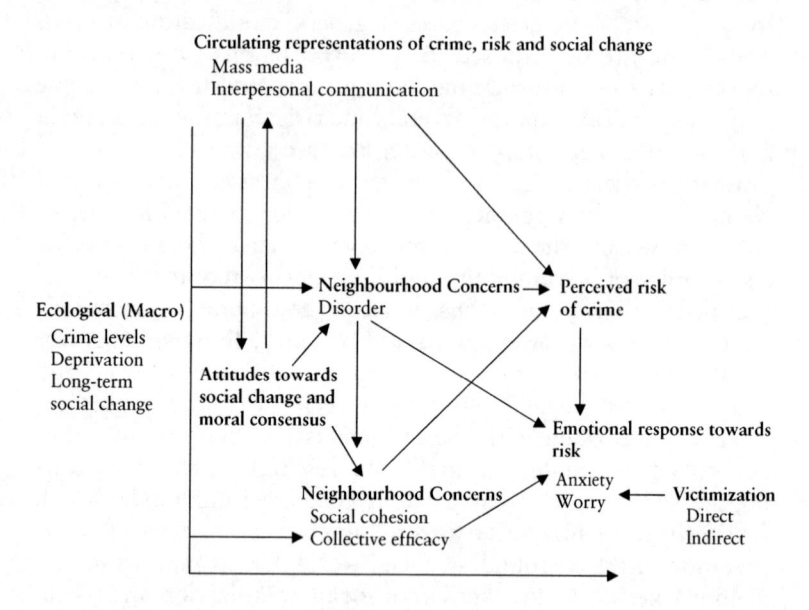

```
                Circulating representations of crime, risk and social change
                Mass media
                Interpersonal communication

                                    Neighbourhood Concerns ──▶ Perceived risk
                                    Disorder                    of crime
Ecological (Macro)
  Crime levels
  Deprivation
  Long-term           Attitudes towards
  social change       social change and
                      moral consensus
                                                              Emotional response towards
                                                              risk
                                    Neighbourhood Concerns    Anxiety
                                    Social cohesion           Worry      ◀── Victimization
                                    Collective efficacy                      Direct
                                                                             Indirect
```

Starting at the left of Figure 4.3, we specify a relationship between beliefs about the actual levels of crime and the prevalence of criminals within one's local and/or national community and fears about crime. These paths capture the sentiments raised by both those concerned with the micro (i.e. community) level and the macro-level (such as the work of Taylor and Jamieson, 1998). We also expect a relationship between actual changes in the local area and fear of crime.

We concur with Smith's suggestion that the fear of crime 'is greatest among people who perceive their communities to be in decline when they are powerless to intervene' (1986: 128), which we see as developing aspects of both the environmental cues thesis and the vulnerability theses. Such beliefs and experiences of crime and change in the local area may also be associated with attitudes towards crime and feelings of confidence in the criminal justice system—the appropriateness of sentences, authoritarian attitudes towards crime, public sensibilities about 'law and order', and attitudes towards long-term social change. We therefore specify paths from the ecological level to attitudes. These paths summarize the thinking of a number of writers, not least of all that of Dowds and Ahrendt, 1995, on the relationship between authoritarianism and fear of crime.

We also expect those who are already concerned about 'broken Britain'—who are concerned about the norms and values that are seen to underpin communities and the society at large—to also seek out information from the mass media and interpersonal communication about crime and about the moral health of the nation. Crime speaks to and dramatizes their concerns about social cohesion, relations, and change. Crime gets into a symbolic tangle with issues of cohesion because the act of crime communicates hostility to the social order of a community and damages its moral fabric. The prevalence of crime may thus signal the community to be suffering from deteriorating standards of behaviour, diminishing power of informal social control, increasing diversification of norms and values, and decreasing levels of trust, reciprocity, and respect. Hearing about crimes and witnessing 'signal events' (Innes, 2004) then feeds into one's sense of neighbourhood stability and one's sense of personal risk. Indeed, ecological factors (crime, deprivation, actual social change) and basic attitudinal issues (sensibilities towards social stability and moral consensus) are also expected to feed into concerns about social disorder, cohesion, and collective efficacy (Figure 4.3). This we see as being in line with Girling et al., 2000, Ferraro, 1995, and also in residents' perceptions of their community's ability to regulate the behaviour of their neighbours. From perceptions of disorder we specify paths directly to the fear of crime (along lines suggested by the social control and environmental cues theses), which includes both *worry* and *anxiety*.

We also specify paths from concerns about community to perceived risk, which includes lay judgements of likelihood, control, and consequence. In line with previous research (Jackson, 2004a, 2008, 2009), we expect lay judgements of likelihood to play the crucial role. But following Jackson (2008) we also propose three roles for control and consequence: (a) shape likelihood; (b) shape worry; (c) moderate the impact of likelihood on worry. Finally (and this is the only aspect in the framework that we cannot address using our quantitative data), we propose that circulating representations of crime, social order, and risk—whether via the mass media or interpersonal communication—will influence most parts of the framework.

Thus, fear of crime involves *experience*—everyday worries about personal risk—and the *expression* of attitudes towards social change, stability, order, and cohesion. We expect individuals who worry on an 'everyday' basis about criminal victimization to live in higher crime areas and to be more concerned about signs of crime and local conditions conducive to crime than individuals who have a more ambient and diffuse sense of anxiety. But we also expect everyday worry and diffuse anxiety to be rooted in how people make sense of their social and physical environment (and in their perceptions of risk). Thus both worry and anxiety are in some sense lay seismographs of perceptions of concerns about cohesion and moral consensus. It is our belief that signs of disorder and low cohesion operate as information about crime, to be sure. However, more fundamental concerns about social change and the direction of society will influence anxieties about more locateable aspects of one's environment (Girling et al., 2000). Moreover, crime is a symbolically dense notion—transportable to a whole range of pressing social issues (Bauman, 2002).

The fear of crime thus is accounted for by elements from all of the major previous theories of the fear of crime (and by emerging findings from our study). Some theories we do not have the data to build into our models. These concern the usage of the fear of crime as a political tool by politicians (see Lee, 1999; Loo and Grimes, 2004). On this question our position is that anxieties about crime exist independently of political rhetoric, although we do recognize that debates around 'law and order', especially those which imply that crime is 'out of control' and which seek to 'stoke up' such fears, can be (and are) used to justify particularly nasty social and criminal policies (see Farrall, 2006). However, the usage of the term and key reference points in the fear of crime debates is not our immediate concern when attempting to explain the incidence and intensity of such fears. Notwithstanding this, we still believe that the fear of crime has become part of a somewhat fashionable political discourse and, in turn, has also become a term which citizens understand and can refer to when discussing crime and social problems.

PART II

In Part II we use the theoretical insights developed during Part I to explore in greater detail a new conceptualization of what the fear of crime is and how it can be approached. In short we categorize survey respondents in to one of four groups: those who do not worry; those who worry; those who worry frequently; and those who are anxious about crime. As fear of crime research is so heavily dominated by survey research, we need to engage directly with survey methodologies and quantitative data analyses, and these groupings represent the outcome of just such an engagement. However, we implore survey researchers to attend more than they have previously done to the meanings of people's answers to questions (both in surveys and during in-depth interviews) on the fear of crime—and the first of the chapters in Part II speaks to these concerns.

5

Conversations about Crime, Place, and Community

'People should worry about each other. Because worry is just love in its worst form. But it's still love.' (Lousia, in *Hidden Laughter*, act 1, scene 2, Simon Gray, 1990).

Introduction

This chapter uses in-depth qualitative interviews to explore the emotional reactions, cognitions, and connections people make when talking about crime, their environment, and community. In line with some of the thinking on the human experience of emotions outlined in Chapter 3, we approach emotions as being complex, episodic, and dynamic. Thoughts, perceptions, and experiences come and go over time and form an integral part of the evolving order of stimuli which make up the life-world of the individual. This contribution attempts to detail the place which the fear of crime takes in the context of people's everyday lives, communities, and important locales. Exploring and presenting participants' in-depth discussion provides a 'thick' layer of analysis and uncovers further avenues for consideration. Through the use of qualitative data this chapter not only attends to the kind of interpretative analysis of how people respond and relate to crime, but contributes to a wider intellectual terrain by refining the broader conceptual framework, developed thus far. We start this chapter, however, by recapping the theoretical framework we first outlined in Chapter 4.

A Summary of Our Theoretical Framework

Our framework starts by assuming that—at some level—the fear of crime is related to actual levels of crime in society and local communities: we specify a relationship between beliefs about the actual levels of crime (local and/or national) and fears about crime. We also propose a relationship between tangible changes in any local area (for example, increases or decreases of amenities or populations, or political shifts) and fear of crime—captured by Smith's suggestion that the fear of crime 'is greatest among people who perceive their communities to be in decline when they are powerless to intervene' (1986: 128). Such beliefs and experiences of local crime and change are also expected to be associated with attitudes towards crime and feelings of confidence in the criminal justice system, the appropriateness of sentences, authoritarian attitudes towards crime and 'law and order', as well as attitudes towards long-term social change. We therefore expect to find relationships between both beliefs about local crime and general change in the local area with respondents' attitudes towards crime and long-term social change (Dowds and Ahrendt, 1995).

In turn, attitudes towards crime and long-term social change, we expect, feed into perceptions of disorder and perceptions of social control and cohesion. This we see as being in line with Girling et al. (2000), Ferraro (1995), and also in our interviewees' perceptions of their community's ability to regulate the behaviour of their neighbours. Similarly, we expect that perceptions of disorder and perceptions of social cohesion and control will be directly related to both levels of fear of crime and assessments of the likelihood of victimization. The perception of the likelihood of victimization is also partly a function of the perceived consequences of victimization, of course, as well as direct experiences (such as victimization) and beliefs about crime produced via indirect experiences (such as from friends and/or the media, for example). This approach is replicated in Figure 5.1.

Conversations about Crime, Place, and Community: Sampling and Methodology

This chapter analyses qualitative data arising from two previous ESRC-funded studies members of the author team have conducted (see our Methodological Appendix for an outline of these). Between them they explored public perceptions of crime, community, and fear of crime in two major UK cities—London and Glasgow. In total, eighty eight individual interviews were conducted in areas of divergent social demographics within both research sites. Our Methodological Appendix describes the data sets we rely upon.

Figure 5.1 A Unified Framework: Experience and Expression in the Fear of Crime

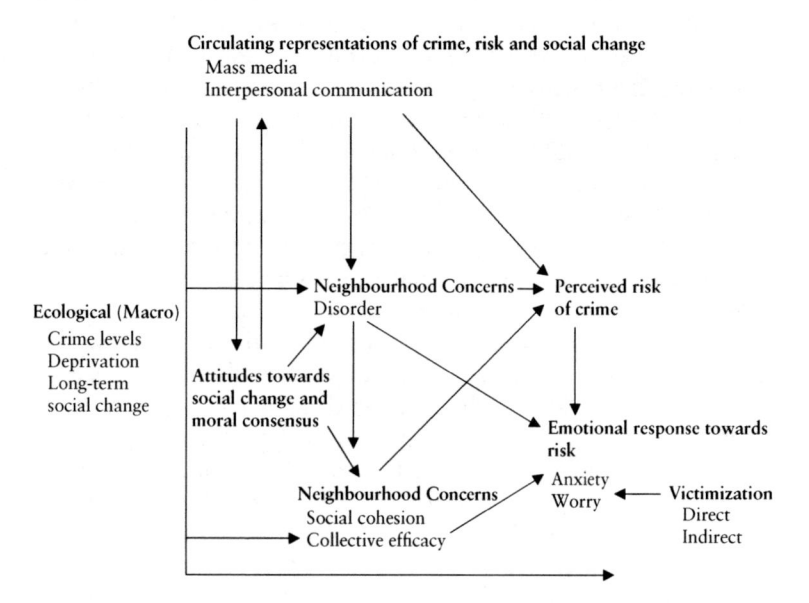

```
                    Circulating representations of crime, risk and social change
                    Mass media
                    Interpersonal communication
                         │    │    │       ╲
                         │    │    │        ╲
                         ▼    │    ▼         ╲
                         ┌──► Neighbourhood Concerns ──► Perceived risk
   Ecological (Macro)    │    Disorder                    of crime
     Crime levels        │       │                          │
     Deprivation         │       │                          │
     Long-term           │    Attitudes towards             │
     social change       │    social change and             │
                         │    moral consensus               ▼
                         │       │                    Emotional response towards
                         │       │                    risk
                         │       ▼                      Anxiety
                         │    Neighbourhood Concerns    Worry  ◄──── Victimization
                         │    Social cohesion                          Direct
                         └──► Collective efficacy                      Indirect
```

Analytic Orientation

During the early stages of the analysis all transcripts were read through and initial notes were taken on anything that appeared significant or of interest. The second stage of analysis consisted of a more thorough reading of the interviews, involving an expansion of all the relevant themes and identifying psychological and theoretical abstractions. Each theme was given a descriptive label which conveyed the conceptual nature of the dynamics therein. The third stage consisted of further organizing the data by establishing connections between the themes and linking them appropriately. In this manner, Smith (2004: 71) suggests that researchers 'Imagine a magnet with some of the themes pulling others in and helping to make sense of them'. Finally, we began to think about how the various issues raised by the participants could be conceptualized theoretically.

The central concern of this work was to explore participants' subjective experiences and responses regarding crime fears. Investigating how events and objects are experienced and given meaning requires interpretative activity on the part of the researcher, which Smith and Osborn (2003: 51) describe as a dual process in which 'the participants are trying to make sense of their world; the researcher is trying to make sense of the participants trying to make sense of their world'. Indeed, in order to produce an authentic picture of what fear of crime actually meant to respondents, the study sought to minimize the potential for measurement errors: the interviewers carefully but persistently probed the relationship between what people thought (cognition), said (account), actually did (behaviour), and felt (emotions). Moreover, the analysis goes into considerable detail to help understand, represent, and make sense of people's ways of thinking, their motivations, and actions. We believe this allows for a detailed and sophisticated understanding of the phenomena of 'worrying' and brings to the fore the complexity of human emotion. This exercise also draws attention to how the interpersonal, material, and social contexts of the participant's life mediate the experience and expression of worry, giving rise to different consequences and interpretations.

The topics discussed in each interview were broad-ranging, concerned with both substantive and theoretical issues. There was, for example, frequent discussion of respondents' concern about macro and meso crime levels, particularly the incidence and perceived threat of 'local' crimes such as burglary, vandalism, car theft, drug use, and more generalized anti-social behaviour. Respondents' experiences of personal as well as vicarious victimization, and their use of security items and experiences and perceptions of the police, were also probed. Naturally, there were a number of questions on the current and changing 'state' of their local environment, the population, and community: by sharing stories about such matters, these narratives invariably touched on wider questions, such as justice, welfare, politics, the economy, the media, security, and the roles and responsibilities of local citizens, all of which lie at the heart of how we, as individuals, relate to crime and our neighbourhoods. Discussions revealed what Girling et al. (2000: xii) call: '. . . the place that crime occupies, not only within people's everyday lives and consciousness, but within contemporary social relations more generally'. As such, this exercise inevitably highlighted the interconnectedness of people's perceptions of crime and their objective and subjective assessments of their community, environment, and change.

This chapter contains four sections—which broadly mirror the processes described diagrammatically in Figure 5.1. The first tackles how people relate to their *physical* environment; their home, the buildings, shops, and green spaces. In exploring these matters, discussion of 'changes over time' and the psychological and sociological importance of 'place' when considering the fear of crime are illustrated. The second section moves on to look at the role and value of important social bonds. Topics herein include how members of the community relate and support each other (or not); the informal control provided by the local population and the identification and social production of particular 'problem populations'. Our third section explores how crime operates in the public's consciousness; what people know about crime and disorder and how and from where this information is absorbed and processed. Finally, the fourth section explores the various constituents of fear of crime; what it represents to people and how it manifests itself in episodic experiences and broader expressions about social life. In addition, we examine how attitudes or opinions are brought forth when people are asked to discuss their feelings about crime, a process we refer to as an 'invocation of attitude' whereby surveys and interviews provoke 'crime talk'.

The Physical Environment: Crime, 'Place', Change, and Perceptions of Order

One of the principal contentions of our study is that when people are asked about and respond to questions concerning crime and fear of crime, they inevitably include assessments of their local environment, both consciously and unconsciously. However, different aspects of the area can have varying degrees of significance for respondents; such stimuli may also invoke different emotions, memories, and opinions, depending on a participant's own circumstances or history. Along these lines, Girling et al. (2000: 5) describe crime as: '. . . a topic that never quite stays still and submits itself for dispassionate examination. Similarly, people's talk about crime is dense and digressive'. In the following section we wish to flesh out in some detail how the respondents we spoke to experienced and expressed fear of crime, and how they related this to their sense of place.

When asked about the area in which they lived—to consider and describe what they liked or disliked about it, how they would characterize the neighbourhood, and how it had changed—it became immediately apparent that the physical appearance was particularly significant to our respondents. There was recognition that a 'clean and tidy' space was important to one's sense of safety and indicative of a 'healthy' place to live:

> I think if your environment looks nice, you feel better. I think psychologically, if the place looks nice, you feel better. If the place looks grim you feel grim, you know that, just the same as in the winter when the park looks dull and wet and damp, you feel dull and wet and damp... so it's the same with living round here. If a lot of things are dumped about and that, if people just come and dump their rubbish down... they forget there's people living here so when you look out on that you feel depressed. G76 (female, 30s–40s, white)

Discussions about the physical aspects of a community prompted mention of 'inner-city council estates', reflecting a preoccupation with deprivation and crime more generally. Such concerns were shared by 'estate' residents as well as those from more suburban areas. Much of the concern was focused on the reputation, appearance, and security of the housing and local businesses. These places were often identified as areas that more affluent respondents neither wanted to live in, visit, nor pass through. Nevertheless, estate residents demonstrated how they had campaigned to maintain and improve the physical aspects of the area including increased security (especially immediately obvious products such as reinforced doors), green spaces, cleanliness, and road safety measures. Some estates were thought of as better—for the moment at least—than those that routinely feature in urban stereotypes:

> Anybody who's down in England, 'oh you come from the Glasgow, oh it's a terrible place', but I don't see any of the things that it's a terrible place. G48 (female, over 50, white)

> There was a time when if people wanted housing and they were offered somewhere on this estate, they'd turn it down... The newspapers used to describe it as 'notorious' which infuriated me. I had words with one or two of the editors. But then when we got the Tenants' Association up and working, we managed to get the security doors fitted. And most of the improvements on this estate have been tenant led. It has got better. H2 (female, over 50, white)

Residents from estates in both London and Glasgow indicated that steady financial investment had contributed to improvements in the physical appearance of the local area—and also their sense of safety more generally. In the quotes above a sense of pride and accomplishment is apparent. Indeed, these residents were satisfied, felt they had some degree of control over their environment, and were happy to continue living there. Invariably, other respondents reported they had not been afforded the attention or investment of the local authorities, and their communities had been seemingly 'abandoned'. Evidence of decay and deterioration had a depressing impact on respondents' sense of safety, equity, and belonging. Indeed, there was a strong relationship between neighbourhood assets and neighbourhood well-being.

The actual buildings are hell. The tower blocks I think make it look sort of a typical run-down urban shit hole . . . there's so much concrete around here . . . I used to sit in the park but there's nowhere for us to sit now . . . I think that's where they've got it wrong. Because they haven't got general areas where people can go anymore. H18 (female, 30s–40s, white)

I think the state [of the neighbourhood] has declined in the sense that this is a fairly affluent area, but I am not sure we get as much from the area as you might think. . . I think what's happening is the physical environment is deteriorating quite badly. H21 (male, over 50, white)

Residents often distinguished between particular estates and identified some as experiencing the 'sharp end' of decline. The loss of local important resources, poor-quality services and planning negatively affected people's enjoyment and use of their public spaces, particularly for those respondents who were financially or practically constrained. One resident gave a discouraging observation about the plight of those 'stuck' in some estates.

Oh aye, we used to have like cafes and places the kids could go to, cinemas and everything but then they tore all of them down and they just built these multi-storeys, put everybody in them but that was it you know, so they took away a lot of the entertainment and things, I mean we haven't got a church, they tore the church down, left us with one chapel . . . we've only got one local secondary school, so all the kids in the area just go there whether they're Catholic or Protestant . . . How're they going to sell these houses they're building? People want to move into an area where you've got schools for your kids—it makes sense. G76 (female, 30s–40s, white)

Certain areas were identified as suffering because the aesthetics of the buildings attracted disorder. Late-night shops and off licences, numerous alley-ways, and poor lighting were a constant irritation to residents. As the following quotes demonstrate, local urban planning was said to have created 'no-go' areas which acquired reputations for drawing unruly young people who were beyond the control of the local people and police.

I think the lighting is bad . . . we are near, unfortunately, to the type of facilities that encourage people from a little bit of a distance away, fish and chips, video shop and [an off licence], so you've got the worst combination. I don't think it's been particularly good for the area. I occasionally use the shops myself but because it's in a bad lighting area and because it's in a residential area it's not well controlled so you have people sitting on the wall drinking, having fish and chips, putting a quarter bottle, half bottle whisky, having drunk it, into your garden, that's two or three times a week. B152 (female, 30s–40s, white)

I think this particular estate is very badly laid out . . . I mean the kids get up to things. There's nothing that kids like more than a game of cops and robbers round here. There are so many places where [police] cars can't go that kids can dive into. And if they're getting up to something pretty horrendous, which some of them do, let's face it, like setting light to the bins and that sort of thing, you know, which can be pretty horrific, somebody'll phone the police. There's nothing they like better than a game of cops and robbers round this estate. It's very badly designed. H2 (female, over 50, white)

In talking about the physical degeneration of local areas, many respondents, particularly those living on estates or in more densely populated areas, described the debilitating long-term effects of crime and anti-social behaviour. Respondents listed incivilities such as graffiti, litter, vandalism, youths hanging around in particular places and destroying property, as a particularly unpleasant and unsettling feature of their environment. Indeed, for some, the continual presence of these problems had a potent impact on their perceptions of the neighbourhood, because they were interpreted as indices of safety and cohesion:

You go out there . . . and you find that mess on the stairs. You find that spitting on the walls, spitting on the floor, peeing. That is to me crime, a crime, it's a disgusting crime. Why should we have to put up with it plus it's a disease. It causes diseases. Would you like anybody pee on your doorstep or in your flat? No. Spit on your doorstep? H20 (female, over 50, white European)

I came up here and you're constantly getting the kids going about with spray paint, which angered me, but that's their life, that's part of their life, that's the way they've been brought up, to wreck bus shelters and things like that, it angers me when I see it happening. Because in about ten years time these kids who are doing it will be saying 'if somebody was doing that to my property I'd be mad', it's just their way of life. K125 (female, under 30, white)

What the quotes above suggest is that for some respondents persistent disorder is not only distressing because it spoils the day-to-day experience of one's environment, but also because it represents an apparent breakdown of previously-accepted conventions of respect and responsibility.[1] When public spaces become unpredictable or 'disgusting' to negotiate, it can lead local residents to feel distressed and insecure. Moreover, mistrust of neighbours, area decline, and crime were key factors behind residents wanting to move away. Moving to 'a better area' was an important goal for many interviewees, and their aspirations were motivated more out of social concerns than material ones—they wanted to live in 'safer' more pleasant areas. However, their choices were highly constrained by income and housing capacity:

Just all the junkies, they were everywhere, street corners, bottom of the flat, shops, everywhere you went they were all round about. Sometimes you'd see needles lying about the streets and things like that, and my wee daughter went out at night, she was in amongst them all cause they were in the swing park where the little ones would play, couldn't let her out, had to keep her in so I thought no, I'll just get away all together, start afresh somewhere else and so I moved up here. D46 (female, under 30, white)

As I say there's good people in the area but it's the minority . . . The good ones are the older ones and they're now, with the houses coming down, they're getting a chance to get off out of the scheme . . . an' that's what most of the people are doing, if they can get the option to leave the scheme they'll do it you know an' they've no intentions of coming back. D34 (female, under 30, white)

---

[1] Research carried out by Innes (2004a) suggests that some crimes and disorders (such as serious domestic violence) may pass relatively unnoticed by the general public, while other incidents are widely perceived to indicate or 'signal' a latent threat to the safety of the community. Drawing on symbolic interactionist sociology he develops the concept of 'signal crimes and disorders' which are important in terms of how people interpret threats to their security and demonstrate how social space is symbolically constructed. Intriguingly, in empirical surveys carried out using the 'signal crimes' concept (see Innes et al., 2004b, 2006), respondents listed various local disorders (persistent graffiti, youths always hanging around in a particular place shouting insults to passers-by etc.) as being actually more threatening to local safety than some more serious crimes like domestic burglary.

Participants explained that when 'respectable' residents left to go to better areas, their homes were either left unoccupied (creating further opportunities for crime) or were occupied by those who were less able to exert control over the local community (if only because they were newcomers).

My Granddad's street was relatively quiet and they're moving everybody into it now, from like junkies hitting up with needles and things like that—they're actually getting houses. [My grandparents have] been brought up there all their lives and they're getting wary now, they're like 'we wouldn't walk down there at night alone' whereas years ago they would've ... I mean in areas that were right good areas and that was hard to get [houses]. I mean they could be letting the houses out to families and keeping it nice, but they're not doing that, instead of keeping the decent areas decent areas, they're moving like all the junkies into them. D36 (female, under 30, white)

The extent to which people's perceptions of disorder feed into a broader sense of insecurity and fear of crime has been of ripe interest to academics for some time (Ferraro, 1995; Jackson, 2004a; Innes, 2004). Predictably, we also found that assessments of the local area, particularly perceptions of disorder, informed participants' assessments of their safety and security from crime. Respondents mentioned that physical examples of decay and disorder often made them feel 'frightened', 'concerned', and 'worried' about potential victimization.

You know, if you go to a place that looks terrible, you start to get a bit frightened. H4 (female, over 50, white Irish)

... so when I went to the Housing Officer, I said 'I don't want [that estate] because I've been told it is a dangerous area'. She said 'you only have one offer, and one offer only'. And I thought 'oh my God, have mercy'. H11 (female, over 50, black)

For respondents living in highly-populated estates or deprived areas, disorder and crime frequently threatened the urban spaces and their quality of life. How they engaged with the local area was an important aspect of managing their personal safety. For example, many categorized different parts of their neighbourhoods as safe or unsafe, 'good', or 'bad', and they had an acute awareness of where boundaries lay. Certain spaces were only considered safe at particular times of the day or week, depending on who would be there. In some areas local crime, specifically prolific drug use, dominated the character and atmosphere of the place.

The following interviewee describes her locale as a 'nightmare'; she mentions that the overwhelming presence of drug users inhibited her mobility and sense of security. A clear sense of isolation, even desperation is engendered in her description:

> What it's like? It's a nightmare, it is, its just, it's a living nightmare, I mean you go to the shops through the day...my daughter can't go to the shop because...there's drunks and junkies hanging about the shops and they're saying things to her and you're finding needles when you go down, they're everywhere. Every day you go round them they're there. Just gangs, they're not doing anything, d'you know what I mean? They're just stoning, they're just standing there but you get the fear...There's a lota badness going about. D34 (female, under 30, white)

This section began with a discussion concerning the significance of physical space in respondents' assessments of their environment, safety, and fear of crime. Despite high levels of drug misuse and disorder, respondents from economically constrained estates or areas were able to identify positive aspects in their physical environment and took pride in keeping their areas tidy, safe, and attractive. However, where local deterioration had not been abated by local campaigning or investment, residents felt 'left' to suffer the affects of neglect, insufficient resources, and ill-conceived planning. Participants from both poor and more prosperous areas reported coping with a range of local 'risks' to their safety and quality of life. Chiefly, their concerns centred on the aesthetic worries, such as vandalism, complex alley-ways, badly-lit spaces which were frightening or attracted disorderly groups of people. Their knowledge, or perceptions, of the characteristics of the neighbourhood helped shape how they assessed their safety and fear of crime. They were also more likely to think of negative environmental cues as representative of a loss of social cohesion and informal control. Indeed, the physical effects of decline, crime, and disorder had a potentially 'profound influence over social relations and the fabric of social life' (Innes, 2006: 50).

Community, Cohesion, and Social Control

Literature on fear of crime research suggests that it is an absorbent topic bound up in how individuals relate to ideas of 'place' *and* 'community' (Banks, 2005; Girling et al., 2000; Jackson, 2004a; Smith, 1986). Ferraro (1995) maintains that an individual's perceptions of their community have a strong influence on their subjective estimates of victimization. These appraisals also influence a respondent's assessment of their relationships with neighbours, their locale, and their sense of 'community cohesion'. Naturally, a mixture of questions concerning the local population and community bonds were addressed in the interviews.

The respondents' personal contexts ranged across household types, age, and length of time spent in the community. Unsurprisingly, many of the older participants were able to identify changes in the dynamics of socio-economic structures during their life-course. Many felt that the 'speeding up' of life and the creation of transient populations forced to move area in the search for employment had had a negative affect on the quality of long-term social bonds and 'neighbourliness':

[There's] not much neighbourliness in the old-fashioned sense of the word 'cause people do, you know, lead really busy lives and to say they're not interested, isn't really true but they're too busy to notice that haven't seen Joe down the road for ages, you know . . . The pattern of work has changed now. Jobs aren't jobs for life, you know, and so there's a lot more part-time working and even my husband and I have done that for a bit recently. So the job situation and that means you can't be a community any more because you're not always there all the time. Nowadays everyone has a car. So we're all doing far more things and far more into our day. We're not at home to be a community. H12 (female, over 50, white)

I think people's, society's cohesion, is splitting up because partly people are moving around a lot for jobs as well, it's partly Americanized influence I think, that's the other thing I would particularly blame, hardened type of uncaring attitude. B152 (female, 30s–40s, white)

'Community' for these respondents was something that had been an important form of social organization and provoked a strong emotional 'pull'. However, contemporary social arrangements were not only perceived as 'busier' and more fluid, but community cohesion was being replaced by more negative influences, namely materialism and 'individualism':

I think society has become more materialistic. I think there is less of neighbourliness than there used to be. And whether this has caused more crime or not, I don't know. I suspect it must have done because there is the underclass which is responsible for the majority of crime, in my experience at least. The underclass says, 'why the hell can't I have my share?'. H6 (male, over 50, white)

Cognate worries about the 'breakdown of family life' were also voiced. Participants explained that families and communities had changed dramatically and become more atomized—rather than fulfilling the traditional role of an 'extended network' of informal social bonds. These types of cultural shifts highlighted a 'lost time' for some of the older respondents, and with it their own sense of belonging, as these changes were wrapped up in their personal histories and anticipated concerns for the future.

You know, it's a combination of the two things, breakdown of family and that sort of thing . . . at one time people used to live and grandma would be around the corner and Auntie Someone would be somewhere else. You had your extended family round about you and your kids didn't ever need to suffer if you had to go out to work or something like that. There was a family unit to look after you or even a social unit, but there isn't these days. That has gone a lot, hasn't it? People have moved, communities have been broken up, they've been destroyed. I suppose that started at the end of the Second World War. H2 (female, over 50, white)

Moreover, these 'losses' were associated with increased vulnerability to crime and social isolation:

People's morals and that are slipping. Really, really slipping, know what I mean, we were living in squalor way back in the 40s and the 50s, we still had a code know what I mean between the area, the people stuck together. The people don't give a damn about what he's doing an' that's doing, it's that bad I get the feeling if a woman was getting raped in front of people, they wouldn't do nothing about it . . . but that's the way people are now. G61 (male, under 30, white)

I don't think I would have been so aware of always locking doors in cars . . . Certainly wouldn't have done it when I was growing up. I certainly wouldn't even lock the front door of the house when I was growing up. Just the way of the world. You just have to be conscious of it and do something about it. H22 (female, over 50, white)

As community cohesion wanes—or is perceived to have waned- and members of the local population become less familiar to one another, the creation and prominence of 'suspicious characters' or 'problem populations' emerges. There were stories about 'notorious' local individuals or categories of people; respondents attributed much of the area's petty crime to indigenous sources, especially, young people, 'drunks', and 'drug addicts'. These groups presented intractable dangers, in terms of causing anti-social behaviour or crime which restricted the aspirations of other members of the community:

There's dodgy people hanging around you know, a lot of drunks . . . Sort of low-lifes, odd-looking people that might just not like the look of you. And I don't know, I don't want to make any generalizations on anybody or assume things of people, I suppose you just automatically think that a whole lot of guys hanging round a street corner . . . I don't know, it's just people that you didn't feel were right, comfortable, set off little bells in your head, I suppose that's how I go by things. B131 (female, 30s–40s, white)

You just don't want to get involved with them. They pick on you and stuff like that, you know. They're just not nice at all. Not, I don't call [them] normal people you know, like most of them are probably on drugs or whatever anyway, so not nice . . . alcoholics, weirdos. H9 (female, over 50, white)

Typically, respondents linked petty crime and low-level disorder in their area with groups of young people—loitering or 'hanging around' in public. Notably, in both affluent and deprived areas, the residents described a 'youth problem' as well as a more digressive problem with 'youth culture'. Specifically, concerns about teenage (mis)behaviour impinged significantly upon how 'liveable' residents considered their local areas to be:

I don't know how children were managed in previous generations, but I am aware of the fact that they don't appear to be managed very well in this generation and I don't know why . . . children are also quite powerful and continuous harassment by kids who are beyond the control of the police, the parents, the school. H19 (male, over 50, white)

All the kids . . . None of them come off the estate. And you've got some poor sod in the concierge and at 12 o'clock he's meant to lock that up, then you get 15 kids sort of 15 to 20 years age and you've got to tell them to get out. It's no joke and they're staying there till three, four o'clock in the morning. Police don't come, I mean I've always got my windows open and doors, you can just hear this effing and blinding, they've got to play about somewhere but not till two o'clock in the morning, three o'clock in the morning. It's like having a noisy party you know, cause the noise is really loud. H18 (female, 30s–40s, white)

In addition to the 'youth problem', appraisals of the local community were strongly influenced by the introduction of immigrant populations. A number of respondents lived on estates which had received a steady influx of migrants over the years. While participants maintained they supported the policy of immigration in principle, they stressed their already 'over-populated neighbourhoods' were negatively affected by unplanned additions. New populations were perceived to have compounded area deprivation and created tensions among the residents. Some noted that their communities had simply not been prepared for the challenges and felt the issues remained largely hidden from the view of the authorities:

> The word 'community' in the twentieth century means you've got to now allow someone else from a different community, national, gender, race, whatever, to come in and feel safe . . . Because they are coming in with their ideas that will infringe and impinge, and of course, people are going to get very upset about that. So, it's no longer, the word community is no longer a word in the twentieth century. It's become obsolete, totally. You will find . . . they use the word 'group', and group just means a lot of people together, where they don't have to be answerable for anyone or anything and that's what some of the communities are like now. H11 (female, over 50, black)

> So this multi-cultural society, a phrase I hate, isn't actually a good thing. Not because one doesn't enjoy living with ethnic minorities, because if you start altering your core you end up with nothing. You don't have anything in particular. So really, you should keep your core values and then other things should be either a bonus or not a bonus, depending on what they are. H16 (female, over 50, white)

Unsurprisingly talk about objective physical cues (run-down areas, graffiti, litter etc.) was prominent when people talked about crime and disorder. But as Sampson and Raudenbush (2004) point out, cultural stereotypes are also relevant. Those groups identified as 'strangers', 'drunks', 'young people', and 'immigrants' were seen as conveying uncertain or ambiguous information about the environment to our participants. Beyond the day-to-day difficulties these groups posed—often expressed in terms of how they occupied social and public space—discussions also focused on more diffuse worries, about the loss of a cultural and moral order. The means by which respondents condensed their concerns was to speak of the loss of 'respect' and 'trust':

> This new generation that's coming up now, I mean, in the late 50s, when I was growing up there was a freer atmosphere, you could go out and leave your door open, nobody would think of going near your house. Or you ran up and down stairs, everybody knew everybody, the rent could come round and lift your rent with no fear of getting mugged. G85 (male, over 50, white)

It's just not the same as it was when I was growing up. My mum and dad used to have people knocking on the door, 'oh your daughter came in and stole a strawberry from my back garden, you know, what are you going to do about it?' But these days, if for instance, this car business, if we had gone up to the child's mother . . . and she's a big terrifying woman . . . there is no way that I would have confronted her and said 'your child has put a brick through my car'. You know, no way in the world. So this is what happens. The kids get away with so much because the parents turn on whomever is the victim. So, you know . . . 'oh, my little Johnnie wouldn't do that'. H7 (female, 30s–40s, white)

Notably, the nature of the sentiments above were not confined to older respondents engaged in wistful nostalgia. Among those who also lamented the loss of important social bonds and relationships were younger people who felt that modern social life could be very lonely and one could not depend on bystanders or neighbours for protection or care:

I've been assaulted about three times now in the town. The last time it was a guy, he was just walking past and he tried to grab stuff out of my bag . . . It was in the town on a Saturday, quite a lot of people about but nobody bothers with you, they just look over and keep walking. G90 (male, under 30, white)

We've had hardly any contact with our neighbours at all . . . If you just knew people around you and they knew when you were going away, you knew when they were going away, you just keep an eye out really, whereas I mean the next house along or something, someone, I don't even know what they look like who live there so anyone could just be breaking in and I wouldn't know a thing . . . people don't seem to have time for each other, it's quite depressing. K99 (male, under 30, white)

The isolation some respondents expressed was compounded by their own reluctance, or anxiety, about mixing with their neighbours. Many respondents explained how they adopted various avoidance tactics and often preferred to 'keep themselves to themselves'.

I'm not involved with the people, you know . . . After 5 o'clock I never go out or been out late or after 5 o'clock. When my children come from school, I just straight away close the door and that's it, you know. Even the courses, I choose the courses in the morning. I don't like to go in the evening. H10 (female, 30s–40s, North African)

Just the area's pretty bad. I'd rather be in ma house watching the telly or listening to the radio or something and if anything's going to happen out there, let it happen, long as I'm no involved. That's about it, I don't hang about. Same at the weekends, I don't hang about. I say I'm going for a drink, [then I take a] taxi. D40 (male, 30s–40s, white)

The accounts above demonstrate a feed-back loop whereby the presence and conduct of unrecognizable, disorderly, or unknown people prompted avoidance strategies and further distanced social players from each other. However, the construction of 'folk devils' involves more than the awkward incursion of anonymous or disorderly people; these unknown faces were seen as providing threats to the community spirit and residents' sense of safety. As these participants explain, while safety-enhancing networks fade, 'unknown others' are not perceived with curiosity, but apprehension and fear:

Like here, the street's empty of people . . . and it's like I don't want to have to walk through groups of guys if I don't have to you know 'cause and they may not, I may not be thinking that they're gonna attack me in any way but there's always the verbal sort of abuse that you get and just hassle, I just, if I can avoid it then I will. K122 (female, 30s–40s, white)

You know how these people come round [selling door to door] and say that they're unemployed, I found some of them quite unpleasant actually, some of the young ones . . . it's maybe lack of training but they're very cheeky sometimes and not nice if you don't want to buy anything and there was one I just did not like and felt a bit suspicious of, and I thought I'd just phone up the police station and ask if they are supposed to come round the doors like that. One of them said to me if you're that worried you should get a chain on the door and he said something about people in places like this who have no sympathy for the unemployed. B148 (female, over 50, white)

These ways of speaking about strangers and 'problem populations' are familiar enough, especially in the media. Yet, such sentiments were not uniform and other participants had different experiences and held different opinions about their neighbours. Many reported the presence of relatives, neighbours, and peers who formed trusted and protective networks; they helped provide knowledge of risks, support, and reciprocal monitoring:

Down here quite a lot of people just look out for each other because there's a couple of times when maybe there's been one of us out, and my pals been out an' there's boys from different areas about to start fighting, there's only drug addicts about, so they go over and help you get away from the fight or whatever, they chase them away for you an' whatever. G90 (male, under 30, white)

Ninety-nine per cent of the people [round here] are good people you know and like everywhere else you've got a wee percentage that's not so good, but put it this way, the good outweighs the bad, as I say I've never felt unsafe in my own area . . . I just feel, well, I wouldn't sit an' let anybody run my area down. We know it's got its faults, we know it's got its problems but we'll not sit an' let anybody else run it down. G76 (female, 30s–40s, white)

Notably, discussion of social bonds was evident across the socio-economic spectrum of participants. Respondents from affluent areas often identified potential threats as 'outside' their community; they trusted and were 'friendly' with their neighbours, taking turns to monitor their houses while either party were on holiday. Notwithstanding, participants from high crime areas proffered interesting and creative examples about how local people organized themselves towards improving feelings of safety, security, and justice. Talk of a local 'code', assistance with retrieving stolen goods, and the protection of vulnerable people were cited by the following interviewees:

H18 (female, 30s–40s, white): I've had things stolen but I know where to go and who to see you know, 'cause I've lived here quite a while now. I've lived here 17 years, you get to know people.

JJ: You get it back you mean?

H18: Get it back, yeah, decent people. You know, there are just one or two places you go to and you say this has been stolen, that's been stolen and they go and have a word with them. Because it all goes through the grapevine. Doesn't matter what's happened, you know, in the estate, it all filters through. And they'll just find out who's got it and then get it back.

I feel quite at home in this area . . . when any elderly person does get mugged or anything like that down here, there is repercussions . . . because there's a lot of people don't like it, and it's very easy to find out who . . . in that respect and there's people that just will not have it. You know, I wouldn't like to think any of my neighbours, especially old Nancy, I wouldn't like anything to happen to her sort of thing. G57 (male, 30s–40s, white)

Other respondents went to considerable effort to explain how they contributed towards the safeguarding, maintenance, and quality of life in their area:

If I see people dropping litter, I tell them. I'm continually warned that I ought not, because one of these days you're going to get bonked. Likewise, if I see people with dogs and they haven't got their little pooper-scoop, then I go and approach them. H13 (female, over 50, white)

What the above quotes describe has resonance with the concept of 'resilience'—which is becoming increasingly popular in urban sociology and describes the methods employed by local people to survive and mitigate the risks and threats they are exposed to (see Vale and Campanella, 2005; Thrift, 2005). While such debates have not been exclusively to the topic of crime, what these studies show is that a community's skill in withstanding harm provides evidence of existing social order or 'collective efficacy'.

This section began with participants' recognition that social life and social relationships had been reorganized over the previous decades; employment patterns had brought more women into work, and employees often moved areas for jobs or worked long hours. These events were said to have detracted from traditional family and community life, specifically in terms of locals' sense of familiarity and trust. In addition, particular groups of people or individuals invoked feelings of suspicion and fear among residents who suggested there had been a steady erosion of informal social control. As such 'unknown others' often acted as indicators about the levels of security afforded to local communities and, in so doing, implied the likely presence of other risks. Indeed, perceptions of one's environment and crime were shown to be complex and involved a dense series of social and physical influences. Intriguingly, respondents from a variety of backgrounds were able to exhibit resilience in the face of crime and disorder problems. As such, the patterns of informal social control areas and the relationship between crime and deprivation may be more complex than previously thought.

Crime Consciousness: Residents' Interpretations of Crime and Risk

Having examined how physical and social cues circuitously inform participants' responses to crime and disorder, we now turn more directly to the processes by which crime enters the imagination or consciousness. In this section we wish to explore how crime and order figure in the everyday lives of our participants; *what* people know about crime, their opinions, emotions, experiences, memories, and from *where* this information is sourced and *how* it is processed and acted upon.

Discussing local crime, residents of highly populated estates and poorer areas commonly complained about street crime, general disorder (littering, noisy and boisterous behaviour, and vandalism), drug abuse, and burglary. Meanwhile, those living in suburban middle-class neighbourhoods emphasized the threat of petty thieving and cars being broken into. However, these respondents were also aware that the desirable reputation of their area might attract burglars of a more professional kind and took steps to protect themselves. Indeed, while the frequency of crime might be reduced in more affluent areas, the threat of victimization continued to occupy a very significant space in their minds and hence their opinions of their safety and environment.

I mean car theft or theft from cars is about as serious as it gets around here. The occasional break-in, kids coming up from the river, throwing your terracotta pots into the water. H5 (female, over 50, white)

Areas seem to go through spates of burglaries. One area is maybe bad for a certain time then they seem to move on to somewhere else. The gardens are all fairly large and it's easier for burglars to be unseen. And they maybe think because the houses are a bit bigger than normal there's something worth stealing. B35 (female, 30s–40s, white)

Knowledge about crime was absorbed from various sources; information travelled via local talk and 'reputations'. Crime stories were also picked up through local people, the media, and police communications.

JJ: Where do you get your information about crime?

H7 (female, 30s–40s, white)

You just hear things. Sitting on buses, you know. Sometimes at the reception, someone saying something about crime or the police and RingMaster, which I think is bloody brilliant. They pick up on the crime at the moment and they just ring round everybody that's on them, and they will describe the crime, when and where it was committed, and then they'll give you a number to ring if you have any information. There was one about the sheds that had been broken into. And sometimes it's literally one particular block of flats.

I've not lived in Glasgow all my life but I hear people mention certain areas. K125 (female, under 30, white)

Knowledge of local crime stories, particularly violent crimes or domestic burglary, provided salient reminders to residents that they, too, might be at risk of victimization. Indeed, awareness of such incidents made some respondents feel unsafe. Moreover, the subsequent 'exchange' of stories supplied an additional layer of significance—the narratives often included assessments of the local environment, the police, and ultimately highlighted the cultural, as well as personal, significance of crime:

I think 'oh don't be silly', it's not going to happen to you just because it's happened to Sheila', you know. 'Get on with your life'. But I think it must be, I think it's very likely that experience of friends and neighbours having problems would tend to make you a little more cautious for a lot of folk. H14 (female, over 50, white)

I think . . . your experiences that you hear from other people. Hearing what happens to them, I think these neighbourhood watch things, when they send round the list of all the things that have gone on, sometimes it's best not to read these, if you're ignorant then ignorance is bliss. If you read this you see exactly what's been stolen, what cars have been nicked and things like that. B131 (female, 30s–40s, white)

Meanwhile, knowledge and discussion of national crime figures indicated that, in the main, participants believed that crime was getting worse—that Britain was more violent and that use of firearms were becoming 'normalized'. For these respondents, awareness of high-profile crimes (however infrequent) functioned as a significant pointer that life had become dangerous and unpredictable.

'I think the whole generation is different, they're more violent . . . it's getting more like America, the guns and everything now, you're hearing the banks getting held up with guns, it is getting like America, it's frightening. G89 (female, over 50, white)

Oh, London—you hear about it every day. It's either guns or vandalism and people wrecking things. Just crime in general in London is what you expect and if you park your car in a street you take your chances. You know, you go by tube you could get mugged. But it doesn't bother me very much. There are certain places I may not go at certain times, dressed in a certain way. H21 (male, over 50, white)

I think the statistics show that crime has got worse compared to say twenty, thirty, forty years ago because I believe the drug question—because more people want money for drugs. But certainly I feel there is more crime than there was when I was young. And I don't necessarily believe it is because more people report it—which most people would say, I don't necessarily think it is. But again I have nothing to base my views on. It is only a gut reaction. H16 (female, over 50, white)

In this manner, it was felt that crime had become an endemic feature of modern life, and was a problem both locally and nationally—in this sense, 'everywhere'. A conclusion emerged that the public had to 'accept' crime because victimization was 'inevitable' and citizens, as well as the police, had little control over it:

I'm aware that in our environment [burglary] seems to be increasing and it's happened to me twice already in flats and in homes ... But, and I think what is probably more worrying now is people's attitude to it, it's happening all the time, people don't worry too much about it, the police seem so frozen and unable to do very much. B152 (female, 30s–40s, white)

In a way I feel it's kind of inevitable because there's so many break-ins round here, there's been a few in this close, so you feel that it will happen at some point, and I obviously don't like the idea of it at all, but I'm kind of resigned to the fact that it could happen. K103 (female, 30s–40s, white)

Up here I think [victimization] is highly likely, I mean I've lived in the country all my life until I came up to the city. Takes a bit of getting used to and you tend to be a bit pessimistic, tend to think 'Oh it's bound to happen', you hear all the stories and you think 'well it's just a matter of time before someone knocks my house off' but I don't know, I suppose I still believe it's fairly likely that it could happen at any time.. I'm quite pessimistic about it really. K99 (male, under 30, white)

The data above provide good examples of how perceptions of crime and disorder can prompt powerful emotional reactions. The circulation of crime 'stories', statistics, and local knowledge of crime functioned as a signal to these respondents and invoked feelings of despair and defeat. Moreover, these sentiments were compounded by the perception that the police were ultimately impotent to manage the quantity and quality of contemporary crime patterns. There was a clear denouncement that the police did not provide a visible or authoritative presence:

I think the police are frustrated by what they can do, what they can't do. I mean the guidelines of what they have to work with now is ... It must be very difficult. But I just think, they've got to the stage where they just don't bother, you know, they know that they're not going to get any joy, so they don't bother. I don't think a policeman even went round to see my mum for her three robberies. I don't think she even saw a copper. H18 (female, 30s–40s, white)

The head, the big people that sold the drugs in this area, they used to come down with swords and everything, it was terrible, really bad an' the police station's right smack up against it and yet you never see a policeman. G69 (female, over 50, white)

Through these quotes, we can begin to see how crime and disorder entered the public consciousness. Respondents seemed to perceive a range of threats and risks from 'everyday' public and social cues and expressed themselves through a narrative of worry. Adding another layer of complexity to this dynamic is the media, an arena in which fear discourses might gather momentum (Loos and Grimes, 2004). It is widely recognized that crime stories and discussions about 'law and order' are the staple diet of the written press, while fictional and semi-fictional criminal representations fill TV and film screens (Sparks, 1992). Similarly, participants noted how they digested large amounts of information about crime, which saturated them with 'rumours', 'statistics', and 'gory tales'. However, respondents were not comforted by this diet and suggested the volume of data actually increased their fear and anxiety:

You're bombarded with information about people who attack you at night, when you read the news, when you read Crime Watch, all these things, most, I mean if something happens in broad daylight, everybody's shocked because you assume it's going to happen at night. H5 (female, over 50, white)

You see that much on the telly and you read that much in the paper—this one getting mugged and an old man, an old woman who's 80 years old, even old women at 80 getting raped, you're reading it constantly now, it's not a case you're reading it once in a while, you're reading it all the time. It's just kept alive in the brain as far as I'm concerned. The media, it's a different world from when I was young. G87 (female, over 50, white)

Certainly there was recognition amongst some that the media overplayed violent and serious crime stories and stimulated public anxieties. In so doing, high-profile crimes could eclipse the 'facts' about crime and the threat of crime:

I think there needs to be a different message got across about the facts. I mean not many people are going to be Jill Dando-ed[2] and shot on

---

[2] Jill Dando was a popular British television presenter who was unexpectedly shot on her own doorstep after returning from a shopping trip. Although convicted of her murder, Barry George was subsequently released on appeal. At present her murder remains unsolved.

their doorstep. Most murders are done by somebody you know. Rape is comparatively rare . . . But that sort of hits the headlines and somehow I think if you could reduce the level of reporting, and make it more factual. H7 (female, 30s–40s, white)

Perhaps more cynically, a number of respondents felt that the government exploited public anxieties and media furore (or 'moral panics') to legitimize repressive social policies:

My concern is more how people react, I think crime is used as an excuse to bring in draconian laws and acts, police powers, whether it's stop and search or it's more an over-reaction to crime, such as the thing with knives a while ago. K112 (male, under 30, white)

To be sure, crime in general was a topic that punctured respondents' imagination, emotions, experiences, and philosophies. As Furedi (2002) suggested, the public can become embroiled in a 'culture of fear', fixated with risk information (research, statistics, political and media spin) and preoccupied with their own safety. This point is well made in terms of how some of our participants felt—that crime was a highly emotive and high-profile topic which invoked a series of dramatic sentiments and actions:

It doesn't matter which area you start from as far as your particular line of enquiry is concerned, you can mention any aspect of life and sooner or later you can relate it to crime, people's perception of crime, it's been with us for so long. B139 (male, over 50, white)

Well, crime is so fundamental to a society, isn't it? If you allow crime to go unchecked, which is why I'm in favour of zero tolerance, it leads to the breakdown of society eventually, if you don't curb it. And we all want to live in a nice world with happy people around us and nothing nasty happening to anybody. I feel very strongly about crime, actually—that is why I am so involved. H16 (female, over 50, white)

It was clear that messages, both explicit and implicit, about the threat of crime had reached those we spoke to, who believed it was their responsibility to protect themselves and their families from crime. Some modified their behaviour, avoided certain places at certain times, or purchased security equipment:

If I'm going to see my son's God-parents, my husband would rather that I drove round there which is always like a minute; whereas I would rather walk and there are sort of shortcuts that go from [here] through the flats just down there, but I've kind of been warned not to go. K103 (male, 30s–40s, white)

The police can't give you 24-hour protection so you just have to be a bit careful yourself. K123 (male, 30s–40s, Chinese)

Interestingly, some respondents took an unsympathetic opinion of those who 'did nothing to protect themselves'—again, mirroring the work of Furedi (2002) who observed that there has been a shift away from perceiving risk-taking as a positive mark of progress, but as the action of irresponsible and culpable citizens:

> I have a couple of friends, and I'm constantly telling them to change their locks, one in particular who lives on her own, and she's got a little Yale lock, and she's elderly, and I keep saying, 'look don't come and tell me when you've been burgled, because you've had ample warning'. I got very angry with these people, and I get very angry with them, because they know it's happening, um, they know it's been done to me and lots of other people, and they're just careless. They think, you see, that it won't happen to them, you know. K167 (female, 50s, white)

> We do nothing to invite break-ins. There are people around here who live flash. And if you live, even if you live an ostentatiously affluent life-style, I don't think that gives anyone the right to help themselves to your lifestyle, but if you're in the habit of keeping large numbers of thousands of pounds in your house and word gets around, it doesn't increase your chances of being secure any, although it doesn't give anyone the right to come in and help themselves, especially with a gun. B159 (female, 30s–40s, white)

The sentiments expressed above invoke Garland's analysis (1996) of the growing importance placed on 'responsibilization' in contemporary crime control strategies. Neo-liberal government policies have increasingly encouraged communities and individual households to 'take responsibility' for crime, perhaps by setting up Neighbourhood Watch programmes, purchasing security products, or taking other preventative measures to protect themselves from crime. The vast majority of respondents in this study were well versed in this discourse and took numerous steps to minimize the effects of crime.

Taking a slight detour from how citizens related and responded to crime, we now consider the unique perspectives of those who have been victims of crime.[3] Those we spoke to explained that victimization is often accompanied, as one might imagine, by

---

[3] This study did not explore the full nature and extent of the impact of criminal victimization. As such this analysis is somewhat limited. However, for a detailed account of the affects of victimization, see Spalek (2006).

feelings of stress, shock, and a sense of an invasion of privacy, along with feelings of heightened fear and vulnerability. In sum, there was a strong relationship between fear, perceived risk, and being a victim of crime, particularly amongst those who suffered repeat victimization:

I worry [about burglary] very much. I do worry very, very much. As I say I've already had it done to me and it was quite a shock when I came in and it was just, it was destructive, really destructive, when the policeman came I just cried into the boy's arms right because I really didn't have very much, I really didn't have very much. I'm afraid to go to bed. I'm on sleeping pills. It's the only thing that'll put me to sleep is sleeping pills and then they can become addictive as well but I can't do without them. D5 (female, over 50, white)

I'd just been attacked and my wallet had been taken and that contained lots of things with my address on it, including something that told people that I was diabetic, an insulin-dependent diabetic and I thought if they bothered reading that, they would know that I had syringes and insulin up here and they would also know where I stayed. D14 (male, under 30, white)

Well after the first [burglary] I felt fearful, the second time I felt fearful and angry they'd come again took the same things 'cause I'd replaced them. But yeah, [I felt worried] for a long time, I would think. I can't remember. I wouldn't have thought years but probably upwards of a year. It's horrible. H12 (female, over 50, white)

It is self-evident that crime does not impact on all members of society in the same way, and it is important to point out that a small, but significant, number of respondents who had suffered criminal victimization did not report amplified levels of fear. In fact the experience of victimization had served to dispel some of the myths and anxieties about what becoming a victim of crime might feel like. It is also worth noting that the following examples include both isolated and repeat victims.

I realize they're isolated incidents, I'm thirty, I go out quite a lot, in fact I go out more, I've had a few, and they're the only incidents in five years and some of them belong to other people, so it's not very regular, not very common, so I mean it's like, and I quickly forget about it, maybe the wee gap, in the days following you're maybe more aware, if someone else came up to you, you might be a bit, hang on what do you want, if someone asked you for a cigarette or something, but quickly gets back to normal. K112 (male, under 30, white)

LG: Did you worry about it before you got all this stuff in, like after the burglary did you worry about it?

G48 (female, over 50, white): No, no, I just thought it was a one-off thing, and that's that. I didn't dwell on it too much, what's done's done. I think the reason I'm not worried about it is because none of our burglaries have upset me particularly. I mean I'm sure if they had stolen something I couldn't replace or if they had vandalized the house, or done something that really did upset, I'm sure I'd be much more worried about burglaries in the future. But because that hasn't happened, I still feel 'Oh well if they're going to break in again we can't really do any more to improve the security of the house now'. It's something you've just got to live with. As insurance premiums go through the roof I'll maybe change my mind. But the insurance company are quite happy with our systems at the moment, so just need to hope nothing else happens. B146 (female, 30s–40s, white)

This section sought to demonstrate how knowledge and experience of crime is gathered and processed through the course of everyday life. Respondents described what they knew about local and national crime and how this information was exchanged through various sources. Respondents lamented the realization that crime had become a prominent feature of modern life. As such crime was identified as a high-profile cultural theme and condensed a variety of diffuse worries and insecurities. Indeed, emotive information about victims, high crime rates, and crime avoidance strategies had become an organizing principle of everyday life, which ultimately contributed to fear of crime. Moreover, a significant number of respondents explained how they believed it was their personal responsibility (not to say duty) to manage the ongoing threats of crime. In this respect, we understand how public concerns about crime have filtered into the public's consciousness, affecting their sense of security as well as their daily cognitive and behavioural processes—in pursuit of protection from crime risks and social ills. As Garland eloquently describes, when it comes to fear of crime 'our fears and resentments, but also our commonsense narratives and understandings, become settled cultural facts that are sustained and reproduced by cultural scripts' (2001: 10).

Experience and Expression in the Fear of Crime

Finally in this last section we explore in further detail the concepts of 'experiential' and 'expressive' fear, and their relationship to the model we specified above. Before we expand this analysis, it is worth reiterating that we believe the two concepts are part of a continuum of fear of crime, rather than independent manifestations of fear (see Chapter 3). In fact, it is likely that the two ends of the fear continuum—experience and expression—have a symbiotic relationship whereby the experience of crime, disorder, and/or victimization shapes the way in which we understand and relate to the local environment. Those who worry may be more likely to interpret their neighbourhood as disorderly and threatening, to see individuals and groups as unpredictable and untrustworthy, and to make links from ecological cues to crime.

Nevertheless, we believe it is not only possible, but empirically and theoretically pertinent, to explore in detail what 'experience' and 'expression' in the fear of crime constitutes and represents. In terms of the experiential features of fear, it is clear when asked whether they worry about crime, some participants tended to convey episodic experiences of fear—which were grounded in the specifics of time and place—such as tangible occasions when they feared their car had been stolen or they had temporarily misplaced a possession (see also Chapter 3). This we refer to as experiential fear. Meanwhile, expressive fear relates to a variety of mental processes—knowledge or perceptions of the characteristics of the neighbourhood and broader socio-cultural concerns which shape an individual's attitudes towards crime, order, and society.

We now wish to put some substantive flesh on the theoretical bones of this argument by exploring in detail the properties, influences, and characteristics of our participants' discussion of fear of crime. What do they worry about? Why do they worry? How do they assess their own worries? And how does crime operate as a way of making sense of one's environment and community?

Experiential fears

The following quotations provide typical examples of the experiential aspects of crime fears. Those anxieties which are aroused when one thinks the threat of crime may be looming large. Such worries accompany clear stimuli, such as a lost bag, footsteps behind you, or the sound of a broken window. What these respondents recall pertains to a specific episode, grounded in time and space:

I think it was two weeks ago, there was a noise from outside and it was just me and my Mum here so and it was quite a loud bang so I went

Experience and Expression in the Fear of Crime 151

outside, round the back with a baseball bat and a torch just in case, but there was nobody there. B157 (female, under 30, white)

I was rushing to get home, dashed out, and as I got to my car, just opening the lock, and I was just conscious of a movement behind me and I turned round and there was a man standing in a doorway, and I mean he gave me a terrible fright, it is a cul-de-sac, I had looked and the street had been empty. I had not seen him at all. There was really no reason that I could see for him being there at all. I won't park in there again. B159 (female, 30s–40s, white)

Just if I'm sitting here myself watching the telly or there's a commotion out in the street or something like that. You get the odd couple of guys running out at the end of the closes banging doors or something like that, playing pranks or fucking some daft thing like that. That's when I worry about it. D40 (male, 30s–40s, white)

Experiential fears are time- and place-specific, and respondents commented how after the 'moment' or 'episode' of fear, it began to drift and fade from their memories. To be clear, this is not to say the memory or the impact of it disappears, but at this point it is subject to retrospective recall (see also Chapter 3). When people discussed how they conceived of their experiences, many reported that the term *fear* was too prescriptive or emotionally loaded. Using their own descriptions participants explained that in the course of their everyday lives they experienced thoughts or feelings of 'concern', 'awareness', 'irritation', and 'anger', to name but a few. In short, the emotional pallet of our respondents was broad and demonstrates the diversity and complexity of emotional responses to crime.

I suppose it's a subconscious thing . . . I don't actually think am I going to be mugged today. I actually think 'oh, how I wear my handbag, where I put things'. So I'm not actually thinking 'am I being mugged?', I'm just thinking what is the safest thing to do. I think that's something that's so ingrained from the job that I did. L22 (female, over 50, white)

I mean you're just alert. D35 (female, 30s–40s, white)

It could be said that the quotations discussed above indicate a 'functional' style of worry (see Jackson and Gray, 2009). Certainly, in some instances worries about crime could be described as advantageous reactions which prompt sensible adaptations to one's environment. Indeed, a number of respondents indicated that crime was in some senses an ordinary aspect of modern daily life, and as such 'worry about crime' was not detrimental to their well-being, but rather an everyday risk management technique:

It would be silly of me to say, no, I don't worry about crime . . . but it's not something I worry about every single day. K103 (female, 30s–40s, white) If you didn't think then it would be a bit worrying because if you didn't think, if no-one thought, then we'd be in a pretty bad state, wouldn't we?" B142 (female, under 30, white)

While for some the experience of worrying about crime had been short lived, for others, especially those living in high crime areas, the regularity of fearful experiences left a more lasting (and harmful) impression. These respondents worried about crime and incivilities of various kinds. Such worries were frequently and intensely felt and were capable of taking a heavy toll on their quality of life. Moreover, the persistence of these experiences generated deeply felt insecurities which could sustain and reproduce negative judgements about one's environment and community. In this respect the experiential and expressive qualities of fear may, in some extreme cases, coincide:

The boy at the top's house got broken in to as well [as mine] and the boy next door, they're all kind of worried about it and I would say more so this time of year, I think everybody worries about it this time of year. I mean Christmas Eve I just don't even go to bed you know. You hear that many stories people get up in the morning, their kids' Christmas presents, that's actually happened to a friend of mine, she got up on Christmas morning and there was not a present under the tree for her kids cause they'd been through the night, so this time of year 'cause people know you've got kids, you're spending money, you're buying, whether its TVs whatever you're buying for them, toys even, even just their clothes. D34 (female, under 30, white)

It is worth noting, however, that high levels of crime and disorder had, for some individuals, become normalized. For example, some calculated that despite the high incidence of local crime, they were unlikely to be victimized as the crime patterns were specific (i.e. drug-related violence or car thefts) and did not pose an immediate risk for them personally. In other instances, however, it was apparent that participants had resigned themselves to living in a 'bad' area, realizing there was little chance anyone, including the police, could do anything to remedy the situation:

I'm getting used to it. I am used to it. I don't expect at times, sometimes you go in there's a fight with the drug addicts, it happens quite a lot, or else the police is chasing them. Down the arcade, it's getting like an everyday occurrence but we're getting used to it, not that we want to see it again, but we are getting used to it. At first, when it first happened we were all panicking and it was the talk of the place but now, it's I don't know. G89 (female, over 50, white)

You do become a little bit streetwise and therefore, I don't feel apprehensive, especially in this area. I might feel apprehensive in some areas but I still drive alone at night and all that sort of thing. I take precautions when I'm driving through certain areas, like locking the doors. Other than that, you know . . . obviously there must be things happening in this area but I never see it, you know. H8 (male, over 50, white)

In summary, we identified experiential fear as a response to direct external stimuli. In that sense we believe it part of a clear sequence of events and recallable as a distinct incident. The memory of the experience is bound in the details of time and place and the retrieval of this information can provide relatively accurate information about the affective experience. For some, such experiences are subtle and infrequent, for others, they are numerous and damaging—especially for those living in poorer areas with higher levels of crime and low levels of 'resilience'.

Expressive fears

As described above (Chapter 3), we believe the expressive qualities of fear of crime can be contrasted with the experiential aspects. We contend that expressive fear is less grounded in day-to-day life, less concerned with the specific details of time and place, and more akin to a set of attitudes or opinions which are brought forth when people are asked to discuss their feelings about crime (a process we have referred to as the invocation of attitude). As such, expressive knowledge may consist of beliefs, perceptions, or attitudes that one has concerning the cultural meaning of crime, social relations, and environmental cues. When respondents discuss expressive fear they may provide 'global' or generalized accounts of particular events or emotions. The following quotes seek to demonstrate what we identify as the 'expressive' nature of fear.

We have been concerned to demonstrate how people understand crime is, in part, related to the way in which they comprehend their physical and social environments—that their 'fear of crime' is grounded in their subjective assessments of 'place' and 'community'. The following quotations reveal how participants' reactions to crime are filtered through a range of latitudinous influences and subjective assessments. Participants indicate how areas in which they live produce signals which point towards both present and potential danger and feelings of despair and apathy.

I think to me it's about how you perceive things, your environment ... I wouldn't say it was all that I'd seen on telly, but the news etc. papers, you do get an interest in certain types of crime, you do get reporting in certain way in terms of say people preying on the elderly, so if you were elderly you might think people are out there to get me, and if you worry about that, and the more you worry about it the more the tension they pick up on it in the newspapers and you have a circle. K112 (male, under 30, white)

[This area] is a piss hole, no matter how much money they spend on tarting it up, it will make no difference ... I remember years ago, there wasn't many drugs over here. It was all like glue sniffing and stuff like that. And you only got walk around the corner now and you can ask someone for a bit of gear, they'll give you what you want. And I don't want my kids growing up in that sort of shit. The council ain't going to do nothing. All the money they spend, £5 million, £10 million, £20 million. H9 (female, over 50, white)

Not only are physical aspects of one's environment significant, but expressive worries about crime are also related to social relations, community bonds, and the informal social control afforded by those resources. In short, expressive fear contains assessments about the relationships local people have with each other and, also, wider society. The quotations below describe how participants perceive that there has been an erosion of social capital and experience a consequent sense of distrust and fear when considering their neighbours and society:

I think everyone needs to have a certain respect and for law, the police, for parents, for elder people. And I think that has disappeared. I don't think there's that same caring community spirit that there used to be. Crime seems to be a bit more horrendous, but I don't know if that's just because the media's changed as well. I'm sure a lot of all these things have always happened, the media's actually exposed to it a bit more. Families have become a little bit more dysfunctional just because I think women working more, you know, for a long time the traditional way, there was a solid base, and now that is not happening. I think there isn't that same ... a bus, an older person, you know, not everyone will [stand up], I'd always give my seat up for an old person, people don't do that any more. I just think it's respect for your environment, for people around you. It certainly has changed. H23 (female, 30s–40s, white)

Apathy, that's what they're suffering from: apathy. Society is suffering from apathy because people just keep themselves to themselves, they don't give a damn, they basically don't want to know. If you're in trouble, I mean, I've seen women getting beaten up and boys won't do anything and you've got to go in and stop it, who cares whether the woman's going to hate you for belting her husband you know what I mean, as long as he's no going to belt her any more. G61 (male, under 30, white)

Broader shifts in society were also identified by participants as influencing their emotional responses to crime. Some participants resented the imposition of responsibilization policies and the 'fortress mentality' that higher crime rates had necessitated. Others lamented the corrosive effects of poverty and inequality as contributing to social tensions as well as public sensibilities about crime and disorder:

I've got locks on my windows, I've got the place like a blooming fortress, you know? And I don't really see that one should have to live like that, I mean I'm vexed with society, for having to live like that. B139 (male, over 50, white)

If you read the papers regularly you're conscious of the fact that so many people are unemployed in this country, there are other people who are employed but have a very minimal living wage, there are so many who are classified as 'have not' and the chances are there are a big number within that category who will contemplate having a go at the house to see if it can relieve them, the chances increase as the economic situation of the country worsens and I think this might very well be a contributory factor, but certainly isn't understood by government, the so-called feel-good factor that they're determined to have everyone experience, there are so many people who just cannot experience the feel-good factor because they don't have anything to feel good about. B139 (male, over 50, white)

While crime and disorder represents a regrettable but commonplace aspect of social life, the public depend on the police and local and national government to protect them and uphold the law. When these agencies appear weak and powerless, however, and fail to prevent or inhibit crime, public anxieties can become amplified.[4] Indeed, many participants, particularly those from deprived and high crime areas, were of the opinion that the police

---

[4] Previous research has demonstrated that rather than reducing public anxieties, the actions of police and other agencies can increase it. Crawford et al. (2002) found that, for a number of reasons, when a local village purchased extra policing presence, residents reported fear of crime actually increased and resident satisfaction with the local police declined. See, too, some of the comments from respondents above.

and council were 'incompetent' and felt effectively 'abandoned' by them. Many people expressed anxieties about the behaviour of the police and local authorities; this was particularly true where the power and visibility of the police was a major concern. Finally, some participants believed these agencies were simply uninterested in their concerns about disorder and crime control, dismissing them as unimportant:

You're lucky if you see police about here, you know what I mean. Only time you see police here is when they've got a warrant to go up somebody's house, that's the only time ye see them. D41 (male, over 50, white)

We are always last to get our streets cleaned, or so we perceive. It may not actually be fact, but we perceive we are always the last. Anything we want done . . . if you approach the council direct you're met with a slightly stony response when you say where you live. And certainly things like CCTV cameras, for example, which this end of the borough thought of first, but we found that the council had applied for cameras for the other end of the borough. I'm not saying they were right or wrong, I am just saying that we weren't altogether surprised that one end of the borough came off better than the other. H16 (female, over 50, white)

The accounts we have documented thus far suggest that 'disappearing' and deficient police and council services offend participants' sense of security and safety and jar with the long-established expectations people had of these agencies. Not only does this undermine participants' sense of attachment they feel towards the police and government, but it leaves in its wake a resulting climate of concern about their future security. Many respondents described future-orientated assessments about the ever-changing nature of society and the loss of familiar and reassuring social behaviours:

I don't know, I don't think I would have been so aware of always locking doors in cars. I don't know that I would always put my handbag out of sight. I mean 10-12 years ago would I have done that? I don't know. Certainly wouldn't have done it when I was growing up. I certainly wouldn't even lock the front door of the house when I was growing up. Just the way of the world. You just have to be conscious of it and do something about it. H22 (female, over 50, white)

Indeed, considerable disquiet was expressed about the future prosperity of society and the potential for crime, disorder, and poor social control to transform life beyond recognition. People voiced particular concerns about the condition and fate of their own community:

I remember one time I was waiting to go in the lift, and I saw this young girl with a baby in a pram, and you could actually see her bending right down, that was her getting a fix, I don't know who, but she did . . . I actually said to her, 'Are you OK?' She couldn't keep her eyes open. It was the wee baby in the pram I was worried about. And then she sort of straightened up and went into the lift, but that was a common thing, you saw that an awful lot. That's what I'm saying. We brought our children up there and that's why a lot of them wanted to leave. G89 (female, over 50, white)

The poor seems to be getting poorer now and you know, old age pensioners and that, they just seem to be getting poorer and poorer. And I don't think, well I don't know. Because of the amount of people we've got coming into the country, you know, and they've stopped building, the country's no longer big enough to keep bringing people in you know. It's going to get, well it's overcrowded now. So where are all these people going to go? We're going to start getting sort of ghettos, you know . . . That I think is what's happening in the inner cities, you know. I think all these estates are becoming kind of ghettos. H18 (female, 30s–40s, white)

Discussion

We have attempted to demonstrate that when we measure public responses to crime and 'fear of crime', we are implicitly including participants' evaluations about the cultural meaning of crime, place, and community. Unravelling this is by no means a simple task. Academics have long argued that fear of crime is a composite and congested concept (e.g. Girling et al., 2000). Certainly, public concerns and perceptions seem more complicated than current research methods disclose. We have sought to demonstrate that fear of crime can express social, psychological, political, and geographic dimensions. Interestingly, some participants recognized the complex nature of crime-related worries; they explained how fear of crime is often a mix of personal and contextual influences—a matter of subconscious reasoning which is often difficult for participants to articulate in a research context:

One of the things [for researchers] would be getting people to actually define what fear is for them. Fear to me is something you worry about, are actually afraid of. Whereas, concern is a thing that happens occasionally but you're not going to be bothered about, no emotion. And probably to get fear, I think you would have to have the stimulus more often. B162 (male, over 50, white)

Again I think fear is a fairly difficult emotion to define, I mean I may be a bit concerned about having my home burgled and having my car stolen and being mugged but then I suppose most women are. I don't know if I would use the word 'fear' but I'm, it's just a consciousness, yeah. Some other form of attack, other than mugging, well, it's such a low possibility that it's not something I go around worrying about. Yes, you could be raped but it's fairly unlikely. It is a high-profile crime but it doesn't actually happen all that often. And I really don't walk around worrying about that. H22 (female, over 50, white)

We have been concerned to discover the role that crime, place, and community play within participants' beliefs and perceptions of crime fears. Our aim has been to explore respondents' reactions to crime and order, and in so doing contribute to a grounded account of everyday worries about crime. As such, we have taken time to document and make sense of the ways in which people talk about and relate to crime and how this naturally connects with their interpretations of their environment, community, as well as wider society.

First, we explored the extent to which physical neighbourhood 'cues', such as visible signs of decay, poor urban planning, and vandalism, were related to participants' fears about crime. This relationship was particularly apparent where negative effects were seen to be getting progressively worse. A number of studies have previously associated urban environmental 'cues' with the fear of crime (see Hunter, 1978; Lewis and Maxfield, 1980; Jones et al., 1986; Bannister, 1993; Maxfield, 1987; Pain, 1993; Hassinger, 1985). However, this relationship was not straightforward, and it was clear from this study that physical cues were subjectively assessed. Indeed, the same 'cue' could be seen in two different areas as being indicative of two different potential crime risks (Sampson and Raudenbush, 2004; Jackson, 2004a). As such, it is how people interpret and perceive crime and all the various ingredients which are associated with the threat of crime that is crucial.

Respondents from 'over-populated' estates or declining areas were able to describe positive features of their physical environment; many made efforts to maintain the aesthetics and safety of their area. Nevertheless, where local deterioration had not been forestalled by general maintenance or regeneration, residents felt 'abandoned' to suffer the effects of decay and neglect. Moreover, because participants were also more likely to associate these cues with a loss of social cohesion and informal control, it was clear the physical effects of decline and disorder had a significant influence over public sensibilities towards crime. As Smith notes (1986: 128), the answer to why the fear of crime is '. . . in some places debilitating, whilst at others it represents simply a healthy awareness of the risks of victimization' is to be found in '. . . the character of the urban environment (built and social) within which fear is experienced'.

Not only were physical cues prominent, but social 'signals' of decline and change also posed a powerful influence over participants' crime fears. The imposition of transient or atomized populations, disorderly behaviour, and the emergence of 'problem' groups or individuals were seen as conveying uncertain or ambiguous information about the environment. As such, insecure social relationships often acted as indicators about the decreasing levels of informal social control within communities. Indeed, the insecurity that was generated by crime and change was shown to have a potent influence over the fabric of social life. Nevertheless, respondents from a variety of backgrounds were able to exhibit 'resilience' in the face of crime problems. In particular, levels of community cohesion and informal social control provided protection in the face of crime and disorder. Jacobs (1961: 31–2) similarly articulates how significant social relations are: 'The public peace . . . is not kept primarily by the police, necessary as the police are. It is kept primarily by the intricate, almost unconscious, network of voluntary controls and standards among the people themselves and [is] enforced by the people themselves'. Thus feelings of security are gained from both formal provisions and informal control. As such, if control is seen to have been exercised, a sense of security is engendered. If control is *not* seen to have been exercised, a sense of *insecurity* is engendered. This model helps us to explain the relationship between the microenvironment and the fear of crime in two ways. First, directly, as signs of crime can indicate real risk of crime. Second, indirectly, as the fear of crime is not solely provoked by the features of the urban environment (i.e. the 'cues') in themselves, rather they are symbolic of the capacity of the community to exercise informal social control. As such the fear of crime can *express* psychic, social, and political anxieties.

Knowledge and experience of crime was seen to play a key role in the respondents' consciousness and many were keenly engaged with these topics through a narrative of fear. Participants described what they knew about local and national crime and how this (often emotive) information was exchanged through local 'stories', journalism, and television dramas. As Garland and Sparks have noted, emotional and detailed information about victims, high crime rates, and consumption of security products have become a prominent feature of everyday life. This has lead, they stress, to the creation of a 'crime complex' which produces a high level of 'crime consciousness' among the populace which: 'produces a series of psychological and social effects that exert an influence upon politics and policy . . . Citizens become crime conscious, attuned to the crime problem and many exhibit high levels of fear and anxiety (2000: 199).

The visible presence of crime was particularly important in relation to participants' 'crime consciousness', as it was experienced firsthand by the majority of the population who occupied those areas. As Bannister notes: 'it is clear that the urban landscape provides signals, directly and indirectly, which are interpreted as indicating the presence of a criminal threat' (1993: 73). Many respondents believed that crime had become a defining and prominent feature of modern life and ultimately concluded they were duty-bound to manage the ongoing threats of crime themselves. Being vigilant and taking steps to secure and defend their own property was essential, not only because informal social control was perceived to have dissipated, but because the police and the local council were often seen as unable to quell the increasing threat of crime. Respondents in both London and Glasgow were of the opinion that the police and council were often indifferent or unresponsive to community crime concerns. Such a refusal to take public fears seriously amplified local anxieties about the community being left vulnerable to other, potentially more serious threats. As such, public concerns about crime had a 'long reach' and articulated worries about their social, psychological, and ontological safety. As Elias (1982: 327) notes, 'the strength, kind and structures of the fears and anxieties that smoulder or flare in the individual never depend solely on his own "nature"'. Rather they are 'always determined, finally by the history and the actual structure of his relations to other people'.

As we indicated at the outset of this book, we believe there is intellectual value in a detailed exploration of the various aspects of fear of crime and that it is possible to identify both experiential and expressive components of fear. Experiential fear was characterized as a response to direct external stimuli—in a particular place at a particular time. It can be a frequent and even subtle experience, brought forward when one wonders about the safety of the house whist away or whether somebody is watching us enter a pin number at a cash desk. The typical experience of this type of fear is a momentary emotional arousal. It is heavily dependent on time and place and subject to the ebb and flow of conscious awareness (Csikszentmihalyi, 1990). These experiences can be recalled as distinct incidents with relatively accurate information. However, it is important to note that one's ability to recall experiential fear declines quickly with the passage of time (Tulving, 1984). Therefore, any delay between a particular emotional episode and its reporting will result in the loss of certain details of that experience (Rubin and Wetzel, 1996).

Meanwhile, the social and cultural meaning of crime was communicated by expressive fear. Expressive fear is located in individuals' understanding of the social and physical composition of their environment, as well as their sense of vulnerability and wider social values. Individuals' attitudes shaped the social meaning of disorder and its links to community features. Participants were also more likely to link physical cues to problems of social cohesion and declining quality bonds. Indeed, when social encounters appeared unpredictable or hostile in the neighbourhood, individuals felt their security and space was threatened. Within communities social cues were interpreted differently due to how much an individual felt part of that community. Between areas, micro features were interpreted differently according to the crime threat that may be present in that area. In summary, we believe that expressive fear reflects more than the experience of a crime-fearing episode, but reaches out further to incorporate social, political, and economic anxieties. Indeed, we find within the conversations among city-dwelling people in Britain, an assortment of ways of comprehending and processing issues to do with crime, each of which can be interpreted as 'projecting' assessments of the environment and society. In Chapter 6 we commence our quantitative exploration of these issues.

6

Types and Intensities of Fear

'There have been several efforts to clarify the meaning of the concept of 'fear of crime'. Most found it troublesome that there is no clear consensus among researchers on what the concept of fear of crime means or how it is best measured. [I] argue that this apparent heterogeneity of meaning simply reflects the fact that the fear of crime is a general concept. It is suited for everyday conversation (Americans talk frequently about fear of crime and its social and political effects), but the concept needs to be refined for research purposes. How it is best defined depends upon the purposes of research and the theoretical framework within which the research is being conducted. Therefore, any specific definition of the fear of crime is not correct or incorrect; rather it is either useful or not useful, and that is revealed by the results of the research.' (Wesley Skogan, 'The Various Meanings of Fear', in Bilsky, W. et al. (Eds), *Fear of Crime and Criminal Victimization*, 1993)

In Chapter 3 we injected into the debate about fear of crime the idea that this 'thing' we call the 'fear of crime' may not, in fact, be *one* 'thing'. That is, when one sits down with respondents and invites them to talk about what they understand by the term 'to be fearful of crime' one finds a rich and nuanced set of experiences. Hitherto, quantitative criminologists have shuffled rather comfortably in their seats, glanced nervously at their feet, and muttered sentiments about measurement error and a broad understanding of what the questions mean. Some have tried (at some level) to disown the substantial qualitatively-based data which suggests that we ought to be approaching the topic at hand in a rather different manner. In this chapter we take up this challenge and, through the use of the British Crime Survey, start to explore what this style of approach to the fear of crime does to our understanding of it, and what it, in turn, does to the sorts of issues which have come to coalesce around this 'magnet' of understanding and thought.

To these ends, then, we embark on the first of two chapters which return to the quantification of fear—however, we do so with qualitative thinking on this topic uppermost in our minds. To some extent—and perhaps inevitably given what we have said directly above and in previous chapters—our interest is as much methodological as it is substantive. In Chapter 3 we focused on what we called two 'streams' of fear: one which was driven by assessments of immediate threat (and which we described as capturing an 'experiential' dimension), and a second which we referred to as the 'expressive' dimension and which tapped into a more diffuse anxiety about risk of crime (the sense that crime must be something to be guarded against) as well as those diffuse sets of feelings which the likes of Girling et al. (2000) and Taylor and Jamieson (1998) had first elucidated. These we measure in the following ways:

- The first is captured by the frequency measures designed by Farrall (2004a and b; Farrall and Gadd, 2004; see also Jackson, 2005) and worded along lines similar to the following: 'In the past year, how often have you worried about being robbed?' Answers to these questions reflect the recall of respondents of concrete episodes when they felt under threat.
- The second stream is captured by a combination of respondent answers to old and new questions. By old questions we mean questions worded along the lines of: 'How worried are you about becoming a victim of robbery?' When individuals say they are worried on this measure, but cannot recall any such incidents in the past year (i.e. using the new measure), 'fear' seems to be a more diffused sense of anxiety rather than a pattern of concrete episodes (everyday worry)—see Hough (2004) and Farrall (2004a and b) for discussions on these issues. Such anxiety has, of course, a basis in the everyday; we are not suggesting for one moment that it has no meaning in people's lives. Rather, since such 'fear of crime' does not 'spike' in concrete moments of threat and danger—people may be successfully avoiding troubling situations, and have the resources to feel safe in most settings—we wonder whether 'fear' in such instances is not best viewed as an intangible awareness of risk and a generalized social attitude, expressing broader concerns about the health of group life.

In this way (and of course in many other ways) methodology shapes our research questions, operationalizes our concepts, and influences our findings. This chapter presents the headline findings from the old and new measures. But it also demonstrates how responses can be combined to form our new definition that differentiates between these two 'streams' of fear: 'anxiety about crime' and the 'everyday worry about crime'. This new definition not only highlights in more detail the actual lived experience of fear of crime, but, as we shall see, it also has a set of rather important empirical implications. Compared to the 'worried', the 'anxious' report that crime has a lesser impact on quality of life than the 'worried'. In terms of the socio-demographic and victim status correlates of 'anxiety' and 'everyday worry' are different: the worried tend to live in higher crime areas, have greater personal (direct and indirect) victimization experience, and view their neighbourhood as being more disorderly, less cohesive, and as posing a greater victimization risk. Lower levels of confidence in criminal justice are associated with being 'worried about crime' but not with being 'anxious about crime'. However, we are getting slightly ahead of ourselves. Let us begin by outlining the wording of the old and new measures.

Outlining Measures of the Fear of Crime

Large-scale representative sample surveys—in many industrialized countries—ask respondents questions along the following lines:

How worried are you about being [burgled/robbed/raped]?

Respondents select one answer from a set of response options, and a standard set would be: very worried, fairly worried, a bit worried, or not at all worried. At first glance this research strategy seems unproblematic. Surveys ask for a brief summary of respondents' worries which respondents are presumably able to provide. Researchers then estimate the distribution in a given population to produce an estimate of the everyday experience of worry among the general populace. One assumes such worry negatively affects individuals and disrupts communities.

Yet greater attention to detail may clarify the nature and impact of fear of crime in people's everyday lives (Farrall et al., 1997). For example, how often do people worry, feel fearful or anxious? The answer could be less often than we think: 'old' standard measures may imply a greater prevalence of fear than specific measures of frequency commonly find (Farrall, 2004a; Farrall and Gadd, 2004). Surveys rarely, if ever, ask how *frequently* people worry, only how worried they are overall (although see Farrall and Gadd, 2004; Jackson, 2004a and 2005). Moreover, which thoughts, feelings, and behaviour best characterize public responses? Anger may be more frequent than fear (Ditton et al., 1999), uneasiness more common than corrosive fear. Yet survey measures only specify 'worry'.

More questions arise. How can we compare the answers of different people if respondents interpret the meaning of 'worry' differently? Some may think of 'physical fear', others of 'a passing moment of anxiety' (cf. Hough, 1995). In addition, how do these emotions shape behaviour and well-being? Surveys rarely enquire into the impact of worry on people's everyday lives, so we simply do not know. And might some level of emotion be a naturally occurring response to crime rather than a pressing social problem in its own right? Why do we always assume worry is negative (Fattah, 1993; Hale, 1996; Warr, 2000; Ditton and Innes, 2005)?

Gladstone and Parker (2003: 347) argue that: 'As a phenomenon, [worry] can range from an innocuous activity possibly associated with positive consequences (i.e. solution finding), through to a distressing and uncontrollable process like the excessive and chronic worry recognised as the cardinal feature of generalised anxiety disorder. It has been defined broadly as repetitive thought activity, which is usually negative and frequently related to feared future outcomes or events'. Intriguingly for fear of crime research, this definition suggests that what might be called *dysfunctional* or *damaging* worry is characterized by the frequency of these experiences. As such, asking people about the regularity of crime fears is both methodologically and empirically meaningful.

Gladstone and Parker go on to suggest that worry has a number of distinctive factors. First, it is predominantly comprized of cognitions (thoughts), often involving a series of future-orientated reflections, involving the embellishment of hypothetical outcomes. Second, it has a 'dynamic (and malleable) and narrative process in which themes are developed and elaborated rather than simply occurring as a string of negative thoughts' (2003: 347). Finally, worry involves awareness of or attention to possible danger, 'which is rehearsed without successful resolution...[and]

usually [self-] described as difficult to dismiss' (2003: 347). Tallis et al. (1994) investigated the everyday experience of normal (i.e. non-pathological) worry. They found that most of the individuals interviewed viewed their worries to be routine, mostly acceptable, with a narrative course and real-life triggers, focusing on realistic, rather than remote problems, which were often beneficial by stimulating activity. Worry was often seen as a problem-solving activity, but Matthews (1990) believes that it is more of a 'mimicry' of problem-solving activity since worry involves the rehearsal of fearful scenarios and the amplification of worse-case scenarios: people who worry also engage in more catastrophic thinking (Davey and Levy, 1998; Vasey and Borkovec, 1992). In Tallis et al.'s (1994) study, negative consequences were noted amongst 'high worriers', including greater frequency, more mood disturbance, a difficulty to stop worrying, and more perceived impairment in everyday functioning.

Of course, and recalling Chapter 3, the experience of some emotions is akin to events or brief episodes which can be located in space and time. In this we include many people's fears about crime. In order to assess the extent of everyday experience of the fear of crime, the new questions explicitly focus on episodes of fear. The old questions ask about a more *general* model of experience ('How worried are you ...'), but it is unclear whether faced with the old questions respondents summarize the frequency with which they worry; whether they assess the intensity of each event and calculate some kind of average; whether the process involves assessing both intensity and frequency; or whether such an overall intensity fuses the everyday experience with other facets of 'fear of crime' (see Hough, 2004; Jackson, 2004a; Farrall et al., 2006; Jackson, 2006; and Chapter 3 above).

Initially piloted as part of an earlier ESRC-funded project (Farrall, 2003), the question set included in the 2003/2004 BCS, attempts to describe the *frequency* and intensity of people's worries. Specifically, the new questions contain a filter question, measure frequency and intensity of fearful episodes, and employ a narrow time frame of 12 months to allow respondents a specific reference period which we believe they will be able to recall more accurately (see also Farrall and Ditton, 1999). The measurement strategy outlined here focuses on *events* of worry; while it explores the intensity of the last fearful event, it does not elicit an overall intensity summary of worry (Farrall and Gadd, 2004):

Q1: 'During the past 12 months, that is since [date], have you ever felt worried about...?' (having your car stolen/having your home broken into and something stolen/being mugged or robbed).

Q2: [if YES at Q1] 'How many times have you felt like this in the past 12 months?' [n times recorded]

Q3: [if YES at Q1] 'And on the last occasion you felt worried about [offence], how worried did you feel?' [not very worried, a little bit worried, quite worried, very worried, or cannot remember].

Questions one and two above focus on the frequency of crime worries, allowing an estimation of the frequency with which people fear crime that is arguably more precise. Specifically, individuals can be classified according to whether they worry and, if they do, how often. Of course, it is an empirical question as to whether this strategy produces different results to standard measures. But as mentioned above, there is early evidence that this might be the case (Farrall et al., 1997; Farrall and Gadd, 2004; Jackson et al., 2006). We shall develop these insights presently.

After the two frequency questions comes one item on the intensity of the last event of worry, and this provides a different type of population estimate. Instead of sampling *individuals* and the number of times each individual worries, this question samples *events*. Consider in any one day that a number of people have worried about crime: a number of events of worry occurred; each event had a level of intensity (as well, of course, as a given context and a set of antecedents and consequents). The new questions, posed in the BCS, ask respondents to think back to the last time they felt worried and to report how intense that episode was.[1] By employing inferential statistics to infer to the population of England and Wales, we can thus produce at the aggregate an estimate of the intensity of all of the individual events of fear that occurred during the past 12 months of individuals throughout England and Wales.

[1] Because of the way memory works, and because of the likely impact of the availability heuristic, we expect respondents to be biased towards the most vivid and easily accessed recent event (Tversky and Kahneman, 1973). The 'most recent event' will thus more likely be the most intense episode that occurred relatively recently rather than previously the most recent (Clore and Robinson, 2002a, 2002b). This is because more emotional episodes are easier to remember than less emotional episodes. As such we expect our estimates to err on the side of exaggeration of the intensity of events of worry.

Basic Frequencies

The following analysis is organized along three different types of crime: being robbed; being burgled; and having one's car stolen. Top-line frequencies are first provided from the 'old' standard measures of worry ('How worried are you about being... [each type of crime]?') and then, second, from the new questions.[2]

Worry about robbery

Table 6.1 shows results according to the old, 'standard' measures of worry.[3] In the 2003/2004 sweep just over one third of respondents reported being worried about being robbed (combining 11 per cent 'very' and 24 per cent 'fairly'). Just under one half were 'not very' worried (45 per cent), leaving one fifth who were 'not at all' worried (20 per cent) about robbery. (Tables may not sum to 100 per cent due to rounding.)

The new questions, asked later in the interview, posed the question slightly differently. When asked: 'In the past 12 months, have you actually worried about being robbed?', only 15 per cent of respondents reported having worried (Table 6.2). Those who said that they had recently worried were then asked how often. Remarkably, just over one third of those who had worried over the past year had only worried between one and three times during that period, with a further one quarter worrying between four and eleven times.

Overall, then, and taking the filter and frequency questions together, 85 per cent of respondents said that they had *not* worried about being robbed in the past year, and only 5 per cent of all respondents had worried once a month or more. This is to be contrasted with the one third who said they were 'fairly' or 'very' worried about being robbed when asked the old standard worry question (Table 6.1).

---

[2] Although both styles of questions were given to respondents in the same sitting, they were asked in separate sections of the questionnaire and they were not asked immediately following each other. The structure and routing of the BCS makes it hard to assess exactly how many questions there were between the old and new batteries, but we estimate this to be between 35 and 96.

[3] Table 6.10 in the Appendix to this chapter graphs the raw frequencies for burglary.

Types and Intensities of Fear

Table 6.1 Standard measure of worry about robbery

Overall intensity of worry	%
Very worried	11
Fairly worried	24
Not very worried	45
Not at all	20
Don't know	0
Total	100

Source: 2003/2004 British Crime Survey, weighted data, entire sample used

Those who reported having worried recently were also asked to think back to the last time and report how worried they had felt. Table 6.3 shows that the vast majority of events were either 'a little bit' (43 per cent) or 'quite' (40 per cent) worried. However, once we include those respondents who had not worried during the previous year, we find that only 8 per cent of all respondents had reported feeling 'quite' or 'very' worried most recently.

Worry about burglary and car crime

In the name of brevity, we direct the reader to another source (Gray et al., 2008) for the same headline findings of the old and new measures of worry about burglary and car crime—which

Table 6.2 New measures of fear of robbery—frequency in the past year?

Filter question	%	Frequency question (raw scores categorized)	% of those who worried	% of all respondents
Not worried in the past year	85	0		85
Has worried in the past year	15	1–3 times	35	5
		4–11 times	25	4
		12–52 times	24	4
		53+ times	9	1
		Don't know	7	1
Total	100		100	100

Source: 2003/2004 British Crime Survey, weighted data, sub-sample Follow-up D

Basic Frequencies 171

Table 6.3 New measures of fear of robbery—how fearful on last occasion?

Intensity of most recent event of worry	% of those who worried	% of all respondents
Not worried		85
Not very worried	4	1
A little bit worried	43	6
Quite worried	40	6
Very worried	13	2
Don't know	0	0
Total	100	100

Source: 2003/2004 British Crime Survey, weighted data, sub-sample follow-up D

mirror those for robbery discussed above. (The eagle-eyed can also find key baseline percentages in Table 6.4 below). But to summarize, Figure 6.1 provides results from the old measures. Overall, 35 per cent of respondents reported being worried (summing 'fairly' and 'very') about being robbed, 47 per cent reported being worried about being burgled, and 45 per cent reported being worried about having their car stolen.

As with robbery, the picture is different when one draws upon data from the frequency of worry about burglary and car theft

Figure 6.1 Worry about robbery, burglary, and car crime (standard measures)

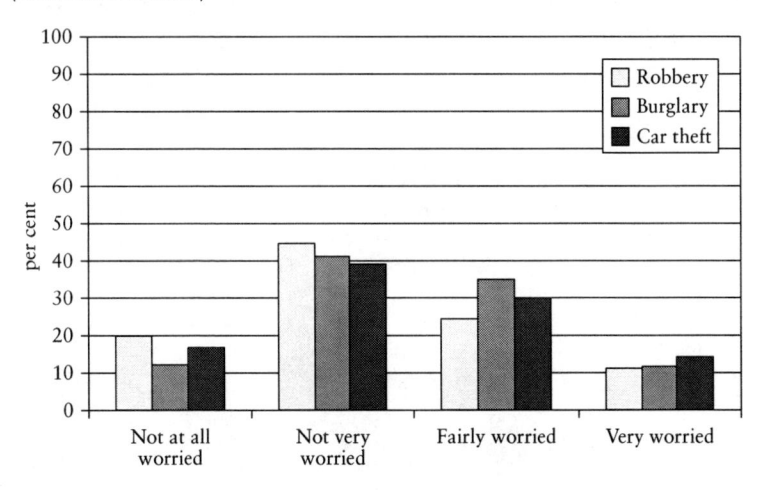

Table 6.4 Cross-tabulation of the old and new measures (raw percentages)

How worried are you …?	In the past year, have you ever actually felt worried about…? If yes, how many times…?							The last time you worried, how worried were you…?				
	Not worried in the past 12 months	1 to 3	4 to 11	12 to 52	53+	Total		Not very worried	A bit worried	Quite worried	Very worried	Total
Robbery												
Very worried (base 10%)	63	9	11	11	7	100		0	34	38	28	100
Fairly worried (base 25%)	71	10	7	8	2	100		2	44	45	9	100
Not very worried (base 45%)	92	4	2	1	1	100		9	53	32	6	100
Not worried (base 20%)	98	1	1	1	0	100		14	48	36	2	100
Full sample base %	*85*	*5*	*4*	*4*	*2*	*100*		*4*	*44*	*39*	*13*	*100*
Burglary												
Very worried (base 12%)	39	13	14	19	14	100		3	30	44	23	100
Fairly worried (base 35%)	53	18	12	13	5	100		6	54	35	6	100
Not very worried (base 41%)	84	9	4	2	1	100		14	64	16	7	100

Not worried (base 12%)	95	3	1	1	1	100	36	68	14	1	100
Full sample base %	*69*	*12*	*7*	*8*	*4*	*100*	*7*	*51*	*32*	*10*	*100*
Car crime										
Very worried (base 11%)	33	14	14	23	16	100	2	37	44	20	100
Fairly worried (base 24%)	51	15	14	14	5	100	7	55	33	5	100
Not very worried (base 30%)	83	8	6	3	1	100	12	63	22	3	100
Not worried (base 13%)	97	1	1	1	1	100	18	57	23	2	100
Full sample base %	*69*	*10*	*9*	*8*	*4*	*100*	*7*	*50*	*34*	*9*	*100*

measures. Sixty-eight per cent had not actually worried about being burgled or having their car stolen. Moreover, of those who had worried, the frequency of these events was surprisingly low—very few people had worried more than once a week during the previous year (Figure 6.2).

Additionally the new questions sampled events of worry, so by asking respondents who had worried recently to think back to the last time and report how worried they felt, the BCS samples *events* rather than *individuals*. We can therefore infer the intensity of individual events of worry about robbery, burglary, and car theft across England and Wales. Figure 6.3 shows that the vast majority of such events involved the individual feeling 'a little bit' or 'quite' worried.

A More Direct Comparison of the Old and New Measures

Thus far, our analysis has shown that when asked standard questions, a relatively large proportion of BCS respondents reported being worried about being robbed (around one third), being burgled (just under one half), and having their car stolen (just under one half of car owners). However, when fielded new questions about the frequency of worry, a smaller proportion had worried once or more during the previous 12 months (robbery 15 per cent, burglary 31 per cent, and car crime 31 per cent; see the relevant

Figure 6.2 Worry about robbery, burglary, and car crime in the past 12 months using new frequency measures

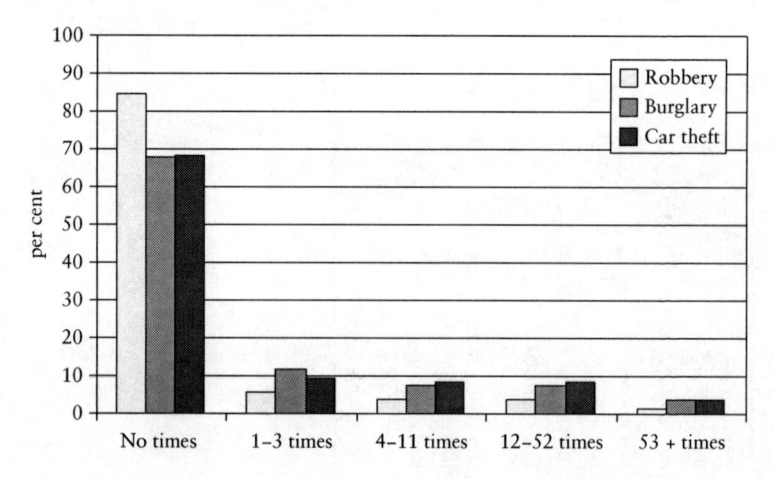

A More Direct Comparison of the Old and New Measures 175

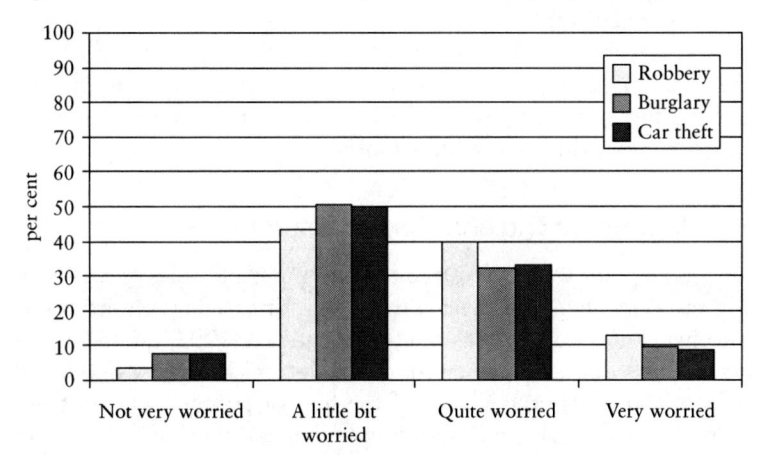

Figure 6.3 Worry about crime using new event-sampling measures

full sample base per cent in Table 6.4); and an even smaller proportion had worried more than once a month (robbery 6 per cent, burglary 12 per cent, and car crime 12 per cent; again see the relevant full sample base per cent in Table 6.4).

In short, the data showed that surprising proportions of people who say they worry about crime also admit that they have *not* actually worried recently; worry seemed to be a relatively infrequent occurrence among the sample. Yet people still reported some level of worry even when they could not recall a single time—in the past 12 months—in which they had actually worried.

To provide a clearer picture of the relationship between old and new estimates of the fear of crime, Table 6.4 cross-tabulates the old (intensity) estimates with frequency and the intensity of the last event. As regards robbery, 63 per cent of those people who earlier in the survey had reported being 'very worried' about being robbed, had not actually worried in the past 12 months (see the shaded cell top left-hand side); 71 per cent of those people who were 'fairly worried' reported the same (the darker cell below that described above). A similar albeit less powerful pattern was apparent in relation to burglary and car theft: 39 per cent and 33 per cent respectively reported they were 'very worried' about being victimized but had not actually worried once recently (see the two 'boxed' cells directly below those already discussed). Turning to the new intensity measures (as they relate to robbery), we see that just under one quarter of those who said they were 'very worried' reported that they felt 'very worried' on the previous occasion (28 per cent—the 'boxed' cell in the top right-hand side). The vast majority of respondents who had been classified by the old measure as 'very' or 'fairly' worried reported that, on the last occasion, they felt 'a bit' or 'quite'.

Combining the Old and New Measures

Until this point we have treated the two differing styles of questioning respondents about their fears about crime separately from one another. But let us reflect on Skogan's advice (1993) quoted at the start of this chapter. How do the questions which we have developed help to illuminate the nature of the fear of crime? How do these help us to refine our understanding of the fear of crime? In order to produce a more sensitive approach to the fear of crime, we combine the above two measures. These two measure we combine in such a manner to differentiate between those who (a) worry on an everyday basis (the 'worried') and those who (b) say that they are worried but do not actually worry during their daily lives (the 'anxious').

- For the 'worried' group, fear of crime appears to manifest itself in some people's lives as concrete events—as the piloting of the frequency questions indicates, people *are* able to recall particular episodes of worry (Farrall, 2003). What the new frequency measures are doing, therefore, is counting 'spikes' of fear. Imagine (for an individual) a 'steady state' of fear that bumps along at something approaching 'not very fearful'. The frequency questions may therefore count sharp increases in fear levels which stand out from the norm—these are fear 'spikes'.
- By contrast, in some people's lives the fear of crime appears to be something more diffuse, more akin to 'anxiety' (Hough, 2004), a representation/image of risk (Jackson, 2006), and an 'invocation of attitude' (Farrall et al., 2006).

In order to differentiate between these two 'streams of fear', we produced a composite variable for each set of questions relating to robbery, burglary, and car crime. This produced the following groups of respondents:

- The 'unworried': respondents who indicated (a) that they were 'not at all' or 'not very' worried, and (b) that they had not worried at all during the past year;

Combining the Old and New Measures   177

- The 'anxious': respondents who indicated (a) that they were 'fairly' or 'very' worried, but (b) that they had not worried at all during the past year;
- The 'worried': respondents who indicated that they had worried between once and 51 times over the past year (their other responses were not taken into consideration in assigning them to this group); and,
- The 'frequently worried': respondents who indicated that they had worried at least 52 times (about once a week) over the past year (again, their responses to the other question were not taken into consideration).

Table 6.5 provides a diagrammatic summary of the grouping of responses into our fourfold classification.

Applying this schema, Table 6.6 shows that just under two thirds of respondents were 'unworried' about robbery, whilst one third were either 'anxious' (23 per cent), 'worried' (13 per cent), or 'frequently worried' (2 per cent). Compared to robbery, more individuals reported some level of fear about burglary or car crime, but in these cases more individuals were 'worried' or 'frequently worried' (31 per cent for burglary and 27 per cent for car crime) rather than 'anxious' (23 per cent for burglary and 16 per cent for car crime).

In order to combine the three crime types, latent class analysis using (full information maximum likelihood estimation in LatentGold 4.0) was conducted. Respondents were assigned to their modal category, indicating whether they were 'unworried', 'anxious', 'worried', or 'frequently worried' with reference to all

Table 6.5 The coding of the answers

		Worried in the past year... (new questions)		
		Not worried	Worried 1-51 times in the past year	Worried >52 in the past year
Old questions	Very	The Anxious	The Worried	The Frequently Worried
	Quite			
	Not very	The Unworried		
	Not at all			

178 Types and Intensities of Fear

Table 6.6 Frequency of the four groups by offence type

	Unworried	Anxious	Worried	Frequently worried	Total
Robbery	62	23	13	2	100
Burglary	46	23	27	4	100
Car crime	58	16	23	3	100

Cells are row %. Individual weights are used

Table 6.7 Frequency of the four groups

Unworried	Anxious	Worried	Frequently worried	Total
54	21	21	4	100

Cells are row %. Individual weights are used

three crimes.[4] Table 6.7 shows that the majority of respondents fell into the 'unworried' group (that is, they were 'not at all worried' or 'not very worried' on the old measures and also report that they had not worried in the past year either). Twenty-one per cent, on the other hand, were anxious. Individuals in this group would typically have said that they were 'very' or 'fairly' worried on the old question, but, seemingly in contradiction to this, had also implied that they had not worried in the past year. The worried (who had worried during the past year) also formed 21 per cent of this sample, whilst the frequently worried formed a mere 4 per cent.

Implications of the New Measure of 'Fear of Crime'

Table 6.8 reports the impact of crime on respondents' quality of life for our four groups, again for each of the three crimes. The 'worried' group typically reported a greater impact on their quality of life than either the 'anxious' or 'unworried' groups, especially with regards to robbery. For example, 11 per cent of the 'worried' about robbery group reported that crime had had a great impact on their quality of life, compared to two

---

[4] Cross-tabulation of the combined measure and the individual measures for each crime category shows that the combination overlaps with each crime category to an extremely strong degree.

per cent of the 'unworried' group and 8 per cent of the 'anxious' (compare the shaded cells in Table 6.8).[5] However, the frequently worried report even higher levels—33 per cent of this group said that crime had a great impact on the quality of their life. Whilst successively fewer of the unworried report greater impact of crime on their quality of life (75 per cent–23 per cent and 2 per cent) the reverse is true for the frequently worried, who tend to report a broadly increasing impact (18 per cent–49 per cent and 33 per cent).

Table 6.8 How much does crime affect your quality of life?

	Unworried	Anxious	Worried	Frequently worried
Fear of robbery				
Minimal (62%)	75%	44%	38%	18%
Moderate (33%)	23%	48%	51%	49%
Great (5%)	2%	8%	11%	33%
Total	100%	100%	100%	100%
Fear of burglary				
Minimal (62%)	79%	55%	43%	30%
Moderate (33%)	19%	39%	49%	49%
Great (5%)	2%	7%	8%	21%
Total	100%	100%	100%	100%
Fear of car theft				
Minimal (62%)	70%	60%	50%	28%
Moderate (33%)	26%	33%	45%	55%
Great (5%)	4%	7%	6%	18%
Total	100%	100%	100%	100%
Fear of the three crimes combined				
Minimal (62%)	78%	53%	38%	27%
Moderate (33%)	20%	41%	52%	52%
Great (5%)	2%	7%	9%	22%
Total	100%	100%	100%	100%

Cells are column %. Individual weights are used

[5] Chi-Square tests of independence for each crime type indicated that these associations were statistically significant (p-values were all below <.001).

Correlates of 'Fear': Socio-Demographics and Crime

The next three tables (6.9–6.11) report various bivariate correlates of our categorization of the fear of crime. The first of these tables reports individual level correlates (gender, age, ethnicity, and the like), whilst Table 6.10 and Figure 6.4 and 6.5 report area-level associates. Table 6.11 focuses on those crime-related associates, such as victimization and witnessing crime.

Table 6.9 Bivariate correlates and associates of 'fear'

	Unworried	Anxious	Worried	Frequently worried	Total %
Gender					
Male	57	20	20	3	100
Female	52	22	22	4	100
Age					
16–19	46	31	21	2	100
20–24	48	23	21	8	100
25–34	51	20	25	4	100
35–44	54	20	22	4	100
45–54	49	22	26	3	100
55–64	53	21	22	4	100
65–74	60	22	15	3	100
75–84	72	16	11	<1	100
85+	87	6	4	3	100
Gender and age groups					
Male 16–29	56	20	20	4	100
Male 30–59	54	20	23	3	100
Male 60+	66	19	13	2	100
Female 16–29	40	25	28	8	100
Female 30–59	47	23	25	5	100
Female 60+	64	19	15	2	100
Ethnicity					
White	54	20	22	4	100
Mixed	57	23	8	12	100
Asian	49	29	14	8	100
Black	50	36	14	1	100
Other	60	32	7	1	100

Household income					
Under £10,000	57	22	17	5	100
£10,000–£14,999	57	23	16	4	100
£15,000–£19,999	53	19	21	7	100
£20,000–£29,999	50	23	24	3	100
£30,000 or more	54	18	25	3	100
Ease of finding £100					
Impossible to find	48	20	25	7	100
A bit of a problem	49	25	20	6	100
No problem	56	20	21	3	100

Cells are row %. Individual weights are used

Table 6.9 shows that whilst slightly more men than women fell into the unworried group, in other respects there were few differences between these two groups in terms of their membership of worried, anxious, or frequently worried groups. Age—another of the commonly cited correlates of fear of crime—provides some interesting insights. Looking first at the unworried, in general, the percentage of each age group being a member of this fear category increases with age, from 46 per cent for the 16–19 year olds, to 87 per cent for the 85 and overs. Accordingly, in general, membership of the anxious and worried groups declines with age. Perhaps of greatest interest are the frequently worried—the age group with the greatest percentage classified as frequently worried are the 20–24 year olds. What these data suggest is that the fear of crime, whilst having a strong relationship with age, operates against commonly held expectations, i.e. that it is the youngest who encounter the fear of crime most frequently, not the older members of society as often presumed.

Of course, age and gender interact, and it is important to explore this issue too. The third block of data in Table 6.9

reports age-gender interactions. What we see is that the percentages of worried and frequently worried fall for both genders as age increases (for males from 20 per cent to 13 per cent, and for females from 28 per cent to 15 per cent in the case of worry, and from 4 per cent to 2 per cent in the case of male frequent worriers and from 8 per cent to 2 per cent in the case of female frequent worriers). Ethnicity also exhibits some interesting patterning. The two groups with the highest percentages of the frequently worried were those of mixed ethnicity (12 per cent) and those of Asian descent 8 per cent), whilst other ethnicities had far lower percentages of membership of this group. Anxiety appeared to be highest amongst non-white groups (ranging from 23–36 per cent) than amongst white people (20 per cent).

Our two next data blocks concern income in some form. Interestingly, household income suggests little substantive or meaningful differences between the different fear categories (for example, the percentage of the unworried by household income ranges from 50–57 per cent). Similarly membership of the anxious group varies little by income (ranging from 18–23 per cent. Worry appears to increase with income, but the pattern is not a clear one, whilst frequent worry appears to have a strange distribution. When the ease of finding £100 (a measure of 'cash flow' rather than income) is used, we again see little variation between the groups. Only the frequently worried group exhibits a trend: those people who report it easier to find £100 are less likely to be in the frequently worried group than those who report that finding £100 would be a bit of a problem or impossible. This generally suggests little support for the financial resources–fear of crime nexus.

Let us turn now to look at area-level correlates (Table 6.10). The broad area type (divided into inner city, urban, or rural) suggests that rural areas remain areas where there is little immediate concern with crime. Of the three area types, rural areas have the highest percentage of the unworried living in them (59 per cent). In terms of where the anxious tend to live, this appears to be in inner city and urban areas, suggesting a confirmation of fear of crime as being an urban experience. The area type with the highest percentage of the frequently worried was also the inner city. That inner city areas are often at the forefront of social change ought not to escape us either.

Table 6.10 Bivariate correlates of 'fear'

	Unworried	Anxious	Worried	Frequently worried	Total %
Area type					
Inner-city	46	26	21	7	100
Urban	53	21	22	4	100
Rural	59	19	19	3	100
ACORN 6 categories					
Thriving	59	19	19	2	100
Expanding	54	18	26	2	100
Rising	53	20	25	2	100
Settling	55	22	20	3	100
Aspiring	53	20	22	5	100
Striving	49	24	20	7	100

Cells are row %. Individual weights are used

ACORN 6 is a classification of neighbourhood types produced by CACI Ltd. This classification describes small geographical areas in terms of the social and economic characteristics of the (typical) residents of that area. Thriving areas include wealthy households in suburban areas and affluent retired households in rural communities. Expanding areas include affluent executives and well-off workers, both living in areas dominated by families. Those areas characterized as Rising include affluent urbanites, prosperous professionals, and better-off executives living in inner-city areas. Settling areas include financially comfortable middle-aged, home-owning households and skilled workers (again who own their own homes). These areas, as Table 6.10 suggests, held few of the frequently worried (two to three per cent). Aspiring areas included more recent home owners in low rise estates, and white collar workers with young families living in multi-ethnic areas. Residents of Striving areas included older people in less prosperous areas, council house residents, those living in areas with high unemployment, communities with the greatest hardship, and multi-ethnic, low-income areas. These last two areas have the highest percentages of all the areas of the frequently worried and the lowest of the unworried.

184 Types and Intensities of Fear

Figure 6.4 compares the averages scores of the Crime and Disorder Index of Deprivation with our fourfold classification.[6] What both boxplots show is that the frequently worried score highest on both of these indices (indicating higher levels of deprivation). For example, whilst the unworried and the anxious (Figure 6.4) have similar profiles, the worried have higher levels of crime deprivation, and the frequently worried higher levels again.

Figure 6.4 Crime and disorder index by fear group (high scores = high levels of crime and disorder)

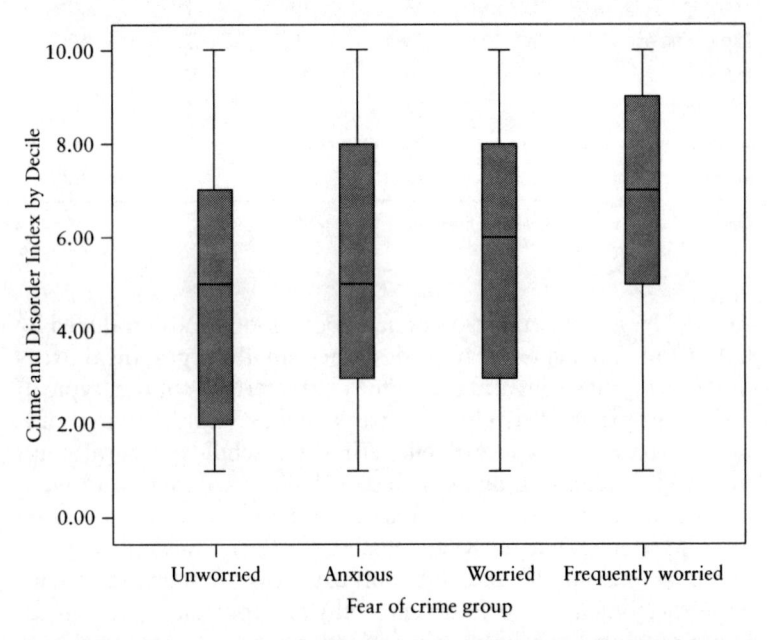

When the full Index of Multiple Deprivation (IMD, Figure 6.5) is used, the unworried, anxious, and worried are broadly similar, whilst the frequently worried stand out as having higher levels of multiple deprivation. Both of these boxplots suggest that the frequently worried in particular live in less advantaged areas.

[6] The boxplots in Figures 6.4 and 6.5 ought to be read like this: The main 'box' contains the middle 50 per cent of cases. The horizontal line in the box represents the median value. The vertical lines extending up and down from each box mark highest and lowest values within 1.5 box lengths (Norusis, 1998: 100-01). As such, boxplots are graphical representations of central tendency.

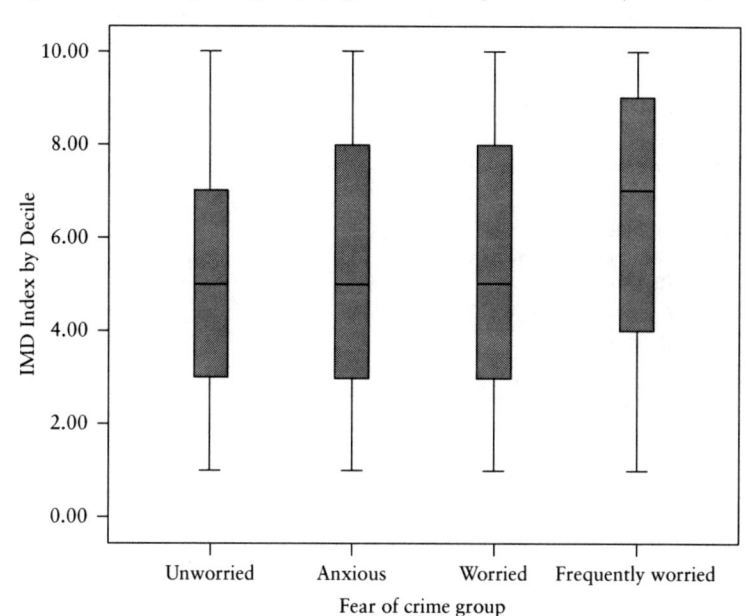

Figure 6.5 IMD by fear group (high scores = high levels of deprivation)

Let us look now at the relationships between common measures of victimization experiences and our classification of the fear of crime. Table 6.11 suggests that, as one might imagine, it is the frequently worried who experience most victimization. For example, 55 per cent of the frequently worried had been a victim of any crime in the previous 12 months, compared to 40 per cent of the worried, 32 per cent of the anxious, and only 20 per cent of the unworried. A similar pattern holds for robbery and burglary victimization. Car crime suggests a different, more equally-distributed patterning. In terms of the number of victimization experiences, we see that a greater percentage of the frequently worried are repeatedly victimized. Only one per cent of the unworried experienced more than five victimizations, whilst for the worried this was three per cent and for the frequently worried this was eight per cent.

Knowing others who are victims of crime also follows a similar pattern (the lower half of Table 6.11). The worried and frequently worried always come out with the highest percentages. For example, when robbery is considered 16 per cent of the unworried knew

186 Types and Intensities of Fear

Table 6.11 Bivariate correlates of 'fear' (percentages)

	Unworried	Anxious	Worried	Frequently worried
Victim of any crime in past 12 months	20	32	40	55
Victim of robbery in past 12 months	<1	<1	1	5
Victim of burglary or attempted burglary in past 12 months	2	2	4	6
Victim of any vehicle crime in past 12 months	<1	2	2	1
Total crimes experienced in past 12 months				
0	80	68	60	46
1	13	21	21	29
2	4	6	9	7
3	1	3	5	4
4	1	1	2	6
5+	1	1	3	8
Total	100	100	100	100
Knows someone who has been robbed or attacked in past 12 months	16	18	29	35
Knows someone who has been burgled in past 12 months	20	26	40	35
Someone in neighbourhood has been burgled in past 12 months	16	21	30	32
Total crimes seen in past five years				
0	68	67	64	59
1	13	15	12	8
2	9	10	9	6
3	6	4	9	13
4	2	2	5	10
5+	1	1	3	4
Total	100	100	100	100

Individual weights are used

someone who had been robbed, but this figure was over twice this for the frequently worried. When one considers knowing victims in one's neighbourhood, the frequently worried again head our list at 32 per cent, whilst half as many of the unworried knew victims of burglary locally (16 per cent). Witnessing crimes follows a—by now—common pattern with more of the frequently worried seeing this more often.

What the foregoing analyses suggest is that the 'typical' frequent worrier is a young female aged 16–29 of mixed ethnicity with low levels of financial resources living in an inner-city (or urban) area. They are likely to live in areas characterized by multiple deprivation, the economic greatest hardship, and high levels of unemployment. They are more likely than not to have been victimized during the past year and probably to have been repeatedly victimized. They will know other victims of crime and also have witnessed crime too. In short, the frequently worried live in some of the worst areas of the UK with the least hopeful outlooks.

Multi-Variate Analysis

Multi-nomial logistic regression allows us to identify differentiating characteristics of the four 'fear' groups. The referent category in the following analyses was 'unworried', so contrasts refer to (a) the 'unworried' versus the 'anxious', (b) the 'unworried' versus the 'worried', and (c) the 'unworried' versus the 'frequently worried'. A stepwise procedure was used, introducing three blocks of variables one at a time:

1. Socio-economic and victimization variables;
2. Attitudes towards social disorder, cohesion, and collective efficacy; and,
3. Judgements of the likelihood of victimization.

Table 6.12 shows the results. Model I includes just the first block of variables (socio-economic and victimization). Let us consider the factors that distinguish the 'anxious' from the 'unworried'. The findings indicate that, compared to the 'unworried', the anxious are more likely: to not have access to a car (a sign of economic hardship); to live in an inner-city area; to have been victimized in the past year; and to know a recent victim of burglary. When we introduce the second block of variables, we see that the anxious are more likely (than the unworried) to have concerns

Table 6.12 What distinguishes the 'frequently worried', the 'worried', and the 'anxious' from the 'unworried'?

Variables	OR	95% CI		OR	95% CI		OR	95% CI	
		Model I			Model II			Model III	
Anxious versus unworried									
Female	1.697	0.961	2.995	1.792*	1.010	3.179	1.672	0.932	2.999
Age	1.029	0.997	1.062	1.018	0.986	1.051	1.010	0.977	1.043
Age squared	1.000*	0.999	1.000	1.000	1.000	1.000	1.000	1.000	1.000
Female * age interaction	0.995	0.984	1.006	0.994	0.983	1.004	0.995	0.984	1.006
Health (very good to very bad)	1.144*	1.028	1.273	1.122*	1.006	1.251	1.084	0.970	1.213
Access to a car/vehicle	0.420***	0.315	0.559	0.417***	0.313	0.556	0.403***	0.301	0.541
Area type: urban versus inner-city	0.583***	0.418	0.812	0.618**	0.441	0.866	0.670*	0.475	0.945
Area type: rural versus inner-city	0.541**	0.364	0.804	0.637*	0.425	0.954	0.712	0.471	1.076
Crime levels (Index of Multiple Deprivation)†	1.016	0.980	1.055	1.003	0.966	1.042	0.999	0.962	1.039
Total number of victimization experiences in past 12 months	1.193***	1.079	1.319	1.112*	1.003	1.233	1.078	0.971	1.197
Total number of crimes witnessed in past 5 years	0.971	0.912	1.034	0.953	0.895	1.015	0.952	0.892	1.015
Know a victim of robbery in past 12 months	1.117	0.874	1.426	1.024	0.799	1.312	0.995	0.773	1.282
Know a victim of burglary in past 12 months	1.378**	1.113	1.708	1.309*	1.054	1.626	1.157	0.927	1.443
Concerns about social and physical disorder				1.622***	1.444	1.822	1.508***	1.339	1.699

	Model I			Model II			Model III		
Concerns about cohesion and collective efficacy				1.008	0.936	1.086	0.980	0.908	1.058
Perceptions of the likelihood of victimization (robbery, burglary, and car crime)							2.071***	1.816	2.363
Worried versus unworried									
Female	2.483**	1.397	4.413	2.705***	1.502	4.871	2.265**	1.215	4.224
Age	1.050**	1.016	1.085	1.039*	1.005	1.074	1.024	0.988	1.061
Age squared	0.999***	0.999	1.000	1.000*	0.999	1.000	1.000	0.999	1.000
Female * age interaction	0.988*	0.977	0.999	0.986*	0.975	0.997	0.989	0.977	1.001
Health (very good to very bad)	1.147*	1.028	1.280	1.097	0.979	1.228	1.043	0.925	1.177
Access to a car/vehicle	0.672**	0.510	0.887	0.645**	0.486	0.856	0.665**	0.494	0.897
Area type: urban versus inner-city	0.739	0.521	1.048	0.809	0.565	1.159	0.911	0.623	1.332
Area type: rural versus inner-city	0.695	0.459	1.052	0.904	0.590	1.386	1.056	0.672	1.660
Crime levels (Index of Multiple Deprivation)†	1.043*	1.005	1.083	1.018	0.979	1.058	1.008	0.968	1.051
Total number of victimization experiences in past 12 months	1.377***	1.258	1.507	1.248***	1.137	1.371	1.190***	1.079	1.314
Total number of crimes witnessed in past 5 years	1.033	0.976	1.094	1.006	0.949	1.066	1.002	0.942	1.066

Table 6.12 (cont.)

Variables	OR	95% CI		OR	95% CI		OR	95% CI	
		Model I			Model II			Model III	
Total number of crimes witnessed in past 5 years	1.033	0.976	1.094	1.006	0.949	1.066	1.002	0.942	1.066
Know a victim of robbery in past 12 months	1.546***	1.236	1.935	1.392**	1.106	1.751	1.298*	1.016	1.659
Know a victim of burglary in past 12 months	2.168***	1.777	2.646	2.027***	1.652	2.486	1.689***	1.359	2.099
Concerns about social and physical disorder				1.895***	1.687	2.129	1.687***	1.490	1.909
Concerns about cohesion and collective efficacy				1.139***	1.056	1.228	1.085*	1.001	1.175
Perceptions of the likelihood of victimization (robbery, burglary, and car crime)							3.629***	3.145	4.187
Frequently worried versus unworried									
Female	4.832**	1.530	15.262	5.205**	1.624	16.686	4.048*	1.218	13.452
Age	1.036	0.972	1.106	1.028	0.962	1.098	1.012	0.946	1.082
Age squared	1.000	0.999	1.000	1.000	0.999	1.000	1.000	0.999	1.001
Female * age interaction	0.975*	0.953	0.998	0.973*	0.951	0.996	0.978	0.955	1.001
Health (very good to very bad)	1.273*	1.036	1.565	1.219	0.988	1.506	1.172	0.942	1.458
Access to a car/vehicle	0.926	0.565	1.518	0.862	0.525	1.416	0.901	0.540	1.505

Area type: urban versus inner-city	0.963	0.512	1.808	1.063	0.561	2.015	1.216	0.630	2.346
Area type: rural versus inner-city	1.550	0.705	3.408	2.018	0.910	4.476	2.414*	1.066	5.470
Crime levels (Index of Multiple Deprivation)†	1.177***	1.089	1.272	1.141***	1.054	1.235	1.133**	1.044	1.230
Total number of victimization experiences in past 12 months	1.513***	1.312	1.744	1.351***	1.166	1.565	1.276**	1.096	1.485
Total number of crimes witnessed in past 5 years	1.115*	1.009	1.233	1.081	0.977	1.197	1.077	0.970	1.196
Know a victim of robbery in past 12 months	1.802**	1.185	2.739	1.615*	1.059	2.465	1.526	0.988	2.359
Know a victim of burglary in past 12 months	2.155***	1.458	3.185	1.987***	1.336	2.954	1.666*	1.109	2.502
Concerns about social and physical disorder				2.014***	1.621	2.502	1.772***	1.418	2.214
Concerns about cohesion and collective efficacy				1.198*	1.035	1.387	1.125	0.968	1.309
Perceptions of the likelihood of victimization (robbery, burglary, and car crime)							4.259***	3.353	5.410

Unweighted data. Model I n = 3495. Model II n = 3495. Model III n = 3495. * significant at 5% level, ** significant at 1% level, *** significant at 0.1% level OR = odds ratio, CI = confidence interval

† Crime levels (Index of Multiple Deprivation) measures recorded crime in the Electoral Ward for violent, theft, burglary, and criminal damage offences. The current index is in deciles, where high scores = relatively high levels of crime.

Social class, education, ethnicity, population density, and interviewer assessment of disorder were included in the model but the parameter estimates are not included here for ease of presentation. Please contact Jackson for more details.

about social and physical disorder. Finally, in the third block, we add judgements of the likelihood of victimization, which again suggests that the anxious score more likely on these than the unworried.

Turning now to the worried compared to the unworried, the findings indicate that, compared to the unworried, the worried are more likely: to have poor health; to not have access to a car (a sign of economic hardship); to live in areas with higher crime rates (according to the crime domain of the Index of Multiple Deprivation); to have been victimized in the past year; and to know recent victims of both robbery and burglary. When we introduce the second block of variables, we see that the worried are more likely (than the unworried) to have concerns about social and physical disorder and concerns about cohesion and collective efficacy. Finally, in the third block, we add judgements of the likelihood of victimization, which again suggests that the worried score more likely on these than the unworried.

Note that the effect size of the concern about disorder and the concern about cohesion/efficacy variables are bigger for the worried (compared to the unworried) contrast than they are for the anxious (compared to the unworried) contrast. Also note that, in both cases, controlling for perceived likelihood (Model III) reduces the impact of concerns about disorder and cohesion/efficacy (compare Model III to Model II) for both the anxious contrast and the worried contrast. This suggests that some of the impact of disorder and cohesion/efficacy on fear of crime is mediated by the perceived probability of crime: people who see problems of disorder and low cohesion around them have elevated perceptions of the risk of victimization (cf. Ferraro, 1995; Jackson, 2004a).

Finally, we turn to the frequently worried as compared to the unworried. Here we see that the frequently worried are more likely (when compared to the unworried) to be: of poor health; to live in high crime areas; to have been victimized in the past year; to witness crimes around them; and to know recent victims of both robbery and burglary. When we introduce the second block of variables, we once more see that the frequently worried are more likely (than the unworried) to have concerns about physical and social disorder and concerns about cohesion and collective efficacy. Finally, in the third block, we add judgements of the likelihood of victimization, which suggests that the frequently worried are more likely to hold perceptions of high risk than the unworried.

It is notable that the very same issues which divide the 'unworried' and the 'worried' also divide the 'anxious' and the 'worried'. Compared to the 'anxious', the 'worried'—who unlike the 'anxious' do report some level of recent experience of worry—are more likely to have had recent (direct or indirect) experience of victimization; to be more likely to judge their neighbourhood to be suffering from problems of social disorder and stability; and are more likely to judge higher levels of risk.

Starting with Model I, we find that the same characteristics distinguish the 'unworried' from the 'frequently worried', and the 'anxious' from the 'frequently worried': age, direct victimization experience, indirect experience, and levels of crime. As with robbery, there is a clear step-function: the effects are stronger for the 'unworried' than for the 'anxious', meaning for example that the 'unworried' are less likely to have been a victim of burglary than the 'anxious' and the 'anxious' are less likely to have been a victim of burglary than the 'frequently worried'. The differences between the 'worried' and the 'frequently worried' are less marked, with direct victimization being a statistically significant predictor (but the effect size is not as large as it is for 'anxiety' or 'unworried') and indirect victimization not a factor.

Figure 6.6 plots the fitted probabilities of being in each 'fear' group for males, tracking the trajectory of 'fear' from ages 15 to 95 (left-hand side plot). We find that elderly males (from 75 onwards) have the highest probability of being 'unworried', although the relationship between age and 'fear' is not very strong. There is a slight tendency for middle-aged men to be more 'worried' than younger and older men. But there seems to be no relationship between age and the chances of being 'frequently worried' (confirmed in Table 6.12). Turning to the same analysis for females, we see a similar pattern for the probability of being 'unworried', albeit with a slightly marked strength of relationship: those of more advanced years are the most likely to be 'unworried'. As with males, there is a slight tendency for middle-aged women to be more 'worried' than younger and older women. Again, there

194 Types and Intensities of Fear

Figure 6.6 Predicted probabilities for age, calculated for men and women separately (Model I)

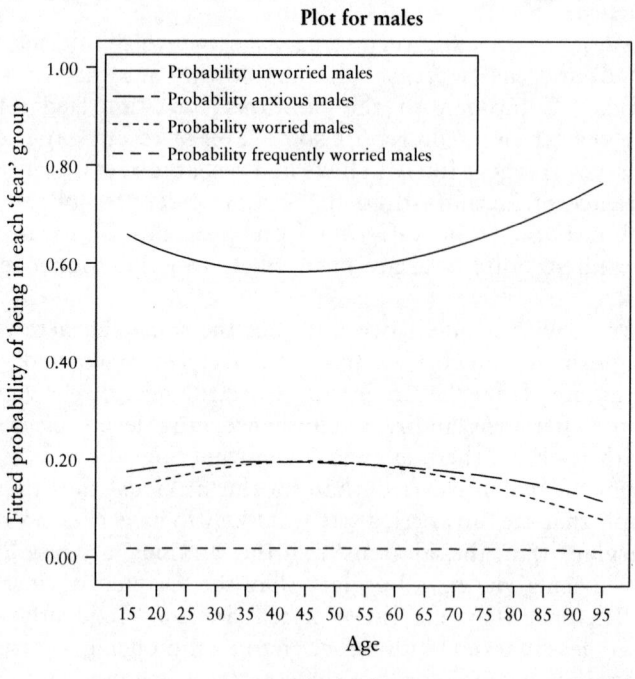

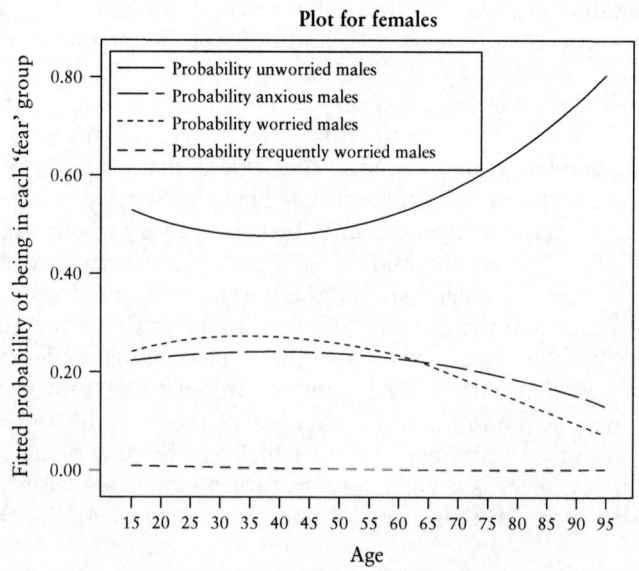

seems to be no relationship between age and the chances of 'frequently worried' (confirmed in Table 6.12).

Moving next to Model II, we now introduce into the model concerns about (a) disorder and (b) social cohesion and collective efficacy. First, we find that many of the effects decrease once we control for these perceptual variables. This suggests that concerns about social stability partly mediate the influence of crime levels on fear (to take one example). Second, we find that (as with robbery) the 'unworried' are the least concerned about disorder and cohesion; the 'anxious' in the middle; and the 'worried' and 'frequently worried' the most concerned.

Model III shows that the introduction of perceived risk reduces the impact of the perceptual variables, and further reduces the impact of variables such as crime rates. As with robbery, this is strong evidence that there is a second mediating relationship at play, sketched out in Figure 6.6.

The other three explanatory variables that were statistically significant in Model III of Table 6.11 were: (a) concerns about disorder; (b) concerns about social cohesion and collective efficacy; and (c) perception of the risk (likelihood) of robbery. Since these variables are continuous (we here treat perceived risk, which runs from a scale of one to four, as continuous), the probabilities are best plotted in a series of graphs (Figure 6.7).

When one includes the second block of variables (which were attitudes towards social disorder, cohesion, and collective efficacy) one finds that the 'unworried' typically hold fewer concerns about local incivilities, social stability, and informal social control (at least compared to the 'worried'). Indeed, controlling for these concerns actually *decreases* the effect sizes for each of crime levels, victimization experience, witnessing crime, and knowing a victim. The final block—lay assessment of victimization probability—further decreases the effects of crime levels, victimization experience, knowing a victim, and witnessing crime. Indeed, by comparing the statistically significant effect of crime levels in Model I to the not significant effects in Models II and III, we can see how judgements of risk, perceptions of neighbourhood stability, and experience of crime mediate the impact of area-level crime rates on worry about crime (Figure 6.8)

196 Types and Intensities of Fear

Figure 6.7 Predicted probabilities for concerns about disorder and concerns about social cohesion (Model II), (high scores = strong concerns)

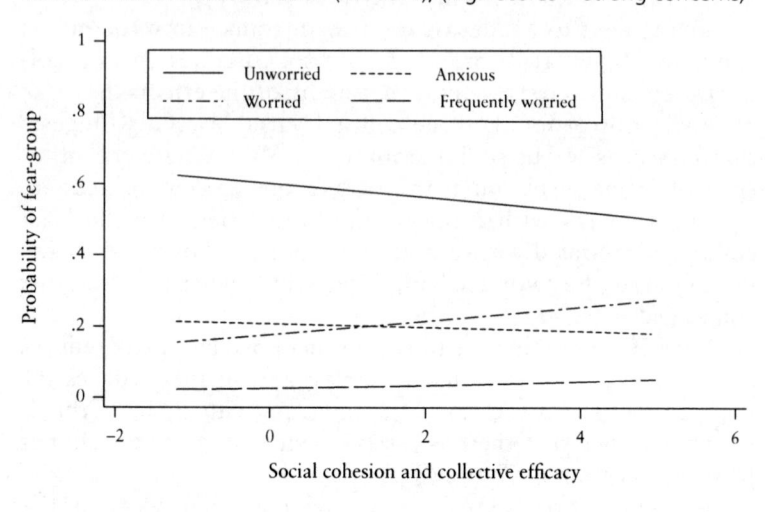

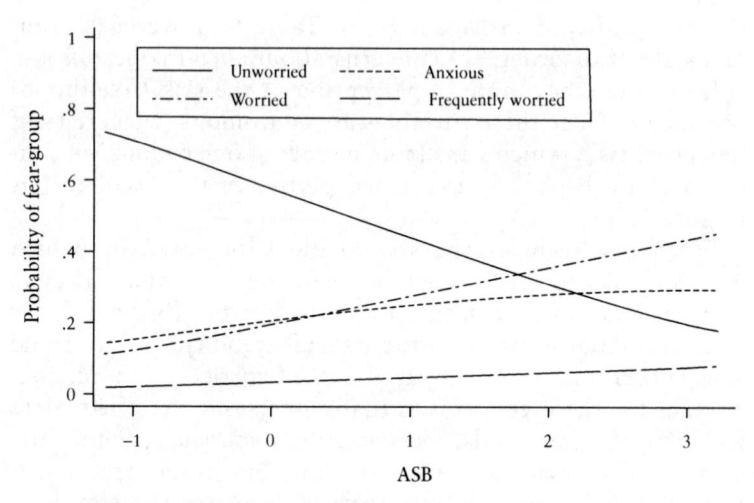

Figure 6.8 Mediational relationships in the fear of crime

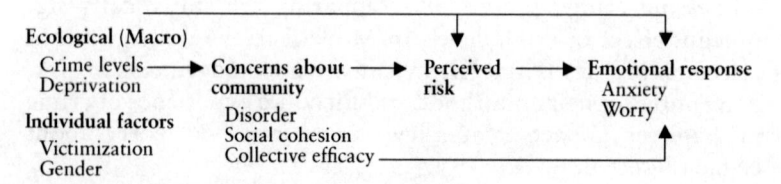

Starting with concerns about disorder, we can see that the probability of being 'unworried' strongly decreases as concerns about disorder increase, holding all other factors in the model constant. The probabilities of being in either the 'anxious' or the 'worried' group increase at similar rates as concerns about disorder increase. Turning to concerns about social cohesion and collective efficacy, the same pattern holds, although the strength of the association is not as strong as it is for concerns about disorder. Finally, the findings for perceived risk are intriguing (Figure 6.9). When individuals judge the likelihood of robbery to be high, the probability of being 'unworried' decreases quite dramatically; the probability of being 'anxious' increases a small amount when perceived risk moves from 1 ('not at all likely') to 2 ('not very likely'), stays the same from 2 to 3 ('fairly likely'), then decreases a small amount in the move to 4 ('very likely'); and for the 'worried' group, increasing perceived risk is associated with much higher probabilities.

Consequences of 'Fear': Public Confidence in Policing

Finally, for this chapter, let us demonstrate what our new approach to the fear of crime tells us about the fear of crime which we could not have achieved had we relied solely upon the old measures.

Figure 6.9 Predicted probabilities for perceived risk (Model III), (high scores = high perceived likelihood)

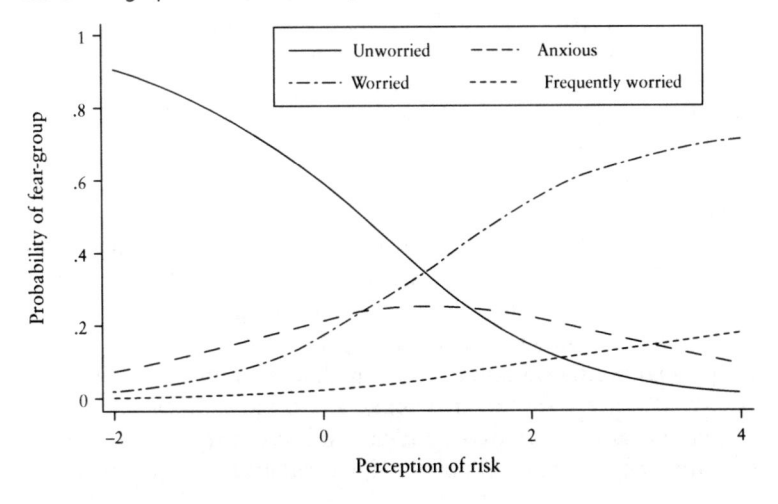

In particular, let us turn to one potential 'consequence' of fear: the draining of trust and confidence in the police. Our point of departure is the idea that people who are especially concerned about disorder and crime—and who are especially concerned about falling victim—are unlikely to express confidence in the police (to maintain order, fight crime, treat citizens fairly, and to be responsible and accountable for community needs and priorities). Skogan (2008) would call this an 'accountability model' where the public hold the police responsible for neighbourhood conditions that include fear, perceived risk of victimization, and crime. Tyler and Boeckmann (1997) would call this an 'instrumental model', where public concern is rooted in judgements about the severity of the crime problem and anxieties about falling victim.

Contrary to such notions of accountability and instrumentality, three consecutive studies found greater empirical support for a contrasting model that stresses symbolic or expressive concerns about social cohesion and moral consensus (Jackson and Sunshine, 2007; Jackson and Bradford, in press; Jackson et al., in press). Public confidence in policing was rooted in lay evaluations of social order, cohesion, trust, and moral consensus. This suggests that people look to the police to defend community values and moral structures, especially when they believe these structures to be under threat. A more 'expressive' model stands in contrast to the instrumental model, holding that confidence in policing is rooted not in fear of crime, nor in perceptions of risk, but in more symbolic yet 'day-to-day' concerns about neighbourhood cohesion and collective efficacy. In essence, low confidence in policing expresses not just an unfavourable assessment of police activities, but also an unfavourable assessment of the strength of local community ties and bonds. Put another way, people hold the police to account for local issues such as young people hanging around and the feeling that local community members have lost control over their neighbourhood.

In short, worry about crime (as measured using standard measures, such as 'how worried are you about being robbed/burgled/etc.?') seems to be only weakly related to public confidence in policing, once one takes into account more fundamental social concerns about neighbourhood stability and breakdown. How, then, does our new measurement set fare in comparison to the old measures?

Below (Table 6.13) are two identical logistic regression models of confidence in the local police—identical except for the fact that

Consequences of 'Fear': Public Confidence in Policing 199

they employ different measures of the fear of crime. The models include measures of social class, education, area type, population density, gender, age, ethnicity, Index of Multiple Deprivation (Crime), interviewer rating of the area, number of victimizations in

Table 6.13 Modelling confidence in the police: old and new measures of fear of crime

Variables	OR	95% CI		OR	95% CI	
		Model I			Model II	
Social class	−0.021*	−0.074	0.439	−0.015	−0.069	0.039
Education	0.134	0.068	0.000	.128***	0.061	0.195
Area Type	−0.080*	−0.208	0.222	−0.067	−0.197	0.064
Population density	−0.053*	−0.128	0.174	−0.041	−0.118	0.036
Female	0.209	0.084	0.001	.188**	0.061	0.315
Age	−0.001***	−0.002	0.348	−0.001	−0.002	0.001
White	−0.533	−0.843	0.001	−.617***	−0.934	−0.300
IMD Crime Rate†	0.016	−0.009	0.205	0.013	−0.012	0.039
Interviewer Rating	0.023	−0.053	0.550	0.034	−0.044	0.112
Total number of victimization experiences in past 12 months	−0.147	−0.211	0.000	−.141***	−0.208	−0.075
Know Robbery victim	−0.108	−0.271	0.195	−0.090	−0.257	0.077
Know burglary victim	−0.229	−0.375	0.002	−.199**	−0.347	−0.050
Concerns about disorder	−0.338	−0.420	0.000	−.343***	−0.426	−0.261
Concerns about cohesion	−0.137	−0.187	0.000	−.125***	−0.176	−0.074
Old worry	*−0.056**	*−0.133*	*0.149*			
Anxious				−0.043	−0.210	0.124
Worried				−0.138	−0.307	0.030
Frequently Worried				−0.635***	−0.986	−0.284

Unweighted data. Model I n = 3538. Model II n = 3438. * significant at 5% level, ** significant at 1% level, *** significant at 0.1% level. Ordinal regression model. OR = odds ratio, CI = confidence interval.
†Crime levels (Index of Multiple Deprivation) measures recorded crime in the Electoral Ward for violent, theft, burglary, and criminal damage offences. The current index is in deciles, where high scores = relatively high levels of crime.

the past year, knowing victims of robbery and burglary, concerns about disorder, and concerns about social cohesion/collective efficacy. In Model I (Table 6.13) we use the old measure of the fear of crime (in italics), and in the second we use three groups: the anxious, the worried, and the frequently worried (in bold). The first thing to note is that the models are very different to one another; in terms of statistical significance, different variables enter into each of the models.

In the first model we see the old measure of the fear of crime reducing confidence in the police with a coefficient of −.056, suggesting that the fear of crime reduces confidence in the police. However, in Model II we see our three different groups having different coefficients: the anxious have a low, statistically nonsignificant coefficient (−.043), the worried is slightly higher, but still does not reach the level of statistical significance. The real change is with the frequently worried for whom the coefficient is −.635 and statistically significant. Another key difference between the models is that both concerns about disorder and concerns about social cohesion enter the model which uses the new classification. Note also that victimization in the past 12 months and knowing a victim also enter Model II. The models suggest that the fear of crime reduces confidence in the local police, but that this is particularly sharply felt amongst the frequently worried. In sum, whilst we have not changed the overall direction of the model, we have identified, via use of our new categorization of the fear of crime, those groups for whom the fear of crime is associated with a particularly rampant loss of confidence amongst the police.

Chapter Summary

A summary of the analysis from the above chapter is provided below. Our methodology employs two measures of the fear of crime. The first line of enquiry asks the standard questions (used in the British Crime Survey) which asks:

How worried are you about being [burgled/ robbed/ having your car stolen/etc.]?

The second line of enquiry uses new measures designed by Farrall (2004a and b; Farrall and Gadd, 2004). Attempting to describe the frequency and intensity of people's worries, they contain a

Chapter Summary

filter question, measure frequency and intensity, and employ a time frame of 12 months:

Q1: 'During the past 12 months, that is since [date], have you ever felt worried about...?' (having your car stolen/having your home broken into and something stolen/being mugged or robbed).

Q2: [if YES at Q1] 'How many times have you felt like this in the past 12 months?' [n times recorded]

Q3: [if YES at Q1] 'And on the last occasion you felt worried about [offence], how worried did you feel?' [not very worried, a little bit worried, quite worried, very worried, or cannot remember].

Both questions were fielded to a sub-sample of the British Crime Survey (2003/2004).

Top-line findings indicated that responses to these two measurement strategies do not neatly map onto one another. Overall, responses to the standard questions demonstrated that 35 per cent of respondents were worried (summing 'fairly' and 'very') about being robbed, 47 per cent reported being worried about being burgled, and 45 per cent reported being worried about having their car stolen. However, the picture was markedly different when one draws upon data from the 'frequency' based questions; 85 per cent said they had *not* worried about robbery in the past 12 months. Similarly, 68 per cent stated they had not actually worried about being burgled or having their car stolen in the preceding year. Moreover, where participants had worried, the frequency of these events was surprisingly low—very few people had worried more than once a week during the previous year.

In short, the data showed that surprising proportions of people who *said* that they worried about crime, also admitted they had *not* worried recently. Worry seemed to be a relatively infrequent occurrence among the sample. Yet people still reported some level of worry even when they could not recall a single time—in the past 12 months—in which they had actually worried. Intriguingly, 63 per cent of those people who earlier in the survey had reported being 'very worried' about being robbed, had not actually worried in the past 12 months; 71 per cent of those people who were 'fairly worried' reported the same. A similar albeit less powerful pattern was apparent in relation to burglary and car theft: 39 per cent and 33 per cent respectively reported they were 'very worried' about being victimized but had not actually worried once recently.

By combining these measures we believe we can identify four empirically and theoretically distinct categories. These include:

- The **'unworried'**: respondents who indicated (a) that they were 'not at all' or 'not very' worried, and (b) that they had not worried at all during the past year;
- The **'anxious'**: respondents who indicated (a) that they were 'fairly' or 'very' worried, but (b) that they had not worried at all during the past year;
- The **'worried'**: respondents who indicated that they had worried between once and 51 times over the past year (their other responses were not taken into consideration in assigning them to this group); and,
- The **'frequently worried'**: respondents who indicated that they had worried at least 52 times (about once a week) over the past year (again, their responses to the other questions were not taken into consideration).

Studying the correlates of our four categories, across all offences, 'worry' about crime was more strongly related to poor personal health, a range of victimization (personal and vicarious), and local crime variables (crimes witnessed and area-level crime measure), as well as concerns about the local community (informal social control, community efficacy). These results suggest that those individuals who live at the 'sharp end of life' vis-à-vis crime and victimization (particularly offences which directly affect individuals and local communities) are most likely to report moments of everyday worry about a range of offences. Meanwhile, 'anxiety' about crime was also related to concerns about disorder and social cohesion, but to a lesser extent.

Conclusion

Let us begin our conclusion by highlighting a number of salient points. We have outlined survey measures of new questions which we propose measure the fear of crime in a different manner to all previous efforts; compared with the old questions, our new questions do indeed appear to paint a different picture of the fear of crime (Tables 6.1–6.3). Instead of embarking on a 'battle of the questions', we sought to illuminate the fear of crime in greater detail by combining these measures, thus producing four groups of respondents based on their answers to these two different styles of questioning. Bivariate analyses suggested that the respondents which comprised these four groups had different experiences from one another (Tables 6.9–6.11), a finding confirmed by quality of life measures (Table 6.8). Our modelling (Table 6.12) refined this approach. Finally, by way of demonstrating the wider utility of the approach we have adopted, in Table 6.13 we explored the ways in which the fourfold classification of the fear of crime operates when used to explore confidence in the police.

In Chapter 7 we complete the quantitative investigation of our new approach to the fear of crime, and return to the model which we first outlined in Chapter 4 and which we first explored in Chapter 5 using qualitative data. This exploration permits us to embed our understanding of these two 'streams' of fear within wider social contexts, and allows us to chart those factors and processes associated with the 'production' of these two forms of fear.

Appendix

The distribution of answers is perhaps best viewed graphically. Figure 6.10 charts the reported frequencies of the new questions as they relate to burglary. The data shows n of respondents reporting n of times worried in the previous year. We include zero for those who said they did not worry in reply to the filter question. The answers given to all three questions follow a very similar pattern to that shown for burglary and the data is positively skewed. As such, the vast majority, over four fifths, said they did not worry about the respective crime or only worried about it up to five times during the year. Just a small percentage of respondents reported more than five episodes of fear in the course of the previous 12 months. In short, if we can assume that counts up to five are likely to be genuine recalls, over four fifths of answers can be assumed to be reasonably accurate while the remainder are estimates and 'rough guesses'.

Figure 6.10 Frequency of worry about burglary over 12 months

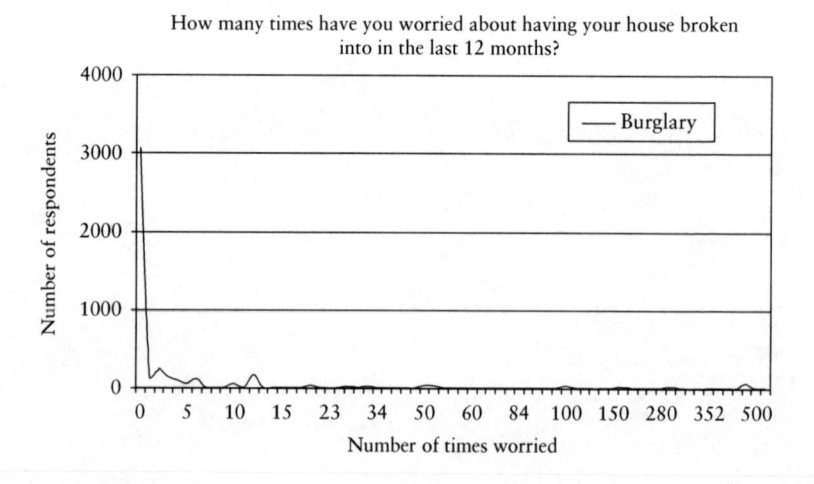

Most notably, when considering the data, there are prominent 'frequency spikes' in the number of reported worries across all three offence types, suggesting common patterns in the calculation of responses more generally. For example, following from zero along the x-axis the number of reported worries reduces exponentially. However, we can see evidence of particularly 'popular' responses or 'spikes' at 6, 10, 12, 20, 50, 52, 100, 300, 365. Following Tourangeau et al. 2000, it is likely these reported frequencies reflect two types of estimation, rounding-up (10, 20, 50 etc.) and calculated averages ('every other month', 'once a month', 'everyday' etc.).

7

Experience and Expression in the Fear of Crime

'The special significance of crime is at the social level. The intensity of public reaction to it is understandable in that it reveals weaknesses of the moral order on which not only everyone's safety depends but also almost everything else that is important and precious in life. Crimes therefore have significance in proportion to the extent to which they affront the moral sensibilities of persons . . . Perceptions of changes in the prevalence of crime can be expected to evoke particularly intense public reactions in that these can be taken as signs of threats to the fundamental moral order. This clearly is the case with much of the current public reaction to news of increasing crime.' (Biderman et al., 1967: 164).

'I'm right in the crime element on the estate—with all the villains and everything.' (Female respondent from London).

The Story So Far...

In the previous chapter we identified and explored some factors associated with four groups of respondents from the British Crime Survey. The four groups were the unworried, the anxious, the worried, and the frequently worried. Focusing on those factors which differentiated the 'anxious' and the 'worried', we demonstrated that everyday worry about crime is associated with feeling at greater risk; with concerns about community order and stability; with having been or knowing a victim of crime; and with living in a high crime area. By contrast, the 'anxious' feel less at risk; are less concerned about disorder and social cohesion; are less likely to have been a victim or know a victim; and are less likely to live in a high crime area. These findings suggest that the fear of crime manifests in specific moments of everyday worry when individuals live at the 'sharp end' of life. By contrast, the 'anxious' are more protected from crime and signs of crime (although not as protected as the 'unworried').

The second phase of our quantitative empirical work herein moves to the theoretical framework we first outlined in Chapter 4 (and examined using qualitative data in Chapter 5). Our model is grounded in a longstanding argument that public perceptions of crime and risk cover a range of circulating representations, sensibilities, and anxieties about social and community life (see Ditton et al., 1999; Jackson, 2004a; Sampson and Raudenbush, 2004; Girling et al., 2000). Redolent of personal vulnerabilities, past histories, and current environments, sentiments are, according to this perspective, infused by broader significance of crime, disorder, cohesion, and social change. Crime and fear of crime are broader 'tokens of cultural preoccupation' (Garland, 2001), emblems of moral outrage and censure that are wrapped up in diagnoses of a society with shifting moral standards, loosening pressures to conform, and broader uncertainties amid rapidly changing conditions.

Our findings so far suggest that concerns about neighbourhood disorder and social cohesion, as well as judgements of risk, are important in explaining emotional response to crime-risk. Moreover, concerns and judgements mediate the impact of neighbourhood crime levels on perceptions of risk and subsequent emotional response. Put another way, our study is beginning to show that perceived risk and worry about crime may be embedded in concerns that certain members of the local neighbourhood are refusing to submit to the rules or rights of others, that social conditions are failing to encourage citizens to treat others with respect—that the physical and social environment is somehow lacking (Figure 7.1). If this analysis is supported by the data, 'crime' may have become intertwined in the public mind with the less dramatic but more everyday matter of social cohesion, consensus, and relations. Concerns about crime would consequently be driven not just by aspects of risk perception and circulating mass-media images of frightening and unsettling events, but also by everyday signs of social stability and moral order. Such concerns may, at the final analysis, be just as much about 'moral outrage' as they are about explicit threat perceptions. Our study is thus developing an account of both the *experience* of the fear of crime (the everyday reality of people

Figure 7.1 A Unified Framework: Experience and Expression in the Fear of Crime

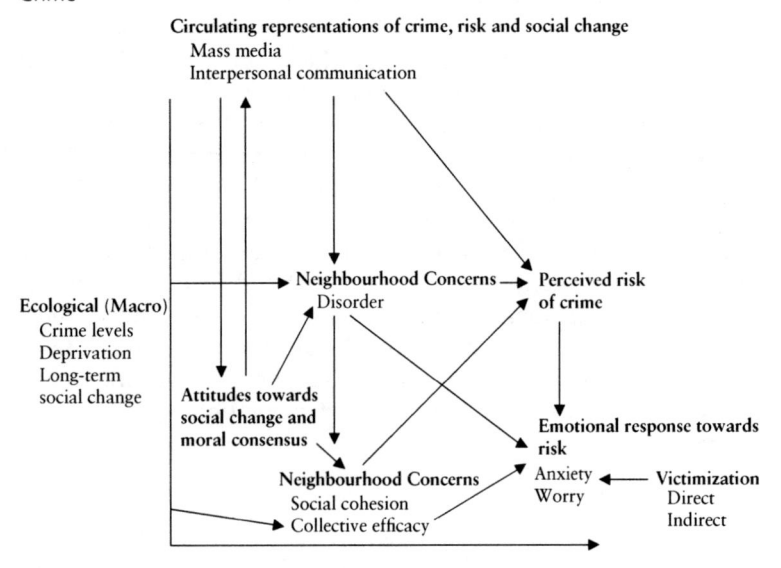

Circulating representations of crime, risk and social change
Mass media
Interpersonal communication

Ecological (Macro)
Crime levels
Deprivation
Long-term social change

Neighbourhood Concerns
Disorder

Perceived risk of crime

Attitudes towards social change and moral consensus

Neighbourhood Concerns
Social cohesion
Collective efficacy

Emotional response towards risk
Anxiety
Worry

Victimization
Direct
Indirect

concerns) and the *expressive* aspect of public concerns, which articulate judgements about persons, groups, behaviours, and social conditions.

In order to submit the model to a more rigorous test, the rest of this chapter moves to structural equation modelling of the quantitative data that we have at hand. The first section draws once again on data from the 2003/2004 BCS. The second section revisits data from a study of public attitudes towards crime and policing in a rural part of Northern England (Jackson, 2004a; Jackson and Sunshine, 2007). Each dataset has its strengths and each dataset has its weaknesses. The first strength of the BCS is that it is a high-quality general-population survey, allowing us to generalize to the population of England and Wales. The second strength is that we have data, from the Index of Multiple Deprivation (ODPM 2004), on crime and deprivation at the Electoral Ward-level, and BCS interviewer assessments of disorder in respondents' neighbourhoods. The weakness of the BCS is that we are constrained by the data: in an ideal world the survey would contain measures of various social and political attitudes and values; the survey would expand the range of perceptions of risk, moving beyond just judgements of likelihood of victimization to include control, consequence, and vividness (Jackson, 2006). The first strength of the local crime survey is that we had full control over the questions asked, giving us data on social and political attitudes and values, as well as a more sophisticated definition of risk perception. The second strength is that there were 1,000 respondents all of whom shared the same environment, meaning that we can explain why different people come to different conclusions about the same neighbourhood. The main weakness is the ideographic nature of this study: the findings cannot be generalized beyond the specific locality studied (although of course the focus here is on the mechanisms that generated the data, not estimated means in a broader population).

Outline of the Analyses

Figure 7.1 gives a summary of our model which we sketched out in Chapter 4, and which develops the work of Ferraro (1995) and Jackson (2004). Beginning with the BCS, we test Ferraro's (1995) risk interpretation model for the first time with UK-based data using structural equation modelling (see Hough, 1995, for a set of regression models that approximate some features). However, the key development is the identification of two separate streams of fear: an expressive dimension (which we refer to as 'anxiety about crime') and an experiential dimension (referred to as 'worry about crime'). Following Jackson (2004), if solid concerns about disorder and social cohesion are identified, we conclude that the interpretative activity involved in these concerns not only provides information about risk, but also constitutes and is expressed by fear of crime. The point here is that the fear of crime is not a function of abstract notions of risk but is instead embedded in how people make sense of social bonds, normative standards, and inter-group relations.

Another key question is whether 'anxiety' and 'everyday worry' operate differently in this model. Is one more highly associated with perceived risk or concerns about disorder, for example? We have seen that 'everyday worry' occurs amongst people who perceive higher levels of risk; are more concerned about disorder, cohesion, and collective efficacy; have greater victimization experience; and live in higher crime areas. The next set of analyses goes beyond identifying the characteristics that differentiate these groups, to highlight the perceptual processes that underpin these two streams of fear.

Analysis of the British Crime Survey

We used structural equation modelling (SEM[1]) to analyse the BCS data. To begin with, a theoretical model is specified. The researcher decides which indicators measure which latent constructs and what the relations between latent constructs are. As with confirmatory factor analysis, the model must be identified—this means that the researcher must determine whether there is enough information to estimate the model. Rules can be followed that will, in practice and in most cases, achieve this (see Bollen, 1989). The parameters of the model are then estimated, usually using Maximum Likelihood Estimation (MLE). If there the data do not conform to a multi-variate normal distribution then polychoric correlations can be used to calculate the covariance matrix and the general least squared estimation method is employed. However, there is evidence that the MLE procedure is robust with ordinal level data (see, for example, Curran et al., 1996). Finally,

---

[1] SEM is a statistical tool used to assess whether a theoretical model of relationships between variables fits a set of data. It has a number of other names, including LISREL (or linear structural relations—Hayduk, 1987; Jöreskog and Sörbom, 1988), causal modelling (Bentler, 1980; Reichardt and Gollob, 1986), latent construct models (Everitt, 1984), covariance structure analysis, and analysis of covariance structures. (The use of 'causal' is misleading: causality is a controversial topic in philosophy and if it can be inferred through social scientific procedures then experimental designs and in-depth qualitative work are amongst the most likely routes. Correlation, of course, does not provide causality). At its most general, this is a linear statistical modelling technique, with confirmatory factor analysis, path analysis and regression all representing special cases of SEM. SEM allows the estimation of latent constructs that are measured by imperfect indicators (measurement models) *and* sets of paths between constructs (structural models). Models can then be tested that conceptualize how these variables (indicators and latent constructs) co-vary or relate to one another in various ways. Each model implies a structure of the covariance matrix of the measures—the resulting model-implicated covariance matrix is then compared to the data-based covariance matrix. If the two matrices are consistent with one another then the covariance structure model can be considered a plausible explanation for relations between the measures. SEM should therefore be treated as a largely confirmatory rather than exploratory technique.

the fit of the model is evaluated.[2] Because SEM can simultaneously estimate a number of regression paths, one has a great deal of flexibility in estimating mediating relationships within quite complex models involving a number of direct and indirect effects (and indeed moderation effects). This means that one can investigate whether one latent construct accounts for, or explains, the relation between two other variables. Baron and Kenny (1986, p 1176) state that '... a given variable may be said to function as a mediator to the extent that it accounts for the relation between the predictor and the criterion'. This may be complete mediation, where a previously significant relation between the independent and dependent variable disappears when controlling for the mediating variable. It may also be incomplete mediation, where the same independent variable has a direct effect on the dependent,

---

[2] Due to the fact that Chi-Square is extremely sensitive to sample size, over-identification, and violations of the assumptions of multi-variate normality, it has become standard not to be too concerned by a significant Chi-Square statistic (see Bentler and Bonett, 1980; Jöreskog, 1981). One alternative is to use a relative Chi-Square statistic that makes the analysis less dependent on sample size (Carmines and McIver, 1981, p 80). The relative Chi-Square statistic is the ratio of the Chi-Square and the degrees of freedom, where <2:1 or <3:1 indicate an acceptable model. Kline (1998) argues that 3:1 is an acceptable cut-off point. An alternative is to use a number of approximate fit indices that have been developed to incorporate factors such as sample size relative to degrees of freedom and model parsimony (i.e. models with fewer parameters to be estimated are, all things equal, preferable) in their assessment of model fit. These non-inferential indices are used in conjunction with the standard Chi- Square statistic relative to degrees of freedom to establish the 'global' fit of models. The fit indices that were used in this thesis were Comparative Fit Index (CFI) (Bentler, 1990) and Root Mean Square Error of Approximation (RMSEA). The CFI has a range of 0 to 1, with 1 indicating perfect fit. Values greater than .90 have traditionally been taken to indicate acceptable model fit, although more recently a cut-off of .95 has been suggested as more appropriate (Carlson and Mulaik, 1993). CFI compares the existing model fit with a null model which assumes the latent constructs in the model are uncorrelated (the 'independence model'). That is, it compares the covariance matrix predicted by the model to the observed covariance matrix, and compares the null model (covariance matrix of 0's) with the observed covariance matrix, to gauge the per cent lack of fit which is accounted for by going from the null model to the specified model. The Root Mean Square Error of Approximation (RMSEA) is an index of approximate rather than exact model fit. It takes into account model parsimony (fewer parameters being estimated) by calculating the discrepancy of the model from the data per degree of freedom. Ranging from 0 (an exact fit to the data) to unity (an extremely poor fit), scores below 0.08 indicate acceptable model fit and scores of around 0.05 or below indicating very good fit (Browne and Cudek, 1993). RMSEA is less affected by differences in sample size than many other measures of global fit.

but also an indirect effect through the third mediating variable. Indeed, Baron and Kenny (1986, p 1173) highlight that the mediator may represent the '... generative mechanism through which the focal independent variable is able to influence the dependent variable of interest'.

Overall, this technique has three clear advantages for the analysis of the survey data arising from the present project. First, through the measurement of latent constructs using multiple indicators one tends to develop or identify more valid measures of that construct (Coovert et al., 1990). This is because not only does the technique allow for the correction for measurement error through the partialling-out of error variance, but also the use of multiple measures allows for a more complete operationalization of the theoretical meaning of an abstract construct than the use of a single indicator. Second, SEM allows for a complex model which can combine direct and indirect relationships to be tested. The technique encourages the researcher to be explicit about the relationships postulated by a theoretical model and allows the empirical test of that model (using global model fit statistics). Finally, AMOS 6.0 allows full information maximum likelihood (FIML) estimation using a missing data analysis technique. This is a more powerful way of dealing with missing data than standard deletion or imputation methods such as replacement by mean (Arbuckle and Wothke, 1999).

Data and Measures

We outline the measures we have relied upon from left to right in the diagram below (that is, we start with the exogenous variables and move towards the endogenous ones).

The *BCS interviewer rating of local disorder* latent construct was measured by asking the interviewers how common each of the following was in the respondents' area ('not at all common', 'not very common', 'fairly common', and 'very common'):

- Vandalism, graffiti, or damage to property;
- Homes in poor condition/run down; and,
- Litter/rubbish.

To measure crime levels, we drew upon data from the IMD and particularly the *Crime Domain*. The 2004 English Indices of Deprivation[3] derived one index from police-recorded crime statistics for four major crime themes:

- Burglary (four recorded crime offence types, Police Force data for April 2002–March 2003, constrained to Crime and Disorder Reduction Partnership (CDRP) level);
- Theft (five recorded crime offence types, Police Force data for April 2002–March 2003, constrained to CDRP level);
- Criminal damage (ten recorded crime offence types, Police Force data for April 2002–March 2003, constrained to CDRP level); and,
- Violence (14 recorded crime offence types, Police Force data for April 2002–March 2003, constrained to CDRP level).

Composite indicators were created for each of these crime types, and then one composite indicator was formed by standardizing and combining using weights generated by factor analysis. The BCS includes this final indicator, measured at the Electoral Ward level and collated into deciles.

The BCS also contains a variable which refers to changing ACORN categories between 1981 and 1991. Although clearly not perfect, we treat this as an indicator of *long-term social change*. We have ordered the categories in this variable to represent something approaching a sliding scale of experiences of macro level social change. At the lowest end we place those people who live in communities which saw decline between 1981 and 1991. As one moves up this scale, so one starts to see descriptions of communities which fared better. We place greenfield developments before rising affluence as in our experience such developments tended to be amongst or alongside the prosperous fringes of cities or 'well-heeled' smaller towns. Even though the descriptors of these areas relate to change between 1981 and 1991 and our data were collected in 2003–2004, we still feel that the use of this variable is acceptable. We suspect that, in conditions in which economic inequalities have become more pronounced, those areas which saw rising affluence up to 1991 have, in all likelihood, seen continuations of this, and vice versa for those areas which saw decline. In addition to this, however, there are good reasons for assuming

---

[3] It should be noted that there are no IMD data available for Wales so all of the information drawn from this variable refer only to England. Recall, however, that the FIML estimation method means that the rest of the model relates to Wales.

that changes up to 1991 still hold some weight in 2003–2004 (the time of data collection). People who move into an area do so, partly, because of that area's past fortunes—in other words rising affluent areas attract only a certain portion of the populous (referred to as 'clubbing' by our colleague Tim Hope). In any case, individuals or families moving into an area become immersed into the dominant cultures of that area—meaning that naturally-occurring area level change happens only slowly. The different categories therefore are:

- Continuing decline;
- Boom then decline;
- Along with the drift;
- Improving but cautious;
- Greenfield developments; and
- Rising affluence.

Moving towards the right, the *concern about disorder/anti-social behaviour* latent construct was measured by asking respondents to what extent they thought each of the following was a problem in their area ('not a problem at all', 'not a very big problem', 'fairly big problem', and 'very big problem'):

- Noisy neighbour parties;
- Teenagers hanging around;
- Rubbish or litter;
- Vandalism, graffiti etc.;
- People using or dealing drugs;
- People being drunk or rowdy; and,
- Abandoned cars.

The *concern about social cohesion and control* latent construct was measured by asking respondents the following six questions:

- How many people do you know in your local area? 'None', 'a few', 'some', and 'many'.
- How many people can you trust in your local area? 'None', 'a few', 'some', and 'many'.
- How likely is a lost wallet to be returned with nothing missing? 'Not at all likely', 'not very likely', 'quite likely', and 'very likely'.
- Is this an area where neighbours look out for each other? 'No', 'yes, to some extent', and 'yes, definitely'.

- Would you say this is an area you enjoy living in? 'No', 'yes, to some extent', and 'yes, definitely'.
- This area is a close-knit community. 'Strongly disagree', 'tend to disagree', 'neither disagree nor agree', 'tend to agree', and 'strongly agree'.

Next, the *perceived risk* latent construct was measured by asking respondents how likely they thought it was that they would become a victim of robbery, burglary, and car crime in the next 12 months. The response alternatives were: 'very unlikely', 'fairly unlikely', 'fairly likely', and 'very likely'.

In order to measure *direct and indirect victimization experience*, we differentiated between (a) witnessing crimes, (b) knowing a victim of crime, and (c) personal experience. The first was measured by a single indicator that measured the total number of different crimes respondents had witnessed in the past five years.[4] The second was measured by summing the scores to two separate questions: 'Do you know someone who has been mugged in the past 12 months?' and 'Do you know someone who has been burgled in the past 12 months?' The third was measured by making a logarithmic transformation of the derived variable provided in the BCS on the total raw incidence of victimization from the previous 12 months.[5]

Finally, we come to our two core endogenous variables: *anxiety about crime* and *worry about crime*. The *anxiety about crime* latent construct was measured using three standard measures of intensity of worry ('How worried are you about being robbed/burgled/having your car stolen?'). Crucially, if an individual reported that they were worried about crime, but also stated

---

[4] The 2003/2004 BCS asked respondents whether or not they had witnessed any of the following over the previous five years: someone vandalizing property or a vehicle; someone stealing a vehicle/from a vehicle; threatening or violent behaviour (including fights); someone being mugged or robbed; someone breaking/attempting breaking into property; shoplifting; anti-social behaviour or disorder; and someone driving dangerously. The composite indicator used here simply summed the number of different crimes that respondents had witnessed; it did not count the number of specific and individual events that individuals had witnessed.

[5] FIML is recommended as the best way of handling missing data in SEMs (see Arbuckle and Wothke, 1999: 333). On the off-chance that there is a bug in the AMOS software—i.e. that the FIML estimation replaces missing values with means despite advertising otherwise—we redid the analysis giving individuals the value of the mean when they had not worried once or more in the past year. Confirming that the FIML estimation did not replace missing values with mean values, we found the results to be very different.

(later in the interview) that they had not experienced an episode of worry in the past 12 months, they were identified as having anxiety about crime, but not worry. This means that the latent construct captures levels of 'anxiety about crime'. One might be concerned about the large amount of missing values in this crucial endogenous variable. However, since we exclude all those who had had any everyday experience, the FIML estimation procedure pools all available data; no deletion or imputation method is used. Therefore, instead of dropping all those who had worried once in the past year—and instead of replacing missing values with the mean—our analysis uses the more powerful technique of drawing upon all information available. The *worry about crime* latent construct was measured using three frequency measures (robbery, burglary, and car crime). The raw frequencies were categorized into five groups: (a) not worried during the past year; (b) 1–3 times; (c) 4–11 times; (d) 12–51 times; and (e) 52 times or more.

Results From the British Crime Survey

Figure 7.2 summarizes the findings from the SEM of the BCS data. As outlined in our discussion of the theoretical models of the fear of crime in Chapter 4, there are a number of mediational layers to this model:

- Macro-level measures of neighbourhood crime and social change;
- Individual-level concerns about social disorder and cohesion (including BCS interviewer assessments of disorder);
- Judgements of victimization risk;
- Victimization experience; and,
- Anxiety/worry about crime.

The fit of the model is acceptable (Figure 7.2). The Chi Square value of 3323 at 329 degrees of freedom was highly significant ($p<.001$), which means that we should reject the proposition that there was an exact fit between the predicted and the observed covariance matrices (or more exactly, the covariance matrix in the population differed from the observed covariance matrix as defined by the theoretical model). However, as discussed above, very rarely does one expect to find non-significant Chi Square statistics in confirmatory factor analysis. Rather, one looks at additional measures of fit that make some adjustment for sample size and model parsimony. Here, the GFI is above .900 (.904) and the RMSEA is below .08 (.045), indicating acceptable fit.

Again, reading the model from left to right, we find that the area-level data on *long term social change* plays a part in *predicting perceptions of disorder and anti-social behaviour*. On this issue our data suggest that it is respondents living in those areas which had poorer experiences of social change up to 1991 (and presumably since) which are likely to report higher levels of concerns about disorder and anti-social behaviour. As such, increases in deprivation appear to create perceptions that the local environment is disorderly amongst some in our data set (albeit a weak relationship). By contrast, crime levels have a weak to moderate association with *concerns about disorder, concerns about social cohesion,* knowing a victim of crime, and personal victimization experience. Turning to environmental perception, *concerns about disorder* predict *concerns about cohesion,* suggesting support for the work of Innes (2004) and others, who propose that disorder signals to observers a weak social structure. Including *BCS interviewer assessments of disorder* allows one to more accurately identify the interpretative activity of the respondent. *Concerns about disorder* have a stronger effect on *concerns about cohesion* than does *BCS interviewer assessments*, highlighting that it is really 'in the eye of the beholder'.

Figure 7.2 and the successful test of the model places *perceived risk* in an important role. It is highly predictive of *anxiety* and *worry*; it mediates the influence of concerns about community (disorder and cohesion); it further mediates the influence of living in a high-crime area. This is consistent with Ferraro's (1995) work and that of Jackson (2004). While neither witnessing crime nor personal victimization experience predicted risk perception, knowing a victim did. Moreover, both *concerns about disorder* and *concerns about cohesion* had moderately strong associations with subjective *probabilities of victimization*.

Anxiety about crime was associated with *perceived risk* and *concerns about disorder*. The higher the perceived risk of robbery, burglary, and car crime, the more anxious respondents tended to be. Levels of anxiety also tended to increase as concerns about neighbourhood disorder increased. However, anxiety about crime was not directly related to *victimization experience* or to *concerns about cohesion*. That said, *concerns about cohesion* and *knowing victims of crime* each predicted *perceived risk*, meaning there were indirect effects of these two variables on *anxiety about crime* through *perceived risk*.

Worry about crime was also associated with *perceived risk* and *concerns about disorder*. Indeed, the effect of *perceived risk* was higher for worry than it was for anxiety (the standardized regression coefficients were .53 and .41); conversely, the effect of *concerns about disorder* was higher for anxiety than it was for worry (the standardized regression coefficients were .25 and .14). However, the biggest difference was that *worry about crime* was associated with each type of *victimization experience*. Having *witnessed* a relatively large number of crimes over the past five years; having been *a victim* of a number of different crimes in the past twelve months; *knowing someone has been victimized* in the past twelve months—all these tended to increase the frequency of everyday *worry* (although it must be said that the effect sizes are considerably smaller than for *perceived risk*).

So in essence, the model supports our contention that public perceptions of crime and risk are the result of a range of circulating representations, sensibilities, and anxieties about social and community life. Such sentiments are, according to this perspective, infused by broader significance of crime, disorder, cohesion, and social change. In this way, crime and the fear of crime are broader 'tokens of cultural preoccupation'; signifying moral outrage about the behaviours of others and the direction in which 'society is heading'. Diagnoses of a society with shifting moral standards, loosening pressures to conform, and broader uncertainties amid rapidly changing conditions appear to find an outlet in anxieties about crime. However, our findings so far suggest that concerns about neighbourhood disorder and social cohesion, as well as judgements of risk, are important in explaining emotional response to crime risks. An individual's concerns and judgements about certain behaviours and general trends in society mediate the impact of their local neighbourhood's crime levels on their perceptions of risk and subsequent emotional response. Or, put another way, perceived risk and worry about crime are embedded in concerns that certain members of the local neighbourhood are refusing to acknowledge the generally accepted rules and the rights of others; that social conditions are failing to encourage citizens to treat others with respect; that the physical and social environment is somehow lacking (Figure 7.1). If these analyses are supported by others using different data, it lends support to those claims that 'crime' has become intertwined in the public's mind with the less dramatic but more everyday matter of social cohesion, consensus, and relations. Concerns about crime would consequently be driven not just by aspects of risk perception and circulating mass-media images of frightening and unsettling events, but also by everyday signs of social stability and moral order. Such concerns may be just as much about 'moral outrage' as they are about explicit threat perceptions. Our study has thus developed an account of both the *experiential aspects* of the fear of crime (the everyday reality of people concerns, and which would appear to be located most commonly in deprived areas) and the *expressive aspect* of public concerns, which articulate judgements about persons, groups, behaviours, and social conditions but which are not exclusively to be found in areas of deprivation.

Analysis of the Local Rural Crime Survey

We now turn to a second source of quantitative data, generated by a single-contact mail survey of a randomly drawn sample of residents of a set of predominantly rural towns and villages in the North-East of England—an area with relatively low levels of crime and disorder. Questionnaires were sent to 5,906 named individuals drawn from the 2001 Electoral Roll.[6]

---

[6] A response rate of 18 per cent yielded 1,023 completed and returned questionnaires. Among the sample there was a slight bias towards females, and the age distribution was somewhat skewed towards older people (M 55.46, SD 15.63, skewness -.13, kurtosis -.67): of those who indicated their age (40 respondents refused), just over half were aged 55 or above (54.7 per cent); only one-tenth were between 18 and 34 (10.9 per cent). However, according to the 2001 Census, this is not that far away from the region as a whole: 40.5 per cent were aged 55 or above and 18.9 per cent aged between 18 and 34. As already mentioned, some of the data from this survey are reported in Jackson (2004) and Jackson and Sunshine (2007); the specific contribution here is to include in the model both *anxiety about crime* and *worry about crime*.

Figure 7.2 A Unified Framework: Experience and Expression in the Fear of Crime: SEM of BCS data

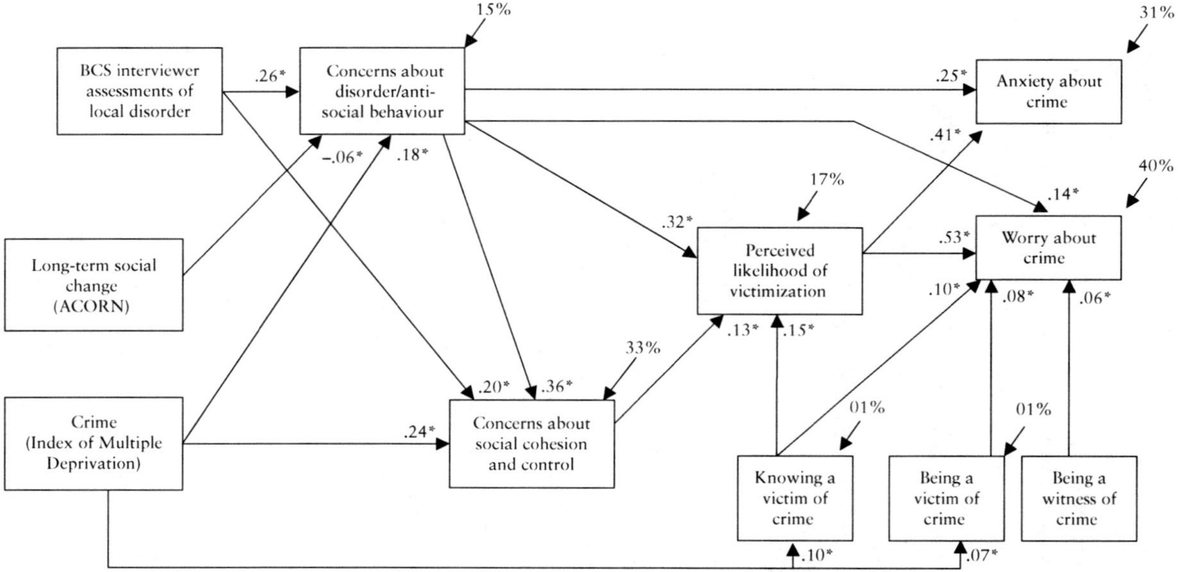

Standardized coefficients
Chi-Square = 3323; 329df; $p < .001$
RMSEA = .045; CFI = .904
* significant, $p < .05$

Please note: the measurement models are not shown for visual ease

The data

Again, starting with the exogenous variables, let us outline the measures we rely upon. The *authoritarian and attitudes towards law and order* latent construct was measured by asking respondents to agree or disagree (five-point scale from strongly agree to strongly disagree) to each of the following statements:

- Young people today don't have enough respect for traditional British values;
- People who break the law should be given stiffer sentences;
- For some crimes, the death penalty is the most appropriate sentence;
- Schools should teach children to obey authority; and,
- The law should always be obeyed, even if a particular law is wrong.

The *attitudes towards social change in the community* latent construct was measured by asking respondents whether they thought each of the following had increased, not changed or decreased in the area in which they lived (five-point scale):

- A sense of belonging to the community;
- A sense of shared values amongst people who live here; and,
- A sense of right and wrong amongst people who live here.

The *attitudes towards social change amongst young people in the community* latent construct was measured by asking respondents whether they thought each of the following had increased, not changed or decreased in the area in which they lived (five-point scale):

- Young people's respect for rules and authority; and,
- Young people's respect for other people and their quality of life.

The *concern about disorder/anti-social behaviour* latent construct was measured by asking respondents to what extent they thought each of the following was a problem in their area ('not a problem at all', 'not a very big problem', 'fairly big problem', and 'very big problem'):

- Teenagers hanging around in streets/in groups;
- Drinking in the street;
- Rubbish and litter lying about; and,
- Vandalism/graffiti/damage to property.

The *concern about social cohesion* latent construct was measured by asking respondents to agree or disagree (five-point scale from strongly agree to strongly disagree) to each of the following statements:

- This area has a close, tight-knit community;
- This area is a friendly place to live;
- This area is a place where local people look after each other;
- I am proud to live in this neighbourhood;
- The things that people in this neighbourhood stand for are important to me;
- When someone praises the achievements of others in this neighbourhood, it feels like a personal compliment to me;
- People in this area share my values;
- People in this area act in ways I find predictable; and,
- People in this area are trustworthy.

The *concern about collective efficacy* latent construct was measured by asking respondents to agree or disagree (five-point scale from strongly agree to strongly disagree) to each of the following statements:

- People act with courtesy to each other in public space in this area;
- You can see from the physical state of public space here that local people take pride in their environment;
- Local people and authorities have control over the state of public space in this area;
- If I sensed trouble whilst in this area, I could 'raise' attention from people who live here for help;
- The people who live here can be relied upon to call the police if someone is acting suspiciously; and,
- If any of the children or young people around here are causing trouble, local people will tell them off.

The *perceived likelihood of victimization* latent construct was measured by asking respondents how likely they thought it was that they would experience the same three events (physical attack, harassment, and robbery) in the next 12 months. The response alternatives were: 'very unlikely', 'fairly unlikely', 'fairly likely', and 'very likely'.

As with the BCS data, the *anxiety about crime* latent construct was measured using three standard measures of intensity of worry ('How worried are you about being mugged/burgled/having your car stolen?'). Again, if these respondents did not confirm any episodes of worry about crime (within the past month in this case) they were classified as anxious and given a missing value on the appropriate value. The use of FIML means that no deletion method was used.

The *worry about crime* latent construct was measured using three frequency measures (be attacked by a stranger in the street in their neighbourhood; be harassed, threatened, or verbally abused in the street in their neighbourhood; and be robbed in the street in their neighbourhood), but unlike the BCS, the time period was the past month and no filter questions were used. The categories were: (a) not once in the past month; (b) once or twice in the past month; (c) about once a week; (d) two or three times a week; and (e) every day.

To recap, the local crime survey allows us to explore in more detail the relationship between social and political attitudes and values and the fear of crime, and provides us with a more sophisticated definition of risk perception. Additionally, because all 1,000 respondents lived in the same environment, we can explore how it is that different people come to different conclusions about the same neighbourhood.

Results from the Local Crime Survey

We had one clear goal for our analysis of the local rural crime survey; this was to take advantage of both the design (the sample comprises people who share the same environment) and data on a range of social and political attitudes and values. This was particularly important, since the BCS data did not contain data on respondents' social and political attitudes. A previous analysis of this dataset found that these attitudes and values shaped the social meaning of disorder and its links to community aspects and criminal threat: respondents who held more authoritarian views about law and order, and who were concerned about a long-term deterioration of community, were more likely to perceive ambiguous cues as 'disorderly' and were more likely to link these cues to problems of social cohesion and consensus, of declining quality of social bonds and informal social control (Jackson, 2004a). They were therefore more likely to judge relatively high levels of risk, and they were therefore more likely to worry relatively frequently about being victimized. Since fear of crime was, in such a way, strongly influenced by a complex set of interpretative activity, the argument advanced was that it expresses that very same interpretative activity: the fear of crime distils how people make sense of social bonds and moral consensus. The present analysis seeks to extend this model to include *anxiety about crime* and *worry about crime*, and to examine whether anxiety and worry operate differently in the model.

Figure 7.3 summarizes the test, using SEM, of the first model. The data are generally supportive. *Concerns about disorder* predict *concerns about social cohesion*. Both of these set of concerns predict subjective *likelihood of victimization*, suggesting that incivilities and indicators of a failure in collective efficacy provide information to observers about crime threat (indeed a new feature in the model is the latent construct *beliefs about crime* which plays a clear mediational role between concerns about community and perceived risk). Finally, *perceived risk*, *beliefs about crime* and *concerns about disorder* all have direct statistical effects on both *anxiety about crime* and *worry about crime*. As such, both streams of fear seem largely to be a product of interpretations of the physical and social environment—particularly disorderly aspects in the environment which are representational of a community that lacked trust, moral consensus, and informal social control. Such disorderly aspects may represent to observers a set of unwelcome social developments into this rural area—hostility to the familiarity and diversity of interaction, to the breakdown of social cohesion and consensus, and to the loosening of moral standards and behavioural norms. Indeed, physical incivilities can create a sense that the neighbourhood is not 'owned' by people and authorities—that social order has been disrupted by certain people who lack acceptable values and a sense of respect.

Finally, wider social attitudes shaped the social meaning of ambiguous cues/disorder. Respondents who held more *authoritarian attitudes towards law and order*, and who were *concerned about a long-term deterioration of community*, were more likely to make the judgement that ambiguous cues in their environment are problematic and 'disorderly' (i.e. identify young people hanging around as a problem, associate young people hanging around with low levels of social cohesion and collective efficacy, and relate all these aspects to crime and criminal threat). Interestingly, *attitudes towards social change amongst young people* predicted

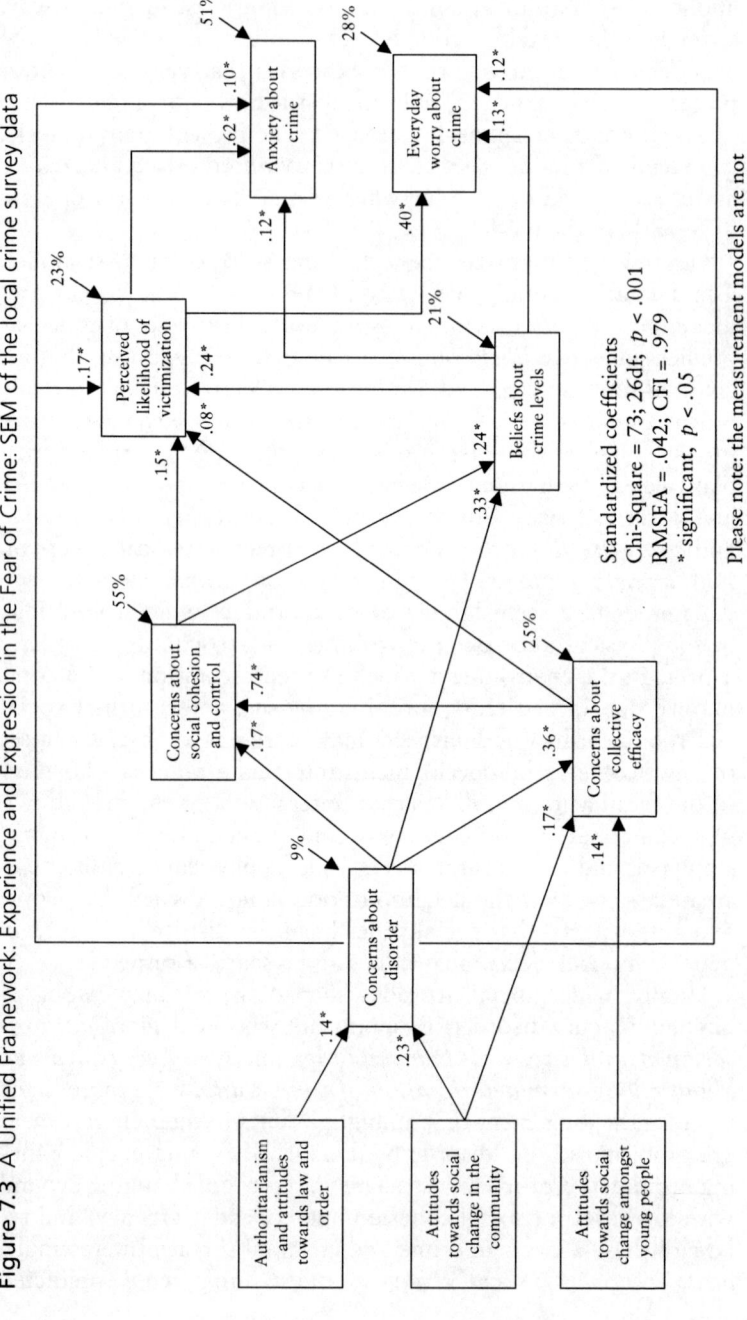

Figure 7.3 A Unified Framework: Experience and Expression in the Fear of Crime: SEM of the local crime survey data

concerns about collective efficacy but not *concern about disorder* or *concerns about social cohesion* (controlling, of course, for the effects of other exogenous latent constructs).

Discussion

Our task was to test an integrative framework that draws on the best qualitative and quantitative research, and that is alive to the trials and tribulations of measuring a complex concept using what can often be rather crude measurement tools. We intended to uncover both the *experiential* element of the fear of crime (how do emotional responses to risk manifest in people's daily lives?) and the *expressive* element of the fear of crime (what interpretative processes underpin representations of risk?). The framework—which we developed in Chapter 4 and pursued using our quantitative data in this and the previous chapter, and using qualitative data in Chapter 5—states that emotional responses to risk and crime manifest in two ways: *anxiety/expressive fears* (without moments of emotion that 'spike' in individuals' daily lives, but rather bubble under in a more diffuse manner) and *worry/experiential fears* (perhaps stimulated by more concrete cues of criminal threat). We found that worry is both less frequent than is commonly believed (replicating Farrall and Gadd, 2004) and more strongly related to the impact of crime on people's quality of life. Moreover, 'everyday' exchanges of crime stories and witnessing crimes in the local neighbourhood contributed to the degree of fear experienced by the 'worried'. These experiences may signal danger and unpredictable social conditions, as such the degree of fear shifts in frequency and intensity as people negotiate different social situations. Coupled with the findings that worry (as opposed to anxiety) is more strongly associated with perceived risk, concerns about disorder and social cohesion, victimization experience and living in areas with higher rates of crime—particularly crimes which directly affect individuals and local communities[7]—'everyday worry' is, we conclude, something that affects people who 'live at the sharp end of life' (in keeping with

---

[7] The key predictors in this model include, personal victimization, knowing victims of burglary and robbery; The Crime Index, which measures recorded crime for violence, burglary, criminal damage, and theft; and observable crimes which can be witnessed by the participant.

our earlier BCS analyses). Indeed, our results show that recent victimization was consistently related to measures of worry and that crime, on average, had a greater impact on the lives of those who say that they are 'worried' about crime.

By contrast, we found that *anxiety* about crime was less related to the realities of a daily life affected by crime. Nevertheless, these individuals continued to be concerned about disorder and social stability. Participants were, akin to the worried, likely to link physical cues to problems of declining quality bonds and social cohesion, perceived disorder, and risk. Their knowledge of their neighbourhood and socio-cultural concerns shaped their attitudes towards crime. However, the anxious were distinguishable from the worried, in that the 'experiential' indicators of crime and victimization were significantly lower than with the worried. The 'anxious' felt less at risk; were less concerned about disorder; were less likely to have been a victim or know a victim; and less likely to live in a high-crime area. In effect, the 'anxious' were more protected from crime and signs of crime (although not as protected as the 'unworried'). As such, we consider this form of anxiety to be borne of a more generalized or discursive 'attitude' towards the broader, social meaning of crime. We hypothesize that this level of anxiety is in fact 'expressive', articulating rich interpretations of the social order of the respondent's environment, even in the absence of concrete episodes of worry.

We also found that the area-level data on long-term social change played a part in predicting perceptions of disorder and anti-social behaviour. On this issue we found that respondents living in those areas which had recently experienced negative social and economic changes were likely to report higher levels of concerns about disorder and anti-social behaviour. As such, increased deprivation appears to create perceptions that the local environment is disorderly amongst some in our data set (albeit a weak relationship). As Gunn and Bell (2002) argue, the past 30 years has seen the erosion of the security enjoyed by the middle classes. The economic changes brought on by the economic depression in the early 1970s damaged the security of this section of society. The socio-spatial changes that gave rise to high crime rates during the 1960s and 1970s also transformed the middle classes' experience of crime too. From being something that normally affected the poor, crime, particularly burglary, vandalism, and robbery, increasingly became a daily consideration for anyone who owned a car, had a house, and travelled on public transport after dark. In short, the group that had been the chief beneficiaries of the post-war consumer boom and growing welfare state felt themselves to be increasingly vulnerable. All the tell-tale signs of crime and social disorder became obvious and openly visible (Garland, 2001). Taylor and Jamieson (1998) have suggested that the professional middle classes have been particularly vulnerable to strategies which emphasize individual risk. Fear of crime, they maintain, is not simply about perceived risks for these people, but about a broader insecurity. The middle class became 'afraid of falling' from their prominent and secure social and economic position which, due to globalization and political change, has come increasingly under threat. Crime fears became a metaphor through which the middle classes were able to express an array of inter-connected anxieties about the current experience of life in England. While the threat of a burglary might be a threat in itself, it also signifies what urban sociologists call 'the urban other' and the increasing threat of social disorder and denigration. In short, it may be that the professional middle classes remain less *objectively* exposed to crime than others in poorer regions, but the mounting *threat* of crime and disorder symbolizes more than an episode of victimization, but a whole host of meanings about their social, economic, and physical position in society. We return to these issues in our final chapter.

All of the foregoing suggests that the different measures of fear discussed herein tap into different aspects of the fear of crime—one of which attracts more of the realities of managing frequent episodes of fear, as well as the deleterious effects of crime on daily life. It is also reasonable to suggest therefore that both questions about fear access these 'daily effects' but also something else—the 'expressive' dimension of the fear of crime which may involve beliefs, perceptions, or attitudes that one has concerning the cultural meaning of crime, social relations, and environmental cues. Indeed, we found (as did Jackson, 2004a) that basic social and political attitudes and values influenced whether individuals interpreted ambiguous cues as disorderly and representational of poor social cohesion and criminal threat.

Our data are also consistent with the idea that there are two stages in the breakdown of trust. The first concerns public judgements of neighbourhood disorder, social cohesion, and collective efficacy. The environment and people's expectations and prior attitudes, values, and anxieties interact to form how they 'see' disorder and how they make sense of the strength of social order, cohesion, and control (Sampson and Raudenbush, 2004; Jackson, 2004a). We show that two individuals who share the same environment can come to different conclusions about neighbourhood breakdown and stability: the individuals who see problems, who lack trust in 'the young people hanging around', who judge a loss of collective authority and erosion of norms and values—these individuals are more likely to have prior concerns about long-term social change compared to the individual who does not interpret these 'cues' as problems. The second stage of breakdown in trust rests between this identification of neighbourhood problems and the subsequent possible conclusions about personal safety and crime risk. Individuals who lack both types of interpersonal trust firstly see young people hanging around in their neighbourhood as a 'problem' and, secondly, view them as a threat and source of criminality.

Suggesting—and demonstrating—that public responses to crime and 'fear of crime' involve participants' evaluations about the broader *meaning* of crime, place, and community, is by no means a simplistic task. Nevertheless, academics have long argued that fear of crime is a composite and 'congested' concept (e.g. Girling et al., 2000). Indeed, in their in-depth study of Macclesfield residents Girling et al. note the complexity of and variation in cultural sensibilities about crime and how people's perceptions and experience of place infuse the meaning of crime and control in contemporary social life. Garland (2001) also notes the pervasive nature of fear and anxiety about crime (and other threats to security) and the process by which the two main responses to it (punitiveness and pragmatism) have come to dominate the crime control field. Certainly, there is no simple relationship between fear and crime, and public concerns seem more complicated than previous research methods have disclosed. Indeed, the results discussed herein suggest emotional reactions to crime are infused by a rich palette of interpretative processes, personal characteristics, experiences, and neighbourhood relationships and conditions. Viewing crime and 'fear of crime' as discursively constructed implies a complex and interactive model of social, psychological, and political formulations. One of our key contributions has been to start to tease apart what we (as an academic community) and what our respondents mean when we (and they) talk of the fear of crime. As we demonstrated in Chapter 3, the fear of crime comes in various shapes and sizes and takes different forms depending on its nature—none of which ought to come as very much of a surprise to anyone. However, moving beyond this we have demonstrated that the nature of the crime-related fears one is likely to report is dependent upon a range of factors. Some of these operate at the macro or meso level (area influences), some are about individual processes of interpretation, and some are about beliefs and attitudes which are more deeply seated and broadly orientated towards social and cultural changes in wider society.

Notably, anxiety, or more precisely the matter of 'security', is an increasingly prominent topic in criminology (Loader and Walker, 2007; Bauman, 2006). Indeed, late-modernity has been characterized by numerous academics as giving way to a rather amorphous, existential, and pervasive anxiety (Giddens, 1992; Glassner, 1999; Furedi, 2002). Moreover, the corrosive effects of 'insecurity' and anxiety about crime and disorder on the wider social fabric is a pertinent subject for politicians and senior figures across the public services. Bauman offers some thoughts on these social forces and suggests that contemporary social life engenders an 'ambient insecurity' (2002). He maintains that aspects of modern life have been perforated by complex and various messages about risk and unsafety, leading to generalized feelings of unease and anxiety. Similarly, Innes and Jones (2006) note that public services and political institutions have felt compelled to 're-balance' their relationships with individual citizens in order to satisfy the worries of the populace. Certainly in the UK 'New Labour' have concluded that criminal justice must be reconfigured around the needs of the victim.[8]

The present study has applied an integrative approach to understanding interviewee responses to traditional standardized items and new frequency-based questions concerning worry about crime. Meanwhile, academics and policy makers continue to debate the nature of fear of crime and 'where it all comes from'. While we do not wish to revise these debates within the boundaries of this book (see, *inter alia,* Lee, 2007; Walklate, 2006; Vanderveen, 2006; Girling et al., 2000; Hale, 1996; Ferraro, 1995; Sparks, 1992),

---

[8] A host of reform initiatives were geared to giving practical effect to the 're-balancing agenda' (Home Office, 2006).

we are able to show, with considerable support, that anxieties and worries about crime cover a wide range of different experiences, attitudes, and vulnerabilities. Questionnaires inevitably struggle to capture the entirety of this dynamic. Nevertheless, with sufficient sophistication it is possible to explore distinctions in the nature of respondents' emotional responses to crime. As we indicated at the outset of this book, we believe there is intellectual and empirical value in a detailed exploration of the various aspects of fear of crime and that it is possible to conceive of both 'experiential' and 'expressive' components of fear.

The improved accuracy of the measurement strategy herein is able to differentiate between everyday episodes of worry (by asking respondents to count such events) and fear of crime as a more generalized social anxiety. In the first instance we have a group of people who closely experience the 'coal face' of crime, and it is in these everyday moments that their opinions are formed and perceptions shaped. In that sense the nature of crime fears is 'productive' (Calderia, 2001). Meanwhile, we also had a group of people who said that they were worried about crime, but had not recently worried and were significantly less affected by crime (and who we have called the anxious). This dimension of the fear of crime we call expressive because it is often not related to any specific event or episode in the respondent's life, but rather encapsulates a general sense of uneasiness on their part. In many cases, we feel, this sense of uneasiness is not directly related to crime, but is an expression of wider concerns about the state of society today. In this sense, consideration and discussion about crime not only produces certain types of interpretations and explanations, but allows respondents to organize and reflect upon the local landscape and public space—shaping the scenario for potential interactions which acquire meaning. The fear of crime is indeed a complex, contested, and congested concept. We have sought to take conceptual and methodological leaps in this work and demonstrate how the latest measurement tools can be taken full advantage of. In so doing we hope to dig into the reality of this social phenomenon—to examine its variety, its effects, its causes, and its nature. Only then will we produce valid and reliable research tools that will facilitate empirically valid frameworks of explanation.

PART III

The third and final Part of this book contains just one chapter. In it we recap what we have learnt from our investigations into the fear of crime, and in the second part, look forward to new areas of research. Our discussion again touches on a number of issues, including economic change, affluence, and the notion of 'winners' and 'losers' during periods of socio-economic change, and—of course—the role of these factors in the (re)production of anxiety. We also explore a number of pressing issues. These include the frequency with which the fear of crime is encountered within the lives of citizens in industrialized nations such as the US, Canada, Australia, and those in the EU, and what governments can 'do' to address popular anxieties about crime.

8
The Anxieties of Affluence

'I will show you fear in a handful of dust.' (T. S. Elliot, *The Waste Land*, 1922).

Overview

In this, our closing chapter, we summarize what we have learnt from our research into the fear of crime, reflect on the implications which stem from this, and explore new areas of research and the ideas which may guide them. Our aim is to be diagnostic rather than prescriptive since we see no easy resolution to the matters we discuss herein.

We have, during the writing of this book, been concerned with the social and cultural meanings of the fear of crime. And we have been keen to identify which social groups in English and Welsh society—and probably further afield—experience anxiety and fear the most. We started this book by locating our work on the fear of crime within a wider set of debates and considerations: the on-going research into the nature and significance of the fear of crime; the prominent position occupied by crime and related matters in the modern era; and the tension between government efforts to administer justice and 'competing' demand for a more punitive set of responses from the public. Let us commence this chapter by reflecting on those insights we have gained.

Summarizing Our Contribution

In Chapter 1 we outlined our basic argument (that the fear of crime has in short been misrepresented as being one 'thing' which all people, more or less, experience along similar lines), and situated our work within a set of wider issues and debates within criminology and allied social sciences. Chapter 2 covered a lot of ground; starting with the social and economic upheavals in the US during the 1960s, we charted the emergence of academic and policy interest in the fear of crime and the ways in which right-leaning administrations and political parties have toyed with and presented the fear of crime in order to generate political capital (see also Hall et al., 1978). This journey took us from 1960s US to contemporary Britain (and by extension Europe and Australia, Lee, 2009). This part of our journey involved our drawing upon a series of interviews with senior academics and policy makers in order to explore the shifting nature of the purposes of surveys such as the British Crime Survey and the debates which it both responded to and in turn triggered.

Having completed the tasks of situating our work within current debates and exploring how we got to where we are today, in Chapter 3 we shifted track slightly and posed a question which surprisingly few who have travelled this road before us appeared to have bothered to ask (at least bothered to ask using empirical data); namely, what is the fear of crime? Our answer entailed us to explore the psychological aspects of how people make sense of and respond to survey questions (this being the *modus operandi* of most researchers exploring the fear of crime) before turning to consider data drawn from in-depth one-to-one interviews with citizens in Scotland and England. We concluded that far from being a unitary construct, the 'fear' 'of crime' turned out to be rather more than 'fear' alone and not as immediately related to crime specifically as one might otherwise imagine.

But this—and we are quite adamant about this—is not to somehow spirit away the fear of crime. Crime fears (and worries and anxieties) are present in the lives of the people we spoke to. Our point is that for different people the language and terminology surrounding the 'fear of crime' is not straightforwardly about *one* type of encounter. In some cases fears are 'in yer face' moments of real threat and potency; whilst at other moments 'fears', or perhaps more appropriately 'worries' or 'anxieties', are ways of speaking about other shifts and changes which are far more subtle and nuanced than a young man with a crow-bar or a knife will ever be able to be. As such the fear of crime is not one thing but rather takes several forms. We focused on two: the terror-laden moments ('experiences') and the use of crime-fears as a metaphor for describing others things (not all crime-related) which made people uneasy (our 'expressive' dimension).

Having charted the rise of, illustrated, and reorganized the fear of crime, in Chapter 4 we retraced the various attempts which others have made in the name of understanding the fear of crime. Our aim was not to reach the conclusion that all which had gone before us was limited or wanting in some fundamental way (since much of the previous work has been of the highest rigour), but rather our motivation was to act like a gang of thieving magpies: to steal the best bits and make off with them in order to build one over-arching model of the fear of crime which accepted at its very core heterogeneity of both the nature of the fear of crime and its antecedents.

In the second part of the book, continuing our commitment of 'overhauling' previous thinking on the fear of crime, we commenced the empirical investigation of the model developed at the end of Chapter 4 via an analysis of in-depth one-to-one interview data collected in Glasgow and London. To the extent to which it was possible (not to say desirable) to do so, our aim in Chapter 5 was to explore the empirical viability of the model we had adopted, adapted, and developed using insights from those people living in a range of communities in two of the UK's largest cities.

Chapter 6 started the analysis of quantitative data sets. Our main focus in this chapter was on describing the survey measures employed, what the data these generate 'mean' empirically (i.e. the everyday phenomena to which the answers to specific questions are orientated), the picture of the fear of crime these paint for us, how such questions can be brought together in a way which mirrors our theoretical position, and the correlates and associates of the four groups which we produce from the resulting data. We then—by way of an empirical demonstration of the utility of (a) the survey questions on the fear of crime which we employ, and (b) our approach to what these can tell us about the nature of popular crime fears—apply the resulting classification of the fear of crime to a topic of contemporary relevance, namely confidence in the police. We find that whilst the old ('unitary construct') model of the fear of crime is weakly associated with reduced levels of confidence in the police, our new approach quickly homes in on the frequently worried as the main group of citizens who lose faith in the police. In short, our survey questions and theoretical approach to them produce (a) a more precise estimation of who is losing confidence in the police, (b) a stronger statistical relationship than was possible using standard measures of the fear of crime alone, and (c) a reasonable explanation of why this group may have lost confidence in the police (they have been victimized in the past 12 months, know victims of burglary, have concerns about social cohesion and disorder, and—understandably given the above—are frequently worried about crime).

Continuing our quantitative investigation of the fear of using more systematic and rigorous apparatus, Chapter 7—in essence—does a very similar task to Chapter 5. That is, the same theoretical model is examined using data from two surveys (the British Crime Survey and a local crime survey). Again, and in line with the qualitative data presented in Chapter 5, this chapter supports the general tenor of our approach to the subject matter.

Crime, Politics, and Insecurity

Our investigation of the *experiential* and the *expressive* elements of public insecurities about crime has examined whether 'fear' rarely erupts in those concrete moments of worry for one's immediate safety (contrary to current thinking). We have assessed whether everyday reality of 'fear' of crime—at least in contemporary England and Wales (and elsewhere we contend)—is best characterized as a backdrop to people's lives rather than a series of concrete moments of worry or fear. We have showed that individuals rarely find themselves in situations in which they feel threatened and 'fear' is most often a sense of insecurity that is managed through precautionary activity. This is evidenced by data from the 2003/2004 British Crime Survey (the BCS, and which fielded new measures of worry about crime developed by Farrall; see Farrall, 2003, 2004a, and b, and Farrall and Gadd, 2004) and expanded upon using qualitative data from interviews conducted in both London and Glasgow.

This has implications for the 'problem status' of the fear of crime. Politicians and social commentators often treat fear as a serious social ill wherever it is to be found (see, for example, Thatcher, 1995: 540). To be sure, widespread fear of crime is an indicator of a society ill at ease with itself. Yet we show that diffuse anxieties and more general insecurities have less of an impact on quality of life than is commonly assumed. Moreover—and echoing some of the concerns of the 'Left Realists'—we have also shown that the everyday experience of worry about crime is more strongly related to crime and experiences of crime than was previously thought.

We also find that symbolic, expressive, and relational concerns lie behind their instrumental concerns. People make judgements about the state of local cohesion and collective efficacy, about the sense of social and physical order, and about the civic pride and collective identity shown by those who inhabit their locale. Not only do people feel less comfortable in an environment that displays (in their eyes) skewed values and social atomism; they also 'read' the environment for information about crime and personal risk, and crucially these symbols of crime extend to community conditions (trust, norms, informal social controls) and the social and physical environment (certain individuals and groups 'hanging around', incivil behaviours, and disorderly features). Thus, we argue, crime is not some abstract category that emerges from nowhere. The risk of crime is projected into a given environment, elaborated with a face (the potential criminal) and a context (the place it might take place), rooted and situated in the everyday (cf. Jackson, 2006, 2008). In some sense, therefore, perceptions of the risk of crime disclose a host of subtle evaluations of and responses to the social world—a way of responding to variable levels of social order and control, a sense of unease in an unpredictable environment, and the association or absence of particular individuals or conditions with deviance and hostile intent.

Commentators often compare the fear of crime to crime itself. In such a comparison the fearful often 'come up short' with a seemingly irrational sense of the crime problem. This disconnect has led scholars, policy makers, and social commentators to argue that public fears are due (in part) to: (a) mass media coverage and political rhetoric which inflames fear and perceptions of criminal threat; (b) growing problems of anti-social behaviour, community cohesion, and diminishing influences of informal relations and taken-for-granted norms; and (c) broader anxieties about the pace and direction of social change.

But we contend that this comparison of fear of crime with crime itself (whether personal victimization or actual area-level crime rates) misses the point. While people may be all too hasty to associate local cues of neighbourhood breakdown and stability to the threat of crime, their experience of personal safety more faithfully reflects their sense of (dis)comfort and (un)ease in that environment. At the heart of this set of relational concerns is the feeling that informal social controls are low, that interactions between strangers are not healthy and respectful, and that the people who occupy public space do not share the norms and values of the local community (indeed that there *is* a local community that defines norms and shared values). Indeed, by associating crime with certain people and certain community conditions, individuals are diagnosing these as hostile to social order (crime is a vivid marker of the failure of group life) with subsequent demands that the police, politicians, and systems of criminal justice restore the 'damaged' social order.

This is not to suggest that people are misguided when they link crime to certain communities and certain individuals and groups. Clearly people may come to the conclusion that their neighbourhood lacks cohesion and informal social control, that the norms and values of others who occupy public space are lacking. This may generate a sense of the possibility of crime, even when crime is extremely unlikely. We do want to retain a sense of proportionality in public perceptions; we would otherwise face the unedifying prospect of treating public intolerance and prejudice at face value. Yet the point here is that, whether it is ultimately out of kilter with statistically estimated risk, fear of crime remains rooted in broader public concerns. Future work might pick up issues of stereotyping and demonization (see Day, 2009 in Lee and Farrall, 2009 on this).

The Nature and Significance of the Fear of Crime

In terms of the nature and significance of the fear of crime, we can make a number of points. How one counts the incidence of the fear of crime depends, naturally, on how one defines it. If previous estimates of the levels of the fear of crime are to be believed, then anywhere between a third and a half of the population can be considered to have some level of crime 'fears'. In this case the fear of crime was defined in an extremely vague fashion, which, we have argued, is open to all sorts of biases (Farrall et al., 1997; Farrall, 2004a and b) and which we have characterized as being 'expressive'. That is, a definition of the fear of crime which leaves it open to acting like a sponge; soaking up a range of other emotions and anxieties, some of which will be about crime, and some of which will relate to other matters (or 'ambient fear' to use Bauman's phraseology, 1998: 22). Furthermore, attempts to approach the fear of crime as if it were 'one thing', one set of experiences with one meaning, are no longer going to pass muster. Yet we have sought to decompose the fear of crime into a number of different sorts of experiences and feelings (see Chapter 3). This can be done with in-depth qualitative work, but also with quantitative data (not always known for its delicacy in handling such matters, see Chapter 6). When we approach the fear of crime along such lines, we find that it manifests itself in a number of different ways in citizens' lives. For some it is a diffuse set of concerns, but for others a more immediate sense of threat and harm. However—and here some good news—the immediate feelings of threat to security are rare. This resonates with the findings of previous studies that have suggested that, by and large: '... the fear of crime is [not] such a prominent feature of most people's lives' (McConville and Shepard, 1992: 58), so long as one gives priority to these countable and recallable mental events of worry. Others have classified fear into differing types. In his wide-ranging discussion of fears, Hankiss (2001: 15–16) suggests two types of fear: existential fears (which relate to 'a deeper, more universal anxiety, the fear of being threatened in one's very existence', 2001: 16); and situational fears (which characterize those moments of fear which relate to immediate threats). Rachman (1978) was another who drew a distinction between (in his terms) 'tangible' and 'existential' fears (cited in Hankiss, 2001: 41).

To return to our data: the vast majority of respondents had not felt fearful of any of the crimes we asked them about in the past year, and of those who had felt fearful, for the majority again these were isolated incidents (Chapter 6). High levels of chronic fear did not appear to feature very much in the lives of respondents of the 2003–04 British Crime Survey. Such feelings appeared to be more common amongst those living in less well-off neighbourhoods where crime itself appeared to be all too common (reinforcing the observations of left realism). The more diffuse sense of anxiety was, however, more common. The nature and the intensity of fear of crime appears therefore to be related to the realities of crime in people's local neighbourhood. However, and importantly, such feelings were related to how they made sense of their local environment and to their understanding and interpretation of wider social changes.

As we have stressed, none of this is an attempt to somehow spirit away the fear of crime. Rather, we are trying to disentangle a series of complex issues in both the lived experiences of the fear of crime and the nature of the psychology of survey responses. The fear of crime 'operates' at a number of levels. On the one hand, the expressive dimension refers to a series of circulating debates about crime and discourses about what ought to be done about crime and criminals (outlined in Chapters 2 and 3; see also Jackson, 2004a, 2006, 2008). People who often have little or no direct experience about the fear of crime or of crime itself are still able to give answers to such survey questions. On the other hand, the experiential dimension represents the 'sharp end', if one will; the questions we designed were aimed at capturing those specific moments of an individual's life at which they felt that they were at risk of immediate harm or loss (Farrall, 2003, 2004a). This dichotomy allowed us both to contrast people's answers and to regroup them along these lines. We have been able to tease apart these two aspects of the fear of crime, and in so doing we have (we think) been able to shed further light on both the *nature* of what we are seeking to describe and the *incidence* with which people encounter it as part of their daily lives (see Chapter 6). In short, the actual incidence of immediate threats to security (or perceptions of these) is rather rare. The extent to which people who do not encounter such experiences but who nevertheless still express (in our terminology) such anxieties is rather higher, and in many cases appears to be related to other issues.

Much of the foregoing discussion of the fear of crime has related to middle-class anxieties about crime and how these relate to wider shifts in social formations and economic systems. This shift (from middle-class security to middle-class insecurity) has been touched on by a number of authors (see Taylor and Jamieson, 1998; Girling et al. on 'middle England'; Garland, 2001). Most notably, David Garland (2001: 10) argues that the fear of crime used just to affect worst neighbourhoods, but since the 1970s has started to become a feature of middle-class social and domestic life. Whilst it is hard to argue against the claim that crime (actual or feared) may have become a more pressing feature of middle-class life (see below also), this draws our attention *away* from the experiences of the working class. One of the benefits of the style of survey questioning which we have adopted is that we have been able to tease apart from one another differing forms of fear about crime. We expect that Garland is correct in his summary that the middle classes have had to face up to greater levels of crime and insecurity than perhaps they have had to prior to the 1960s.

However, the forms of fear which they appear to report (so long as one aligns the middle classes with people who live in areas with lower crime levels, who have less experience of crime, and who see their neighbourhood to be relatively orderly and cohesive) are of what we have termed the expressive nature—that is, they encapsulate a wider set of concerns and preoccupations than just crime alone. Those people who we classified on the basis of their answers as worried or frequently worried about crime were, on the basis of our analyses, differentiated from the unworried and anxious along the following lines; they perceived themselves to be at greater risk of crime; they were more likely to have concerns about social order and social cohesion; they were more likely to be victims of crime; they were more likely to know victims of crime and to have witnessed crime; they were more likely to live in areas which the BCS interviewers described as being disorderly; and, finally, they lived in areas with higher scores on the Index of Multiple Deprivation (IMD)—see Chapter 6. In short, those people who we classified as being worried or frequently worried lived in the sorts of areas one might expect them to: in neighbourhoods characterized by disorder, crime, and low levels of social cohesion and social order. The anxious, on the other hand, appear to be expressing anxieties through the language of crime without ever really experiencing the 'sharp end' of disorder in the UK. This supports the work of the left realists (e.g. Young, *Confronting Crime*, 1986, p 23; or Lea and Young, *What Is To Be Done about Law and Order?*, 1984, p 264–5), namely that crime and the fear of crime are more pressing problems for those amongst our society living in some of the poorer sections of it.

However, we also find that those people who live in 'mid-range' areas, with 'mid-range' levels of crime, who have 'middling' perceptions of disorder and risk (sometimes referred to as 'middle England'), have (as mentioned above) a more generalized fear of crime. This finding echoes Garland's discussion of the middle classes becoming more aware of crime since the late 1970s. We also find that both worry and anxiety are about trust in strangers and changes in assessments of local collective efficacy, the perceived loss of collective authority and control over norms and values (Chapters 5 and 7). Crime—especially when we move to discussion of the fear of crime—is a vivid and dramatic marker of the failure of society to regulate its members.

The Prominent Position of Crime and Security in Contemporary Times

In short, part of the reason why crime has attained a place in the modern consciousness is its growing prominence in political analysis, debate, and discussion (see also Chapter 2). Concerns about crime, justice, and punishment have been fuelled by media coverage, by broader anxieties about social change, and by a loss of trust in government. One of the reasons why this has occurred is that public and political discourse has merged the issue of crime in the public's mind with issues of social change and declining social cohesion and moral authority (see Hall et al., 1978; Hall, 1978; Hay, 1996). Such anxieties—although these were already in existence—have been exploited by rightwing politicians and, as the political agenda has slipped ever rightwards, has come to obtain a hegemonic position in discourses about crime, and law and order. And this in turn helps to explain the persistence of crime in social and political debate: such debates have a strong symbolic charge because they speak to and dramatize social stability and moral consensus. We feel that one of our lasting contributions to such debates is the development of a survey methodology and statistical technique for 'teasing apart' the fear of crime along the ways outlined above. In so doing we provide a way of assessing the fear of crime along the lines suggested by both Garland, Taylor, Girling et al. and those approaches (most notably inspired by left realist thinking on the issues of crime and victimization) which have emphasized economic inequality and crime fears.

The Tension between Government Administration of Justice and Competing Public Perceptions and Demands (The 'Punitive Turn' and 'Penal Populism')

As mentioned in Chapter 1, both Garland (2001) and Loader (2006b) have documented how liberal elites took on the role of 'looking after' criminal justice policy prior to the mid-1980s. The criminal justice system during this era was organized along dispassionate and rational lines, arrived at via an assessment of 'what worked'. However (as documented elsewhere and in Chapter 2 above), this started to unravel during the late 1970s and throughout the 1980s. The public started to make (and importantly voice) assessments of risk that differed to those produced by rational and technical judgements. To a large extent what governments and policy makers should do depends on how they perceive the fear of crime. We submit that there is a moral, social value and normative component to the fear of crime: by associating certain individuals, groups, and social conditions with crime, people may be articulating their sense that these run counter to their idea of a stable and cohesive society. As such the fear of crime is an important attitudinal social indicator, reflecting concerns about the erosion of traditional sources of authority, and anxieties about the cohesion and stability of communities. But the fear of crime is not *only* this; it is also a sense of immediate threat to one's security. On the basis of our findings, those in greatest need of security are those living in some of the least advantaged communities in England and Wales. They see more crimes, live in areas with greatest policing need (on the basis of the IMD and other area level assessments) and are more victimized than those living in other areas (see Chapter 6). As such it may appear tempting to provide such communities with extra resources. However, as we stated previously, we argue that one misunderstands the fear of crime if we approach it as simply about either crime or a way of making sense of social change. Therefore 'what' one 'does' about 'the fear of crime' depends very much on which element of this phenomenon one wishes to 'tackle'. The trick is to tackle the fear of crime as both symptomatic of crime (*à la* left realists) whilst articulating a set of policy responses which chime with the concerns of 'middle England', 'middle America', or 'middle elsewhere'. Such a balancing act is not an easy one, but we shall return to this issue towards the end of this chapter. Let us, however, reflect on the causes of all this worry and anxiety.

The causes of worry we understand as the quite sensible and rational responses to living in areas in which crime appears common, and so require very little further comment, we feel. Anyone who lives in an area with multiple sources of deprivation, where they knew many victims of crime, saw crimes and the effects of crime regularly, and felt likely to be victimized themselves is entitled to worry about crime. What these communities need is for crime to be tackled directly (of course), but what they also need is for there to be a sense of a worthwhile future inculcated amongst others in their communities. This means providing people with those things which neither the police nor (since the mid-1970s) governments can easily (or want to?) provide: jobs and a hope for a better future. Criminal justice policies based not on 'trashing' the lives of former miscreants (Simon, 2007) but on helping them and other people towards law-abiding lives (employment, decent homes, good schools, and so on) are what is needed. This may sound like namby-pamby, 1970s social work, but the best forms of control are informal forms of social control (Sampson and Laub, 1993) and as such the best way of tackling worry about crime is to tackle crime itself through social interventions aimed at encouraging informal social controls to flourish. In short, if crime underpins the *fear* of crime for the worried (and our analyses suggest that it *does*), then, as Jock Young argued some time back:

> It is not the Thin Blue Line, but the social bricks and mortar of civil society which are the major bulwarks against crime. Good jobs with a discernible future, housing estates that tenants can be proud of, community facilities which enhance a sense of cohesion and belonging, a reduction in unfair inequalities, all create a society which is more cohesive and less criminogenic. (Young, 1992: 45).

But what of the other side of the coin: What of all this anxiety?

Economic and Social Change and Anxiety

Our models (Chapter 7) suggest that similar processes may lie behind anxiety about crime. We saw, for example, that negative experiences of long-term social change were associated with increases in concerns about disorder and anti-social behaviour, which were in turn strongly associated with anxiety about crime (Figure 7.2). Similarly, attitudes towards social change in the local community were also associated with concerns about disorder in the local crime survey, which in turn were related to anxiety about crime (Figure 7.3).

That the UK, Europe, and many other parts of the world (both industrialized and developing) have undergone a period of sustained economic changes in the past forty to fifty years ought not to be news to anyone. However, of late, there has been a recognition, at least amongst some, that the increasing levels of affluence experienced by many in Europe, North America, and elsewhere may not be making people happier—in fact, such developments may in fact be making people less happy and more insecure. How might such approaches assist us in understanding anxieties about crime?

Amongst the authors who have documented the negative outcomes of rising affluence are Avner Offer (2006), Rober H. Frank (2007), and, albeit in a populist style, Oliver James (2007). Anver Offer argues that affluence, which he sees as driven by novelty (2006: vii), and rising material abundance leads to a number of potential harms, such as obesity, mental disorder, violence, economic fraud, and insecurity (2006: 2). In short, he claims, 'the paradox of affluence and its challenge is that the flow of new rewards can undermine the capacity to enjoy them' (2006: 2).

If affluence is measured by average income per head, then, as Offer suggests (2006: 7), the US has led the UK by one generation in terms of rises in affluence. Furthermore, and possibly part of this process, towards the end of the 1960s attitudes began to shift away from common welfare and public service as a form of well-being, and private benefits were seen as replacing these as sources of well-being (2006: 7–8). Interestingly, this is also the same approximate point at which we see the widespread recognition (or 'invention' and 'production' for some; see Lee, 2007; Loo, 2009) of the fear of crime in the US and then the UK (see Chapter 2).

The work underpinning Offer's critique of contemporary societies can be traced back to the early 1980s. Offer approvingly quotes Zolotas (1981) who along similar lines claimed that 'When an industrial society reaches an advanced state of affluence, the rate of increase in social welfare drops below the rate of economic growth, and tends ultimately to become negative' (1981: 1). Or, put more simply, as a society's wealth increases, so increases in welfare slow and then decline. In short, increases in affluence result in decreases in social welfare. As Offer demonstrates, rises in levels of income provide no increases in well-being (2006, Ch 12). But why should this be the case? One possible answer is that as income increases, people adjust to it and raise their standards—remaining on what Easterlin termed 'a hedonistic treadmill'. Another possible answer, and one which resonates with our own concerns, is the thesis put forward by Inglehart. Stated simply, this suggests that as a result of their experience of post-war economic security, cohorts of Europeans and North Americans have shifted the preferences from economic to non-economic rewards. In other words, economic security drives us towards wanting non-economic goals—including non-economic security. Offer argues that there have been two stages of economic growth since the end of the Second World War. In the first period, economic growth produces high welfare payoffs as basic deprivations are remedied. Homes are built, healthcare is improved, education is provided, and basic needs are met. In the second period, the return from increases in GDP is diminishing and at extremes, negative (2006: 36). Likewise, psychic rewards under conditions of affluence lead to habituation (2006: 37), mirroring Easterlin.

As such, in first the US and then the UK, economic growth led to rising prosperity, which, roughly from around the late 1960s, started to produce not only diminishing rewards, but also increases in levels of anxiety (Offer, 2006: 282). At around this time we see a shift in those sorts of forms of security which people sought (having had, in many cases, their immediate economic needs met). Also, as others have documented (Loo, 2009), rightwing politicians started to emphasize the 'problem of crime' (see Chapter 2). These sentiments resonated with members of the middle class, who, as Frank (2007) notes, often felt as if they had lost most during the period of rising affluence. As Offer himself notes:

Since the 1970s, the risks [of social falling associated with un- or underemployment] have increasingly embraced a growing proportion of the so-called 'middle class' in the US, people with families, houses of their own in a safe neighbourhood, and seemingly steady jobs. Once the two-earner family had become the norm, the risks and the stakes rose (2006: 293).

As such, the fear of crime arguably became a topic of study in the late 1960s in the US and the late 1970s in the UK not simply because of rising crime rates, but also because of background economic factors and the implications which these had for value systems in industrialized nations.[1] Rising levels of affluence, to which people became habituated and which were then challenged by the oil crisis in the early 1970s, produced increased levels of anxiety. Added to this, according to some authors, was a desire to shift political debates from 'New Deal'/Kennedyian politic towards an agenda which would favour neo-conservative policy concerns (Loo, 2009). Offer, too, argues something close to this position:

My hypothesis is that the shift from the New Deal to the New Right, from social democracy to market liberalism, the largest historical shift of the

---

[1] Maruna and King (2004: 93) similarly report various studies which have found a relationship between economic conditions and the lynching of black men in Southern US states in the early part of the twentieth century.

last fifty years, has worked up from technologies, to new opportunities and rewards, which unsettled the individual psyche, to consequences both unintended and desired, the level of society and politics (2006: 365–6).

In this analysis, the rise of the fear of crime was the result of a 'perfect storm': rising affluence, shifts in values as a result of this, an economic crisis in the case of the UK and an attempt to shift the agenda by the political rightwing in the US and the UK.

At around this time there emerged another key plank in our story: the rise of the social survey. Murray Lee (2001, 2007) has used a Foucaldian analysis to help describe the ways in which government has incorporated 'the science of statistics' deeply into the ways in which policies are shaped and promoted. Statistics, he says, allow a problem or population to be explored, dissected, and made manageable. It allows for computation and assessment and is a convincing tool with which to establish 'facts'. This style of 'governmentality' is government power that exerts its influence through the development of knowledge and technologies that allow the most minute and specific forms of governance to occur. The use of survey data and crime prevention literature, he stresses, are intimately involved in the complex relationship between fear of crime, knowledge, power, individuals, and the state. Specifically, he maintains that there is 'little doubt that the genealogy of the "fear of crime" is intimately entwined with the development and deployment of crime statistics more generally' (2001: 472). He describes how, since the 1960s, there has been an increasing emphasis on the development of research techniques and collection of data which have been able to quantify information about crime, victims, and fear. These data have been fundamental in hoisting the issue of crime up the political agenda and led to 'the emergence of fear of crime as a disciplinary and governmental object of inquiry and regulation' (2001: 480). He cites the volumes of crime prevention literature—particularly those aimed at women—which are as much about fear management as they are about crime prevention (see Stanko, 2000). But reminiscent of the responsibilization strategies as already mentioned above, Lee notes how citizens are now expected to govern their own risks; they are subjected to intimate details of potential threats and the consequences of those threats. As such he believes we are asked to become 'fearing subjects'. Lee (2001: 480–1) argues that once the fear of crime has been 'discovered', it becomes almost impossible to escape from—what he refers to as the 'fear of crime feed-back loop'.

In summary, the works discussed above suggest the growth and sophistication of statistics and information, combined with a new governmental focus on individual responsibility and self-assessment of risk, have contributed to the emergence of fearing and anxious individuals. Lee eloquently notes that the development of fear is borne from a complex milieu; it has 'no locatable birth moment and its emergence is not somehow teleological' (2001: 481). To be clear, fear is not simply about the objective day-to-day risks we are faced with, in terms of any particular crime or disease, but we are directly encouraged to consider and calculate all potential short- and long-term threats to our well-being and safety. We focus on our *ill health* rather than our good health, we ponder the risk of becoming a victim, as opposed to our general safety from offending behaviour.

Furthermore, as Garland (2001: 153) and Taylor and Jamieson (1998) have highlighted, the emergence of 'fear of crime' must be considered in a broader social and political context. Fear of crime has evolved during a specific time period, where the professional middle classes are experiencing greater threats to their position and safety more generally, and they have consequently been particularly vulnerable to 'fearing strategies' (see also Gunn and Bell, 2002: 187). It would appear that this anxiety about crime has increasingly preoccupied the middle classes: research by Tim Hope and his colleagues (Hope et al., 2001) found that areas of Lancashire with greater levels of social need (i.e. poorer ones with greater levels of poverty) called the police for assistance *less* often than their objective needs and crime rates would suggest they ought to have. In more affluent areas, although the need for policing was lower, relative to their needs, residents called the police for assistance *more* often than their needs suggested they would do. Similarly, Walklate (2002: 306–12) recounts how upper middle-class residents in villages in Cheshire found their influence over local matters (such as policing) swept away by a tide of 'financial management' and 'resource allocation' (for want of better descriptions) which left their constabulary unable to continue to pay for the upkeep of a local police station. Such concerns left the traditionally powerful with neither a police officer nor a way of effectively altering this situation. One could argue that their anxieties about losing their local police officer came about, in part, from their lack of political control over these decisions—where once they had voice and control, in the face of economic and political choices they were left impotent.

Considering the position of the professional middle classes, Garland notes they have historically lived 'separately' from high crime and insecurity—they occupied low-crime areas of the city and the suburbs. As Gunn and Bell (2002) note, over the past thirty years or so the middle classes have experienced an erosion of the traditional career pathway and the development of long hours and short-term contracts. However, the economic changes wrought by the global depression in the early 1970s destroyed the security of the middle classes. Social and spatial changes that gave rise to new high crime rates during the 1960s and the subsequent decades also transformed the middle-class experience of crime too—or at least their perceptions of it. From being something that normally affected the poor, crime, particularly burglary, vandalism, and robbery, increasingly became a daily consideration for anyone who owned a car, had a house, and who travelled on public transport after dark:

> The group that had been the prime beneficiaries of the post-war consumer boom now found themselves to be more vulnerable than before in the face of the massively increased levels of property crime that this boom brought in its wake. And the tell-tale signs of crime and disorder became more visible in the streets—in the form of vandalism and graffiti, the incivility of unsupervised teenagers, or the erratic behaviour of the newly deinstitutionalised mentally ill—fear of crime became an established part of daily existence (Garland, 2001: 359).

Similarly, Taylor and Jamieson, taking inspiration from Barbara Ehrenreich's 'Fear of Falling' (1989), have suggested that the professional middle classes have been particularly vulnerable to strategies which emphasize individual risk. Fear of crime, they maintain, is not simply about perceived calculated risk for these people, but about a broader insecurity. This group of people are 'afraid of falling' from their prominent and secure social and economic position which, due to globalization and political change, has come increasingly under threat. Crime fears become a catalyst through which the professional middle classes express an array of inter-connected anxieties about the current experience of middle-class life in England. While the threat of a burglary might be a threat in itself, it also signifies what urban sociologists call 'the urban other' and the increasing threat of social disorder and denigration. In short, it may be that the professional middle classes remain less *objectively* exposed to crime than others in poorer regions, but the mounting *threat* of crime and disorder symbolizes more than an episode of victimization, but a whole host of meanings about their social, economic, and physical position in society. Or, as Bauman (2006: 130) observes:

> It is the people who live in greatest comfort on record, more cosseted and pampered than any other people in history, who feel more threatened, insecure and frightened, more inclined to panic, more passionate about everything related to security and safety than people in most societies past and present.

Thus those people we have referred to as the anxious (those who express worry about crime but who do not encounter any such worries) and which others have termed (in the health arena) the 'worried well' appear to be from amongst the 'middle mass' of society and appear to express anxieties about crime which are out of kilter with their objective risks (see Farrall et al., 2007 on this concept more widely). Why are these seeming 'winners' in our societies so concerned about their health, their safety, their security? One answer, perhaps, and as we have hinted at above, lies in wider social and economic transformations—and another in the sorts of political cultures and rhetoric (if not policy actions) of the neo-liberal right. Let us take each in turn.

Political Culture

In Chapter 2 we discussed the origins of the fear of crime as a concept (and hence as a topic for research, debate, and political use) and discussed how popular alignment with this concept was manipulated by political and academic interest groups. We argued—following others, naturally—that the fear of crime started as something of a rightwing toy, which chimed with popular anxieties about 'disorder' in the US and which was adopted as a useful sound bite by Thatcher in her 1979 general election campaign in the UK. If the 'spiritual home' of fear of crime research is the US, then the UK represents its main base in Europe. Until very recently, there was little sustained research on the fear of crime from researchers outside of these two countries. However, as both criminology and neo-liberal social and economic policies strengthened in Europe throughout the 1980s, 1990s, and

Political Culture 253

into the twenty first century, so we have witnessed an increase in research into the fear of crime. For sure, some of the research into the fear of crime is inspired by individual criminologists exploring in their own countries what is (or appears to be) happening in neighbouring countries. But there is also evidence to suggest that this transference of interest in crime and the fear of crime is driven by other, less benevolent, interests. In her *Making People Behave* (2005), Burney charts the rise of interest in the control of antisocial behaviours in The Netherlands and Sweden.

The Netherlands, famously, of course, was for a long time considered to be the home of European tolerance (Downes, 1988). However, one rightwing politician (Pim Fortuyn) started to explore and bring to the fore what Burney (2005:146) referred to as 'simmering discontents' about crime and criminal justice. As Pakes also notes (2004: 290), Fortuyn also used concerns about crime and immigration to bolster his standing amongst the electorate (recall our observations about the fear of crime and right-leaning politicians in Chapter 2). In this way the concept of 'veiligheid' (safety) came to occupy the central ground of political debates about crime in The Netherlands (Burney, 2005: 146–7)—assisted greatly of course by his assassination in May 2002. Sweden (another of the European countries long held to embrace a more enlightened approach to social issues, including crime) has not been able to escape this rightwards drift (Burney, 2005: 155); however, it has been able, thus far at least, to avoid the worst excesses of both neo-liberalizm (Burney, 2005: 160) and the fear of crime (Heber, 2007: 244—who finds that when asked about crime fears, many respondents express concerns for *other* people, not themselves; 2007: 246).

David Green (2008) reflects on the relationship between political culture and sentiments about crime in his compelling account and comparison of the child murders of James Bulger (1993, UK) and Silje Marie Redergård (1994, Norway). In the UK politicians (from both the right, in the form of the Conservative Party leader and, then, Prime Minister, John Major, and the right of centre Labour Party leader, Tony Blair) appeared to find it impossible to refrain from commenting on the Bulger case. In Norway, however, there was almost no comment on the murder, except for a 'comparatively reasoned' (2008: 256) set of comments from the Norwegian Culture Minister. Green concluded that while the legitimacy of elite expertise appears to survive in Norway, it has fallen to the wayside in Britain, and addressing this absence of public confidence has become a political priority. Moreover, the political culture in Norway makes its politicians less susceptible to the temptations experienced by adversarial English politicians to politicize high-profile crimes. He describes English political culture as being highly susceptible to late-modern anxieties brought by rapid social change, which have steered government towards emotional and popular penal actions.

What is particularly interesting, however, from our perspective is the ways in which politicians in the UK used the Bulger murder (which was to all intents and purposes a random act of violence) to launch commentaries on the 'state of the nation'. John Major argued that society needed to 'condemn a little more' and 'understand a little less' (speaking to a set of punitive attitudes which were growing in volume at the time), whilst Tony Blair used the murder as evidence that 'there [was] something very wrong and sick at the heart of our society' (Green, 2008: 258). Green eloquently summarizes the differences between the UK and Norway (2008: 270):

> Ways of doing politics complicatedly interact with the ways that media cover and contextualise crime. These often antagonistic relationships are nonetheless mutually supporting, and they seem to conduce to cultural and political attitudes in citizens that in turn support the status quo. It seems that distrustful English citizens expect and value a news media that is aggressively antagonistic toward and distrustful of government. This distrust, on emotive crime and punishment issues at least, extends to those who call themselves experts—the woolly-minded 'ologists' vilified in the tabloids—and is rhetorically reinforced by opposition party politicians eager to discredit those in power and regain power themselves. In contrast, the apparently more trustful and deferential Norwegian citizen still retains considerable trust in fellow citizens, elected leaders and elite expertise.

Thus—as Green argues (2008: 272)— 'consensus democracies' (such as Norway) have been able to limit the incentives to politicize crime and criminal justice responses to it in exactly the way in which a more conflictual political system cannot.

'Winners' and 'Losers' in Socio-Economic Transformations

It is possible to see the anxious in our data sets and the wider notion of the 'worried well' as a social phenomenon as falling somewhere between those who have, during recent social and economic transformations, 'won' and those who have 'lost'. Crow and Rees (1999) remind us that in between the 'winners' and the 'losers' there are several classes of intermediate groups (1999: Abstract). Just as we have found, Crow and Rees point out that the gap between those who 'have' and those who 'have not' does not lie neatly along class lines (1999: 2.2). Social class appears, for many sociologists, to bear little relationship to those who have 'won' and those who have 'lost' (e.g. Offe, 1996; Ferge, 1993). As such, what is being 'won' or 'lost' during and after social changes may no longer (if it ever were) be simply about material gains (in keeping with Inglehart).

Crow and Rees point out that even those who look like they may have 'won' may feel like they have lost. Even upward social mobility may bring a sense of personal unhappiness (1999: 3.2) as the upwardly mobile find themselves in surroundings which are unfamiliar and (perhaps) alienating (see Runciman, 1998; James, 1998). During periods of quite far-reaching social change, people may come to feel and view themselves as more insecure. Writing about the changes in post-communist countries, Standing remarks that 'the economic, social and psychological shocks of the restructuring have precipitated a profound and widespread sense of *insecurity*, reflecting an inability to adjust to ... new and difficult circumstances' (1996: 250). Los (2002: 176–8) suggests that levels of fear of crime rose in Poland in the years following the collapse of communist rule there, partly in response to wider social and political projects associated with risk privatization. 'Eternal' (Ferge, 1993) or 'total' (Latouche, 1993) losers characterized by extreme forms of isolation and exclusion have been identified by some sociologists. Maybe these are who the worried in our data sets are most like: certainly their social and criminological characteristics appear to support this view. They are more likely to be victimized, to have seen crimes taking place, to be poorer, to live in poorer neighbourhoods, and so on. The anxious, on the other hand, had broadly better material conditions, and were more likely to be living in areas which were improving and less likely to be in areas which were declining—but as noted above even positive change can produce anxiety. Bauman (2000: 213–7) notes how the promotion of deregulated, market capitalism by neo-liberal states has served to increase anxiety and insecurity via the concept of the flexible workforce and its application in many arenas of the economy.

Such analysis and debates chime with other recent work (Sennett, 1998; Beck, 2000; Bauman, 2001; Rifkind, 1995; Therborn, 1989) on the changing nature of work in what some have referred to as 'fast capitalism' (Furlong and Kelly, 2005), This work—known as the Brazilianization thesis—argues that the modern labour market has become characterized by employment insecurity, casualization, informality, and precariousness (all conditions which haunted the labour markets of the world's less developed economies—hence the title). As such, the working conditions and therefore the social lives of many of the law-abiding, middle mass of society have come to be characterized by uncertainty. Therborn refers to this as the two-thirds, one-third society, whereby one third are near-permanently un- or under-employed, one third are stably employed (or re-employable) and one third are top business managers who 'appeal to the bulk of employees as the guarantors of the latter not falling into the abyss of unemployment' (1989: 112). For Bauman, this uncertainty has the effect of individualizing society; instead of uniting people, it fragments collective interests. As Furlong and Kelly (2005) note, since there is no guessing who will 'sink' and who will 'swim', the notion of common interests evaporates. In these conditions it is easy for politicians to re-articulate inchoate anxieties and troubles back to the public as fears about specific harms (ill-health, the economy, immigrants—and crime).

Interestingly, and scanning the broader fields of sociological and social theory literature, the ubiquity of 'risk' in contemporary Western social life has been widely discussed; beyond crime and health fears as discussed above, the increasing significance of risk has been identified in relation to work, relationships, education, travel, and food consumption. Indeed, few would dispute the idea that risk has become an important driver of recent government policies and private enterprise, while academic debates have led to the concept becoming a key term of reference. However, it was Beck (1992) who emphasized the negative transformatory qualities of this framework. This new 'risk society' he maintains is epistemologically pessimistic and encourages one to be constantly vigilant to potential threats. To summarize his theory, he stresses that modern capitalist societies are best described as seeking protection from dangers (crime, AIDS, pollution, and anti-social behaviour) as opposed to the positive quest for 'goods' (a home, income, or education). Curiously, however, Giddens (1991) notes the paradox of risk in modern capitalist societies whereby, 'abstract systems' such as insurance, health screening, security items, and financial services have been able to protect people from potential risks, but there nevertheless exists an amplified perception of risk awareness in everyday life. Giddens says the crux of modern mentalities is that it 'becomes less and less possible to protect any lifestyle, however pre-established, from the generalized risk climate' (1991: 126). Specifically, Garland (2001) suggested that it was after the 1970s that people in the US and UK began to feel that life was becoming more risky in general. Not only was the rehabilitative ideal of prisons and probation seemingly failing, leaving crime on the increase, but there emerged a sense of social malaise related to the idea that common values were deteriorating and that modern life was unfamiliar, unpredictable, and hazardous.

Both Garland and Beck accused the media and politicians of being involved in shifting the sensibilities of the public; they had become increasingly preoccupied with risk conflicts to the point where risk matters were not rationally communicated to the public, but sensationalized. Garland (2001) noted how policy documents were designed with obvious sound bites in mind and spun in the press to increase their potential newsworthiness. The media responded and gave considerable attention to these matters. Moreover, not only did new neo-liberal debates erupt throughout written and televised journalism, but such debates also arose in well-known TV dramas and films. The messages were clear—people were at greater risk and the government could not protect the public. As such, the public's anxieties and sensibilities were, in part at least, shaped by the nature and intensity of political rhetoric and media attention. Moreover, as Sparks's work on crime in the media illustrates, the public appeared to have an insatiable appetite for crime stories in particular, to the extent that consumption of crime reports and fiction has become a popular pastime (1992a, 2000).

These analytic frameworks help us understand how concerns about crime have perforated the public's consciousness, impacting on their sense of safety as well as their daily cognitive and behavioural processes, shaped how they perceive risks in their own environs, and why it is they seem so continuously in pursuit of protection from new risks and social ills. However, the perceptions of the public are worth further consideration to help understand why so many people responded to the 'call to arms' of the responsibilization lobby—why people might be persuaded to buy into more security items, live in gated communities, purchase private healthcare or move towards other neo-liberal social policies. Indeed, Garland and other writers do not suggest the public were blindly following a media pied piper. As Cavender explains, the public 'had genuine concerns that reflected a changing social reality' (2004: 346)—which were amplified in the media (see Lee, 2001; Loo, 2009), and constructed in ways which were more readily understood and which could be used for political gain (Hall et al., 1978; Hay, 1996). Indeed, media scholars agree that the narrative structure of news items, programmes, and the written press strike at the heart of how we experience our environment. As Fiske puts it, these narratives help us to make sense of the world, to make the events we experience understandable (1987: 129). Furthermore, he continues, some of the most potent social and moral narratives emanate from the media, in particular television, and these have an important role in how we understand and make sense of our own daily lives. Indeed, in order to fully understand the basis of public anxieties, we need to examine more deeply what the public understand about their position and safety, because as Tudor (2003) points out, fear includes both a macro- and micro-level response which is influenced by a wide range of factors including everyday habits, cultural practices, social structures, personalities, and political rhetoric.

In particular, literature on the fear *of crime*, (the subject we are primarily interested in here), suggests it is a topic often bound up in how individuals relate to 'place' and their immediate environment (Banks, 2005; Chadee and Ditton, 2005; Girling et al., 2000; Ferraro, 1995). Ferraro (1995) maintains that an individual's perceptions of their community have a strong influence on their subjective estimates of the chances of victimization. More explicitly, it is the physical environment and local crime rates that impact on how people define their environment; by interpreting local cues they make judgements about their safety and security (findings we confirm; see Chapter 7). These appraisals also influence respondents' perceptions of their social relationships with neighbours, their locale, and their sense of 'community cohesion' and trust. Writing more recently, Burney (2005) notes how antisocial behaviour (ASB) has come to dominate Britain's law and order discourse and become a potent signal of disorder. While

ASB is a vague term that can mean anything, it is also a strongly symbolic and evocative label. It is apparent that the perception of ASB in the public and media sphere goes beyond what it witnessed outside the home, or in the local community, or even in the newspapers and television, but reaches out to wider concerns about crime and society more generally. As Jackson (2004) contends, fear of crime and anxiety about ASB acts as a kind of lay seismograph of social cohesion and moral consensus.

These writers suggest that understanding the *expressive* as well as the experiential content of individuals' perceptions is central to disentangling the complex process of fear of crime. As such, Sparks et al. (2001) agree that crime discourse is a particularly pertinent area in which to discover the impact of social and political change on people's everyday experience of life, but fear of crime is also very much grounded in a sense of location and people's appraisal of fear is deeply contacted to their unconscious interpretation of their environment and space. They conclude:

> ... crime works in everyday life as a cultural theme and token of political exchange; it serves to condense, and make intelligible, a variety of more difficult to grasp troubles and insecurities—something that tends to blur the boundary between worries about crime and other kinds of anxiety and concern. In speaking of crime, people routinely register its entanglement with other aspects of economic, social and moral life; attribute responsibility and blame; demand accountability and justice; and draw lines of affiliation and distance between 'us' and various categories of 'them'. In short, 'fear of crime' research is at its most illuminating when it addresses the various sources of in/security that pervade people's lives (and the relationship between them) and when it makes explicit (rather than suppresses) the connections that the 'crime-related' anxieties of citizens have with social conflict and division, social justice and solidarity. (2001: 895–6)

> people's worries and talk about crime are rarely merely a reflection of behavioural change and 'objective' risk (although they represent lay attempts to make sense of such changes and risks), but are also 'bound up in a context of meaning and significance, involving the use of metaphors and narratives about social change. (Sparks, 1992b: 131)

Thus the fear of crime is at some level related to how people make sense of wider (i.e. social and economic) changes. It expresses, through metaphor and analogy, concerns and troubles which are hard to find the right words to otherwise describe. In this respect, it is interesting to reflect on what John Hills in a lecture to support the launch of *Inequality and the State* (2004) at the LSE has referred to as the 'onion-shaped class distribution'. Unlike other models of class distribution which have a triangular or diamond shape, Hills argues that wealth has become so concentrated amongst the super rich that the class shape is now onion-shaped: a bulbous 'mass' (the 'onion') at the bottom, but a very long stem growing from the top of this, which represents the 'super rich' (see also Frank, 2007: 117). The lesson is that it does not matter how far up the stem one goes, there are always people above you. Similarly, the higher up one gets, the greater the fall one may experience. As such, inequalities in wealth produce poor outcomes for the financially well-off as well as for the less well-off members of society.

Perhaps, then, one reason why North America and the UK led the way in terms of research into the fear of crime during the 1980s was because they were presided over by neo-liberal political administrations who 'played up' the problem of crime for their own political purposes and shifted the tax base in such a way as to increase economic inequalities (see Farrall, 2006: 263 on the UK; Brandolini, 1998 on the US). Timmins (2001: 375) is not alone in noting the 'marked widening in the gap between rich and poor during the Thatcher years' (see also Young, 1993: 606; Walker, 1990), reporting that as early as the late-1980s the first signs that the UK was becoming a more unequal society were emerging (2001: 449). The inequalities were, in part, the result of government changes to income tax law. Timmins (2001: 375, 448, and 508) reports that the top rate of tax was dropped from 60 pence in the £ to 40 pence, whilst the bottom rate changed from 33 pence in the £ to 30 pence—much less of a reduction. As Wilkins and Pease (1987) note, the greater a society's tolerance of economic inequality, the greater the levels of punishment meted out by the society will be. What makes this issue particularly difficult to resolve is the intractability of the gap which has developed between rich and poor. In 2007 the Joseph Rowntree Foundation reported that inequality was the widest it had been for 40 years. Households in already wealthy areas had become disproportionately richer compared with society as a whole, while the number of 'poor' households had risen over the past 15 years. A further report stated that in 2006–07, 2.9 million children were living in poverty and it was estimated that the proportion of children living in poverty had doubled in the past generation (JRF, 2006).

Psychosocial Understanding of the Fear of Crime

As we noted in Chapter 4, no review of recent work on the fear of crime would be complete without some discussion of that body of work which takes as its starting point the key ideas emanating from psycho-analysis. In this work the individual is re-cast into academic study to learn how he/she personally integrates and responds to psychological, sociological, and psychosocial influences. The approach incorporates the complex and contradictory nature of human emotion—which often operates in difficult and cross-pressured circumstances, but is nevertheless the reality of our everyday lives (Gadd and Jefferson, 2007). It suggests that all individuals suffer from anxiety, and that individuals need to 'defend' themselves against such anxieties. This will often mean that individuals are drawn to those discourses which offer ways of controlling such anxieties. The manner in which individuals are attracted to such discourses and the reasons for their attraction to one discourse rather than another are partly dependent upon their own biographies (Hollway and Jefferson, 1997: 261). As such the fear of crime is 'an unconscious displacement of other fears which are far more intractable' (Hollway and Jefferson, 1997: 263). Anxieties which perhaps cannot be properly identified or fully understood by the individual in question are projected onto 'knowable' and 'name-able' fears. For example, when cotton prices were deflated, the frequency of lynching increased in Southern US states (Hovland and Sears, 1940). We argue—as do others, naturally—that crime is a convenient receptacle for anxieties associated with modern life for a number of reasons. First, it represents one of the last remaining 'others' in a complex society. The 'criminal other' represents a traditional figure of hate where anxieties can be safely projected and attacked (Maruna and King, 2004: 94). What sets the 'criminal other' apart from, for example, the 'racial other' is that in modern societies many people know people from ethnic minorities—as such, processes of racial othering are harder to successfully achieve without censure. This has not happened, however, with those people identified as 'criminal'—in fact, the opposite is probably true (see our discussion above). Thus the 'criminal other' represents an expedient and convenient location for the projection and storing of anxieties (Scheingold, 1995). Second, the discourse associated with the fear of crime brings with it a series of actions which promote feelings of control over uncertainty (Hollway and Jefferson, 1997; Lupton, 1999: 14). In part, these feelings of uncertainty, as we mentioned immediately above, are related to the economic forms which underpin society (Bauman, 2000). Similarly, our work supports this general line of reasoning: our anxious group report anxieties about crime (and in the qualitative data could become quite animated on the topic) but have little or no direct experience of either crime or of feeling fearful about specific criminal threats in particular. As such, this group of people appear to be attracted to the discourse around 'fear' and 'crime' and are able to use it to express anxieties about crime—but also other matters which are important to them. However, as Gadd and Jefferson highlight, these people are susceptible to having their anxiety manipulated and to being drawn into emotionalized, political debates, which inevitably lead them nowhere particularly satisfying. The authors conclude:

> If governments were to take psychoanalytic insights more seriously they would focus their efforts on protecting their citizens from the 'spiralling mutual aggression' projective processes engender, think very carefully about the long term effects of agitating anxieties for political advantage, and avoid, wherever possible, deflecting responsibility for difficult, almost irresolvable, problems onto those communities least able to cope with them (2007: 190).

What, Then, *Can* the State 'Do'?

Building on his notion of a fear of crime feed-back loop, Lee (2007: 134) questions whether our various attempts to reduce fears about crime are not just increasing such anxieties. Letters to residents from local police services may only serve to raise fears rather than suppress them, after all. In a similar vein, Crawford (2002: 11) reflects that governments can do little to guarantee security (of any sort)—and in fact actually promote it via flexible labour markets and the corrosion of long-term commitments. Similar lines of argument are not hard to uncover. Loader (2009), for example, draws on the work of Sennett (2006) who reflects on the present political climate in which governments feel quite unhindered in their ability to abandon new policies almost without waiting to see the sorts of outcomes these produce. This does two things, in Sennett's view; first, it damages confidence in the government of the day. Second, it also raises expectations that 'zero risk' environments are a realistic possibility. These two outcomes, set against a period of reduced state control over many mundane aspects of citizens' lives (such as housing, transport, healthcare, and so on), combined to produce a third outcome (we believe): governments are increasingly pressurized by their electorates to act in ways which *will* produce the zero risk utopia, yet they are unable to do so since they no longer directly control many aspects of daily existence, leading them to increasingly 'knee jerk' reactions which tend (in the long run) to pander to illiberal desires. As Loader (2009) notes, this produces a situation in which the sorts of outcomes most needed (sensible debate about crime, relative risks, and long-term solutions to these problems) become increasingly hard to propagate.

The work of Bauman offers some further support in this respect. Bauman (2000) argues that, in the modern world, security is traded in against the exercise of free choice (driven by market forces) and that this creates, as a by-product, anxiety. These anxieties are then channelled into issues surrounding law and order (2000: 213). Governments, however, are relatively powerless in the face of both the market and the anxieties it engenders (see also Castells, cited in Sparks, 2006: 43); they have conceded power to the market and its 'forces' which, in an increasingly globalized system of capital transfer, are harder and harder for any one government to control and almost impossible to predict with any degree of certainty. Instead, governments focus on efforts to 'do something' (2000: 215), which often translates as increasingly harsh punishments and increasing the statutes of criminal offences (Scheingold, 1995: 156). One might add, following Lee, that this serves only to highlight the apparent 'need' for such policies. Of course, many of these policies will either fail (in the long term) or will make no discernible impact on the problem at hand. This is partly because, in our opinion, many of the policies aimed at tackling crime since the 1970s are ill-conceived, or, following Hollway, Jefferson, and Bauman, *not* the prime source of many of the fears anyway, since this is the anxiety brought on by social and economic changes. In sum, it becomes increasingly hard to 'slow down' or 'dampen' the speed and tenor of public debate in any way sufficient in order for reasoned debate to be fostered.

Our work, whilst not directly concerned with issues related to policing, touches on some of the recent debates about the nature of policing in the UK and the forms this ought to take. We use, as a way into these debates for us, Loader's critique (2006) of the notion of 'ambient policing' (also referred to as reassurance policing or neighbourhood policing and associated with the signal crimes perspective). Loader takes one recent paper on this topic (that by Innes, 2004) in order to critically examine the theory and practice which underlines this approach. Our aim herein is not to 'take sides', but rather to reflect on this debate given what we have learnt from our studies of the fear of crime.

As Loader notes, the reassurance policing model (RPM hereafter), amongst other things, argues that the police need to respond to 'more demanding customer expectations' (Loader, 2006a: 205), and also via perceptual interventions (i.e. making the local environment a more pleasant or less aversive one in which to live). However, given what we have said above about the increasingly shrill demands for a zero risk environment, responding to such calls may serve only to add to the problem. (This is not to suggest for one moment, however, that we ought not to attend to the conditions of many public areas or of many of our housing estates—for such conditions ought to be improved anyway, regardless of how these impact upon crime). One of the downsides of the RPM for us is the assumptions which this position makes about demands on police resources. First, it is assumed (as Loader notes too, 2006a: 206–07) that all demands for policing are benign. However, this is not always the case. Calls upon police time need to be seen as (in Loader's words, but backed up by our own findings) 'giving voice to a series of fears about, and hopes for, the political community in which they live and to the insecurities that flow from their sense of place within it' (2006: 207). Our studies have suggested that for some (those who we have characterized as the anxious, and who it must be remembered form a large part of the sample we relied upon) the language associated with the fear of crime may not only be related to their experiences of crime. As such the anxious would appear to be expressing a set of concerns through the language of crime and the fear of crime which do not wholly chime with their everyday experiences of crime or fear. They appear to be using the discourse of the fear of crime in order to express a set of anxieties which do not, at least to us, appear to be solely about that topic. In this respect the fear of crime is a 'sponge', soaking up other sorts of anxieties and concerns.

This chimes with earlier research members of our team were involved in (Hope et al., 2001), which uncovered a higher than

What, Then, *Can* the State 'Do'? 265

predicted demand for police action not from 'problem estates', but from leafy middle-class areas (see also Hope and Trickett, 2004: 445). Such calls were often about relatively less serious forms of crime (if indeed the calls were related to crime). Similarly we have found that it is the relatively better positioned (Loader's 'wealthy, active, noisy, well connected, [and] organized', 2006a: 213), who enjoy greater levels of social and economic protection and who, by and large, live more secure lives who are still, nevertheless, likely to report being worried about crime, despite often not having worried about it in the recent past. The RPM, via its assumption that demands for policing are (a) benign and (b) actually about crime, misses some of the nuances of both crime and insecurity, the forms and intensities of these, and how these are distributed in modern societies.

Furthermore, as Loader again argues (but see also Lee, 2007, discussed above), ambient policing risks making 'security' a pervasive feature of social life, and in so doing only serves to make *in*security more pervasive, since the practices (both personal and policing-led) often do little to tackle the sources of those insecurities. Our research, which has pointed to a large section of society who report being worried but who have not worried recently and whose anxieties appear to be related not just to crime but to all sorts of other considerations, speak to this agenda in two ways. First, it confirms Loader's point that often the causes of anxiety are not solely crime related. Second, and perhaps more worryingly for all concerned, the anxious in our study could be seen as evidence that the demand (and supply) of ambient security has already started to make insecurity more pervasive. Or, as Loader writes (2006a: 209):

> By treating security as an unmediated relation between police and citizen that requires the former to be routinely displayed in front of the latter, and by pandering to, rather than calling into question, popular fantasies of total security, ambient policing makes security pervasive in ways that, in the end, foster and sustain the very insecurity it purports to tackle.

All of the above leaves the State (and by implications, ourselves too) with a rather thorny set of problems. What can be done by the primary actor in the provider of 'safety and security', namely the State, when so much of what they do appears only to exaggerate fears (Lee, 2001, 2007) or appears to have limited or short-lived outcomes? Inevitably, we are not the first to consider this question. For Sennett (2006) one solution is for governments to have faith in their own policies and not refrain from their wide-scale abandonment. This slower, more reflective approach to policy making may serve to limit the damage done to public confidence in the government of the day and their policies. Second, it may also serve to communicate that any notions of 'zero risk' environments are unrealistic. A further set of suggestions comes from Loader (2009). Loader suggests that, in order to escape from an 'insecurity treadmill' (whereby governments respond to public demands for greater safety in ways which only serve to fuel such demands and which lead to the notion of security becoming a pervasive feature of contemporary life), societies need to embrace more fully enhanced democratic participation. We see this as a possible way forward if approached in the correct manner. One practical solution which chimes with Loader's suggestions lies in what some have referred to as 'deliberative polling' (Green, 2006; Hough and Park, 2002). Deliberative polls involve citizens and experts breaking down the traditional boundaries between those 'who know' and 'those who give opinions'. Such sessions involve citizens being given briefings on a particular issue and being asked over the course of some period of time to listen to expert presentations and to debate the issue at hand. The evaluations of such processes which have been undertaken suggest that participants are likely to change their minds over key issues, and often in a liberalizing direction (Green, 2006: 134). In this way—by moving away from the traditional one-to-one survey tool—criminologists might be better able to draw an informed opinion from citizens. Such debates would serve as useful correctives against the grandstanding on crime issues by politicians in order to legitimize increasingly punitive measures noted by Lee (2001).

A second possible solution involves rethinking the levels of economic inequality we presently tolerate in society. As Frank (2007: 115–6) notes, income inequality is the root cause of many social problems. Frank, like Offer (2006: 369–72), argues for an increase in consumption taxes (whereby certain key goods are taxed more heavily than other basic goods). Certainly the proposal is an interesting one (despite the sorts of strange outcomes in consumption preferences it may produce; Frank, 2007: 104). Perhaps what is needed is not taxes on consumption, but a redistributive tax regime which attempts to close the gap in inequalities of wealth (and hence, we contend, experiences of and anxieties about crime).

Is there any evidence to suggest that reductions in economic inequalities will reduce anxieties about crime? Kristjansson, in an analysis of Scotland's and Finland's relative levels of the fear of crime, finds that income inequalities are associated with greater levels of fear (2007: 79). These findings support those by Hope (2000), Currie (2003), and Burney (2005: 162). We fully accept, however, that in the current political climate, in which the UK's taxation policies have been aimed at increasing inequalities rather than reducing them, our suggestion that one of the solutions to the problem of the fear of crime is to reorganize taxation policies is unlikely to win any friends in the places which matter. However, one set of questions which criminologists have not yet grappled with revolves around this very issue: what sorts of emotions are the general thrusts of our political and economic systems and taxation policies encouraging in us, both at the level of the individual, and at the societal level? How might these inequalities in economic resources—and the likely changes in them—shape both our direct experiences of crime and the emotions they provoke (frequent worry, fear, and anger) and our responses to feelings (anxiety, a sense of general uncertainty) about social and political change and the shifting moral order?

Methodological Appendix

Interviews with Academic and Government Criminologists

A list was drawn up of academic and Home Office researchers who have been influential in the debate. Particular attention was given to those who have authored widely cited publications; who were described in the literature as important contributors to the debate; and who have steered the debate into new ground in the past or who have been most vocal in the main discussions. For example, a number of individuals have recently written articles that have raised doubts about survey measurement tools. An effort was made to approach those most vocal on this matter and those who were key in overseeing, analysing, and writing up key quantitative studies.

There was also a snowballing element to the sampling procedure. Many interviewees recommended people for interview based on their perceived impact on the debate. Nearly all these were then approached, although many had already been identified.

Thirty-six individuals were approached via email and letter. Twenty-six interviews were carried out, with two interviews involving talking simultaneously to two researchers who had worked closely together, making a total of twenty-eight individuals who were interviewed, five of whom were researchers with current or previous roles at the Home Office. Nearly all had conducted research into the fear of crime; those who had not had written on the subject. Refusals mostly involved individuals feeling that they had not carried out sufficient work in this area; the small remainder simply did not respond. All the interviews were conducted in 1999 and 2000 and took place where the individuals were based. The interviews lasted on average one and a half hours. The tapes were fully transcribed. Discussion focused on the history of the debate and its context, with a particular emphasis on how fear of crime has been researched and conceptualized alongside accounts of how they currently think about the phenomenon.

A note on the topic guide: Each interview began with an explanation of the aims and the topics to be covered—to trace the history of the debate and its context, with a particular emphasis on the way in which fear of crime has been conceptualized. Interviewees were presented with a sheet of A4, on which was printed the 'domains of interest' of the current investigation:

- What *is* the fear of crime?
- The history of the debate:
  - How has the concept of fear of crime been constructed within academic and political research and debate?
  - How have the ways in which the fear of crime has been conceptualized and researched affected the debate?
  - What have been the most important arguments and contexts within the history of the debate?
- How has the issue of the fear of crime affected policy?
- The future—impediments and promising lines of enquiry.

After the aims were explained, the interview took an unstructured form. A topic guide was used as an aide-memoire, stating all the relevant topics of discussion. It served as a reminder to Jackson of the goals of the interviews and was used to direct individuals to all of the issues of interest that had not sprung up during the conversation. However, the majority of interviewees launched into a prolonged narrative that touched upon many of the issues of interest.

The topic guide divided into four sections. The first section introduced the interviewee's interest in the topic and their opinions on its importance. This began with an enquiry into the interviewee's research interests, how they came to the topic of the fear of crime, and what research they had done. This then led into whether it is an important issue academically, social and politically, and if so, why? This elicited opinions on differences between the importance across these three levels. For example, did one field of activity fuel the salience of the issue in another?

The second section of the topic guide related to the history of the debate and its political context. Interviewees were asked: If you were writing a history of the emergence and development of the debate, what issues would you isolate as being particularly important? Have the parameters of debate and research been shaped by policy concerns?

Interviews with Academic and Government Criminologists 271

The third section began with the rather crude question: 'What is the fear of crime?' This moved on to a discussion on how conceptual and methodological issues have directed the research and debate. Have the methods been valid and reliable? How has the object of study been theoretically defined and interpreted? Have inadequate theoretical and methodological tools interacted to limit research, knowledge, and interpretation?

The final section looked backwards and forwards—interviewees were asked if they thought there have been any past impediments to understanding and researching the fear of crime. They were then asked for their impressions on promising goals for future research. How do they conceptualize fear of crime? What methods do they support? How could the current theoretical frameworks be improved?

The data from the transcripts of the interviews were analysed using a technique developed in a specialist qualitative unit at the National Centre for Social Research in London. 'Framework' is a method of qualitative data analysis designed to facilitate systematic analysis of often unstructured and 'unwieldy' data from transcripts of interviews and other written documents (Ritchie and Spencer, 1994). It seeks to assist the researcher in imposing coherence and structure on a cumbersome data set whilst keeping one 'close' to the original text. Such imposition includes creating typologies, finding associations, seeking explanations, and mapping the range and nature of phenomena. All of this involves the detection and interpretation of data by coding pieces of text in order to address the particular research problem at hand.

A qualitative data analysis software package entitled ATLAS/ti was used to manage, examine, and code these data. The two basic functions of this program are the management of text, much like a word processor, and the coding of words, sentencing, paragraphs, or any other unit of analysis. Furthermore, one can run searches for words and phrases, query the presence of patterned relationships, collect all the text assigned to particular codes, and create code classifications of networks. These more advanced functions of this program were not used here. Rather, text was coded and queries run in order to collate those pieces of text assigned to certain themes or sub-themes.

'Framework analysis' involves a number of: '... distinct though highly interconnected stages... [that involve] a systematic process of sifting, charting and sorting material according to key issues and themes' (Ritchie and Spencer, 1994, p 177). The first is familiarization with the material. The tapes of the interviews were listened to and the transcripts read and re-read (and saved in a text format that ATLAS/ti can read). Key ideas and recurrent themes were noted as an overview of the data was gained. The second stage was then to identify a thematic framework within which to sift and sort the data; to: '...identify the key issues, concepts and themes according to which the data can be examined and referenced' (Ritchie and Spencer, 1994, p 179). Creating an index of themes was a result of the interplay between drawing upon *a priori* issues (the original research questions as played out in the topic guide), emergent issues from the data, and what Ritchie and Spencer (1994: 180) describe as: '...analytical themes arising from the recurrence or patterning of particular views or experiences'. But this was also an iterative process for a thematic framework was developed and refined by repeatedly going back to the data or the original research problem. The final result was a: '...mechanism for labelling data in manageable "bites" for subsequent retrieval and exploration' (1994: 180).

The next stage was 'indexing'. Here, the thematic framework was systematically applied to the data through the assigning of codes to the text using ATLAS/ti. Of course, this was an interpretative exercise that involves judgements on meaning and significance, bearing in mind the context of particular passages of text within an individual interview, for example. Having applied the index, data were then rearranged accordingly in a process labelled 'charting' by Ritchie and Spencer (1994). An Excel file was created with columns denoting themes and rows representing each individual transcript. In each cell was a distilled summary of what each interviewer said about a particular theme or sub-theme, along with sometimes sparse, other times extensive, quoting. The pages from the transcript were noted in this Excel file to facilitate quick access if one wished to explore the point in more detail.

The final step was 'mapping and interpretation'. This was where key characteristics were pulled together and the data as a whole were mapped and interpreted (1994). The charts were reviewed, attitudes, experiences, and arguments were compared and contrasted on key moments in the fear of crime debate, patterns and explanations were sought within and across individual accounts, and definitions and accounts of current conceptualizations of fear of crime were catalogued.

Qualitative Data Sets from Glasgow and London

Both of our qualitative data sets come from ESRC-funded projects award numbers L210252007 (Glasgow) and R00429834481 (London).

In Glasgow, four sites were selected along two dichotomies (outlying/inner city and poor/affluent). The two inner city areas (Kelvinside and the Gorbals) both fell within two miles of Glasgow city centre. The outlying areas (Bearsden and Drumchapel) were both approximately five miles out from the centre of the city. Both of the areas selected as 'poor' had been identified by Strathclyde Regional Council as being Priority One Areas (the most deprived) under their 'Social Strategy for the Nineties'. These types of areas the Regional Council describe as being '. . . large areas of severe multiple deprivation . . .' (SRC, 1994: 2). Unemployment rates for these two neighbourhoods stood at (respectively) 39 per cent and 41 per cent; overcrowded households at 6 per cent and 8 per cent; non-elderly illnesses at 15 per cent and 21 per cent; long-term illnesses at 19 per cent and 27 per cent; and households lacking amenities at 0.2 per cent and 0.3 per cent (all statistics from SRC, 1994). One (the Gorbals) had experienced significant problems associated with prolific opiate-based drug use (acquisitive crime, visible dealing, and consumption), although at the time of the interviews the area was benefiting from substantial investment and regeneration. Data for the two 'affluent' neighbourhoods were harder to find, as neither were 'priority' areas nor did they form a distinct geographical region. The data reported here refer to only one of these areas (Kelvinside); the unemployment rate was 5 per cent, with overcrowding at 0.5 per cent, and non-elderly illnesses at 3 per cent (Muir, 1994).

Respondents were selected using the 'random walk' method. Approximately 40 people in each of the four areas took part in short interviews (N = 167) and were asked if they would be prepared to take part in a second in-depth interview. The response rate for agreeing to be recontacted for the longer interview was 90 per cent; 64 follow-up interviews were completed. The data were collected in 1994–95.

Meanwhile, in London, the two contrasting areas were selected within Hounslow (West London). The first area was a wealthy suburb with a predominantly white ethnic mix. It had low personal crime rates but a relatively high incidence of burglary and car crime. The physical environment was well kept and typical of an affluent London suburb. The second area was a high-rise, high-density, local authority housing estate. With reasonably close proximity to the first area, it had high rates of inter-personal crime and public incivilities, although it was also at that time undergoing considerable physical regeneration. A high proportion of residents came from low-income brackets and the population included a diverse blend of ethnicities and religions.

To begin with, a convenience sample of residents in both of the London sites was recruited via contacts at Hounslow Council and the local police office. There was also a 'snowballing' of recruits, where those being interviewed suggested others who might be willing. Letters were the first contact in almost all cases. There were 24 interviews conducted and 25 refusals. Many letters were sent with no reply, and a local police officer rang a number of residents to enquire about their willingness to take part; most declined. All interviews took place in participants' homes and were recorded. The interview data were transcribed in full. The interviews took place in 1999.

The British Crime Survey

The BCS is run by the Home Office's Research, Statistics and Development Directorate, and is one of the largest social science surveys run in the UK, and certainly the largest to focus on crime. First run in 1982, the survey moved to an annual basis from 2001 (Bolling et al., 2004: 1). The BCS is primarily a face-to-face victimization survey, with questions relating to experiences in the previous 12 months. Members of the public are asked directly about their experiences of crime, regardless of whether or not they have experienced victimization or reported it to the police. As well as collecting information on victimization, the BCS collects information on a range of beliefs about the CJS, the causes of crime, lifestyle variables, and a host of other information of interest to researchers at the Home Office. The survey sampling is structured in such a way as to be representative of two groups, namely residential households in England and Wales, and adults (aged 16 years and over) living in those households (Bolling et al., 2004: 4). The survey does not collect information from those living in residential institutions such as prisons, detention centres, military accommodation, care homes, or university accommodation (Bolling et al., 2004: 4).

The 2003–04 BCS used the postal address file (PAF) as the sampling frame, widely accepted as one of the most thorough sampling frames for the UK (Bolling et al., 2004: 5). The exact process of sampling is described in full in Bolling et al. (2004: 5–14); however, for our purposes it is enough to report that the survey was a stratified random sample (police force area, level of ethnic concentration, population density, and social status of head of household being the chief stratification criteria) with each individual selected for interview being chosen via a Kish grid. In order to assist interviewees recall events, a life event calendar was used to help interviewees temporally locate events within the previous 12 months.

The interview consisted of sections on the following topics: time living in the area, the causes of crime, changes in the crime rate, evenings out, other life style questions, experience of victimization, victim follow-up forms, a module on mobile phone theft, and the performance of the CJS. After this interviewees were routed into one of four strands of questions, and in some of these modules further splits were made. Thus the new questions about the fear of crime were asked of one-eighth of the whole sample. Following this, interviewees received questions on technology crimes, antisocial behaviour, their socio-demographics (age, gender, marital status, and so on), and drugs and alcohol (if under 60 years old). All interviewers were fully briefed (Bolling et al., 2004: 33), and several quality control measures were put in place.

All addresses selected for interview were sent a letter from the Home Office in advance of the interviewer calling. Although respondents were given the opportunity to 'opt out' of the survey at this point, only 2 per cent did so (Bolling et al., 2004: 35). In all 37,213 interviews were successfully completed, representing a response rate of 74 per cent with a refusal rate of just under 15 per cent (Bolling et al., 2004: 35, 45). The remaining 10 per cent were made up of ineligible addresses or addresses where the selected respondent could not be contacted. The average interview time was estimated at 47 minutes, but this varied greatly with n of victimization experiences reported (Bolling et al., 2004: 41). Various options for weighting the data were produced (Bolling et al., 2004: 65–71).

The Rural Crime Survey

Data were drawn from a single-contact mail survey of a randomly drawn sample of residents of seven sets of towns and villages within the Tynedale District, a predominantly rural area in the North-East of England. According to the 2001 Census, Tynedale has a population of 58,808 with the vast majority white (99.3 per cent compared to 90.9 per cent across England) and an equal gender mix (49 per cent male, 51 per cent female). There was a significantly lower incidence of crime and disorder than the North East as a whole and England and Wales more widely, according to the 1998 Crime and Disorder Audit and police figures relating to the period of April 2000 to March 2001. But despite the comparatively low crime levels, the Tynedale Citizens' Panel Baseline Survey (1999) found that, of 600 people interviewed, around 80 per cent felt that the safety and security of the community was the issue that mattered most to them.

Questionnaires were sent to 5,906 named individuals drawn from the 2001 Electoral Roll. Because of an arrangement with Royal Mail, those that could not be delivered (e.g. residents had moved) were returned to sender. There were 223 of these. A total of 1,023 completed questionnaires were returned, yielding a response rate of 18 per cent. This meant that fewer than one in five of those sampled returned the questionnaire completed (although a low response rate is almost guaranteed with one-contact postal surveys). While there was enough statistical power to perform the analyses, such a low response rate must surely have an impact. The question is: how much of an impact?

When considering this issue one begins by comparing known quantities of the sample and population. The socio-demographic breakdown of the sample was close to that of the population of the area according to Census data, albeit with a slight bias towards females and older individuals. Yet despite this, one supposes that those who did not complete the questionnaire are likely to be busy and not interested in the topic; they may also be rather cynical about public opinion research and the more specific benefits of this study. In many other respects those who did not return the questionnaire may also differ to those who did.

Yet, the extent of the impact of a low response rate depends to some degree on what you are estimating. One worries particularly about the representativeness of a sample when one estimates more basic population attributes such as means or proportions; relationships between constructs, as well as the measurement models in these structural equation models, are arguably less susceptible to low response rates. Following this logic, these findings—based on the estimation of measurement and structural elements of a number of models—may have greater validity than other studies that have low response rates but do not focus so heavily on relationships between variables.

Furthermore, some parts of the model may be more robust than others. The relationships between the more psychological aspects, such as threat appraisal, vulnerability, and emotion, seem unlikely to be specific to the sample—even if effect sizes might vary somewhat. In contrast, perhaps the sociological or social-psychological processes are more contextually specific. As suggested above, this particular sample may have contained more people with an interest in the topic. Crime might therefore be more salient to them, containing a wider range of social meaning. Relationships between social attitudes and environmental perceptions may therefore have been attenuated, so these particular aspects of the model might be more applicable to individuals who place greater importance on social cohesion and law and order.

Bibliography

Agnew, R.S. (1985) 'Neutralising the Impact of Crime', *Criminal Justice and Behaviour*, 12: 221–39.
Anderson, E. (1999) *Code of the Street: Decency, Violence, and the Moral Life of the Inner City*, New York: W.W. Norton.
Arbuckle, J.L. and Wothke, W. (1999) *AMOS 4.0 User's Guide*, Chicago, Il. Small Waters Corporation.
Arnold, H. (1991) 'Fear of Crime and its Relationship to Directly and Indirectly Experienced Victimisation: a Binational Comparison of Models' in K. Sessar and H.J. Kerner (eds) *Developments in Crime and Crime Control Research*, London: Springer-Verlag.
Averill, J. (2004) 'Everyday Emotions: Let Me Count the Ways', *Social Science Information*, 43(4): 571–80.
Balkin, S. (1979) 'Victimization Rates, Safety and Fear of Crime', *Social Problems*, 26(3): 343–58.
Banks, M. (2005) 'Spaces of Insecurity: Media and Fear of Crime in a Local Context', *Crime, Media, Culture*, 1(2): 169–87.
Bannister, J. (1993) 'Locating fear: Environmental and ontological security' in H. Jones (ed) *Crime and the Urban Environment*, Aldershot: Avebury.
Baron, R.M. and Kenny, D.A. (1986) 'The Moderator–Mediator Variable Distinction in Social Psychological Research: Conceptual, strategic and statistical considerations', *Journal of Personality and Social Psychology*, 51: 1173–82.
Bauman, Z. (1998) *Globalization: The Human Consequences*, New York: Columbia University Press.
—— (1999) *In Search of Politics*, Cambridge: Polity Press.
—— (2000) 'Social Issues of Law and Order', *British Journal of Criminology*, 40(2): 205–21.
—— (2001) *The Individualized Society*, Oxford: Blackwell.
—— (2002) 'Violence in the Age of Uncertainty' in A. Crawford (ed) *Crime and Insecurity: The Governance of Safety in Europe*, Cullompton, Devon: Willan.
—— (2006) *Liquid Fear*, Cambridge: Polity Press.
Beck, U. (1992) *Risk Society*, London, Sage.
—— (2000) *The Brave New World of Work*, Cambridge: Polity Press.
Ben-Ze've, A. (2000) *The Subtlety of Emotions*, Cambridge, MA: MIT Press.
—— and Revhon, N. (2004) 'Emotional Complexity in Everyday Life', *Social Science Information*, 43(4): 581–9.

Bennett, T. (1990) 'Tackling Fear of Crime', *Home Office Research and Statistics Department Research Bulletin*, 31(28).

Bentler, P.M. (1980) 'Multivriate Analysis with Latent Variables', *Annual Review of Psychology*, 31: 419–56.

—— (1990) 'Comparative Fit Indexes in Structural Models', *Psychological Bulletin*, 107: 238–46.

—— and Bonett, D.G. (1980) 'Significance Tests and Goodness of Fit in the Analysis of Covariance Structures', *Psychological Bulletin*, 88: 588–606.

Berryman, J. (1942) *Poems*, Norfolk, CT: New Directions Press.

Biderman, A.D., Johnson, L.A., McIntyre, J. and Weir, A.W. (1967) 'Report on a Pilot Study in the District of Columbia on Victimization and Attitudes toward Law Enforcement', *President's Commission on Law Enforcement and Administration of Justice, Field Surveys I*, Washington, DC: US Government Printing Office.

Bishop, G. and Klecka, W. (1978) 'Victimization and Fear of Crime Among Elderly Living in High Crime Urban Neighborhoods', *Paper presented at the annual meeting of the Academy of Criminal Justice Science*, New Orleans, LA.

—— Tuchfarber, A. and Oldendick, R. (1986) 'Opinions on Fictitious Issues: The Pressure to Answer Survey Questions', *Public Opinion Quarterly*, 50: 240–50.

Bollen, K.A. (1989) *Structural Equation with Latent Variables*, New York: Wiley.

Bolling, K., Clemens, S., Grant, C., Smith, P. and Brown, M. (2004) 2003/04 British Crime Survey (England & Wales), Technical Report, London: BMRB.

Bowling, B. (1993) 'Racial Harassment and the Process of Victimisation', *British Journal of Criminology*, 33: 231–50.

Box, S., Hale, C. and Andrews, G. (1988) 'Explaining Fear of Crime', *British Journal of Criminology*, 28: 340–56.

Brandolini, A. (1998) 'A Bird's-Eye View of Long-Run Changes in Income Inequality', Rome: Banca d'Italia Research Dept.

Brandstatter, H. (1983) 'Emotional Responses to Other Persons in Everyday Life Situations', *Journal of Personality and Social Psychology*, 45: 871–83.

Browne, M.W. and Cudek, R. (1993) 'Alternative Ways of Assessing Model Fit' in K.A. Bollen and J.S. Long (eds) *Testing Structural Equation Models*, Newbury Park, CA: Sage, 136–62.

Burgess, J. (1994) *The Politics of Trust: Reducing Fear of Crime in Urban Parks*, Working Paper No. 8, Stroud, London: Comedia in association with Demos.

Burney, E. (2005) *Making People Behave: Anti-Social Behaviour, Politics and Policy*, Devon: Willan.

Bursik, R.J. (1988) 'Social Disorganization Theories of Crime and Delinquency: Problems and Prospects', *Criminology*, 26: 519–51.
—— and Grasmick, H. (1993) *Neighborhoods and Crime: The Dimensions of Effective Community Control*, New York: Lexington Books.
Butler, G. and Mathews, A. (1983) 'Cognitive Processes in Anxiety', *Advances in Behaviour Research and Therapy*, 25: 51–62.
—— and —— (1987) 'Anticipatory Anxiety and Risk Perception', *Cognitive Therapy and Research*, 11: 551–65.
Calderia, T. (2001) *City of Walls: Crime, Segregation, and Citizenship in São Paulo*, California: University of California Press.
Carlson, M. and Mulaik, S.A. (1993) 'Trait Ratings from Descriptions of Behaviour as Mediated by Components of Meaning', *Multivariate Behavioural Research*, 28: 111–59.
Carmines, E.G. and McIver, J.P. (1981) 'Analysing Models with Unobserved Variables' in G.W. Bohrstedt and E.F. Borgatta (eds) *Social Measurement*, Beverly Hills, CA: Sage.
Carvalho, I. and Lewis, D.A. (2003) 'Beyond Community: Reactions to crime and disorder among inner-city residents', *Criminology*, 41: 779–812.
Castells, M. (1998, Second Edition 2000) *End of Millennium, The Information Age: Economy, Society and Culture Vol. III*, Oxford: Blackwell.
Cavender, G. (2004) 'Media and Crime Policy: A reconsideration of David Garland's the Culture of Control', *Punishment and Society*, 6: 335–48.
Chadee, D. and Ditton, J. (2003) 'Are Older People More Afraid of the Fear of Crime?', *British Journal of Criminology*, 43: 417–33.
—— and —— (2005) 'Fear of Crime and the Media: Assessing the lack of relationship', *Crime Media Culture*, 1(3): 322–32.
Chiricos, T., Hogan, M. and Gertz, M. (1997) 'Racial Composition of Neighborhood and Fear of Crime', *Criminology*, 35(1): 107–29.
Clore, G.L. and Gasper, K. (2000) 'Feeling is Believing: Some affective influences on belief' in N.H. Frijda, A.S.R. Manstead and S. Bem (eds) *Emotions and Beliefs: How Feelings Influence Thoughts*, Cambridge: Cambridge University Press.
Cohen, S. (1972) *Folk Devils and Moral Panics*, London: Paladin.
Conklin, J.E. (1975) *The Impact of Crime*, New York: Macmillan.
Connell, R. (1987) *Gender and Power*, Palo Alto, CA: Stanford University Press.
Converse, P. (1964) 'The Nature of Belief Systems in the Mass Publics', in D.E. Apter (ed) *Ideology and Discontent*, New York: Free Press.
Coovert, M.D., Penner, L.A. and MacCallum, R. (1990) 'Covariance Structure Modeling in Personality and Social Psychological Research: An introduction' in C. Hendrick and M. Clark (eds) *Review of Personality and Social Psychology (Volume 11)*, Newbury, CA: Sage.

Covington, J. and Taylor, R.B. (1991) 'Fear of Crime in Urban Residential Neighbourhoods: Implications of Between- and Within-Neighborhood Sources for Current Models', *The Sociological Quarterly*, 32(2): 231–49.

Crawford, A. (1998) *Crime Prevention and Community Safety: Politics, Policies and Practices*, London: Longman.

—— (2002) (ed) *Crime and Insecurity: the Governance of Safety in Europe*, Cullompton, Devon: Willan Publishing.

—— Lister, S. and Wall, D. (2002) *Great Expectations: Contracted Community Policing in New Earswick*, York: Joseph Rowntree Foundation.

Crow, G. and Rees, T. (1999) '"Winners" and "Losers" in Social Transformations', *Sociological Research Online*, 4(1).

Csikszentmihalyi, M. (1990) *Flow: The Psychology of Optimal Experience*, New York: HarperCollins.

Curran, P.J., West, S.G. and Finch, J.F. (1996) 'The Robustness of Test Statistics to Non-normality and Specification Error in Confirmatory Factor Analysis', *Psychological Methods*, 1: 16–29.

Currie, E. (2003) 'Social Crime Prevention Strategies in Market Societies', in E. McLaughlin et al. (eds) *Criminological Perspectives*, Second Edition, London: Sage.

Curtis, L.P. (2001) *Jack the Ripper and the London Press*, New Haven, CT: Yale University Press.

Darwin, C. (1872) *The Expression of the Emotions in Man and Animals*, London: Oxford University Press.

Davey, G.C.L. and Levy, S. (1998) 'Catastrophic Worrying: Personal Inadequacy and a Perseverative Iterative Style as Features of Catastrophizing Process', *Journal of Abnormal Psychology*, 107: 576–86.

Davidson, R.J., Scherer, K.R., and Goldsmith, H.H. (eds) (2003) *Handbook of Affective Sciences*, New York: Oxford University Press.

Day, K. (2009) 'Bearing Feared: Masculinity and race in public space', in M. Lee and S. Farrall (eds) *Fear of Crime: Critical Voices in an Age of Anxiety*, London: Routledge.

Ditton, J., Bannister, J., Gilchrist, E. and Farrall, S. (1999) 'Afraid or Angry? Recalibrating the "fear" of crime', *International Review of Victimology*, 6(2): 83–99.

—— and Farrall, S. (2000) 'Introduction' in J. Ditton and S. Farrall (eds) *Fear of Crime*, Aldershot: Ashgate.

—— and Innes, M. (2005) 'The Role of Perceptual Intervention in the Management of Crime Fear' in N. Tilley (ed) *Handbook of Crime Prevention and Community Safety*, Cullompton, Devon: Willan.

Dobash, R.E. and Dobash, R.P. (1979) *Violence Against Wives*, New York: Free Press.

—— and —— (1992) *Women, Violence and Social Change*, London: Routledge.
Dolan, P. and Peasgood, T. 'Estimating the Economic and Social Costs of the Fear of Crime', *British Journal of Criminology*, 47: 121–32.
Douglas, J.D. (1971) 'The Sociological Analysis of Social Meanings of Suicide' in A. Giddens (ed) *The Sociology of Suicide*, London: Frank Cass and Co.
Douglas, M. and Wildavsky, A. (1982) *Risk and Culture: An Essay on the Selection of Technical and Environmental Dangers*, Berkeley, CA: University of California Press.
Dowds, L. and Ahrendt, D. (1995) 'Fear of Crime' in R. Jowell et al. (eds) *British Social Attitudes: 12th Report*, Aldershot: Dartmouth.
Downes, D. (1988) *Contrasts in Tolerance*, Oxford: Oxford University Press.
DuBow, F., McCabe, E. and Kaplan, G. (1979) *Reactions to Crime: A Critical Review of the Literature*, Washington, DC: National Institute of Law Enforcement and Criminal Justice, US Government Printing Office.
Ehrenreich, B. (1989) *The Fear of Falling: The Inner Life of the Middle Class*, New York: Harper Perennial.
Ehrlichmann, J. (1970) *Witness to Power*, New York: Simon and Schuster.
Elias, N. (1982) *The Civilizing Process, Vol. 2, State Formation and Civilization*, Oxford: Basil Blackwell.
Elliot, T.S. (1922) *The Waste Land*, New York: Harvester Wheatsheaf.
Elster, J. (2004) 'Emotion and Action' in R.C. Solomon (ed) *Thinking about Feeling*, Oxford: Oxford University Press, 151–62.
Emde, R.N. (1980) 'Levels of Meaning in Infant Emotions: A biosocial view', in W.A. Collins (ed) *Development of Cognition, Affect, and Social Relations: The Minnesota symposium of child psychology*, Hillsdale, NJ: Lawrence Erlbaum, 1–37.
Ennis, P.H. (1967) 'Criminal Victimization in the United States: A Report of a National Survey', *President's Commission on Law Enforcement and Administration of Justice, Field Surveys II*, Washington DC: US Government Printing Office.
Evans, E.J. (1997) *Thatcher and Thatcherism*, First Edition, London: Routledge.
Evans, K., Fraser, P. and Walklate, S. (1996) 'Whom Can You Trust? The Politics of "Grassing" on an Inner City Housing Estate', *Sociological Review*, 44(3): 361–80.
Everitt, B.S. (1984) *An Introduction to Latent Variable Models*, London: Chapman-Hall.
Farrall, S. (2003) 'Measuring the Fear of Crime With Greater Accuracy', End of Award Report to Economic and Social Research Council, Swindon, UK.

Farrall, S. (2004a) 'Revisiting Crime Surveys: Emotional Responses without Emotions', *International Journal of Social Research Methodology*, 7(2): 157–71.
—— (2004b) 'Can We Believe Our Eyes: A Response to Mike Hough', *International Journal of Social Research Methodology*, 7(2): 177–9.
—— (2006) '"Rolling Back the State": Mrs Thatcher's Criminological Legacy', *International Journal of the Sociology of Law*, 34(4): 256–77.
—— and Bannister, J. (1997) *Putting Fear in Its Place*, Queens University, Belfast: British Society of Criminology.
—— Bannister, J., Ditton, J. and Gilchrist, E. (1997) 'Questioning the Measurement of the Fear of Crime: Findings from a major methodological study', *British Journal of Criminology*, 37(4): 657–78.
—— and Gadd, D. (2004) 'The Frequency of the Fear of Crime', *British Journal of Criminology*, 44(1): 127–32.
—— Gray, E. and Jackson, J. (2007) 'Combining the New and Old Measures of the Fear of Crime: Exploring the "worried well"', ESRC project: *Experience and Expression in the Fear of Crime, Working Paper #4*.
—— Jackson, J. and Gray, E. (2006) 'Everyday Emotion and the Fear of Crime: Preliminary findings from experience and expression', ESRC project: *Experience and Expression in the Fear of Crime, Working Paper #1*.
—— and Lee, M. (2009) 'Critical Voices in an Age of Anxiety: A Reintroduction to the fear of crime' in M. Lee and S. Farrall (eds) *Fear of Crime: Critical Voices in an Age of Anxiety*, London: Routledge, 1–11.
Fattah, E.A. (1993) 'Research on Fear of Crime: Some common conceptual and measurement problems' in W. Bilsky et al. (eds) *Fear of Crime and Criminal Victimisation*, Stuttgart: Ferdinand Enke Verlag.
Ferge, Z. (1993) 'Winners and Losers After the Collapse of State Socialism' in R. Page and J. Baldock (eds) *Social Policy Review 5*, Canterbury: Social Policy Association.
Ferraro, K.F. (1995) *Fear of Crime: Interpreting Victimization Risk*, New York: SUNY Press.
—— and LaGrange, R. (1987) 'The Measurement of Fear of Crime', *Sociological Inquiry*, 57(1): 70–101.
Figgie, H.E. (1980) *The Figgie Report on Fear of Crime: America Afraid. Part 1: The General Public*, Willoughby, OH: A-T-O Inc.
Fiske, J. (1987) *Television Culture*, London: Routledge.
Frank, R.H. (2007) *Falling Behind*, Berkeley, CA: University of California Press.
Franzini, L., Caughy, M.O., Nettles, S.M. and Campo, P.O. (2008) 'Perceptions of Disorder: Contributions of neighborhood characteristics to subjective perceptions of disorder', *Journal of Environmental Psychology*, 28: 83–93.

Fredrickson, B.L. and Kahneman, D. (1993) 'Duration Neglect in Retrospective Evaluations of Affective Episodes', *Journal of Personality and Social Psychology*, 65: 45–55.

Frijda, N.H., Manstead, A.S.R. and Bem, S. (2000) 'The Influence of Emotions on Beliefs' in N.H. Frijda, A.S.R. Manstead and S. Bem (eds) *Emotions and Beliefs: How Feelings Influence Thoughts*, Cambridge: Cambridge University Press.

Furedi, F. (1998) *Culture of Fear: Risk Taking and the Morality of Low Expectation*, London: Cassell.

—— (2002) *Culture of Fear: Risk Taking and the Morality of Low Expectation. Revised Edition*, London: Continuum.

—— (2006) *Culture of Fear Revisited: Risk-taking and the Morality of Low Expectation*, London: Continuum.

Furlong, A. and Kelly, P. (2005) 'The Brazilianisation of Youth Transition in Australia and the UK', *Australian Journal of Social Issues*, 40(2): 207–25.

Furstenburg, F.N. (1971) 'Public Reactions to Fear in the Street', *American Scholar*, 11: 601–10.

—— (1972) 'Fear of Crime and its Effect upon Citizen Behaviour' in A. Biderman (ed) *Crime and Justice: A Symposium*, New York: Nailberg.

Gabriel, U. and Greve, W. (2003) 'The Psychology of Fear of Crime: Conceptual and methodological perspectives', *British Journal of Criminology*, 43: 600–14.

Gadd, D. and Jefferson, T. (2007) *Psychosocial Criminology: An Introduction*, London: Sage.

Gardner, C.B. (1990) 'Safe Conduct: Women, Crime, and Self in Public Places, *Social Problems*, 37(3): 311–28.

Garland, D. (1996) 'The limits of the sovereign state', *British Journal of Criminology*, 36: 445–71.

—— (2001) *The Culture of Control*, Oxford: Oxford University Press.

—— and Sparks, R. (2000) 'Criminology, Social Theory, and the Challenge of our times', in D. Garland and R. Sparks (eds) *Criminology and Social Theory*, Oxford: Oxford University Press.

Garofalo, J. (1979) 'Victimisation and the Fear of Crime', *Journal of Research in Crime and Delinquency*, 16: 80–97.

—— and Laub, J. (1978) 'The Fear of Crime: Broadening Our Perspective', *Victimology*, 3: 242–53.

Giddens, A. (1991) *Modernity and Self-Identity. Self and Society in the Late Modern Age*, Cambridge: Polity Press.

—— (1992) *The Transformation of Intimacy*, Cambridge: Polity Press.

Gilbert, D.T. and Ebert, J.E. (2002) 'Decisions and Revisions: The affective forecasting of changeable outcomes', *Journal of Personality and Social Psychology*, 82: 503–14.

Gilling, D. (1997) *Crime Prevention*, London: University College London Press.
Girling, E., Loader, I. and Sparks, R. (2000) *Crime and Social Change in Middle England*, London: Routledge.
Gladstone, G. and Parker, G. (2003) 'What's the Use of Worrying? Its function and its dysfunction', *Australian and New Zealand Journal of Psychiatry*, 37(3): 347–54.
Glassner, B. (1999) *The Culture of Fear: Why Americans Are Afraid of the Wrong Things*, New York: Basic Books.
Godfrey, B., Cox, D., and Farrall, S. (2007) *Criminal Lives: Family Life, Employment, and Offending*, Oxford: Oxford University Press.
Goffman, E. (1971) *Relations in Public*, New York: Basic Books.
Goldie, P. (2004) 'The Life of the Mind: Commentary on emotions in everyday life', *Social Science Information*, 43(4): 591–8.
Gordon, M. and Riger, S. (1988) *The Female Fear*, New York: Free Press.
Gray, E., Jackson, J. and Farrall, S. (2008) 'Reassessing Fear of Crime in England and Wales', *European Journal of Criminology*, 5(3): 309–36.
Gray, S. (1990) *Hidden Laughter*, London: Samuel French Ltd.
Green, D. (2006) 'Public Opinion Versus Public Judgement About Crime', *British Journal of Criminology*, 46: 131–54.
—— (2008) 'Political Culture and Incentives to Penal Populism', in H. Kury (ed) *Fear of Crime – Punitivity: New Developments in Theory and Research*, 251–76, Bochum, Univ Brockmeyer.
Greenberg, S.W. (1986) 'Fear and Its Relationship to Crime, Neighborhood Deterioration, and Informal Social Control' in M. Byrne and R.J. Sampson (eds) *The Social Ecology of Crime*, New York: James Springer-Verlag.
Gunn, S. and Bell, R. (2002) *Middle Classes: Their Rise and Sprawl*, London: Phoenix.
Hale, C. (1996) 'Fear of Crime: A Review of the Literature', *International Review of Victimology*, 4: 79–150.
Hall, S., Critcher, C., Jefferson, T., Clarke, J. and Roberts, B. (1978) *Policing the Crisis: Mugging, the State and Law*, London: Macmillan.
Hankiss, E. (2001) *Fears and Symbols*, Budapest: CEU Press.
Harcourt, B.E. (2001) *Illusion of Order: The False Promise of Broken Windows Policing*, Cambridge, MA: Harvard University Press.
Harris, R. (1969) *The Fear of Crime*, New York: Praeger.
Hartnagel, T. 'The Perception and Fear of Crime', *Social Forces*, 58: 176–93.
Hassinger, J. (1985) 'Fear of crime in public environments', *Journal of Architectural and Planning Research*, 2: 289–300.
Hay, C. (1996) *Re-Stating Social and Political Change*, Milton Keynes: Open University Press.

Hayduk, L.A. (1987) *Structural Equation Modeling with LISREL*, Baltimore, MD: John Hopkins University Press.
Heber, A. (2007) *Var Rädd om Dig!*, Stockholm: Stockholm University Press.
Hills, J. (2004) *Inequality and the State*, Oxford: Oxford University Press.
Hochschild, A. (1983) *The Managed Heart: The Commercialization of Human Feeling*, Berkeley, CA: University of California Press.
Hollander, J.A. (2001) 'Vulnerability and Dangerousness: The construction of gender through conversation about violence,' *Gender and Society*, 15: 83–109.
—— (2002) 'Resisting Vulnerability: The social reconstruction of gender in interaction', *Social Problems*, 49: 474–96.
Hollway, W. and Jefferson, T. (1997) 'The Risk Society in an Age of Anxiety: Situating Fear of Crime', *British Journal of Sociology*, 48(2): 255–66.
—— (2000) *Doing Qualitative Research Differently: Free Association, Narrative and the Interview Method*, London: Sage.
Home Office (2006) *Rebalancing the Criminal Justice System in Favour of the Law-abiding Majority*, available at <http://www.homeoffice.gov.uk/documents/CJS-review.pdf/>
Hope, T. (2000) 'Inequality and the Clubbing of Private Security' in T. Hope and R. Sparks (eds) *Crime, Risk and Insecurity*, London: Routledge.
—— Karstedt, S. and Farrall, S. (2001) *The Relationship Between Calls and Crimes*, End of Award Report to Home Office.
—— and Sparks, R. (2000) 'Introduction' in T. Hope and R. Sparks (eds) *Crime, Risk and Insecurity*, London: Routledge.
—— and Trickett, A. (2004) 'Angst Essen Seele Auf ... But it Keeps Away the Burglars!', *Kölner Zeitschrift für Soziologie und Sozialpsychologie*, 43: 441–68.
Horlick-Jones, T., Sime, J. and Pidgeon, N. (2003) 'The Social Dynamics of Environmental Risk Perception: Implications for risk communication research and practice' in N. Pidgeon, R.E. Kasperson, and P. Slovic, (eds) *The Social Amplification of Risk*, Cambridge: Cambridge University Press, 262–85.
Hough, M. (1995) *Anxiety About Crime: Findings from the 1994 British Crime Survey*, Home Office Research Study No. 147, London: Home Office.
—— (1985) *Taking Account of Crime: Key Findings From The Second British Crime Survey*, London: HMSO.
—— (2004), 'Worry about Crime: Mental Events or Mental States?', *International Journal of Social Research Methodology*, 7: 173–6.
—— and Mayhew, P. (1983) *The British Crime Survey: First Report*, Home Office Research Study No. 76, London: Home Office.

Hough, M. and Park, A. (2002) 'How Malleable Are Attitudes to Crime and Punishment?' in J. Robert and M. Hough (eds) *Changing Attitudes to Punishment*, Cullompton, Devon: Willan Publishing, 163–83.

Hovland, C.I. and Sears, R. (1940) 'Minor Studies of Aggression', *Journal of Psychology*, 9: 301–10.

Hunter, A. (1978) 'Symbols of Incivility: Social disorder and fear of crime in urban neighborhoods', Paper presented to the Annual Meeting of the American Criminological Society, Dallas.

Innes, M. (2004) 'Signal Crimes and Signal Disorders', *British Journal of Sociology*, 55: 335–55.

—— and Jones, V. (2006) *Neighbourhood Security and Urban Change: Risk, Resilience and Recovery*, York: Joseph Rowntree Foundation.

—— Hayden, T., Lowe, H., Mackenzie, C. Roberts and Twyman, L. (2004) 'Signal Crimes and Reassurance Policing Volumes 1 and 2', Research Report, Guildford: University of Surrey.

—— —— —— and C. Roberts (2005) 'Signal Crimes and Reassurance Policing Volume 3', Guildford: University of Surrey.

Jackson, J. (2004a) 'Experience and Expression: Social and cultural significance in the fear of crime', *British Journal of Criminology*, 44(6): 946–66.

—— (2004b) 'An Analysis of a Construct and Debate: The fear of crime' in H. Albrecht, T. Serassis and H. Kania. (eds) *Images of Crime II*, Freiburg: Edition Iuscrim (Max Planck Institute, 35–64).

—— (2005) 'Validating New Measures of the Fear of Crime', *International Journal of Social Research Methodology*, 8(4): 297–315.

—— (2006) 'Introducing Fear of Crime to Risk Research', *Risk Analysis*, 26(1): 253–64.

—— (2008) 'Bridging the Social and the Psychological in Fear of Crime Research' in M. Lee and S. Farrall (eds) *Fear of Crime: Critical Voices in an Age of Anxiety*, London: Routledge-Cavendish, 143–67.

—— (2009) 'Revisiting Sensitivity to Risk in the Fear of Crime', *Working Paper*, London: LSE.

—— (in press) 'A Psychological Perspective on Vulnerability in the Fear of Crime', *Psychology, Crime and Law*.

—— Allum, N. and Gaskell, G. (2006) 'Bridging Levels of Analysis in Risk Perception Research: The case of the fear of crime' in *Forum Qualitative Sozialforschung/Forum: Qualitative Social Research* (online journal), 7(1): Art. 20. Available at <http://www.qualitative-research.net/fqs–texte/1–06/06–1–20–e.htm> (accessed 4 July 2006).

—— and Bradford, B. (in press) 'Crime, Policing and Social Order: On the expressive nature of public confidence in policing', *British Journal of Sociology*.

—— and Gray, E. (2009) 'Functional Fear and Public Insecurities about Crime', *LSE: Working Paper*, London: LSE.

—— Gray, E. and Brunton-Smith, I. (2009) 'Crime, Norms and Neighborhood Disorder: Notes on the tolerance of low-level deviance', *Working Paper*, London: LSE.
—— and Stafford, M. (2009) 'Public Health and Fear of Crime: A Prospective Cohort Study', *British Journal of Criminology*, doi: 0.1093/bjc/azp033.
—— and Sunshine, J. (2007) 'Public Confidence in Policing: A Neo-Durkheimian Perspective', *British Journal of Criminology*, 47: 214–33.
Jacobs, J. (1961) *The Death and Life of Great American Cities*, New York: Vintage Books.
James, O. (1998) *Britain on the Couch*, London: Arrow Books.
—— (2007) *Affluenza*, London: Vermillion.
Jaycox, V.H. (1978) 'The Elderly's Fear of Crime: Rational or Irrational?', *Victimology: an International Journal*, 3(3–4): 329–34.
Jones, T., Maclean, B. and Young, J. (1986) *The Islington Crime Survey*, Aldershot: Gower.
Jöreskog, K.A. (1981) 'Analysis of Covariance Structures', *Scandinavian Journal of Statistics*, 8: 65–92.
—— and Sörbom, D. (1988) *LISREL-6 User's Reference Guide*, Mooresville, IN: Scientific Software.
Joseph Rowntree Foundation (2006) 'Monitoring Poverty and Social Exclusion in the UK 2006' (Ref 1979), online research findings available at <www.jrf.org.uk/knowledge/findings/socialpolicy/1979.asp> (accessed 20 November 2008)
—— (2007) 'Poverty and Wealth Across Britain 1968 to 2005' (Ref 2077), online research findings available at <www.jrf.org.uk/knowledge/findings/housing/2077.asp> (accessed 20 November 2008)
Kahneman, D. (1994) 'New Challenges to the Rationality Assumption, *Journal of Institutional and Theoretical Economics*, 150: 18–36.
—— Krueger, A., Schkade, D., Schwarz, N. and Stone, A. (2004) 'A Survey Method For Characterizing Daily Life Experience: The Day Reconstruction Method (DRM)', *Science*, 306: 1776–80.
Kanan, J.W. and Pruitt, M.V. (2002) 'Modeling Fear of Crime and Perceived Victimization Risk: The (in)significance of neighborhood integration', *Sociological Inquiry*, 72(4): 527–48.
Karstedt, S. (2002) 'Emotions and Criminal Justice', *Theoretical Criminology*, 6(3): 299–317.
Kasperson, J.X., Kasperson, R.E., Pidgeon, N. and Slovic, P. (2003) 'The Social Amplification of Risk: Assessing fifteen years of research and theory' in N. Pidgeon, R.E. Kasperson and P. Slovic (eds) *The Social Amplification of Risk*, Cambridge: Cambridge University Press, 13–46.
Katz, J. (1999) *How Emotions Work*, Chicago, IL: University of Chicago Press.

Katz, J. (2004) 'Everyday Lives and Extraordinary Research Methods', *Social Science Information*, 43(4): 609–19.
Keller, H. (1957) *The Open Door*, Garden City, NY: Doubleday.
Kelly, L. (1987) 'The Continuum of Sexual Violence' in J. Hamner and M. Maynard (eds) *Women, Violence, and Social Control*, Atlantic Highlands, NJ: Humanities Press International, 46–60.
—— (1988) *Surviving Sexual Violence*, Minneapolis, MN: University of Minnesota Press.
Kemper, T.D. (1990) *A Social Interactional Theory of Emotions*, New York: John Wiley.
Killias, M. (1990) 'Vulnerability: Towards a better understanding of a key variable in the genesis of fear of crime', *Violence and Victims*, 5(2): 97–108.
—— and Clerici, C. (2000) 'Different Measures of Vulnerability in Their Relation to Different Dimensions of Fear of Crime', *The British Journal of Criminology*, 40(3): 437–50.
Klein, S.B., Babey, S.H. and Sherman, J.W. (1997) 'The Functional Independence of Trait and Behavioural Self-knowledge: Methodological considerations and new empirical findings', *Social Cognition*, 15: 183–203.
Kline, R.B. (1998) *Principles and Practices of Structural Equation Modelling*, New York: Guildford Press.
Kristjansson, A.J. (2007) 'On Social Inequality and Perceptions of Security', *European Journal of Criminology*, 4(1): 59–86.
Kuran, T. and Sunstein, C. (1999) 'Availability Cascades and Risk Regulation', *Stanford Law Review*, 51: 683–768.
Kury, H. and Ferdinand, T. (1998) 'The Victim's Experience and Fear of Crime', *International Review of Victimology*, 5: 93–140.
LaGrange, R.L., Ferraro, K.F. and Supancic, M. (1992) 'Perceived Risk and Fear of Crime: The role of social and physical incivilities', *Journal of Research in Crime and Delinquency*, 29: 311–34.
Latouche, S. (1993) *In the Wake of the Affluent Society*, London: Zed Books.
Lavrakas, P.J., Herz, L. and Salem, G. (1981) 'Community Organization, Citizen Participation, and Neighbourhood Crime Prevention', Paper presenting at the annual meeting of the American Psychological Association.
Lavakras, P. 'Fear of Crime and Behavioural Restrictions in Urban and Suburban Neighborhoods', *Population and Environment*, 5: 242–64.
Lea, M. and Young, J. (1984) *What Is To Be Done about Law and Order?*, London: Harmondsworth.
Lee, M. (1999) 'The Fear of Crime and Self–governance: Towards a Genealogy', *The Australian and New Zealand Journal of Criminology*, 32(3): 227–46.
—— (2001) 'The Genesis of Fear of Crime', *Theoretical Criminology*, 5(4): 467–85.

—— (2007) *Inventing Fear of Crime: Criminology and the Politics of Anxiety*, Cullompton, Devon: Willan.
—— (2009) 'The Enumeration of Anxiety' in M. Lee and S. Farrall (eds) *Fear of Crime: Critical Voices in an Age of Anxiety*, London: Routledge.
Lewis, D.A. and Maxfield, M.G. (1980) 'Fear in the Neighborhoods: An investigation of the impact of crime', *Journal of Research in Crime and Delinquency*, 17: 160–89.
—— and Salem, G. (1980) 'Community Crime Prevention: An analysis of a developing strategy', Unpublished manuscript, Evanston, IL: Northwestern University.
—— and —— (1981) 'Community Crime Prevention: An analysis of a developing strategy', *Crime and Delinquency*, 27: 405–21.
—— and —— (1986) *Fear of Crime: Incivility and the Production of a Social Problem*, New Brunswick: Transaction Books.
Liska, A.E., Sanchirico, A. and Reed, M.A. (1988) 'Fear of Crime and Constrained Behaviour: Specifying and estimating a reciprocal effects model', *Social Forces*, 66: 760–70.
Loader, I. (1999) 'Consumer Culture and the Commodification of Policing and Security', *Sociology*, 33/2: 373–92.
—— (2006a) 'Policing, Recognition and Belonging', *Annals of the American Academy of Political and Social Science*, 605: 202–21.
—— (2006b) 'Fall of the Platonic Guardians', *British Journal of Criminology*, 46: 561–86.
—— (2008) 'The Anti-politics of Crime', *Theoretical Criminology*, 12(3): 399–410.
—— (2009) 'Ice Cream and Incarceration: On appetites for security and punishment', *Punishment and Society*, 11(2), 241–57.
—— Girling, E. and Sparks, R. (2000) 'After Success: Anxieties of influence in an English village' in T. Hope and R. Sparks (eds) *Crime, Risk and Insecurity: 'Law and Order' in Everyday Life and Political Discourse*, London: Routledge.
—— and Walker, N. (2007) *Civilizing Security*, Cambridge: Cambridge University Press.
Loo, D. (2009) 'The "Moral Panic" that Wasn't' in M. Lee and S. Farrall (eds) *Fear of Crime: Critical Voices in an Age of Anxiety*, London: Routledge.
—— and Grimes, R.-E. (2004) 'Polls, Politics and Crime: The "law and order" issue of the 1960s', *Western Criminology Review*, 5(1): 50–67.
Los, M. (2002) 'Post Communist Fear of Crime and the Commercialisation of Security', *Theoretical Criminology*, 6(2): 165–88.
Loury, G. (2002) *The Anatomy of Racial Inequality*, Cambridge, MA: Harvard University Press.
Lupton, D. (1999) 'Dangerous Places and the Unpredictable Stranger', *Australian and New Zealand Journal of Criminology*, 32(1): 1–15.

Lupton, D. and Tulloch, J. (1999) 'Theorizing Fear of Crime: Beyond the rational/irrational opposition', *British Journal of Sociology*, 50(3): 507–23.

Madriz, E. (1997) *Nothing Bad Happens to Good Girls: Fear of Crime in Women's Lives*, Berkeley, CA: University of California Press.

Markowitz, F.E. and Felson, R.B. (1998) 'Social-demographic Differences in Attitudes and Violence', *Criminology*, 36: 117–38.

Marsh, H.W. and Yeung, A.S. (1998) 'Top-down, Bottom-up, and Horizontal Models: The direction of causality in multidimensional, hierarchical self-concept models', *Journal of Personality and Social Psychology*, 75: 509–27.

Maruna, S. and King, A. (2004) 'Public Opinion and Community Sanctions' in A.E. Bottoms, S.A. Rex and G. Robinson (eds) *Alternatives to Prison*, Cullompton, Devon: Willan Publishing, 83–112.

Matthews, A. (1990) 'Why Worry? The cognitive function of anxiety', *Behaviour Research and Therapy*, 28: 455–68.

Maxfield, M.G. (1984) *Fear of Crime in England and Wales*, London: HMSO.

—— (1987) *Explaining the Fear of Crime: Evidence from the 1984 British Crime Survey*, Home Office Research Paper No. 41, London: Home Office.

McConville, M. and Shepard, D. (1992) *Watching Police, Watching Communities*, London and New York: Routledge.

McCoy, H.V., Woolredge, J.D., Cullen, F.T., Dubeck, P.J. and Browning, S.L. (1996) 'Lifestyles of the Old and Not So Fearful: Life situation and older persons' fear of crime', *Journal of Criminal Justice*, 24(3): 191–205.

Melanson, P. (1973) *Knowledge, Politics, and Public Policy*, Cambridge: Winthrop.

Merry, S. (1981) *Urban Danger: Life in a Neighborhood of Strangers*, Philadelphia, PA: Temple University Press.

Meyer, T.J., Miller, M.L., Metzger, R.L. and Borkovec, T.D. (1990) 'Development and Validation of the Penn State Worry Questionnaire', *Behaviour Research and Therapy*, 28: 487–95.

Miethe, T. and Lee, G.R. (1984) 'Fear of Crime Among Older People: A reassessment of the predictive power of crime related factors', *Sociological Quarterly*, 25: 397–415.

Moeller, G.L. (1989) 'Fear of Criminal Victimization: The effect of neighborhood racial composition', *Sociological Inquiry*, 59(2): 209–21.

Muir, C. (1994) Personal Communication, 1991 Census Data.

Myrtek, M. (2004) *Heart and Emotion. Ambulatory Monitoring Studies in Everyday Life*, Gottingen: Hogrefe and Huber.

Norusis, M. (1998) *SPSS Guide 8.0*, Chicago, IL: SPSS.

Offe, C. (1996) *Varieties of Transition*, Cambridge: Polity Press.

Offer, A. (2006) *The Challenge of Affluence*, Oxford: Oxford University Press.
Osborne, T. and Rose, N. (1999) 'Do the Social Sciences Create Phenomena?', *British Journal of Sociology*, 50(3): 367–96.
Pakes, F. (2004) 'The Politics of Discontent: The emergence of a new criminal justice discourse in the Netherlands', *Howard Journal of Criminal Justice*, 43(3): 284–98.
Pain, R. (1993) 'Women's Fear of Sexual Violence: Explaining the spatial paradox' in H. Jones (ed) *Crime and the Urban Environment*, Aldershot: Avebury.
—— (1997) 'Whither Women's Fear? Perceptions of sexual violence in public and private space', *International Review of Victimology*, 4: 297–312.
Pattillo, M.E. (1998) 'Sweet Mothers and Gangbangers: Managing crime in a black middle-class neighborhood', *Social Forces*, 76(3): 747–74.
Pearson, G. (1983) *Hooligan: A History of Respectable Fears*, London: Macmillan.
Perkins, D.D. (1990) 'The Social and Physical Environment of Residential Blocks, Crime, and Citizens' Participation in Block Associations', Unpublished doctoral dissertation, Department of Psychology, New York University.
—— and Taylor, R. (1996) 'Ecological Assessments of Community Disorder: Their relationship to fear of crime and theoretical implications', *American Journal of Community Psychology*, 24: 63–107.
Phillips, L.M. (1999) 'Recasting Consent: Agency and victimization in adult–teen relationships' in S. Lamb (ed) *New Versions of Victims: Feminists Struggle with the Concept*, New York: New York University Press, 82–107.
—— (2000) *Flirting With Danger: Young Women's Reflections on Sexuality and Domination*, New York: New York University Press.
Pidgeon, N., Kasperson, R.E. and Slovic, P. (2003) *The Social Amplification of Risk*, Cambridge: Cambridge University Press.
Pratt, J. (2007) *Penal Populism*, Oxford: Routledge.
President's Commission on Law Enforcement and the Administration of Justice, Task Force Report (1967), Washington, DC: US Government Printing Office.
Quillian, L. and Pager D. (2001) 'Black Neighbors, Higher Crime? The role of racial stereotypes in evaluations of neighborhood crime', *American Journal of Sociology*, 107(3): 717–67.
Rachman, S.J. (1978) *Fear and Courage*, San Francisco: Freeman.
Reichardt, C.S. and Gollob, H.F. (1986) 'Satisfying the Constraints of Casual Modeling' in W.M. Trochim (ed) *Advances in Quasi-experimental Design and Analysis*, San Francisco: Jossey-Bass.

Reiner, R., Livingstone, S. and Allen, J. (2000) 'No More Happy Endings? The media and popular concern about crime since the Second World War' in T. Hope and R. Sparks (eds) *Crime, Risk and Insecurity: 'Law and Order' in Everyday Life and Political Discourse*, London: Routledge.

Reiss, A.S. Jr (1967) 'Studies in Crime and Law Enforcement in Major Metropolitan Areas, Volume I', *President's Commission on Law Enforcement and Administration of Justice, Field Surveys III*, Washington DC: US Government Printing Office.

Riddell, P. (1985) *The Thatcher Government*, Second Edition, Oxford: Basil Blackwell.

Rifkind, J. (1995) *The End of Work*, New York: G P Putnam.

Ritchie, J. and Spencer, L. (1994) 'Qualitative Data Analysis for Applied Policy Research' in A. Bryman and R.G. Burgess (eds) *Analyzing Qualitative Data*, London: Routledge.

Roberts, D. (1999) 'Foreword: Race, vagueness, and the social meaning of order-maintenance policing', *Journal of Criminal Law and Criminology*, 89: 775–836.

Robinson, J.B., Lawton, B.A., Taylor, R.B. and Perkins, D.D. (2003) 'Multilevel Longitudinal Impacts of Incivilities: Fear of crime, expected safety, and block satisfaction', *Journal of Quantitative Criminology*, 19(3): 237–74.

Robinson, M.D. and Clore, G.L. (2002a) 'Belief and Feeling: Evidence for an accessibility model of emotional self report', *Psychological Bulletin*, 128: 934–60.

—— (2002b) 'Episodic and Semantic Knowledge in Emotional Self-report: Evidence for two judgment processes', *Journal of Personality and Social Psychology*, 83: 198–215.

Rock, P. (1990) *Helping Victims of Crime: The Home Office and the Rise of Victim Support in England and Wales*, Oxford: Clarendon Press.

Ross, C.E. and Jang, S. (2000) 'Neighborhood Disorder, Fear and Mistrust: The buffering role of social ties with neighbors', *American Journal of Community Psychology*, 28: 401–20.

Rountree, P.W. (1998) 'A Reexamination of the Crime–Fear Linkage', *Journal of Research in Crime and Delinquency*, 35(3): 341–72.

—— and Land, K.C. (1996a) 'Perceived Risk Versus Fear of Crime: Empirical evidence of conceptually distinct reactions in survey data', *Social Forces*, 74: 1353–76.

—— (1996b) 'Perceived Risk Versus Fear of Crime', *Journal of Research in Crime and Delinquency*, 33: 147–80.

Rubin, D.C. and Wetzel, A.E. (1996) 'One Hundred Years of Forgetting: A quantitative description of retention', *Psychological Review*, 103: 734–60.

Runciman, W. (1998) *The Social Animal*, London: HarperCollins.

Russell, M. and Davey, G.C.L. (1993) 'The Relationship Between Life Event Measures and Anxiety and Its Cognitive Correlates', *Personality and Individual Differences*, 14: 317–22.

Sacco, V.F. (1993) 'Social Support and the Fear of Crime', *Canadian Journal of Criminology*, 35: 187–96.

—— (2005) *When Crime Waves*, London: Sage Publications.

Sampson, R.J. (2004) 'Seeing Disorder: Neighborhood stigma and the social construction of "broken windows"', *Social Psychology Quarterly*, 67(4): 319–42.

—— and Earls, F. (1997) 'Neighborhoods and Violent Crime: A multilevel study of collective efficacy', *Science*, 277: 918–24.

—— and Jeglum-Bartusch, D. (1998) 'Legal Cynicism and (Subcultural?) Tolerance of Deviance: The neighbourhood context of racial differences', *Law and Society Review*, 32: 777–804.

—— and Laub, J.H. (1993) *Crime in the Making: Pathways and Turning Points Through Life*, London: Harvard University Press.

—— and Raudenbush, S.W. (1999) 'Systematic Social Observation of Public Spaces: A New Look at Disorder in Urban Neighborhoods.' *American Journal of Sociology*, 105:603–51.

Savage, S. (1990) 'A War on Crime?', in S. Savage and L. Robins (eds) *Public Policy Under Thatcher*, London: Macmillan.

Scheingold, S. (1995) 'Politics, Public Policy and Street Crime', *The Annals of the American Academy*, 539: 155–68.

Scherer, K.R., Wranik, T., Sangsue, J., Tran, V. and Scherer, U. (2004) 'Emotions in Everyday Life: Probability of occurrence, risk factors, appraisal and reaction patterns', *Social Science Information*, 43(4): 499–570.

Schuman, H. and Presser, S. (1996) *Questions and Answers in Attitude Surveys*, Second Edition, London: Sage.

Sennett, R. (1998) *The Corrosion of Character*, New York: Norton and Co.

—— (2006) *The Culture of the New Capitalism*, New Haven, CT: Yale University Press:

Shakespeare, W. (1603) *Macbeth*.

Shaw, C. (1931) *The Natural History of the Delinquent Career*, Chicago, IL: The University of Chicago Press.

Silvermann, R.A. and Kennedy, L.W. (1985) 'Loneliness, Satisfaction and Fear of Crime: A test for non-recursive effects,' *Canadian Journal of Criminology*, 27(1): 1–13.

Simon, J. (2007) *Governing Through Crime: How the War on Crime Transformed American Democracy and Created a Culture of Fear*, Oxford: Oxford University Press.

Skogan, W. (1981) *Issues in the Measurement of Victimisation*, Washington DC: US Government Printing Office, US Department of Justice.

—— (1986) 'Fear of Crime and Neighborhood Change', *Crime and Justice*, 8: 203–29.

Skogan, W. (1990) *Disorder and Decline: Crime and the Spiral of Decay in American Neighborhoods*, New York: Free Press.
—— (1993) 'The Various Meanings of Fear' in W. Bilsky, C. Pfeiffer and P. Wetzels (eds) *Fear of Crime and Criminal Victimization*, Stuttgart: Enke, 131–40.
—— (1995) 'Crime and the Racial Fears of White Americans', *The Annals of the American Academy*, 539: 59–71.
—— and Maxfield, M. (1981) *Coping with Crime*, Beverly Hills, CA: Sage.
Smith, J.A. (2004) 'Reflecting on the Development of interpretative Phenomenological Analysis and its Contribution to Qualitative Research in Psychology', *Qualitative Research in Psychology*, 1: 39–54.
—— and Osborn, M. (2003) 'Interpretative Phenomenological Analysis' in J.A. Smith (ed) *Qualitative Psychology. A practical guide to research methods*, London: Sage.
Smith, L.N. and Hill, G.D. (1991) 'Perceptions of Crime Seriousness and Fear of Crime', *Sociological Focus*, 24(4): 108–31.
Smith, S. (1987) 'Fear of Crime: Beyond a geography of deviance', *Progress in Human Geography*, 11: 1–23.
Smith. S.J. (1985) 'News and the Dissemination of Fear' in J. Burgess and J. Gold (eds) *Geography, the Media and Popular Culture*, London: Croom Helm.
—— (1986) *Crime, Space and Society*, Cambridge: Cambridge University Press.
Spalek, B. (2006) *Crime Victims: Theory, Policy and Practice*, London: Palgrave.
Sparks, R. (1992a) *Television and the Drama of Crime*, London: Open University Press.
—— (1992b) 'Reason and Unreason in Left Realism: Some problems in the constitution of the fear of crime' in R. Matthews and J. Young (eds) *Issues in Realist Criminology*, London: Sage, 119–35.
—— (2000) 'The Media and Penal Politics', *Punishment and Society*, 2(1): 98–105.
—— (2006) 'Ordinary Anxieties and States of Emergency' in S. Armstrong and L. McAra, (eds) *Perspectives on Punishment: The Contours of Control*, New York: Oxford University Press, 31–47.
—— Girling, E. and Loader, I. (2001) 'Fear and Everyday Urban Lives', *Urban Studies*, 38(5–6): 885–98.
Stafford, M.C. and Galle, O.R. (1984) 'Victimization Rates, Exposure to Risk, and Fear of Crime', *Criminology*, 22: 173–85.
Stafford, M., Chandola, T. and Marmot, M. (2007) 'Association Between Fear of Crime and Mental Health and Physical Functioning', *American Journal of Public Health*, 97: 2076–81.
Standing, G. (1996) 'Social Protection in Central and Eastern Europe' in G. Esping–Anderson (ed) *Welfare States in Transition*, London: Sage.

Stanko, E.A. (1985) *Intimate Intrusions: Women's Experience of Male Violence*, London: Routledge and Kegan Paul.

—— (1987) 'Typical Violence, Normal Precaution: Men, women and interpersonal violence in England, Wales, Scotland and the USA' in J. Hanmer and M. Maynard (eds) *Women, Violence and Social Control*, London: Macmillan.

—— (1988) 'Hidden Violence Against Women' in M. Maguire and J. Pointing (eds) *Victims of Crime. A New Deal?*, Milton Keynes: Open University Press.

—— (1990) 'When Precaution Is Normal: A feminist critique of crime prevention' in L. Gelsthorpe, and A. Morris (eds) *Feminist Perspectives in Criminology*, Milton Keynes: Open University Press.

—— (1997) 'Safety Talk: Conceptualising women's risk assessment as a "technology of the soul"', *Theoretical Criminology*, 1(4): 479–99.

—— (2000) 'Victims R Us: The life history of "fear of crime" and the politicisation of violence' in T. Hope and R. Sparks (eds), *Crime, Risk and Insecurity: 'Law and Order' in Everyday Life and Political Discourse*, London: Routledge.

Stapel, D.A., Reicher, S.D. and Spears, R. (1994) 'Social Identity, Availability and the Perception of Risk', *Social Cognition*, 12(1): 1–17.

—— and Velthuijsen, A.S. (1996) 'As If It Happened To Me: The impact of vivid and self-relevant information on risk judgments', *Journal of Social and Clinical Psychology*, 15: 102–19.

Sterngold, A., Warland, R. and Herrmann, R. (1994) 'Do Surveys Overstate Public Concerns?', *Public Opinion Quarterly*, 58: 255–63.

Strathclyde Regional Council (1994) *Social Strategy for the Nineties: Priority Areas*, Glasgow, July.

St John, C. and Heald-Moore, T. (1996) 'Racial Prejudice and Fear of Criminal Victimization by Strangers in Public Settings', *Sociological Inquiry*, 66(3): 267–84.

Sunstein, C. (2005) *Laws of Fear: Beyond the precautionary principle*. Cambridge: Cambridge University Press.

Sutton, R. and Farrall, S. (2005) 'Gender, Socially Desirable Responding, and the Fear of Crime: Are women really more anxious about crime?', *British Journal of Criminology*, 45(2): 212–24.

—— and —— (2009) 'Untangling the Web: Deceptive responding in fear of crime research' in M. Lee and S. Farrall (eds) *Fear of Crime: Critical Voices in an Age of Anxiety*, 108–24, London: Routledge.

Tallis, F., Davey, G.C.L. and Capuzzo, N. (1994) 'The Phenomenology of Non-pathological Worry: A preliminary investigation' in G.C.L. Davey and F. Tallis (eds) *Worrying: Perspectives on Theory, Assessment and Treatment*, London: Wiley, 61–89.

Tallis, F., Eysenck, M.W. and Mathews, A. (1992) 'A Questionnaire for the Measurement of Nonpathological Worry', *Personality and Individual Differences*, 13: 161–168.

Taub, R.P., Taylor, D.C. and Dunham, J.D. (1984) *Paths of Neighborhood Change*, Chicago, IL: University of Chicago Press.

Taylor, I. (1990) 'Sociology and the Condition of the English City – Thoughts from a Returnee', *Salford Papers in Sociology*, No. 9, University of Salford.

—— (1996) 'Fear of Crime, Urban Fortunes and Suburban Social Movements: Some reflections from Manchester', *Sociology*, 30(2): 317–37.

—— Evans, K. and Fraser, P. (1996) *A Tale of Two Cities*, London: Routledge.

Taylor, I. and Jamieson, R. (1998) 'Fear of Crime and Fear of Falling: English anxieties approaching the millennium', *Archives Europeanee de Sociologie*, 19(1): 149–75.

Taylor, R.B. (1999) 'The Incivilities Thesis' in R. Langworthy (ed) *Measuring What Matters*, Washington, DC: National Institute of Justice.

—— (2000) *Breaking Away from Broken Windows*, Boulder, CO: Westview Press.

—— and Hale, M. (1986) 'Testing Alternative Models of Fear of Crime', *Journal of Criminal Law and Criminology*, 77: 151–89.

—— Shumaker, S.A. and Gottfedson, S.D. (1985) 'Neighborhood-level Links Between Physical Features and Local Sentiments: Deterioration, fear of crime, and confidence', *Journal of Architectural and Planning Research*, 2: 261–75.

Thatcher, M. (1995) *The Path to Power*, London: HarperCollins.

Therborn, G. (1989) 'The Two-Thirds, One-Third Society' in S. Hall and M. Jacques (eds) *New Times*, London: Lawrence and Wishart Ltd.

Thrift, N. (2005) 'But Malice Aforethought: Cities and the natural history of hatred', *Transactions of the Institute of British Geographers*, 30: 133–250.

Tien, J.M., O'Donnell, V.F., Barnett, A. and Michandani, P.B. (1979) *Street Lighting Projects. National Evacuation Program. Phase I Report*, Washington, DC: National Institute of Law Enforcement and Criminal Justice.

Timmins, N. (2001) *The Five Giants*, London: HarperCollins.

Tourangeau, R., Rips, L.J. and Rasinski, K. (2000) *The Psychology of Survey Response*, Cambridge: Cambridge University Press.

Tucker, C., Baxter, J.C., Rozelle, R.M. and McCreary, J.H. (1979) 'Group Differences in the Utilisation of Cues of Danger: The potential for rape on a university campus', Unpublished paper, University of Houston.

Tudor, A. (2003) 'A (Macro) Sociology of Fear?', *The Sociological Review*, 51(2): 218–37.

Tulloch, J., Lupton, D., Blood, W., Tulloch, M., Jennett, C. and Enders, M. (1998) *Fear of Crime*, Canberra: Centre for Cultural Risk Research for the NCAVAC Unit for the NCAVAC, Attorney-General's Department.

Tulloch, M. (2003) 'Combining Classificatory and Discursive Methods: Consistency and variability in responses to the threat of crime', *British Journal of Social Psychology*, 42(3): 461–76.

Tulving, E. (1984) 'Precis of Elements of Episodic Memory', *Behavioral and Brain Sciences*, 7: 223–68.

Turner, J.H. (1996) 'The Evolution of Emotions in Humans: A Darwinian–Durkheimian analysis', *Journal for the Theory of Social Behaviour*, 26: 1–33.

—— and Stets, J.E. (2005) *The Sociology of Emotions*, Cambridge: Cambridge University Press.

Tversky, A. and Kahneman, D. (1973) 'Availability: A heuristic for judging frequency and probability', *Cognitive Psychology*, 4(1973): 207–32.

Tyler, T.R. (1980) 'Impact of Directly and Indirectly Experienced Events: The origin of crime-related judgements and behaviours', *Journal of Personality and Social Psychology*, 39: 13–28.

—— (1984) 'Assessing the Risk of Crime Victimization: The integration of personal victimization experience and socially transmitted information', *Journal of Social Issues*, 40: 27–38.

—— and Boeckmann, R. (1997) '"Three Strikes and You're Out" But Why?', *Law and Society Review*, 31(2): 237–65.

—— and Cook, F.L. (1984) 'The Mass Media and Judgements of Risk: Distinguishing impact on personal and societal level judgement', *Journal of Personality and Social Psychology*, 47: 693–708.

—— and Rasinski, K. (1984) 'Comparing Psychological Images of the Social Perceiver: Role of perceived informativeness, memorability, and affect in mediating the impact of crime victimisation', *Journal of Personality and Social Psychology*, 46(2): 308–29.

Vale, L.J. and Campanella, T.J. (2005) *The Resilient City: How Modern Cities Recover from Disaster*, Oxford: Oxford University Press.

Valentine, G. (1989) *Women's Fear of Male Violence in Public Space: A public expression of patriarchy*, PhD thesis, Reading University.

van der Wurff, A. and Stringer, P. (1988) 'Measuring Fear of Crime in Residential Surroundings' in L.G. Stephenson, L. Sozzka, C. Jesuino and D. Cantor (eds) *Environmental Social Psychology*, The Hague: Nijof.

Vanderveen, G. (2006) *Interpreting Fear, Crime, Risk and Unsafety*, Cullompton, Devon: Willan.

Vasey, M.W. and Borkovec, T.D. (1992) 'A Catastrophising Assessment of Worrisome Thoughts', *Cognitive Therapy and Research*, 16: 505–20.

Verkuil, B., Brosschot, J.F. and Thayer, J.F. (2007) 'Capturing Worry in Daily Life: Are trait questionnaires sufficient?', *Behaviour Research and Therapy*, 45(8): 1835–44.

Villarreal, A.B. and Silva, B.F.A. (2006) 'Social Cohesion, Criminal Victimization and Perceived Risk of Crime in Brazilian Neighborhoods', *Social Forces*, 84(3): 1725–53.

Walker, A. (1990) 'The Strategy of Inequality: Poverty and income distribution in Britain 1979–89' in I. Taylor (ed) *The Social Effects of Free Market Policies: An International Text*, London: Harvester.

Walklate, S. (2002) 'Issues in Local Community Safety' in A. Crawford (ed) *Crime and Insecurity*, Cullompton, Devon: Willan Publishing.

—— (2006) *Imagining the Victims of Crime*, Berkshire: Open University Press.

Warner, M. (1998) *No Go the Bogeyman*, London: Chatto and Windus.

Warr, M. (1984) 'Fear of Victimization: Why are women and the elderly more afraid?', *Social Science Quarterly*, 65: 681–702.

—— (1985) 'Fear of Rape Among Urban Women', *Social Problems*, 32(3): 238–50.

—— (1987) 'Fear of Victimisation and Sensitivity to Risk', *Journal of Quantitative Criminology*, 3/1: 29–46.

—— (1990) 'Dangerous Situations: Social context and fear of victimization', *Social Forces*, 68(3): 891–907.

—— (1994) 'Public Perceptions and Reactions to Violent Offending and Victimization' in A.J. Reiss, Jr and J.A. Roth (eds) *Consequences and Control*, Volume 4 of *Understanding and Preventing Violence*, Washington, DC: National Academy Press.

—— (2000) 'Public Perceptions of and Reactions to Crime' in J. Sheley (ed) *Criminology: A Contemporary Handbook*, Third Edition, Belmont, CA: Wadsworth, 13–31.

—— and Stafford, M.C. (1983) 'Fear of Victimization: A look at the proximate causes', *Social Forces*, 61: 1033–43.

Wiedemann, P.M., Clauberg, M. and Schutz, H. (2003) 'Understanding Amplification of Complex Risk Issues: The risk story model applied to the EMF case' in N. Pidgeon, R.E. Kasperson and P. Slovic (eds) *The Social Amplification of Risk*, Cambridge: Cambridge University Press.

Wilhelm, P. (2001) 'A Multilevel Approach to Analyze Ambulatory Assessment Data: An experiment of family members' emotional states in daily life' in J. Fahrenberg and J. Murtek (eds) *Progress in Ambulatory Assessment: Computer Assisted Psychological and Psychophysiological Methods in Monitoring and Field Studies*, Kirkland, WA: Hogrefe and Huber, 173–89.

Wilkins, L. and Pease, K. (1987) 'Public Demand for Punishment', *International Journal of Sociology and Social Policy*, 7(3): 16–29.

Williams, S. (2001) *Emotions and Social Theory*, London: Sage.

—— and Bendelow, G. (eds) (1998) *Emotions in Social Life: Critical Themes and Contemporary Issues*, London: Routledge.

Williams, F.P., McShane, M.D. and Akers, R.L. (2000) 'Worry About Victimization: An alternative and reliable measure for fear of crime', *Western Criminology Review* 2(2) available at <http://wcr.sonoma.edu/v2n2/williams.html>

Wilson, J.Q. (1968) 'The Urban Unease: Community vs. city', *Public Interest*, 12: 25–39.

—— and Kelling, G.L. (1982) 'Broken Windows', *Atlantic Monthly*, March, 29–38.

Wilson, L.A. (1976) 'Private and Collective Choice Behavior in the Provision of Personal Security from Criminal Victimization', Ph.D. Dissertation, Department of Political Science, University of Oregon.

Winkel, F.W. (1998) 'Fear of Crime and Criminal Victimisation: Testing a theory of psychological incapacitation of the "stressor" based on downward comparison processes', *British Journal of Criminology*, 38(3): 473–84.

—— and Vrij, A. (1990) 'Fear of Crime and Mass Media Crime Reports: Testing similarity hypotheses', *International Review of Victimology*, 1: 251–65.

Wouters, C. (1986) 'Formalization and Informalization; Changing tension balances in civilizing processes', *Theory, Culture and Society*, 3(2): 1–18.

—— (1992) 'On Status Competition and Emotion Management: The study of emotions as a new field', *Theory, Culture and Society*, 24(4): 699–717.

Yin, P.P. (1980) 'Fear of Crime Among the Elderly: Some issues and suggestions', *Social Problems*, 27(4): 492–504.

Young, H. (1993) *One of Us*, Final Edition, London: Pan Books.

Young, J. (1986) 'The Failure of Criminology: the need for a Radical Realism', in R. Matthews and J. Young (eds) *Confronting Crime*, London: Sage.

—— (1992) 'Ten Points of Realism' in J. Young and R. Matthews (eds) *Rethinking Criminology*, London: Sage.

—— (1999) *The Exclusive Society: Social Exclusion, Crime and Difference in Late Modernity*, London: Sage.

Zaller, J. (1992) *The Nature and Origins of Mass Opinion*, Cambridge: Cambridge University Press.

—— and Feldman, S. (1992) 'A Simple Theory of the Survey Response: Answering questions versus revealing preferences', *American Journal of Political Science*, 36(3): 579–616.

Zedner, L.H. (2003) 'Too Much Security?', *International Journal of the Sociology of Law*, 31: 155–84.

Zolotas, X.E. (1981) *Economic Growth and Declining Social Welfare*, Athens.

Index

administration of justice
  priorities 14
  resources 14, 16
affluence *see* anxieties of affluence
Agnew, R.S. 83
Ahrendt, D. 96, 103, 115, 119, 124
Anderson, E. 94
anti-social behaviour
  Anti-social Behaviour Orders (ASBOs) 38
  area-level data 228
  community issues 136
  focus on 38
  local crime survey 222
  policy 39, 40, 43
  public fears 239, 246
  public perception 259
  social cohesion 59
anxieties of affluence
  class distribution 260
  consumer boom 251
  crime rates 248
  economic growth 247, 248
  economic inequalities 260
  economic security 247
  economic/social change 246, 247, 251
  education 248
  housing 248
  income levels 247
  levels of affluence 248, 249
  middle-class concerns 228, 229, 242, 243, 245, 250, 251, 252
  neo-conservative influences 248
  neo-liberal influences 260
  non-economic rewards 247
  paradox of affluence 247
  policing 250, 265
  political control 250
  private benefits 247

  social surveys 249, 250
  social welfare 247
  socio-economic transformations *see* socio-economic transformations
  taxation rates 260, 266
  wealth 260, 266
  'worried-well' 252, 254
anxiety
  anti-social behaviour 246
  anxiety about crime 165, 176, 177, 178, 210, 216, 217, 218, 223–6, 228, 232
  disorder 246
  future-orientated anxiety 51, 66
  index of anxiety (USA) 24, 47
  middle-class concerns 228, 229, 242, 243, 245, 250, 251, 252
  psychosocial understanding 261, 262
  public anxiety 1, 9, 14, 15–17, 22, 23, 42, 91, 104, 106, 107
  social change 246
Arbuckle, J.L. 213, 216
area-level data
  anti-social behaviour 228
  disorder 228
  social change 228
Arnold, H. 85
attitudinal questions
  use of 54, 55, 56
authoritarianism
  attitudes to crime 5, 118, 119
Averill, J. 62

Babey, S.H. 66
Baker, Kenneth 36
Balkin, S. 82
Banks, M. 258
Bannister, J. 91, 94, 98, 99, 114, 158, 160

Index

Baron, R.M. 212, 213
Bauman, Z. 12, 104, 110, 231, 240, 252, 255, 256, 262, 263
Beck, U. 256, 257
Bell, R. 228, 250, 251
Bendelow G. 60
Bennett T. 82
Ben-Ze've, A. 61, 63
bibliography 280–301
Biderman, A.D. et al. 24, 25, 28, 46, 47, 48, 49, 96, 207
Bishop, G. 56, 57, 96
Blair, Tony 35, 36, 40, 44, 105, 253, 254
Boeckmann, R. 100, 198
Bolling, K. 275
Borkovec, T.D. 167
Bowling, B. 84
Box, S. 85, 91
Bradford, B. 198
Brandolini, A. 260
Brandstatter, H. 65
British Crime Survey (BCS)
  ACORN categories 214
  audit culture 39
  environmental perception 100
  function 30, 31, 236
  interviewees 275
  methodology 49, 50, 51
  operation 277
  results 217–21
  sampling frame 275
  source of information 5, 33, 44, 163, 167, 168, 170, 171, 174, 200, 201, 207, 209, 216, 238, 241
  structural equation modelling (SEM) 211 *see also* **structural equation modelling (SEM)**
  topic guide 275
  victimization survey 277
Brixton Riots
  significance 34
Bulger, James 35, 253, 254
Burgess, J. 92
Burney, E. 39, 40, 95, 253, 258, 267
Bursik, R.J. 93, 102, 106
Bush, George (Snr) 105
Butler, G. 114

Calderia, T. 232
Campanella, T.J. 141
Caravalho, I. 87, 99, 100, 101
Castells, M 263
Cavender, G. 258
CCTV
  use of 35, 37
Chadee, D. 49, 258
child curfews 38
Child Safety Orders 38
Chiricos, T. 85, 97, 99, 102
Chi-square statistics 212, 217, 218
Clarke, Kenneth 36
Clerici, C. 86
Clore, G.L. 65, 66, 114, 168
Cohen, S. 108
commodification of security 44, 104
community
  anti-social behaviour 136
  breakdown of family life 135
  community cohesion 134, 239
  community conditions 239, 240
  community deterioration 225, 239
  community efficacy 93
  community trust 108
  disintegration 94
  emotional attachments 134
  employment patterns 141
  feed-back loop 139
  immigrant populations 136, 137
  local crime survey 225
  low-level disorder 136
  materialistic influences 134
  multi-cultural society 137
  neighbourhood familiarity 108
  neighbourhood relationships 134
  personal safety 138
  protection/care 138, 139, 140
  quality of life 140
  resilience 141
  respect/trust 137, 138, 139, 141
  social bonds 135, 138, 139, 140
  social cohesion 134, 135
  social isolation 135, 138, 139
  socio-economic structures 134
  youth culture 136
community safety
  audits 38
  legislation 38

Index

responsibility
  local authority 38
  police 38
comparative fit index (CFI) 212
Conklin, J.E. 83, 94
Connell, R. 30
consumer boom
  anxieties of affluence 251
  increase in crime 9, 229
control
  judgements of control 87, 88
  loss of control 86
  risk control 87
  social/physical environment 87
Cook, F.L. 88
Coovert, M.D. 213
correlates of fear
  ACORN classification 183
  age 180, 181, 182
  area-level correlates 182, 183
  ethnicity 180, 182
  gender 180, 182
  household income 181, 182
  victimization 185, 186, 187
Covington, J. 83, 85, 91, 94, 97, 98, 99
Crawford, A. 38, 262
crime
  anxiety about crime 165, 176, 177, 178, 210, 216, 217, 218, 223–6, 228, 232
  authoritarian attitudes 118
  behavioural standards 117, 119
  breakdown of trust 229
  cascade effects 116
  collective efficacy 229, 239
  commodification of security 44, 104
  community cohesion 239
  community conditions 239, 240
  connected anxieties 106, 107
  contemporary importance 244
  crime consciousness *see* **crime consciousness**
  crime control 90, 104
  crime risk 90, 91
  cultural factors 9, 107
  daily effects 229
  direct/indirect experience 91

emotional reactions 123, 208, 227
erosion of security 228
everyday experience 9, 10, 33, 34, 42
government response 17, 18, 40
group polarization 116
increase in 9, 14, 33, 34, 42, 91, 228
law and order 118
liberal sensibilities 42, 90
location
  mental maps 107
  symbolic locations 107
media influences 10, 11, 16, 33, 34, 37, 42, 46, 88, 89, 90, 91, 116, 117, 208, 239, 244
middle-class concerns 228, 229, 242, 243, 245, 250, 251, 252
moral authority 244
moral decay 16
moral order 208
moral outrage 208, 219
moral standards 5
neighbourhood crime
  see **neighbourhood crime**
neighbourhood pride 239
penal populism 16
perpetually contemporaneous offences 96
personal safety 239
physical environment 208
physical order 239
policy-making 18
political analysis 244
political influences 239
political rhetoric 9
prevention 9
private security 9
public anxiety 1, 9, 14, 15–17, 22, 23, 42, 91, 104, 106, 107
public beliefs 96
public emotions 5
public feelings 8
public perception 4, 22, 42, 91, 105, 208, 219
public responses 106, 230
right-wing policies 105
risk management 9, 15, 239
risk perception 116, 208, 210
salience of crime 42, 91
security 231, 238, 242

crime (cont.)
   social breakdown 5
   social change 5, 12, 22, 42, 117, 118, 119, 239, 244
   social cohesion 90, 117, 119, 208, 229, 230, 239, 240, 244, 245
   social conditions 245
   social control 99, 117, 119, 230, 239, 240
   social/economic factors 9, 12, 13, 14, 19, 43, 208
   social inequality 107
   social interventions 246
   social order 117, 119, 230, 239, 240
   social/political issues 9, 229
   social relations 107, 108, 117, 119
   social significance 10, 40
   stimulus similarity 116
   symbols of crime 10, 239
   transfer of interest 253
   vandalism 42, 91
   victimization 11, 33–5, 42, 210
      see also victimization
   welfare state 229
   worry about crime 165, 176, 177, 178, 210, 217, 224–6, 232
   zero tolerance 16
Crime and Disorder Index of Deprivation 184
Crime Commission on Law Enforcement and Administration of Justice
Katzenbach Commission 23, 26
crime consciousness
   crime stories 144, 145
   Crime Watch 145
   culture of fear 146
   emotions 141
   experiences 141
   government influence 146, 147
   highly populated areas 142
   knowledge of crime 141–4, 159
   media influences 145, 146, 159
   memories 14
   middle-class neighbourhoods 142
   murder 146
   narrative of fear 159
   Neighbourhood Watch 147
   opinions 141
   personal safety 160
   police attitudes 160
   protective behaviour 146, 147, 160
   rape 146
   responses to crime 146, 147
   responsibilization 147, 258
   victimization 142, 147, 148, 149
      see also victimization
   vigilance 160
criminal justice system
   crime control 34
   expenditure 34
   liberal influences 244
   objectives 3
   policy 15, 34, 35, 110, 244
   populist influences 15, 16
   public confidence 40, 118, 124
   public perception 16, 17
   rehabilitation 15
   resources 15
   risk assessment 244
   social issues 245, 246
Crow, G. 255
Csikszentmihalyi, M. 161
Currie, E. 267
Curtis, L.P. 22, 46

Dando, Jill 145
data and measures
   anti-social behaviour 215, 218
   anxiety about crime 216, 217, 218
   burglary 214
   composite indicators 214
   crime levels 213
   criminal damage 214
   disorder 215, 218, 219
   endogenous variables 213, 216
   exogenous variables 213
   judgements of risk 219
   local disorder 213
   perceived risk 216, 218, 219
   social change 214, 215, 218, 219
   social cohesion 215, 218, 219, 220
   social conditions 220
   social control 215
   social relationships 220
   sources of information

Index 307

British Crime Survey 5, 33, 44,
    163, 167, 168, 170, 171, 174,
    200, 201, 207, 209, 216, 238, 241
  Crime Domain 213
  Index of Multiple Deprivation
    213, 243, 245
  local crime survey 238
  theft 214
  victimization 216, 218, 219
    see also victimization
  violence 214
  worry about crime 217
Davey, G.C.L. 114, 167
Davidson, R.J. 60
Day, K. 240
disorder
  area-level data 228
  community standards 91
  criminalization 38
  decreasing tolerance 39
  impact 93
  judgements of disorder 93
  lack of concern 91
  lack of control 91
  local authority powers 40
  local crime survey 222, 225,
    226, 227
  low-level disorder 9
  moral consensus 100
  neighbourhood breakdown 99
  neighbourhood stimuli 100
  objective signs 99
  perception of risk 91
  personal distancing 100, 101
  police powers 40, 43
  public fears 243
  public perception 96, 97, 98,
    99, 100
  public sensibilities 95
  sensitivity 99
  'signal crimes' concept 95
  social change 99, 100, 120
  social cohesion 100, 120
  social control 96, 100
  social cues 96, 97
  threat of crime 114
  victimization 91
    see also victimization
  visible signs 95

worry 202, 227
young persons 38
Ditton, J. 21, 25, 38, 49, 166, 167,
    208, 258
Dobash, R.E. 30
Douglas, J.D. 8
Dowds, L. 96, 103, 115, 119, 124
Downes, D. 253
DuBow, F. 83
Durkheim, E. 60

Easterlin 247
Ebert, J.E. 65
Economic and Social Research
    Council (ESRC) 37, 39, 124
Ehrenreich, B. 251
Ehrlichman, J. 41
Elias, N. 60, 160
Elster, J. 117
emotion
  anger 62
  basic emotions 62, 63
  contempt 62, 63
  criminology 60
  ecological distribution 51
  emotional complexity 60–2
  emotional experiences
    appraisal theory 65
    concurrent reports 65
    emotional digestion 64
    emotional responses 64, 66, 73
    emotion-eliciting events 65
    episode memory 65
    episodic knowledge 65, 66
    future-orientated anxiety 66
    retrospective reports 65
    semantic knowledge 65, 66
  envy 62, 63
  ethnographic studies 60
  everyday experience 51, 62, 80
  fear 62, 63 *see also* fear
  happiness 62
  hate 62, 63
  hope 62, 63
  indicators 48–50
  jealousy 62, 63
  love 62, 63
  psychological lessons 60
  psychosocial understanding 261

308 Index

emotion (*cont.*)
  public emotions 5
  research *see* research (emotions)
  shame 62, 63
  sociology of emotions 60
  symbolism/significance 63
Ennis, P.H. 31, 47
environmental factors
  environmental cues 91, 92, 98, 99, 119, 133, 158, 159, 229, 258
  environmental perception
    community efficacy 93
    control/consequence 115
    danger signs 92, 93, 111
    environmental relationships 114
    fear of unknown 92
    first-person assessments 95
    informal control 133, 158
    lack of control 94
    local disorders 95
    local environment 114
    neighbourhood breakdown 114, 158, 159, 230
    neighbourhood characteristics 114, 129
    neighbourhood crime 94
    neighbourhood trust 230
    physical decay 98
    presence of others 91, 92
    psychological effects 95
    racial composition 95, 97, 114
    secondary sources 95
    sense of place 127
    sense of security 92, 93
    'signal crimes' concept 95, 131
    social change 115
    social cohesion 93, 96, 115, 133, 158
    social consensus 115
    social control 92, 93, 94, 96, 115
    social disorder 95
    social/economic deprivation 94, 95
    victimization 115, 116
    visual control 92
    vulnerability 115
  physical cues 92
  social cues 92
  urban issues
    abandoned streets 92
    broken windows theory 94, 95, 114
    discarded needles 92
    disorderly behaviour 92
    drug use 131, 132, 133
    graffiti 92, 130
    hiding places for criminals 92
    highly populated areas 142, 158
    litter 92, 130
    noise pollution 92
    no-go areas 130
    poor lighting 91
    state of buildings 92
    stray dogs 92
    urban decline 94
    vandalism 92, 130, 133, 158
error approximation 218
Evans, K. 31, 105, 108
experience and expression
  anxiety about crime 210
  experiential fear 150–3, 160, 161, 164, 227, 236, 238, 242
  expressive fear 150, 153–7, 161, 164, 227, 229, 232, 236, 238, 242
  local crime survey 210
  outline of analysis 210, 211
  risk interpretation 210
  significance 149, 150, 209
  worry about crime 210
expert views
  criminologists 29
  feminist sociologists 29
  moral panic theorists 29

Fattah, E.A. 105, 166
fear
  ambient fear 240
  anticipated fear 51
  anxiety about crime 165, 176, 177, 178
  attitude/perception 51
  causes 81
  chronic fear 76, 77, 78, 241
  correlates of fear *see* correlates of fear
  definition 51, 112
  development of fear 250

Index

everyday experience 51, 66, 238, 250
existential fear 241
experiential fear 150–3, 160, 161, 164, 227, 236, 238, 242
expressive fear 66, 150, 153–7, 161, 164, 227, 229, 232, 236, 238, 242
frequency 80
genetic modification 117
immediate threat 164
individual experience 63, 64
intensity 80
macro-level influences 101
management of fear 36
measurement 113
media influences 10, 11, 16, 33, 34, 37, 42, 88, 89, 90, 91, 116, 117, 208, 239, 244
momentary effective state 64
multi-variate analysis *see* **multi-variate analysis**
nagging doubts 79
neo-conservative policy 34
precautionary actions 64, 79, 109
quantification 164, 165
risk-fear paradox 32, 83
risk of crime 164
risk sensitivity 113
shock events 78
situational fear 241
streams of fear 164, 165, 203, 210
tangible fear 241
threats to well-being 250
worry about crime 165, 176, 177, 178
fear of crime
academic research 39
authoritarianism 118, 119
background concerns 75, 76, 79
categorization of others 106
causes 1
community disintegration 94
community trust 108
complex nature 157, 163, 231, 232, 236
concept 1, 7, 21–3, 252
connected anxieties 106, 107
constituent elements 157
control over uncertainty 109
correlates of fear *see* **correlates of fear**
crime complex 104
criminological interest 19, 21, 22
critical commentary 6
economic factors 246
empathy 74, 75
everyday reality 238
experience/expression 114–8, 120
experiential dimension 242
expressive dimension 242
feed-back loop 41, 57, 105, 139, 249, 262
frequency 242
generally 1
government reaction 3, 40
'hoodies' 40
individual anxieties 109, 110
industrialized nations 233
integrative position 6, 110, 111
see also **unified framework (fear of crime)**
intensity of worry 7, 8, 241
lived culture 104
lived reality 70, 72, 78
meaning 45, 78, 112, 163, 240
measurement 8, 38, 46, 47
media influences 10, 11, 16, 33, 34, 37, 42, 88, 89, 90, 91, 208, 239, 244
middle-class concerns 242, 243, 245, 250
misrepresentation 235
moral consensus 6
moral decline 6
moral value 18
multi-variate analysis *see* **multi-variate analysis**
nature of 7, 8, 236, 240, 241
negative influence 3
neighbourhood order 5
origins 43
penal populism 16, 40
personal/contextual influences 157
pervasive insecurity 3
political economy 40
political influence 105, 120, 236, 252, 253

fear of crime (*cont.*)
  precautionary action 64, 79, 109
  problem status 238
  psychological significance 7
  public anxiety 22, 23, 106
  public emotions 4
  public insecurities 4
  research *see* research (fear of crime)
  risk
    evaluation 111
    perception 40, 111, 112
  security/insecurity 231
  significance 240
  social attitude i8
  social change 5, 75, 103, 246
  social cohesion 6, 104
  social consensus 104
  social/cultural meaning 235
  social/economic changes 110
  social indicator 245
  social perception 4, 111
  social/political issue 3
  social values 6
  socio-economic transformations *see* socio-economic transformations
  subconscious reasoning 157
  theoretical development 6, 81
  theoretical model 19
  unified framework *see* unified framework (fear of crime)
  USA experience *see* United States of America
  victimization 4, 8, 72, 74, 78, 79, 111 *see also* victimization
feed-back loop
  effect 41, 57, 105, 139, 249, 262
feelings
  behavioural responses 73
  reality of feelings 45
  transitory experiences 70–4
Feldman, S. 53, 57
Felson, R.B. 94
feminist views
  feminist sociologists 29
  harassment 29
  male violence 29, 30
  patriarchy critique 29
  victimization 30, 32 *see also* victimization

Ferdinand, T. 83
Ferge, Z. 255
Ferraro, K.F. 7, 45, 48, 49, 85, 87, 88, 91, 111, 112, 114, 117, 119, 124, 132, 133, 192, 210, 218, 231, 258
Figgie Report
  perception of safety 48
  security threats 46
  victimization 46
Fiske, J. 258
Fortuyn, Pim 253
Frank, R.H. 13, 247, 248, 260, 266
Franzini, L. 99
Fredrickson, B.L. 65
frequency items
  accurate count 58
  decomposition 59
  estimation 58
  example 58
  guesses 59
  meaning 57, 58
  set of possible responses 59
  socially desirable responses 59
Frijda, N.H. 114
full information maximum likelihood (FIML) 213, 214, 216, 217
Furedi, F. 11, 35, 108, 146, 147, 231
Furlong, A. 256
Furstenberg, F.N. 25, 27, 94

Gabriel, U. 63, 80, 87
Gadd, D. 7, 52, 54, 57, 80, 164, 166, 167, 168, 200, 227, 238, 261, 262
Galle, O.R. 83
Gardner, C.B. 85
Garland, D. 9, 11, 15, 33, 34, 35, 42, 73, 90, 91, 104, 111, 147, 149, 160, 208, 229, 230, 242, 244, 250, 251, 257, 258
Garofalo, J. 47, 83, 106
Gasper, K. 114
George, Barry 145
Giddens, A. 231, 256, 257
Gilbert, D.T. 65
Gilchrist, E. 70
Gilling, D. 35

Index

Girling, E. 12, 22, 38, 45, 49, 99, 106, 111, 117, 119, 120, 124, 126, 127, 133, 157, 164, 208, 230, 231, 242, 244, 258
Gladstone, G. 68, 166
Glassner, B. 231
Goffman, E. 92
Goldie, P. 64, 65
Goldwater, Barry 26, 105
Gordon, M. 30
government action
  economic inequality 266, 267
  law and order 29, 31, 32, 34, 35, 44, 118, 222, 225, 258, 263
  penal policy 263
  policing 263, 264, 265
  policy-making 18
  public confidence 262, 266
  redistributive tax regimes 266, 267
  security issues 262, 265, 266
  social/economic changes 263
  see also socio-economic transformations
  zero risk environments 263, 264, 266
  zero tolerance 16
Grasmick, H. 93, 102, 106
Green, D. 253, 254, 266
Greenberg, S.W. 103, 111
Greve, W. 63, 80, 87
Grimes, R.E. 25, 26, 41, 105, 120, 145
Gunn, S. 228, 250, 251

Hale, C. 81, 82, 83, 85, 88, 91, 97, 99, 108, 166, 231
Hall, S. 22, 29, 39, 236, 244, 258
Hankiss, E. 241
Harcourt, B.E. 38, 95
Harris, R. 25, 26, 105
Hassinger, J. 92, 158
Hay, C. 29, 244, 258
Hayle, M. 49
Heald-Moore, T. 99, 102
Heber, A. 253
Herz, L. 96
Hill, G.D. 83
Hills, J. 259, 260
Hochschild, A. 60

Hollander, J.A. 85
Hollway, W. 38, 109, 110, 261, 262, 263
'hoodies'
  public anxiety 40
Hope, T. 17, 104, 215, 250, 264, 265, 267
Horlick-Jones, T. 90
Hough, M. 31, 32, 49, 83, 85, 164, 166, 167, 176, 210, 266
Hovland, C.I. 261
Howard, Michael 36, 37
Hunter, A. 48, 91, 158
Hurd, Douglas 36

Index of Multiple Deprivation 184, 185, 192, 209, 213, 243, 245
Innes, M. 84, 91, 95, 119, 131, 132, 166, 231
invocation of attitude 79, 127, 153, 176

Jacobs, J. 93, 159
James, O. 13, 247
Jamieson, R. 12, 43, 103, 107, 111, 118, 164, 229, 242, 250, 251
Jang, S. 49, 93
Jefferson, T. 38, 109, 110, 261, 262, 263
Jeglum-Bartusch, D. 94
Jones, T. 84, 91, 92, 158, 231

Kahneman, D. 65, 168
Kanan, J.W. 94
Karstedt, S. 60
Kasperson, J.X. 89
Katz, J. 60, 61
Kelling, G.L. 91, 94, 95
Kelly, P. 84, 85, 256
Kemper, T.D. 60
Kennedy, John F. 23, 25
Kenny, D.A. 212, 213
Killias, M. 85, 86
King, Martin Luther 25
Klecka, W. 96
Klein, S.B. 66
Kristjansson, A.J. 267
Kuran, T. 116
Kury, H. 83

Land, K.C. 91
LaGrange, R.L. 7, 45, 48, 49, 84, 85, 91, 92
Latouche, S. 255
Laub, J. 47, 106, 246
Lavrakas, P.J. 96
Lee, M. 12, 14, 16, 25, 28, 29, 34, 35, 38, 39, 41, 42, 45, 57, 80, 83, 104, 105, 110, 120, 231, 236, 240, 243, 247, 249, 250, 258, 262, 265
Levy, S. 167
Lewis, D.A. 26, 82, 87, 91, 99, 100, 101, 158
linear structural relations
 use of 211
Liska, A.E. 82
Loader, I. 9, 12, 15, 17, 38, 104, 106, 107, 231, 244, 262, 263, 264, 265, 266
local crime survey
 anti-social behaviour 222
 anxiety about crime 223, 224, 225, 226
 authoritarian views 5
 collective efficacy 223, 226, 227
 community deterioration 225
 data 222, 275
 differing conclusions 224
 disorder 222, 225, 226, 227
 evaluation 276, 277
 exogenous variables 222
 experience and expression 210
 geographical area 275, 276
 law and order 222, 225
 perceived risk 224
 questionnaires 220, 276
 response rate 276
 results 224, 225
 social change 225
 social cohesion 5, 223, 225, 226, 227
 social control 5
 social/political attitudes 224
 socio-demographic breakdown 276
 source of information 238
 structural equation modelling (SEM) 226 see also **structural equation modelling (SEM)**
 victimization 223, 225, 226
 see also victimization
 worry about crime 224, 225, 226
 youth culture 222, 225, 226
Loo, D. 13, 14, 25, 26, 41, 105, 120, 145, 247, 248, 255, 258
Loury, G. 99
Lupton, D. 107, 109, 262

Madriz, E. 85
Major, John 36, 253, 254
Markowitz, F.E. 94
Marsh, H.W. 66
Matthews, A. 114, 167
Maxfield, M.G. 48, 85, 91, 92, 96, 97, 99, 158
maximum likelihood estimation (MLE)
 use of 211
Mayhew, P. 31, 32, 49
McCoy, H.V. 83
McGonville, M. 104, 105, 241
media
 amplification of risk 90
 crime consciousness 159
 crime risk 90, 91
 influence 10, 11, 16, 33, 34, 37, 42, 46, 88, 89, 90, 91, 116, 117, 208, 239, 244
 perception of crime 10, 11
 public concerns 46, 90, 239
Melanson, P. 28
Merry, S. 102, 106, 108
Methodological Appendix
 data analysis 270, 271, 272
 framework analysis 70
 indexing 272
 interpretation 272
 interviews
  academic criminologists 269
  discussion 269
  domains of interest 270
  duration 269
  government criminologists 269
  sampling procedure 269
  topic guide 270, 271
 local crime survey
  data 275
  evaluation 26, 277

geographical area 275, 76
questionnaires 276
response rate 276
socio-demographic
 breakdown 276
mapping 272
qualitative data sets
 Glasgow 273
 London 273, 274
migrants
immigrant populations 136, 137, 159
multi-cultural society 137
neighbourhood composition 95, 97, 114
Moeller, G.L. 102
multi-nominal logistic regression 187
multi-variate analysis
disorder/cohesion/collective efficacy 187, 192, 195, 196, 197, 210
mediational relationships 195, 196
perceived risk 197
predicted probabilities (female) 193, 194
predicted probabilities (male) 193, 194
unworried 187
unworried versus frequently worried 187, 190, 191, 192
unworried versus worried 187, 189, 192
victimization variables 187, 192, 193
worried versus anxious 187, 188
Myrtek, M. 62

neighbourhood crime
community conditions 239, 240
community trust 108
crime levels 101, 208
declining neighbourhoods 91, 94, 114
economic factors 103
emotional response 208
environmental perception 94
ethnic composition 101, 102
group conflict 102
local disorders 95
moral order 208
neighbourhood breakdown 94, 99, 114, 158, 159, 230, 239
neighbourhood disorder 208, 229

neighbourhood familiarity 108
neighbourhood stability 5, 208
neighbourhood trust 230
perception of risk 208, 10
physical environment 208
social disorder 101
social environment 208
social stability 208
victimization 102, 210 *see also* victimization
New Labour policy
criminal justice 36, 37, 39, 44, 105
Nixon, Richard 26, 41, 43, 105

Offer, A. 13, 14, 247, 248, 255
Osborn, M. 126
Osborne, T. 56, 57

Pain, R. 85, 92, 158
Pakes, F. 253
Parenting Orders 38
Park, A. 266
Parker, G. 68, 166
Pattillo, M.E. 94
Pearson, G. 22, 29, 39, 46
Pease, K. 260
penal populism
effects 16
increase 40
Perkins, D.D. 91, 97, 98, 99
Phillips, L.M. 84
Pidgeon, N. et al. 89
police
crime consciousness 160
patrols 37, 43
performance indicators 43
public confidence 198, 199, 200, 237, 238
policing
ambient policing 264, 265
community-led 40
community safety 38
disorder 40, 43
government policy 263, 264, 265
intelligence-led 40
middle-class concerns 265
nature of 263
neighbourhood-led 40

314 Index

re-assurance policing model (RPM) 40, 264, 265
resource levels 250
zero risk environment 264
political culture
  Conservative Party policy (UK) 30, 31, 32, 36
  high profile crimes 253, 254
  immigration issues 253
  neo-liberalism 253
  Netherlands 253
  New Labour policy (UK) 36, 37, 39, 44
  Norway 253, 254
  public confidence 254
  right-wing influences 41, 43, 105, 251, 252, 253
post-traumatic stress disorder
  effects 64
Pratt, J. 12, 40
Presser, S. 56
Pruitt, M.V. 94
psychology of risk
  emotion 113, 114
  exposure to risk 86
  fear 112
  perceptions of risk 85, 86, 87, 113
  sensitivity to risk 86, 87, 113
  social perception 113
  vulnerability 86
  worry 113
psychology of survey response(s)
  attitudinal questions 54, 55, 56
  cognitive aspects 53
  comprehension 53
  formation of judgement 53
  frequency items 57–9 *see also* frequency items
  leading questions 54
  no-attitudes 56, 57
  presuppositions 54
  psychological issues 53
  retrieval of relevant information 53
  selection/reporting of answer 53
  socially desirable responses 54, 55
psychosocial understanding
  anxiety 261, 262
  human emotion 261
  uncertainty 262

Rachman, S.J. 241
Rasinski, K. 53, 83, 116
Raudenbush, S.W. 93, 97, 99, 102, 114, 137, 158, 208, 230
Redergard, Silje Marie 253
Rees, T. 255
Reiner, R. 37
Reiss, A.S. 47
research (emotions)
  cognitive interviewing techniques 67
  data collection 67
  frequency of emotion 67
  measurement errors 67, 68
  methodological issues 66, 67, 68
  qualitative/quantitative techniques 69, 73
research (fear of crime)
  day reconstruction method 50
  ecological momentary assessment methods 50
  event reconstruction method 50
  increased research 252, 253
  indicators
    emotion 48, 49, 50
    worry 48, 49, 50
  inter-disciplinary analysis 46
  measurement 45–9
  methodological issues 45, 202 *see also* Methodological Appendix
  multi-disciplinary perspective 46
  outlining measures
    impact of worry 166
    prevalence of fear 165
    representative sample surveys 165
    research method 165
  psychology of everyday emotions 45
  qualitative data 70, 111
  quality of life measures 203
  quantitative data 111
  reality of feelings/fear/anxiety 45
  risk perceptions 48
  safety issues 47–9
  survey measures 202, 203
  survey responses 45, 80 *see also* psychology of survey response(s)
  theoretical under-specification 45
  trait questionnaires 50
  victimization 48, 49

responsibilization 35, 147, 258
Revhon, N. 63
Riddell, P. 31, 105
Rifkind, J. 256
Riger, S. 30
Rips, L.J. 53
risk
  crime risk 90, 91
  evaluation 111
  media influences 90
  psychology of risk
    emotion 113, 114
    exposure to risk 86
    fear 112
    perceptions of risk 85, 86, 87, 113
    sensitivity to risk 86, 87, 113
    social perception 113
    vulnerability 86
    worry 113
  risk control 87
  risk-fear paradox 32, 83
  risk interpretation model 111, 112
  risk management 15
  risk perception 40, 48, 85, 86, 87, 90, 111, 112, 116
  Social Amplification of Risk Framework (SARF)
    communication processes 89
    perception of risk 89
    risk events 89
    risk signals 89
Ritchie, J. 271, 272
Roberts, D. 38
Robinson, J.B. 65, 66, 91, 168
Rock, P. 30, 31
Root Mean Square Error of Approximation (RMSEA) 218
Rose, N. 56, 57
Ross, C.E. 49, 93
Rountree, P.W. 83, 91
Rubin, D.C. 161
Runciman, W. 255
rural crime *see* local crime survey
Russell, M. 114

Sacco, V.F. 49, 51, 66, 88, 102
Salem, G. 26, 82, 91, 96
Sampson, R.J. 93, 94, 97, 99, 102, 114, 137, 158, 208, 230, 246

Savage, S. 31, 105
Scheingold, S. 105, 109, 110, 261, 263
Scherer, K.R. 60, 61, 62, 63, 64, 69, 80
Schuman, H. 56
Sears, R. 261
Sennett, R. 256, 262, 266
Shaw, C. 22, 46
Shepard, D. 104, 105, 241
Sherman, J.W. 66
Silva, B.F.A. 94
Simon, J. 246
Skogan, W. 48, 82, 83, 85, 91, 95, 96, 97, 102, 163, 176, 198
Smith, J.A. 83, 88, 91, 94, 98, 106, 107, 118, 124, 125, 126, 133, 159
Social Amplification of Risk Framework (SARF)
  communication processes 89
  perception of risk 89
  risk events 89
  risk signals 89
social change
  area-level data 228
  disorder 99, 100, 120
  effects 5, 12, 22, 42, 46, 75, 103, 117, 119, 239, 244
  local crime survey 222, 225
social cohesion
  anti-social behaviour 259
  disorder 100, 120
  environmental perception 93, 96, 115, 133
  fear of crime 6, 90, 104, 117, 119, 239, 240, 244, 245
  local crime survey 5, 223, 225, 226, 227
  public fears 243
  worry 202, 227
social control
  disorder 100
  environmental perception 92, 93, 94, 96, 115, 159
  incidence of crime 90, 91, 117, 119
  local crime survey 5
social inequality
  effects 107
social relations
  significance 107, 108
socio-economic transformations

Brazilianization thesis 256
community cohesion 258
environmental cues 258
fast capitalism 256
insecurity 255
media influences 257, 258
neo-liberal debate 257
paradox of risk 257
perceptions of community 258
perceptions of risk 257
political influences 257
protection from danger 256
responsibilization 258
significance of risk 256, 257
social class 255
social mobility 255
social relationships 258
uncertainty 256
victimization 255 *see also* **victimization**
winners/losers 254–60
Spalek, B. 147
Sparks, R. 17, 18, 38, 104, 145, 160, 257, 259, 263
Spencer, L. 271, 272
Stafford, M. 48, 83, 88
Stanko, E.A. 23, 25, 26, 28, 55, 74, 83, 85, 249
Stapel, D.A. 89
St John, C. 99, 102
Sterngold, A. 56
Stets, J.E. 60, 61
Stringer, P. 92
structural equation modelling (SEM)
confirmatory technique 211
direct/indirect relationships 212, 213
flexibility 212
local crime survey 226
results 217, 221
statistical tool 211
Sunshine, J. 91, 100, 117, 198, 209, 220
Sunstein, C. 10, 116, 117
Sutton, R. 55, 84, 86

Tallis, F. 167
Taub, R.P. 102
Taylor, I. 12, 43, 49, 83, 85, 91, 94, 95, 97, 98, 99, 103, 105, 107, 111, 118, 164, 229, 242, 244, 250, 251
Thatcher, Margaret 29, 30, 31, 105, 238, 260
Therborn, G. 256
Thrift, N. 141
Tien, J.M. 91, 98
Timmins, N. 260
Tourangeau, R. 53, 55, 56, 58, 59, 205
Toxteth Riots
significance 34
Trickett, A. 265
truancy
control of 38
Tudor, A. 258
Tulloch, M. 87, 88, 107
Tulving, E. 161
Turner, J.H. 60, 61
Tversky, A. 168
Tyler, T.R. 83, 85, 88, 96, 116, 198

unified framework (fear of crime)
analytic orientation
invocation of attitude 127
knowledge of crime/disorder 127
physical environment 127
social bonds 127
social relations 126
subjective experiences 125, 126
subjective responses 125
victimization 126
community concerns 119
control/consequence 119
establishment of 237
experience/expression 118, 120, 125, 127, 149–57 *see also* **experience and expression**
interpersonal communication 118, 119
judgements of likelihood 119
levels of crime 117, 118, 123, 124
media involvement 118, 119
moral consensus 118
neighbourhood concerns 118, 124
perceptions
disorder 124
perceived risk 119
social cohesion 124, 158

Index

social control 124, 159
victimization 124, 126, 132
physical environment
  disorder 129, 131, 132, 133
  drug use 131, 132, 133
  environmental cues 158, 159
  graffiti 130
  highly populated areas 158
  informal control 158, 159
  insecurity 159
  litter 130
  local environment 127
  neighbourhood assets 129
  neighbourhood decay 158, 159
  neighbourhood deprivation 245
  neighbourhood well-being 129
  no-go areas 130
  physical appearance 128, 129
  physical degeneration 130, 131
  resilience 141, 159
  safety 130
  sense of place 127
  social conditions 245
  social relationships 159
  transient populations 159
  vandalism 130, 133, 158
prevalence of criminals 118
representations of crime/social order/risk 119
sampling methodology 124, 125
social change 118, 124

United Kingdom
academic research 35
anti-social behaviour 38, 258, 259
British Crime Survey *see* **British Crime Survey**
Brixton Riots 34
CCTV usage 35, 37
community safety 38 *see also* **community safety**
Conservative Party policy 30, 31, 32, 36
Crime and Disorder Act (1998) 38, 39
crime prevention 34, 35
crime rates 30, 33, 34
crime survey 44
criminal behaviour 35
delinquency 29
law and order 29, 31, 32, 34, 35, 44, 258
management of fear 36
media influences 37
neo-conservative policy 34
New Labour policy 36, 37, 39, 44, 105
personal safety concerns 31, 32
political rhetoric 35
public anxiety 32
race/class issues 34
responsibilization 35, 258
risk-fear paradox 32
security services 44
socio-economic issues 32, 33
Toxteth Riots 34
vandalism 3
victimization 33, 35 *see also* **victimization**
youth crime 29

United States of America
Bureau of Justice Statistics 24
civil rights 25, 43
crime surveys
  black crime 25
  crime statistics 24
  fear of attack 24
  index of anxiety 24, 47
  National Crime Surveys 24, 46
  personal safety 28, 47, 48, 49
  police powers 25
  public anxiety 24, 25, 28, 46, 47
  public perceptions 24, 27
  social tensions 28
  victimization 24, 46, 48
criminal procedure
  detention incommunicado 27
  police questioning 27
  right of silence 27
fear of crime
  feed-back loop 41
  political usage 41
  public anxieties 41
  right-wing politics 41, 43
inner-city riots 25, 26
Katzenbach Commission 23, 26, 46, 47
Melone Commission 23, 26

United States of America (cont.)
  Omnibus Crime Control and Safe
    Streets Act 23, 26
  social change 27
  social/economic upheaval 235

Vale, L.J. 141
Valentine, G. 92
vandalism 3, 42, 91, 92, 130, 132, 158
Van der Wurff, A. 92
Vanderveen, G. 82, 84, 231
Vasey, M.W. 167
Velthuijsen, A.S. 89
victimization
  crime consciousness 142, 147, 148, 149
  direct/indirect experience 4, 82, 83, 84
  effects 33–5
  empirical data 83
  fear 4, 8, 48, 49, 72, 74, 78, 79
  feminist views 30, 32
  gender effects 86
  harassment 84, 85, 87
  imagined victimization 85, 90
  impact 84
  indirect 85–8
  legal definitions 84
  levels of criminal activity 82, 83, 84
  likely victimization 82, 83, 84
  local crime survey 223, 226
  perception of risk 85, 86, 87, 90, 94, 96, 134
  personal knowledge of victims 84
  property victimization 83
  risk-fear paradox 83
  social groups 86
  surveys 84
  threat of 111
  unwanted behaviour 84
  worry 53, 85, 227 *see also* **worry**
Villarreal, A.B. 94
Vrij, A. 88, 89, 116
vulnerability
  anticipation of consequences 86
  exposure to risk 86
  loss of control 86

Walker, A. 12, 231, 260
Walklate, S. 17, 231, 250
Warr, M. 48, 51, 65, 66, 86, 87, 88, 92, 96, 97, 113, 166
welfare state
  influence on crime 229
Wetzel, A.E. 161
Wiedemann, P.M. 90
Wilhelm, P. 62
Wilkins, L. 260
Williams, F.P. 49
Williams, S. 60
Wilson, J.Q. 91, 94, 95
Wilson, L.A, 48
Winkel, F.W. 83, 88, 89, 116
women
  fear of crime 101, 102
  feminist sociologists 29
  harassment 29, 84, 85, 87
  male abuse 29, 30, 85
  patriarchy critique 29
  rape 87
  victimization 30, 32, 84, 86
    see also **victimization**
  violence towards 85
  vulnerability 86
worry
  basic frequencies
    intensity/frequency
      measures 174–9
    worry about burglary 170–4, 179, 185, 186, 200, 201, 204, 205, 219
    worry about car crime 170, 171, 173, 174, 179, 185, 186, 200, 201, 219
    worry about robbery 169–72, 174, 175, 179, 185, 186, 200, 201, 218
  categorization of results 202, 207
  chronic worry 166
  control/consequence 113
  damaging worry 166
  disorder 202, 227
  dysfunctional worry 166
  elements 166
  events, focus on 167
  everyday experience 51, 52, 120, 165, 176, 177, 178, 207, 208, 227, 238

excessive worry 166
frequency (generally) 52, 87, 113, 200, 201, 227
functional properties 68
future-orientated anxiety 51
impact 166
indicators of worry 48, 49, 50
intensity (generally) 7, 8, 52, 167, 168, 174, 175, 200, 201
knowledge of victims 227
local collective efficacy 243
local crime variables 202
momentary worry 73
moral consensus 120
multi-variate analysis *see* **multi-variate analysis**
nature of 113
neighbourhood concerns 245
negative effect 166, 167
negative information 113
Penn State Worry Questionnaire (PSWQ) 50
perceived risk 227
positive consequences 166
precautionary actions 68, 71
problem-solving 166, 167
quality of life concerns 179
social cohesion 120, 202, 227
victimization 53, 85, 120, 201, 202, 227 *see also* **victimization**
'worried-well' 252, 254
Worry Domains Questionnaire 50
Wouters, C. 60
Wothke, W. 213, 216

Young, J. 66, 107, 243, 246, 260

Zaller, J. 53, 55, 57
Zedner, L.H. 12
zero tolerance
effects 16
Zolotas, X.E. 13, 247